AF598911

History of the Mauser Rifle in Chile

Mauser Chileno Modelo 1895, 1912, and 1935

David Nielsen

Library of Congress Control Number: 2018958789

Cover design by Justin Watkinson
Type set in Buenos Aires & Minion Pro

ISBN: 978-0-7643-5676-6
Printed in China

Published by Schiffer Publishing, Ltd.
4880 Lower Valley Road
Atglen, PA 19310
Phone: (610) 593-1777; Fax: (610) 593-2002
E-mail: Info@schifferbooks.com
Web: www.schifferbooks.com

Contents

Preface

To understand the Mauser, one also needs to understand the origins of German industrialization. In the late nineteenth century, Germany realized that it could effectively compete with established trading nations—particularly Britain—only if it offered vastly superior quality and design in its products. Ludwig Loewe, along with numerous formative German industrialists such as August Borsig and Emil Rathenau, initially relied on foreign designs that were then steadily improved on through top-quality manufacturing. As part of this process, Loewe created a new industrial concern—based mostly on American knowhow and technology—that produced the machines, process, and facilities for the mass production of precise interchangeable parts of the highest quality. After the failure of his early foray into sewing-machine manufacturing, Loewe then sought a well-designed and highly profitable product to sustain his fledgling factory. Following an introduction to rifle manufacturing, Loewe acquired a controlling interest in Waffenfabrik Mauser in 1887. Having thus assimilated the design excellence of the Mauser, Loewe then systematically transformed his growing company into one of the dominant small-arms manufactures of its time.

Mausers are fascinating objects because of their technical innovation, flawless functioning, and top-quality manufacturing. However, the Mausers that were exported to South America possess an additional quality. This quality, while exceptionally hard to quantify, undoubtedly has something to do with the fact that these examples are additionally items of beauty and historical significance. Of the many countless millions of Mausers that have been exported globally, approximately 170,000 were purchased by Chile from 1894 to 1935. Debatably, these Chilean rifles and carbines are some of most noteworthy and collectible of all South American Mausers.

Because of the War of the Pacific (1879–1883), the Chilean Civil War of 1891, and growing tensions with its neighbors, Chile realized that it needed to modernize its armed forces. Therefore, Chile decided to emulate the highly successful Prussian military, which had decisively defeated the French in 1870. As a result of this victory and an earlier defeat of the Austrian Empire in 1866, Prussia had emerged as the dominant European military power of the time. Along with emulating Prussian military organization, Chile likewise decided to equip its army with the very latest small arms that Germany had to offer. To fulfill this desire, from 1894 to 1898 the Chilean government contracted to procure 115,800 rifles and carbines following the Mauser 1893 pattern, which were officially designated as the *Mauser Chileno Modelo 1895* (Chilean Mauser Model of 1895). In 1912, Chile procured a further 43,100 Mauser 1898 pattern rifles and carbines that were officially designated as the *Modelo 1912*. To conclude Chile's Mauser purchases, in 1935, 10,000 *Modelo 1935* carbines were acquired.

The introduction of Mauser rifles played an instrumental role in the Prussianization and subsequent modernization of the Chilean military. Chile thus emerged as one of the dominant military powers of the region. This fact was significant not only for Chile, but also for most of South America, since it played a crucial role in fueling a local arms race, particularly with Argentina.

This book has been written for the historian and collector. Thus, in the three chapters that follow that detail the Modelo 1895, 1912, and 1935, respectively, the period context and actual process that led to the eventual procurement of each model will first be outlined before a detailed technical explanation of each model is offered.

The availability of primary sources is paramount when constructing a historical narrative. In this regard, the Chilean National Archives in Santiago has been a treasure trove of information, having contributed a substantial volume of the documents that have been essential in the writing of this book. While many of these papers have been discovered and recognized, there are still many more that remain hidden. Mauser historian Jon Speed has been a further vital source of these essential resources, particularly those employed to compose chapter 3.

The technical specifics that are offered in chapters 1 and 2 have been obtained from observation and a number of *cartilla* (manuals) that were originally intended for the instruction of military personnel. For the Modelo 1895 and

1912, these *cartilla* were written by José Boado y Castro and José Mercado, respectively. For the chapter on the Modelo 1935, no such *cartilla* are available; therefore, information has been procured from primary sources provided by Speed, as well as through observations by the author.

Chapter 1 will detail the Mauser Chileno Modelo 1895, arguably one of the finest military Mausers ever produced. This chapter will start with a brief explanation of its immediate heritage and the companies that produced it. It would be folly to detail the Modelo 1895 without first understanding the reasons for its procurement. Thus, a brief explanation of the War of the Pacific and the Chilean Civil War are included for essential contextual information. Apart from the specifics of the rifles and carbines that constituted the Modelo 1895, a further detailing of certain "oddities" is also offered. This section will discuss the Modelo 1895s that were procured for the Chilean navy, the differences in stock cartouches (FAEME, ME, MF, 1895, 1898, and 1902), the changes from Ludwig Loewe to Deutsche Waffen und Munitionsfabriken manufacture, the missing "I" and "J" serial number prefixes, the conversion from 7 × 57 mm to 7.62 × 51 mm, the Boer War rifles that were redirected to Chile, the rear-sight conversion for spitzer ammunition, and the Steyr-made 1895s.

Chapter 1, on the Modelo 1895, is the largest in this book, simply because the vast majority of primary-source information obtained from the Chilean National Archives meticulously details the events and facts that surrounded the procurement and production of this model. For this reason, it is proposed that one of the primary contributions of this book is in providing the first comprehensive narrative that systematically documents these events.

This Modelo 1895 information also importantly sets the context for chapter 2, which details the Modelo 1912 through an explanation of the procurement of spare parts and ammunition from Österreichischen Waffenfabrik Gesellschaft in the period 1910–1912. Notably, the history and details surrounding the procurement of the Modelo 1912 have already been established by authors who have scrupulously researched this topic through the use of impeccable primary sources. In this regard, the initial work of Jürgen Schaefer (1974) and the later work of William Sater and Holger Herwig (1999) are authoritative. In an attempt to respect the significant impact of these authors, the chapter on the Modelo 1912 includes only a summary of the procurement process on the basis of their findings. Likewise, chapter 1 will also include some information from these three authors. Starting with a brief explanation of Mauser technical developments that resulted in the iconic model of 1898, chapter 2 also includes a discussion on the specifics of the carbines and rifles of the Modelo 1912. Also offered is a detailing of a small number of Modelo 1912s that were used by the British during World War I, and the conversion by the Chileans of large numbers of rifles and carbines from 7 × 57 mm to 7.62 × 51 mm in the early 1960s. These facts mean that, on face value, chapter 2 on the Modelo 1912 is the shortest of this book.

Chapter 3, which details the Modelo 1935, is much like chapter 1, in that it is based on extensive primary sources that are largely unpublished. However, these are of a different type, because unlike chapter 1, which details events mainly from the perspective of the Chilean government, these chapter 3 sources detail the viewpoint of Mauser Werke and its representatives in Santiago. Starting with an explanation of the effects of the Treaty of Versailles on Deutsche Waffen und Munitionsfabriken and Waffenfabrik Mauser, chapter 3 will expose Chile's initial desire for an additional 45,727 Mausers. It will also show how the renamed Mauser Werke then proposed to circumvent the manufacturing restrictions imposed by the treaty in the proposed supply of these weapons. However, with the advent of the Great Depression and the associated political upheaval in Chile, this large order was then canceled, reduced, and eventually delivered only as 10,000 Modelo 1935s.

Jon Speed has requested that both Hans Lockhoven and Walter Schmid receive special acknowledgment for their vital contributions in preserving many of the original documents referenced in this book. In early 1945, with the end of World War II fast approaching, many Mauser employees and Oberndorf residents had already seen fit to remove or duplicate and then hide a countless number of Mauser documents and records. When French troops arrived in Oberndorf in April 1945, Schmid and others chose—instead of simply destroying documents subsequently deemed unnecessary—to hide documents of all kinds. Lockhoven was a military historian from Cologne who then found many of these hidden documents and preserved them for posterity. As well as Speed, many other people have contributed their valuable time and resources to the writing of this book. In this regard, Pedro Bello and Jon Magnuson have also offered invaluable assistance.

Chapter 1: The Chilean Mauser Model of 1895

Mauser Developments, 1889–1894

On 28 August 1888, the Belgian Inspectorate of Arms invited tenders for the supply of 150,000 repeating rifles. To fulfill this tender, on 3 July 1889 the Fabrique Nationale d'Armes de Guerra (National Factory for Weapons of War, or simply FN) was incorporated by twelve arms manufacturers based in the city of Liège. Nine days later, FN's chairman, Allard Bormans, and its managing director, Henri Pieper, signed a contract with the Belgian War Ministry that committed them to supply the 150,000 rifles for seventy-nine francs each (Francotte and Gaier 1989, pp. 30–31). While the inspectorate's tender called for price and supply terms, it did not mandate the model of rifle. This might seem odd to the casual observer, and it thus deserves further explanation.

Because of Germany's adoption of the Mauser Model 1871, which was modified in 1884 to incorporate a tubular magazine (Model 1871/84), the Belgian army hastened the development of a repeating rifle. In 1880, they had already experimented with the Krnka loading device on their Albini rifles. However, these tests proved indecisive, since even with this device the very best marksmen failed to significantly increase their rate of fire, and their accuracy was significantly decreased. In August 1886, the Manufacture d'Armes de l'Etat (State Arms Manufacturer) experimented with rifle designs from Kropatschek, Nagant, Francotte, Jahrmann, Schulhof, and Remington-Lee. This was then followed in October by additional tests on three further designs by Comblain, Martini, and Nagant, as well as a Jahrmann action. A month later, a commission was established to conduct comparative tests among Mannlicher, Schulhof, Pieper, and a number of Nagant systems. The results of this were inconclusive, and therefore further tests were conducted in July and August 1888. These were followed by final tests that started in November 1888 and ended on 8 August 1889. During these final trials, designs by Mannlicher, Nagant, Pieper, Mauser, and Engh were evaluated. Finally, on 21 October 1889, in a report by the minister of war, the Mauser Model 1889 was adopted (Leconte 1910).

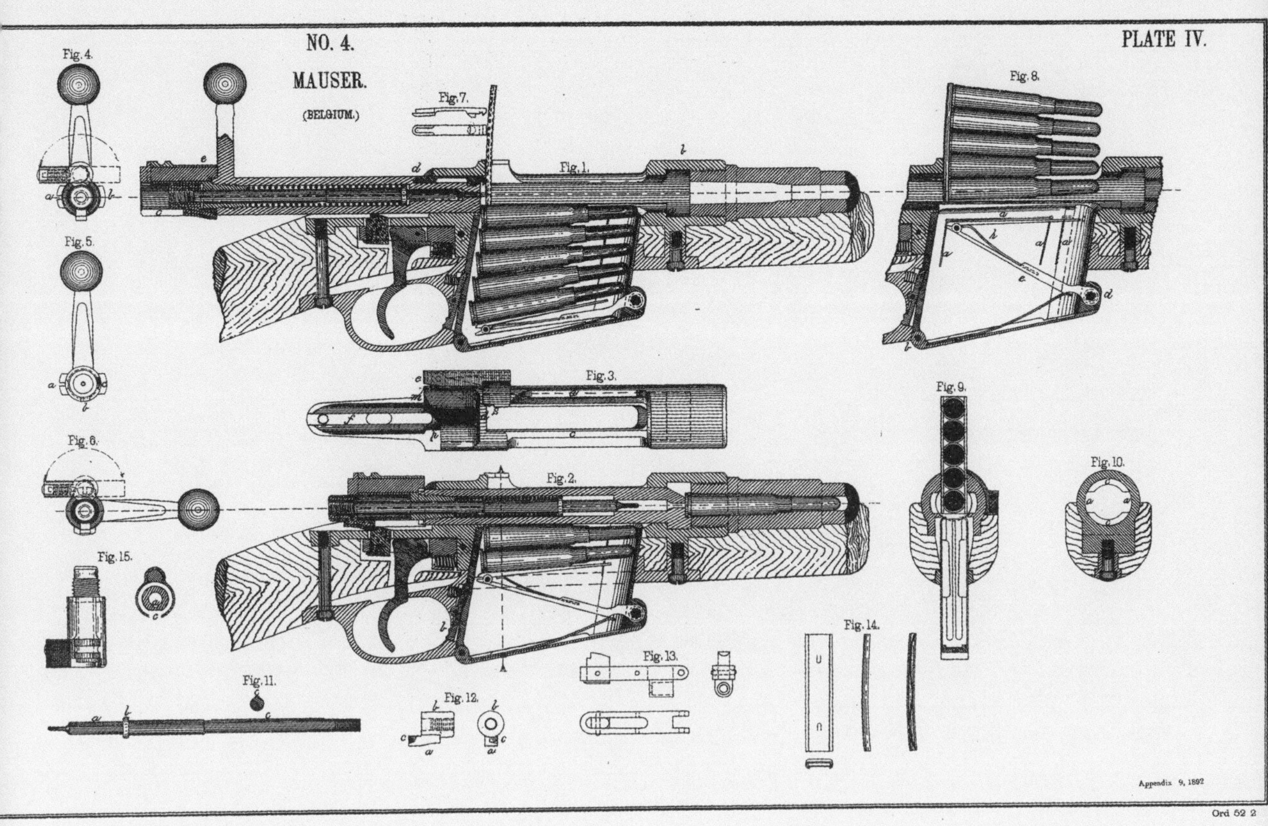

Belgian Mauser Model 1889.
Unknown author. 1892a. *Annual Report of the Chief of Ordnance to the Secretary of War for the Fiscal Year Ended June 30 1892.* Washington, DC: Government Printing Office.

The following day, the Belgian minister of defense, Gen. Pontus, obtained a license to produce Mauser Model 1889 rifles from Mauser's representative in Belgium, Alexandre Résimont (Francotte and Gaier 1989, p. 32). On 25 October 1889, Belgium's new rifle was made public in the Belgian *Government Gazette*. As important as the announcement of this new repeating rifle was, the proclamation that it would fire a new 7.65 mm caliber, rimless cartridge that used smokeless powder was of additional significance (Léopold and Pontus 1889). The consequences of Belgium's decision would be substantial and would resonate across the globe.

In February 1887, Turkey signed a contract for 500,000 Mauser Model 1887 rifles and 50,000 carbines. These were essentially the German black powder Model 1871/84 chambered for an optimized 9.5 × 60 mm cartridge with a smaller trigger guard and the addition of two locking faces to the bolt. After becoming aware of the Belgian Model 1889, Turkey decided to invoke the "upgrade clause" in their contract (Ball 2011, pp. 374–377). This clause stated that any improvement or modification that the German government made to its Model 1871/84 that then appeared desirable to the Turkish government would have to be incorporated into the remainder of the Turkish order. More importantly, the clause also specified that any further technical inventions made by Paul Mauser would likewise be incorporated into the remaining Turkish rifles (Seel 1986, p. 34). Because the Belgian Model 1889 offered numerous technical improvements—notably two symmetrical locking faces at the front of the bolt, a nontubular magazine design, and a smokeless cartridge—the Turks decided on 20 July 1890 that production of their Model 1887/84 would cease, and the remaining 280,000 rifles and 46,000 carbines would be manufactured according to a new Model 1890 specification (Seel 1986, p. 41). Essentially a Belgian Model 1889, the Turkish Model 1890 also included some significant innovations, such as a stepped barrel that omitted the metal barrel shroud, replacing it with a wooden handguard and an improved rear sight (Ball 2011, p. 377).

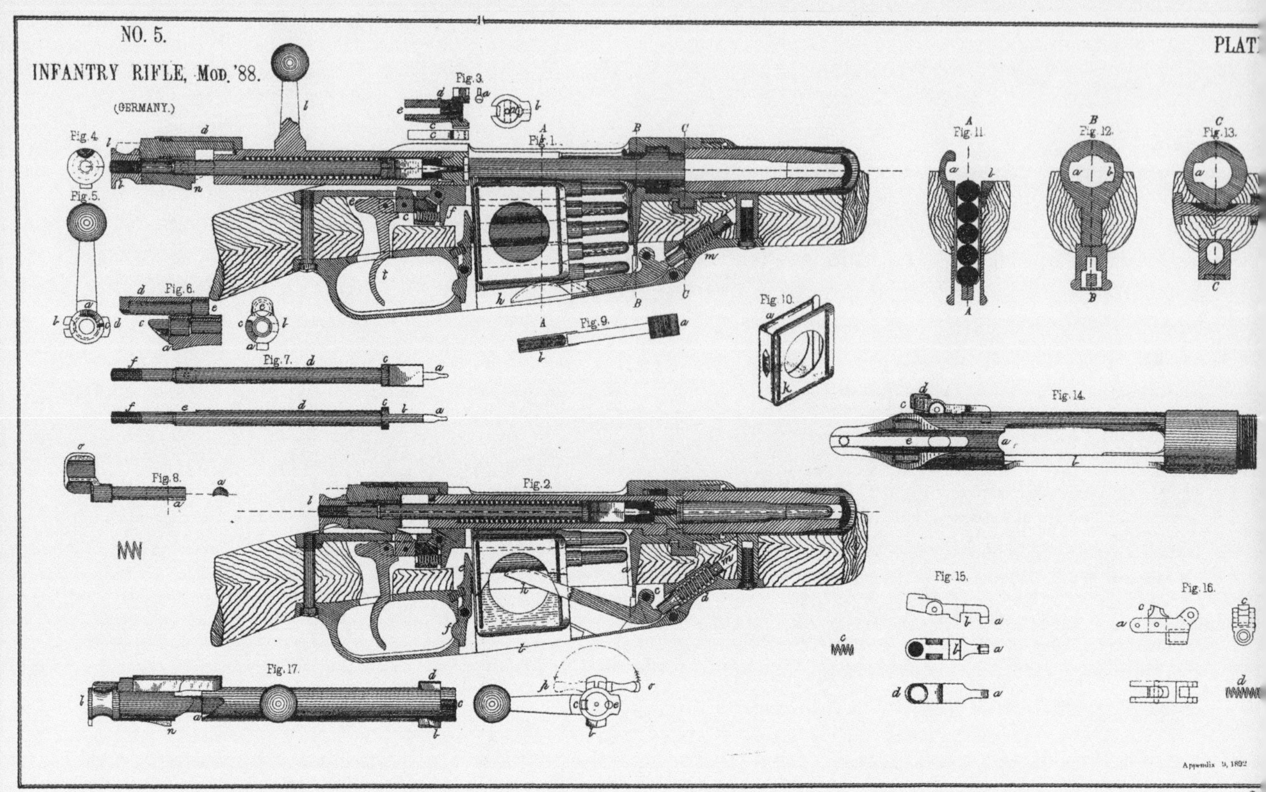

German Commission 1888 Rifle.
Unknown author. 1892a. *Annual Report of the Chief of Ordnance to the Secretary of War for the Fiscal Year Ended June 30 1892*. Washington, DC: Government Printing Office.

On the South American continent, in 1887, Argentina decided that it needed 15,000 new rifles because of growing tensions with its Chilean neighbor. While the Argentines initially sought to procure these according to the *Gewehr 1888* design, it was soon identified that this design was already obsolete. Thus, in early 1888, the Argentines, via the intermediary of Krupp, approached Mauser and requested rifles according to the Model 1871/84 specification. Mauser quickly declined the Argentine advances, since the order stipulated rifles in 11 mm caliber. Because the Waffenfabrik Mauser (Mauser Armaments Factory) in Oberndorf was owned by Ludwig Loewe & Cie (Ludwig Loewe & Co.), it was logical that any business that Mauser declined could therefore be considered by the parent company. The desperate Argentines proceeded to negotiate directly with Ludwig Loewe & Co. for an increased procurement of 30,000 Model 1871/84 rifles. Even though the Argentines eventually sought to obtain 50,000 rifles and 10,000 carbines, Ludwig Loewe & Co. also declined their business because of the Argentines' steadfast insistence on the 11 mm caliber. For Loewe, which had already converted its factories to the production of small-caliber technology, the execution of a relatively small order based on obsolete technology made little sense. Accepting that their 11 mm caliber specification was not viable, the Argentines then returned to their original position and on 20 July 1889 requested a Gewehr 1888 design in 8 mm. The German government declined this request, since it was still arming its forces with the rifle, and as such its export was prohibited. To take matters in hand, the Argentines decided that effective from 22 October 1889, an arms-purchasing commission was to be established in Paris. The foresight of this decision soon proved its worth. On 28 October 1889, a copy of the Royal Decree authorizing the Belgian Model 1889 arrived at the new commission's offices. Two days later, a member of the commission—Maj. Pablo Riccheri—set off for Brussels to obtain copies of the Belgian Commission's report; Riccheri was the very same officer who in 1887 had pointed out that the Gewehr 1888 was an obsolete design. Having grasped the significance of the report's contents, and having met with Paul Mauser and viewed a sample of the Model 1889, the commission quickly arrived at a decision and recommended on 28 December that Argentina purchase the Belgian Model 1889. Consequently, on 25 February 1890, Argentina signed a contract with Loewe for 100,000 rifles and 20,000 carbines, which would later become known as the Argentine Model 1891 (Webster 2003, pp. 26–29).

Because of its fear of Chilean aggression, Argentina saw fit to include Article 18 in their contract with Loewe, stipulating that Ludwig Loewe & Co., including all of its subsidiary companies, should make no deliveries of Mauser 1889 weapons to any other Latin American power. Argentina further stipulated that this prohibition would be in place until three-quarters of both the rifles and carbines had been delivered (Webster 2003, pp. 39, 244). Turkey had also stipulated a somewhat similar condition in its contract with Mauser: Waffenfabrik Mauser could not perform any work for any foreign government until the Turkish contract was completed (Seel 1986, p. 34).

The Argentine Model 1891 was an evolved Mauser design that incorporated all of the changes already introduced by the Belgians, as well as some of the improvements introduced by the Turks; most notably, the elimination of the barrel shroud and the use of a stepped barrel profile. However, the Argentines also incorporated further changes, including the addition of a locking screw to the magazine and the adoption of newer Krupp-Marcotty steel for its barrels (Webster 2003, p. 45).

This latest Mauser, initially designed as the Belgian Model 1889 and then further refined by Turkey and Argentina, marked a radical moment in firearms development. Nonetheless, a truly revolutionary Mauser system and caliber combination was about to make its appearance.

As early as 1882, Spain—like most nations of that period—had started the process of reequipping its military with a modern repeating rifle (Ball 2011, p. 435). On 16 February 1891 the Spanish military attaché ordered ten Model 1890 Turkish specification rifles from Mauser, which were delivered on 6 March. Following extensive testing, in December 1891 and January 1892, small orders were placed with Waffenfabrik Mauser for 1,200 infantry rifles, 640 navy rifles, and 400 cavalry carbines. The infantry and navy rifles were completed by April 1892 (Seel 1986, p. 44). Like the Turkish Model 1890, these rifles were chambered in 7.65 × 53 mm but also included other improvements to facilitate the feeding of ammunition from the magazine: an undercut to the bolt face and a spring-loaded plunger installed in the right locking lug (Ball 2011, pp. 335–336). These Model 1891 rifles (not to be confused with the Argentine Model 1891) were used in month-long, large-scale troop tests by Savoy Infantry Regiment 6 and Light Infantry Regiment of Puerto Rico 19 (Boado y Castro 1895). Following these troop trials, Spain decided to adopt the Mauser with the following modifications: a new extractor, an improved trigger system that would not disengage the cocking piece until the bolt was fully closed, a detachable magazine floorplate and follower, a bolt guide rib to the inside of the left receiver channel, a firing pin that was attached to the cocking piece via interrupted lugs, and the introduction for a third position to the safety that facilitated bolt disassembly. These rifles became known as the Spanish Model 1892 (Ball 2011, pp. 337–338) and were officially adopted on 30 November 1892 (Ball 2011, p. 435). On 17 February 1893, Paul Mauser delivered a rifle chambered in a new 7 × 57 mm cartridge to the Spanish military representative in Berlin. The advantages of the new cartridge became apparent once submitted to the Spanish Ministry of War, and 400 carbines were ordered. These 400 carbines were manufactured from early May to early August 1893. Further Spanish tests were conducted during summer 1893, during which time Mauser's seminal integrated, staggered five-round magazine made its appearance (Seel 1986, pp. 44–45). With this latest improvement in hand and specifying the new 7 × 57 mm instead of the 7.65 × 53 mm cartridge, Spain proceeded to amend its 1892 order and substitute it with a revised Model 1893 specification. On 7 December 1893, Spain officially adopted the Model 1893 rifle and placed an initial order for 70,000 rifles and 5,000 carbines (Ball 2011, p. 436). Loewe executed this order because Waffenfabrik Mauser was constrained by the Turkish contractual clause

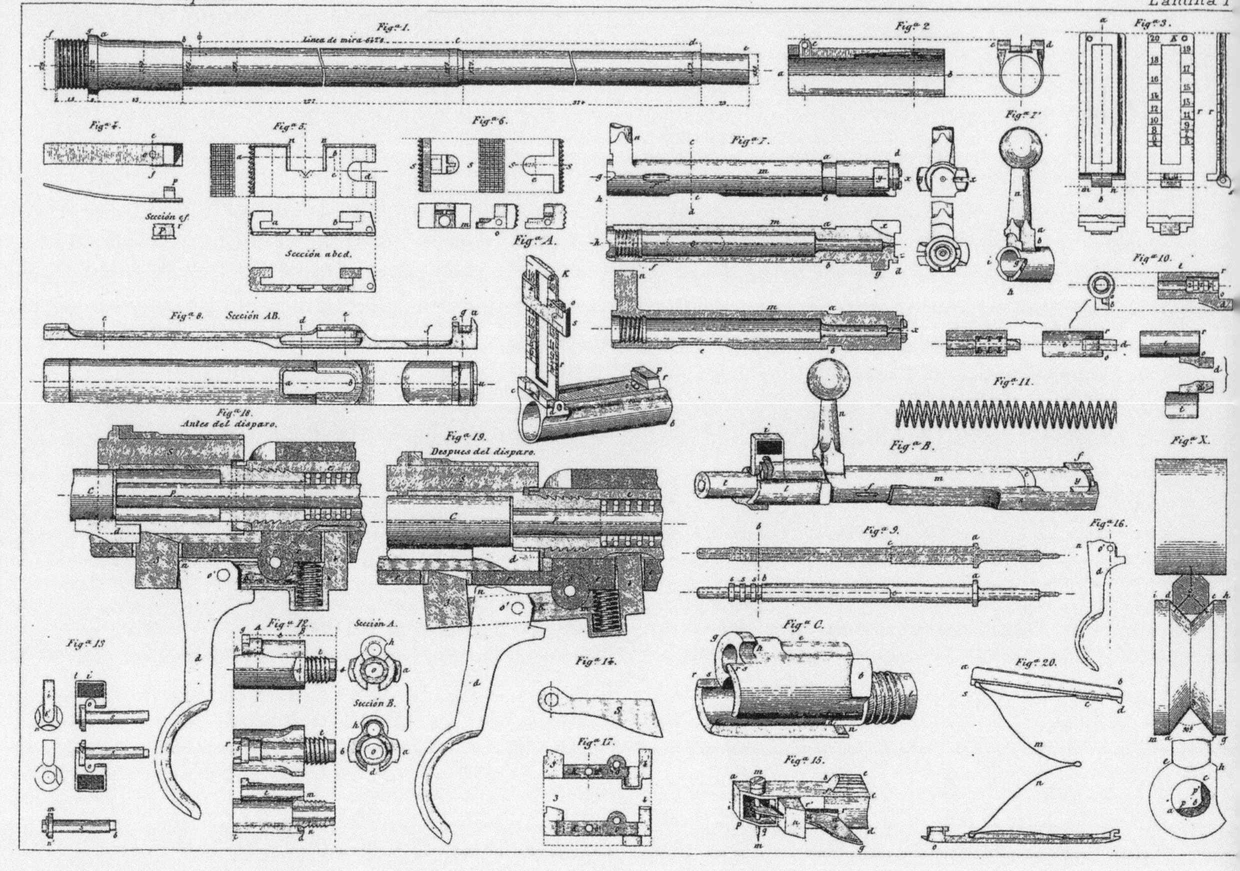

Receiver, bolt, and barrel of the Spanish Model 1893.
Fuente, J. 1894. "El fusil Mauser español." *Memorial de Ingenieros del Ejército* 49, no. 12: 361–369.

that restrained it from fulfilling any order to a foreign government. But considering that the last of the Turkish rifles left Waffenfabrik Mauser on 5 December 1893, the timing must have been extremely close. In November 1895 the Spanish government awarded a contract for 30,000 rifles to Waffenfabrik Mauser in response to production difficulties at Loewe. When the last of Spain's rifles were delivered on 20 August 1896, both Waffenfabrik Mauser and Ludwig Loewe & Co. had produced a total of 251,800 rifles and 27,500 carbines (Seel 1986, pp. 44–45).

Following a predictable pattern toward an ever-smaller caliber, in 1889 Sweden decided to convert its 100,000 existing Remington Model 1867s to the then newly adopted 8 × 58 mm rimmed cartridge. When the Swedes began to seriously consider the adoption of a repeating rifle in about 1890, one of their primary concerns was to obtain a weapon that employed a reduced caliber with a long range and a flat trajectory. Because of Sweden's close association with Norway at that time, this choice was fixed on the 6.5 mm caliber that had been recommended for Norwegian infantry rifles by the Rifle Committee of 1891. Very soon, the Swedes realized that technical innovations introduced by Mauser were of a superior standard. As a first step in deciding Sweden's new repeating rifle, from 1 April 1892 to early January 1893, two Mauser Model 1892s, two Gewehr 1888 rifles, and a Belgian Model 1889, together with various carbines, were tested. Subsequently, in September 1892, three Swedes from the Ministry of Defense—A. Gibson, Capt. Carl Hylten-Cavallius, and engineer Wilhelm Sundell—visited Waffenfabrik Mauser to test Mauser's latest model, conduct some test firing, and inquire as to the processes of Mauser rifle manufacture. At the same time as this visit, further separate trials were conducted both in Sweden and Norway on various rifles and magazine types. After these trials, three rifles—the Krag-

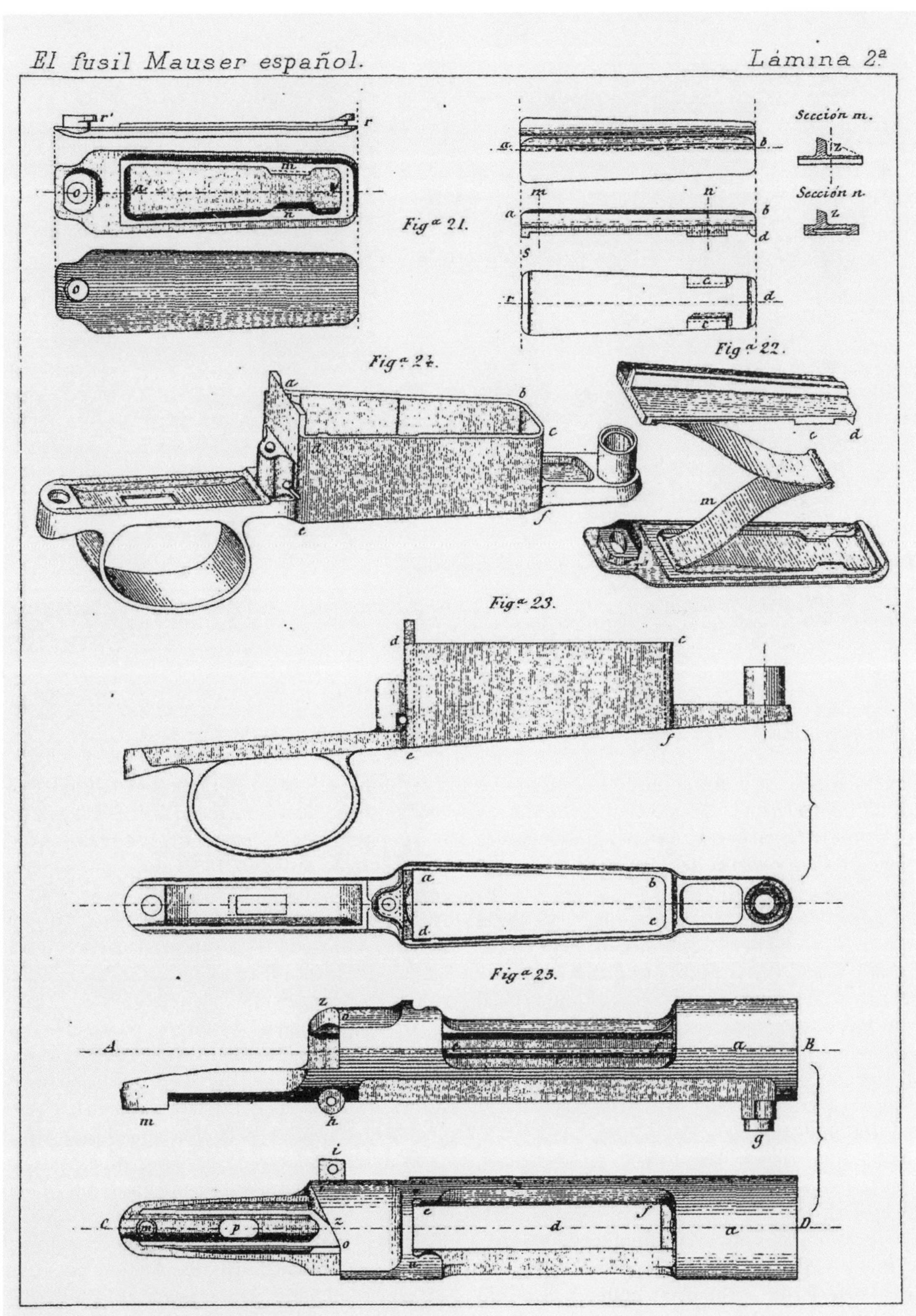

Trigger guard, magazine, and receiver of the Spanish Model 1893.
Fuente, J. 1894. "El fusil Mauser español." *Memorial de Ingenieros del Ejército* 49, no. 12: 361–369.

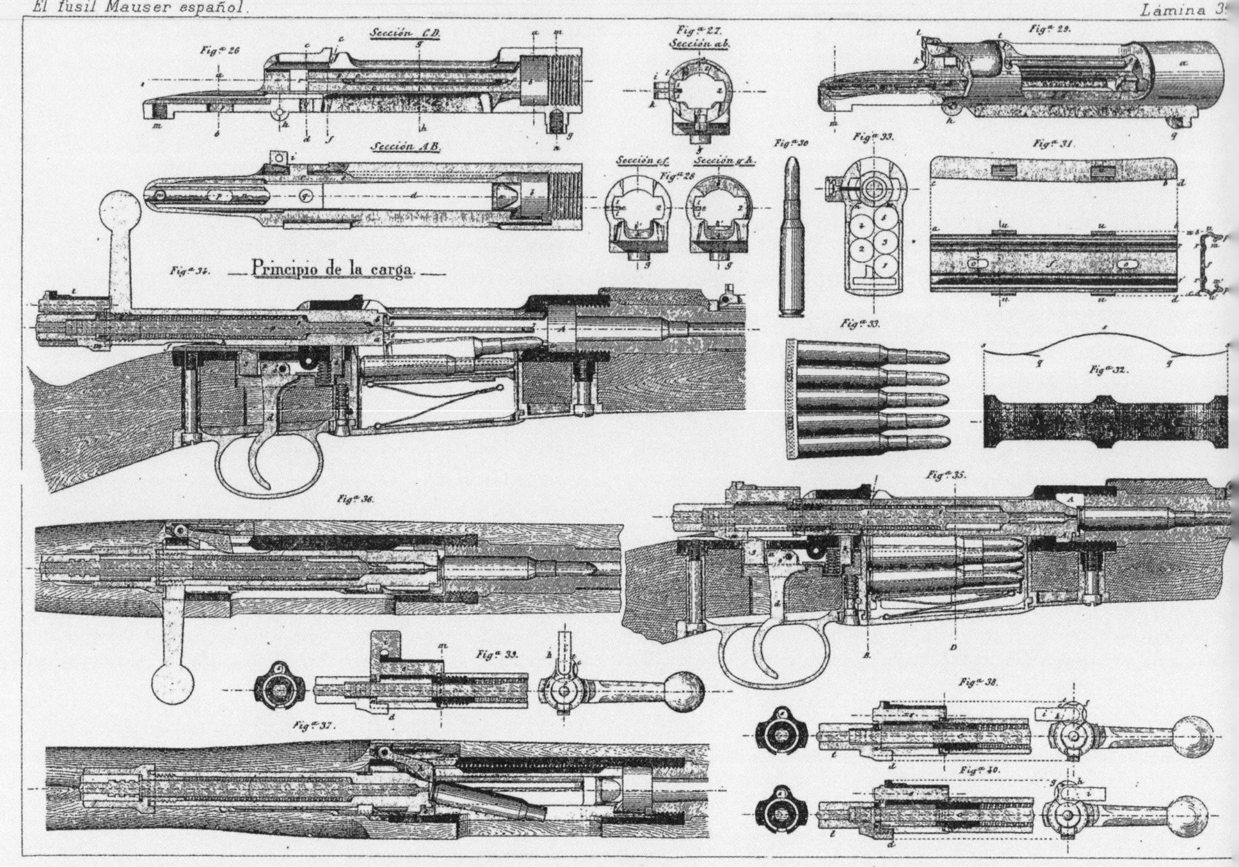

Cross-sections through major components of the Spanish Model 1893.
Fuente, J. 1894. "El fusil Mauser español." *Memorial de Ingenieros del Ejército* 49, no. 12: 361–369.

Jorgensen, Mauser, and Mannlicher—were chosen for additional testing (Jones 2003, pp. 16–18).

In the *Crown Jewels*, Dana Jones includes original correspondence between Paul Mauser and Mauser's agent in Sweden, Franz Marcotty. This correspondence, apart from exposing the technical intricacies of the new lug connector between the firing pin and the cocking piece and magazine concerns, also importantly exposed the crucial role of Mauser's agents in the whole testing and procurement process. The crucial importance of the agents' role will become increasingly evident when the matter of Chile's Mausers is discussed in the sections that follow.

The final tests between the Krag-Jorgensen, Mauser, and Mannlicher were conducted from 24 February to 13 April 1893. On 23 May 1893, a telegram was sent to Waffenfabrik Mauser, stating that the Swedish committee had decided on Mauser's rifle with an integrated five-round magazine, wide-leaf spring to the magazine, and the rimless 6.5 mm cartridge. On 1 June 1893, Marcotty placed an order for eighty rifles to be used in troop testing. The first ten rifles were shipped to Stockholm on 8 August 1893, and the remaining seventy between 9 and 12 August. Shipped on 13 August were a further thirty trial carbines. In the first few months of 1894, fifty of Mauser's original eighty rifles were then deployed in troop trials (Jones 2003, pp. 23–35).

In a strange twist of fate, when Sweden ordered its first repeating small arms, it was not rifles but carbines that were procured. On 7 August 1894, Sweden officially adopted the *1895 ars karbin*, which was later changed on 6 April 1895 to *6.5 mm karbin m/1895* (Jones 2003, p. 37). On 16 August 1894, Sweden ordered 12,000 Model 1894 carbines from Waffenfabrik Mauser (Seel 1986, p. 46). This order comprised an initial order of 5,000, which was then later extended by a further 7,000. Delivery started on 24 July 1895 and was finished on 19 February 1896 (Jones

2003, pp. 38, 42). A further extension of the initial contracts was made on 20 October 1895 for a small batch of *Kammarkarbin* (chamber carbines). These 185 carbines were intended for the firing of light, short-range loads at indoor shooting ranges and were delivered on 21 December 1895 (Jones 2003, p. 41).

Interestingly, Sweden, like Belgium (Francotte and Gaier 1989, p. 32) and Spain (Seel 1986, p. 45), while initially procuring only completed weapons, also decided to obtain the machinery, technical expertise, and licenses for the local manufacture of Mauser rifles. To start local manufacture at the Carl Gustafs Gevarsfaktori (Carl Gustaf's Rifle Factory) in Eskilstuna, Sweden bought three milling machines for the local production of Model 1894 carbines on 11 April 1896 (Jones 2003, p. 41). Presumably, these machines were bought from Loewe, which had earlier also supplied both Belgium and Spain.

Sweden officially adopted its infantry rifle *6.5 mm Gevar m/96*—or Model 1896—on 20 March 1896. Because of delivery delays in the supply of machinery from Loewe to Carl Gustafs Gevarsfaktori, local manufacture of the Model 1896 did not start until 1889; during this year, approximately 3,200 rifles were then locally produced. To rectify this shortcoming, Sweden ordered 38,600 Model 1896 rifles from Waffenfabrik Mauser, of which approximately 15,000 rifles were delivered in 1889, with the remainder delivered in 1900 (Jones 2003, pp. 64–66).

The Swedish Model 1896 was essentially a Spanish Model 1893 with some minor differences. Four of the most obvious of these differences related to the rear thumb protrusion to the cocking piece, the round instead of square bottom to the bolt face, a unique rear sight, and a thumb notch in the left of the receiver to aid the loading of stripper clips. Other smaller differences include aspects such as a slimmer cleaning rod and a hole in the upper barrel band for the attachment of a monopod.

These developments demonstrate that in the few short years between 1889 and 1893, Mauser's technical development, coupled with Loewe's business acumen, had established the Mauser brand as being at the forefront of firearms design. But who exactly was Ludwig Loewe and how did he come to be associated with Mauser?

Ludwig Loewe & Cie

Germany was a relative latecomer to the Industrial Revolution, having started its industrialization only in the first half of the nineteenth century. At the forefront of the formative industrialization were the railways and companies that supported their growth. August Borsig, with his famous Berlin locomotive *Maschinenfabrik* (machinery factory), and the Krupp family, whose name was synonymous with steel, were early pioneers. In the late nineteenth century, Germans realized that they could effectively compete with established trading nations—particularly Britain—only if they offered improved design and vastly superior quality. The sheer quantity of goods required for this competition could be achieved only if Germany married its long-standing tradition of craft with machine production. It was within this context that Ludwig Loewe & Co. emerged as the preeminent small-arms manufacturer.

The son of a Jewish community teacher, Ludwig Loewe was born in 1837 in the town of Heiligenstadt, in Eichsfeld (Lower Saxony), Germany. In the 1860s, Ludwig operated a small machine tool shop in Berlin, where he became interested in American mass-production techniques. In December 1869, he, together with a group of associates, formed a company for the mass production of sewing machines. On 8 January 1870 the company Ludwig Loewe & Cie—a partnership limited by shares for the manufacture of sewing machines—was entered into the Companies Register of the Berlin city council. Shortly thereafter, Loewe left for the United States on 25 January 1870 to observe firsthand its mass-production techniques (Matscoss and Schlesinger 1930, pp. 5–8), with Colt and New England Machine Tools among the factories he visited. When Loewe returned to Germany on 3 April 1870, he did so with Pratt & Whitney machine tools and a complete design for a sewing-machine factory (Wengenroth 2002, p. 259). Because American industry could not satisfy the demands of German industrialization, Loewe soon started to copy and sell under license the manufacturing machines, particularly those of Pratt & Whitney, which he had acquired. By 1873, Loewe's copies, along with the original Pratt & Whitney machines, were exhibited at the Vienna World's Fair. Loewe's copies were well considered and were made heavier than the originals because of the lower machinability of German steel and the lesser skills of German operators (Buxbaum 1919, pp. 118–119).

Sadly, the economic crisis of 1873 and the resultant dramatic reduction in consumer demand dashed Loewe's hopes of selling vast numbers of sewing machines. Loewe thus desperately sought a means to keep his modern facility occupied. When Germany decided to adopt the Mauser Model 1871, it likewise decided to adopt factory mass production, or the *American way of manufacture*. To this end, it had also acquired Pratt & Whitney machine tools, gauges, and jigs to the value of 350,000 US dollars to reequip their armories in Spandau, Erfurt, and Danzig. So successful was the adaptation of the American way of manufacture that by 1874, the number of rifles produced per annum rose from 10,000 to between 40,000 and 50,000 at each rifle factory. When it became obvious that the state armories could not keep pace with the increasing demands of the army, private industry was co-opted to the production of small arms. Considering that some of Loewe's first clients were the Prussian armories, and Loewe also had the same machines and production philosophy, he was perfectly situated to fully exploit this opportunity (Wengenroth 2002, pp. 259–260). As such, on 2 May 1872, Ludwig Loewe reported to his board that he had secured a contract with the Prussian armories for the delivery of Mauser Model 1871 parts; in particular, large volumes of sights and extractors. By 1875, Loewe's production of rifle and ammunition components had reached such proportions that night shifts had to be introduced to cover the tremendous demand. Only in 1877 did working hours return to normal once the large Model 1871 orders were complete (Matscoss and Schlesinger 1930, p. 19). What this all meant for Ludwig Loewe was that he transformed his fledgling sewing-machine business into a preeminent supplier of small arms and one that had the means to produce them. While he had secured the intellectual property needed to manufacture machine tools, he lacked this for small arms. With the death of Ludwig Loewe on 11 September 1886, and the succession of his brother Isidor Loewe to the leadership of Ludwig Loewe & Co. (Matscoss and Schlesinger 1930, pp. 26–30), the company soon satisfied this criterion.

Mauser's association with Loewe appears to have started in the early 1880s with the purchase of Loewe machinery (Unknown author 1938, p. 91). On 2 May 1886, Paul Mauser and the Loewe brothers met at the Frankfurter Hof in Frankfurt am Main. During this meeting, a contract was finalized that confirmed their collaboration in obtaining and executing the aforementioned rifle contract from Turkey. This initial agreement stipulated that if a contract was forthcoming, it would be signed in Mauser's name, and the price per rifle, excluding bayonet, would be sixty marks (Yorulmaz 2014, pp. 110–111). This initial agreement and the subsequent Turkish contract with Loewe would eventually have catastrophic implications for Paul Mauser. Before 1884, Paul and his brother Wilhelm were the sole owners of Gebrüder Mauser & Cie (Mauser Brothers & Co.). This changed on 5 March 1874, when the need for capital drove Gebrüder Mauser & Cie to form an association with Württembergische Vereinsbank (Wurttemberg Bank). On 1 April 1884, Waffenfabrik Mauser was formed, with Paul Mauser having 334 shares and Württembergische Vereinsbank having 1,666, respectively. Significantly, this resulted in Paul Mauser transferring all of his past and future intellectual property to the company. This meant that when Ludwig Loewe & Co. acquired all the shares of Waffenfabrik Mauser on 28 December 1887, it owned both the company and the technical genius of Paul Mauser (Unknown author 1938, pp. 86–91). In my personal communication with Jon Speed in 2017, he contended that it was Württembergische Vereinsbank's director Alfred Kaulla who facilitated the transfer of the bank's holding to Loewe without informing Mauser.

Not satisfied with acquiring only Waffenfabrik Mauser, Loewe was further set on building a small-arms manufacturing empire. Isidor Loewe soon realized that he could achieve this supremacy only if his company worked in intimate combination with cartridge and propellant manufacturers. To achieve this aim, Loewe entered into an agreement with Germany's two leading propellant manufacturers in 1888—Vereinigten Rheinischen-Westfälische Pulverfabriken (United Rhineland and Westphalia Propellant Factory) in Cologne and Pulverfabrik Rottweil (Rottweil Propellant Factory) in Hamburg—to create or acquire a cartridge manufacturer. The Deutsche Metallpatronenfabrik von Lorenz (German Metal Cartridge Factory Lorenz) in Karlsruhe was subsequently acquired and converted to a public limited company (Matscoss and Schlesinger 1930, pp. 32–34). This took place as a direct result of Wilhelm Lorenz succumbing to the overwhelming pressure applied by Loewe for the massive ammunition order that accompanied the Turkish order. Consequently, Lorenz sold his company to Loewe on 6 February 1889 for six million marks (Yorulmaz 2014, p. 119). This development was quickly followed by the forced acquisition of the Ungarische Waffenfabrikations A.G. (Hungarian Arms Manufacturing) in Budapest. Interestingly, because of the later-discussed repercussions of a patent dispute between FN and Loewe regarding FN's wish to supply Chile with Model 1893 Mausers, Loewe also managed to acquire a majority shareholding in FN in February 1896. At an extraordinary general meeting on 7 November 1896, Loewe's board approved a request by Isidor Loewe that the Deutsche Metallpatronenfabrik von Lorenz be transformed into the Deutsche Waffen und Munitionsfabriken (German Armaments and Munitions Factories, or simply DWM), with its headquarters in Berlin and a branch in Karlsruhe. As share capital of the DWM was increased from six to twelve million marks, the Waffenfabrik Ludwig Loewe & Cie, Ungarische Waffenfabrikations, Waffenfabrik Mauser, and FN were also incorporated into DWM (Hassler and Bihl 1939, pp. 53–54; Matscoss and Schlesinger 1930, pp. 32–34). Following this event, the only European competitors of any consequence that remained outside the DWM conglomerate were the Österreichischen Waffenfabrik Gesellschaft (Austrian Armaments Factory Incorporated, or simply OEWG) in Steyr, Austria, and cartridge manufacturer Hirtenberger Patronen-, Zündhütchen- und Metallwaarenfabrik Aktiengesellschaft (Hirtenberger Cartridge, Primer and Metalware Factory, or simply Hirtenberg) (Schaefer 1974, p. 165).

In terms of the small-arms market at the end of the nineteenth century, Ludwig Loewe & Co., with its Mauser product, had gained an almost insurmountable position as the supplier of choice. Despite this, Austrian manufacturers started to gain market share both through rationalization and innovation in handguns. To ward off the ruinous consequences of competitions for orders, in October 1905 a cartel agreement was reached among DWM, FN, and OEWG that was further modified in 1907. This agreement stated that all three would divide the market according to spheres of influence. Likewise, it was agreed that the minimum price per rifle would be seventy-five francs, of which fifteen francs would be paid into a common fund that was to be divided by the constituent DWM companies and OEWG. Initially this agreement included only Russia, Japan, China, and Ethiopia. In 1907, this was extended to all other countries, with the exceptions of Germany, which was the exclusive domain of DWM; Belgium and the Belgium Congo, which belonged to FN; and Turkey and Spain, which were placed off limits to OEWG, while Bulgaria and Romania were the exclusive domain of OEWG. Thus, whichever company won any given contract in Latin America and Chile would then have to share the profits with the other through the common fund (Schaefer 1974, pp. 166, 267; Seel 1986, p. 64).

Chile Immediately before the Introduction of the Mauser

Chile's entanglement with Mauser can be argued as a direct result of two seminal events in its history. The first of these events was the War of the Pacific that took place among Bolivia, Peru, and Chile from 1879 to 1883. The second was the Chilean Civil War of 1891, which pitted a majority congressional-supported navy against the mostly presidential-backed army.

Map of South America.

Miller, J. M., and L. G Stahl. 1909. *The Twentieth Century Atlas of the Commercial, Geographical and Historical World with a Description of Every Known Land, Both Near and Remote, Ancient and Modern, Embracing Complete, Original and Authentic Maps of the Present Development of All Countries, Empires and States of the World Comprising Graphic Description of the People: Their Civilization, Their Religion, Their Government, Their Cities, Their Imports and Exports, Their Wealth, Their Railways, Their Canals, Their Cables, Their Telegraphs, etc., etc., Including Useful and Timely Statistics, Educational, Industrial Military, Naval.* 3rd ed. Chicago: L. W. Walter.

Chile's prosperity, which was initially driven by agriculture and trade, was later sustained by a thriving mining industry. In the second half of the nineteenth century, silver and, to a lesser extent, copper as well as nitrate mineral salts, were Chile's major mineral resources. Because of their high nitrogen content, nitrates were very desirable for the making of fertilizer, gunpowder, and explosives (Rector 2005, p. 97). Before the invention of viable artificial nitrate production by Fritz Haber and Carl Bosch in 1909, the primary supply of nitrates was, by far, the mining of nitrate deposits (Laylin 1993, p. 118). In this context, Chile and its nitrate resources offered a ready and cheap supply. Unfortunately for Chile and its neighbors, the majority of the nitrate deposits were in arid areas in the north, the ownership of which was contested.

In 1866, Chile had agreed with its northern neighbor Bolivia that the border between the two countries would be demarcated by 24 degrees south latitude. Problems soon arose because major deposits of nitrates existed on Bolivian and Peruvian territory that was heavily exploited by Chilean companies. To counter the perceived threat of Chilean domination, Bolivia and Peru signed a secret mutual defense treaty in 1873 (Rector 2005, p. 99). As mentioned, this was the year the world entered a decade-long economic recession (Barreyre 2011), and as such nitrate prices declined. In an attempt to control weakening international prices, Peru nationalized all nitrate mines in 1875 and issued interest-bearing certificates that were to be repaid after two years. In 1877, when it was time to repay the certificates, Peru lacked the funds and their values dropped significantly. To complicate matters even further, in 1878 Gen. Hilarion Daza overthrew the Bolivian government and proceeded to increase taxes on nitrates. The Antofagasta Nitrate and Railroad Company, which was jointly owned by Chilean and British investors, subsequently refused to pay these increased taxes. Daza and the Bolivians responded by embargoing the company's machinery. Chile responded by invading the Bolivian port of Antofagasta, after which Bolivia declared war. Peru initially offered to mediate the conflict, but after Chile became aware of the mutual defense pact between Bolivia and Peru, it responded by declaring war on Peru (Rector 2005, p. 100).

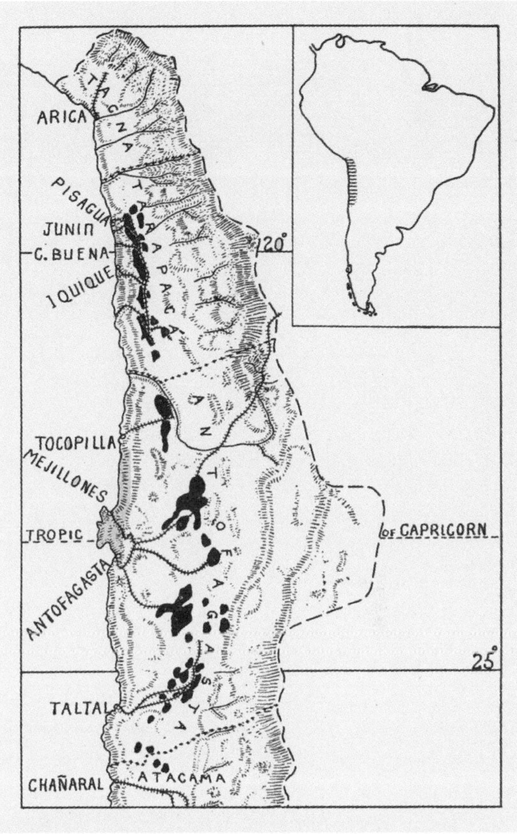

Map of northern Chile indicating the major nitrate deposits (black areas).
Tower, W. S. 1913. "The Nitrate Fields of Chile." *Popular Science Monthly* 83 (September), 209–230.

At the outbreak of war, Chile's army comprised approximately 2,700 regular troops equipped with Belgian Model 1874 Comblain rifles in 11 mm caliber. Along with a stockpile of 13,000 Comblain rifles, the Chilean army also had numerous Gras, Minie, Remington-Lee, and Beaumont rifles that fired the same cartridge. The Chilean cavalry was armed with Spencer and Winchester carbines. Peru was armed with dated weaponry acquired in 1866, including Chassepot and Minie rifles. In stark contrast, the small Bolivian Presidential Guard appeared to be the only unit armed with "modern" Remington rifles (Scheina 2003, pp. 376–377). Following years of cost cutting, the Chilean army had lost 20 percent of its manpower. Likewise, the Chilean navy had decommissioned warships,

Hammer and pick used in the extraction of nitrates. These basic tools are arguably depicted as one of the acceptance marks on Chile's Mauser Model 1895 and 1912.
Tower, W. S. 1913. "The Nitrate Fields of Chile." *Popular Science Monthly* 83 (September): 209–230.

and the Territorial Reserve (Guardia Nacional) had been reduced in size by almost two-thirds. Thus, with the Chilean army lacking weaponry, logistics, and medical supplies, the only viable option left was to attack from the sea (Collier and Sater 2004, p. 129). After neutralizing the Peruvian navy in October 1879, Chile proceeded over the next three years to launch a number of campaigns, culminating in the capture of Lima in January 1881. With this event Peru was officially defeated and could then offer only sporadic guerrilla warfare until October 1883, when it signed the Treaty of Ancon. The war was ended in April 1884, when Bolivia, which had played a secondary role in the war, signed an indefinite truce (Collier and Sater 2004, pp. 131–136). Under the Treaty of Ancon, Chile unconditionally gained the Peruvian province of Tarapaca, while the provinces of Tacna and Arica were ceded for ten years, after which a plebiscite would decide if they would remain Chilean or return to Peru (Nova Vidal et al. 1883). As will be explained, the stipulation concerning Tacna and Arica would eventually prove the pretext for further provocation and subsequent Mauser rifle purchases in 1901 and 1910.

Before explaining the Chilean Revolution of 1891, key figures, institutions, and concepts in the story of Mauser and Chile need introduction. Chile's victory in the War of the Pacific highlighted the serious inadequacies of its military. The notion of modeling the Chilean army after that of Prussia was advocated as a solution (Boonen Rivera 1888; Lara 1929, pp. 3–4). As this thinking gained strength, it later became known as "Prussianization." To achieve this aim, Chilean president Domingo Santa Maria instructed Guillermo Matta, as head of the Chilean legation in Paris, to find a competent Prussian officer to serve as instructor and subdirector of the military school in Santiago. The candidate eventually chosen in 1885 was Capt. Emil Körner, who assumed his duties as a lieutenant-colonel in early 1886. Subsequently, on 9 September 1886, the Chilean War Academy was founded, whose role was to promote the technical and scientific instruction of officers so that Chile could utilize modern tactics and armaments in future wars. Before capable officer candidates could progress to the war academy, the military school also had to be reformed. Körner thus devised Prussianization plans both for the military school and the war academy, and the event that allowed him to implement and advance these plans was the revolution of 1891. Körner's involvement in the 1891 revolution was not driven by any strong political ideals on his part; rather, he realized that only by siding with the congressionalists' cause could he fully implement his radical reforms (Nunn 1970, pp. 303–305).

The revolution of 1891 was essentially the result of a squabble between the Chilean congress and the president. On 4 January 1891, President José Manuel Balmaceda announced that the budget for 1891 would be unilaterally passed by his office. Congress responded to this act by accusing Balmaceda of high treason. The Chilean navy, having sided with congress, steamed from its home port of Valparaíso on 7 January 1891 and commenced hostilities against the army, which had sided with Balmaceda, who remained in Santiago. After securing a foothold in the northern port of Iquique, the navy proceed to train and equip a force of approximately 10,000 with newly acquired European weapons (Collier and Sater 2004, pp. 154–155). Körner, having been dismissed by Balmaceda, traveled north and joined congressional forces. Here he quickly trained the new army and reorganized it into three infantry regiments, an artillery detachment, an engineering battalion, and an all-important sanitation group. Along with indoctrinating modern tactics, constant drill and rifle shooting were emphasized. Modern weapons—notably Krupp cannons and Mannlicher rifles—were acquired (Resende Santos 2007, pp.

Emil Körner at the Chilean Cavalry School, 19 December 1905. Körner is ninth from the left, and to his immediate right is then Chilean minister of war Manuel Fóster Recabarren.
Unknown author. 1905. *Escular de caballería, revista final, 19 diciembre 1905*. Santiago, Chile: Biblioteca Escuela Militar.

143–145). On 3 July 1891 the transport *Maipo* arrived in Iquique with European armaments acquired by Augusto Matte Pérez and Agustín Ross. These included six Krupp Mountain Cannons with ammunition and 5,000 Gras rifles with two million rounds of ammunition (Unknown author 1892b, p. 245). *Maipo* also delivered 1,970,000 rounds of Mannlicher 8 mm cartridges (Unknown author 1892b, p. 393). Having captured 4,500 Mannlicher rifles on 8 January 1891, the congressional army greatly needed this Mannlicher ammunition. They had taken these 4,500 rifles from the German steamship *Cleopatra*, which was anchored in Valparaíso, and then transferred them to the commandeered ship *Aconcagua* that belonged to the Campania Sud-Americana de Vapores (Unknown author 1892b, p. 2). The problem facing the congressional army was that while it had Mannlicher rifles, it had very little ammunition for them (Unknown author 1892b, pp. 97, 99). At this point, it is worth mentioning that before the 1891 revolution, Chile had acquired a substantial stock of Mannlicher Model 1888s in 8 mm caliber. The total amount of these is somewhat unclear, with one source mentioning 12,000 as having been supplied in 1889–90 (Neubauer 1974) and another stipulating a total of 32,000 (August Schriever & Compagnie 1895).

Chile's decision to replace its existing frontline store of Comblain, Gras, Winchester, and, to a lesser extent, Minie, Beaumont, Peabody, Spencer Remington, Bomsmueller, and Kropatschek rifles, was driven by a decision made by President Balmaceda in 1888. This resolution dictated that Chile needed 100,000 rifles, 100 cannons, 8,000 sabers, and 5,000 carbines. The only unresolved question was whether these would come from France—which was Chile's traditional supplier of arms—or Germany. As we can see, it was neither; rather, the Austrian Mannlicher prevailed in this instance (Sater and Herwig 1999, p. 136). Interestingly, when offering his final accounting of the congressional army's European acquisitions, Agustín Ross revealed that it had also acquired an additional 10,000 11 mm caliber Mannlicher rifles with five million rounds of ammunition, 2,000 .44-caliber Winchester carbines with two million rounds of ammunition, and an additional

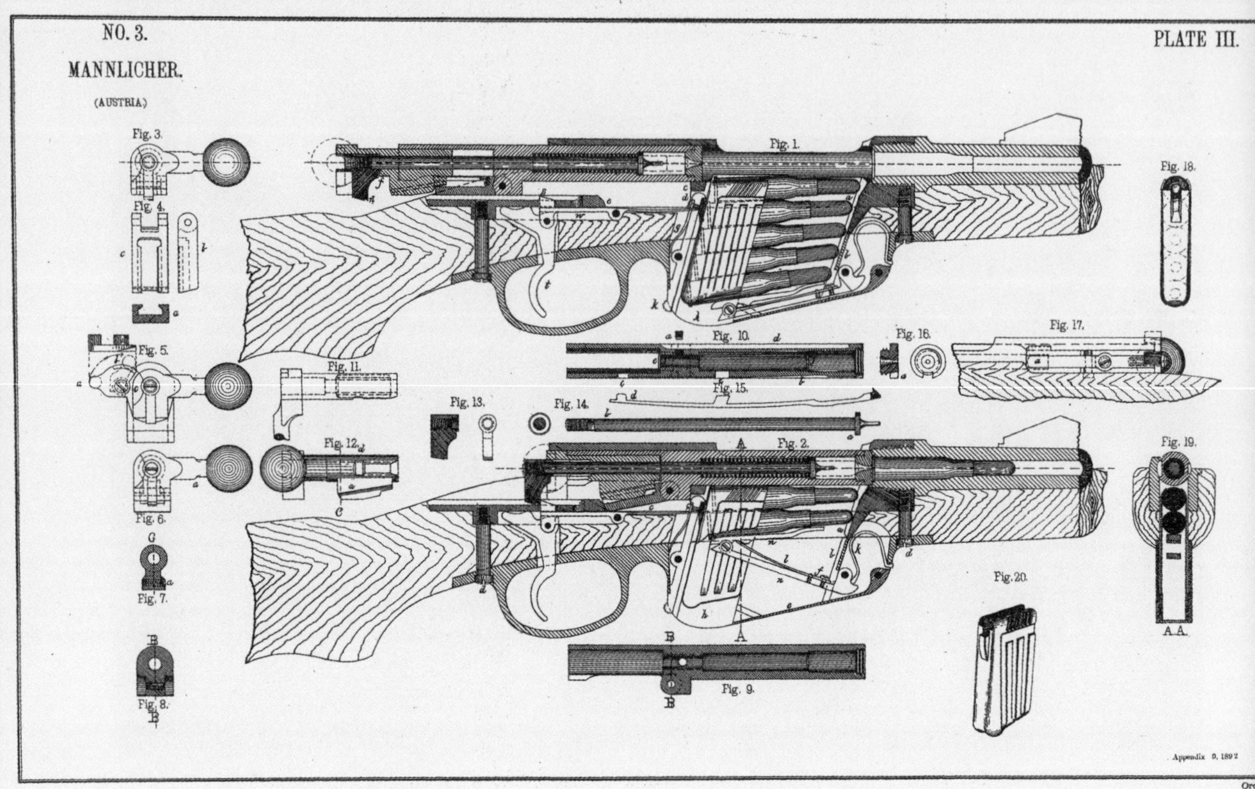

Mannlicher 8 mm Model 1888.
Unknown author. 1892a. *Annual Report of the Chief of Ordnance to the Secretary of War for the Fiscal Year Ended June 30 1892.* Washington, DC: Government Printing Office.

one million rounds of Mannlicher 8 mm ammunition. Ross openly mentioned that the 10,000 11 mm Mannlicher rifles were obsolete in Europe because of their 11 mm caliber, and this would create supply problems with Chile's other 8 mm Mannlicher rifles; they were thus bought only out of necessity (Unknown author 1892b, pp. 392–401). Interestingly, in 1907, Chile sold 28,000 Mannlicher Model 1888s and 11.2 million rounds of ammunition to Bulgaria, with the deal being facilitated through the Hamburg firm Gleissner & Co. for one million francs (Sater and Herwig 1999, p. 148).

On 20 August, Körner's new army went on the offensive and landed at Quintero, near Valparaíso. Swift congressional victory followed the initial Battle of Concon on 21 August 1891 and culminated in the Battle Placilla on 27 August (Sater and Herwig 1999, pp. 50–54). At the Battle of Concon, the congressional army comprised 4,000 troops armed with Mannlichers, 5,000 with Gras, and the remainder with Comblain rifles. The Balmaceda forces comprised 8,000 men armed with Gras and Comblain rifles. Remarkably, the author of an account of the battle, while mentioning the effectiveness of the Mannlicher, conceded that the congressionalists' success was mainly due to the low morale of the Balmaceda army (Unknown author 1891b). Period reports of these two battles noted the devastating effects of the new Mannlicher rifles coupled with its small caliber. One report by US naval observers stated that these rifles terrorized and caused untold confusion in the ranks of Balmaceda's forces (Sears and Wells 1893, p. 58). Körner likewise praised the superiority of the Austrian Mannlicher (Unknown author 1892b, pp. 300–307); a newspaper article quoted him as saying that he considered the Mannlicher to be the best rifle made to date, with an unequaled range and trajectory. He did mention that its two weaknesses were the rear springs in the breach that raised the cartridges from the magazine to the barrel and its 8 mm caliber, which should be reduced to 7.5 mm. Körner stated that recruits found the Mannlicher simple to handle and operated it with ease, even when using it for the first time. More interestingly for this book, Körner dramatically implied that the Mannlicher was superior to the Mauser: "Its action is simple, there being but one motion in loading against the two in the Mauser rifle" (Unknown author 1891a).

With the congressional victory thus assured, the Prussianization of Chilean armed forces could then proceed.

Mauser and Chile

Before the Chilean Revolution of 1891, Alex Résimont, as Mauser's Brussels agent, wrote to a Mr. Mauser on 7 January 1890. He stated that as Mauser well knew, the Chilean government had ordered 60,000 Mannlicher rifles from Steyr-Werke of Österreichischen Waffenfabrik-Gesellschaft. He proceeded to state that only 20,000 of these rifles had so far been confirmed, and the contract had a clause that allowed cancellation after this amount. Résimont continued to state that Col. Martínez—responsible for overseeing delivery of these rifles—had suggested to the Chilean government that it take delivery of only 20,000 rifles. Martínez is further quoted as suggesting that the remaining 40,000 rifles be respecified for a better design. A gentleman who worked with Martínez on the acceptance of the 20,000 Mannlichers is then quoted as having suggested that Martínez consider the new Belgian Model 1889 Mauser. Résimont then stated in the letter that Martínez had informed him that Mauser had already sent a sample of a Mauser rifle; he would therefore like to know if it was a Model 1889 (Résimont 1890b).

On 27 August 1890, Résimont again wrote to Mr. Mauser. In this letter, Résimont stated that he had again met with Col. Martínez from the Chilean legation. During this meeting, Martínez informed Résimont that he was not happy with the choice of the Mannlicher rifles selected by his country, and as such, he would like to stop their manufacture and replace them with Mauser rifles. Martínez then asked if Mauser could inform him in the next eight days if it was possible to manufacture a rifle that fired the Austrian 8 mm cartridge, and what the cost of this would be. Martínez likewise stated that if manufacture was possible, then he would cancel the remaining Mannlicher rifles and redirect the outstanding 28,000 rifles toward a Mauser system. Martínez then stated that if it were possible to totally discard the Mannlicher and rearm the Chileans with new Mausers, then 60,000 to 68,000 rifles would be ordered. Résimont then asked Mauser what each of these new Mauser rifles in 8 mm would cost and where they could be manufactured, and specified initial deliveries either for 1891 or 1892 (Résimont 1890a).

Chilean initial interest in Mauser's rifles was the focus not only of the military. On 16 July 1892, a Mr. Theodor Dohse from the Café del Pacífico in Valparaíso wrote to Mauser, inquiring if the company could sell him a custom-made rifle. Paul Mauser personally replied to Dohse on 7 September 1892, stating that custom rifle manufacture was not possible, since their business was focused on the supply of military small arms. He did go on to state that he was willing to supply three of their newest 7.65 mm caliber rifles, with trigger guard and magazine in one part—including seaworthy packaging to Chile—for 105 marks each. Mauser quoted a price of 150 marks per 1,000 rounds of associated ammunition. Mauser further informed Dohse that if he would like to reload or manufacture his own ammunition, these components could also be supplied: metal cartridge cases that used primers at sixty marks and projectiles with nickel-plated steel jackets at forty marks. (Although it was not mentioned, it is assumed that these prices are per 1,000.) Mauser also quoted prices for one kilogram of smokeless powder at twelve marks. Mauser concluded by stating that he welcomed future orders and had enclosed a brochure for further information on the benefits of small-caliber projectiles and smokeless powders (Mauser 1892b).

The last sentence of this letter exemplifies the marketing intent of Mauser's letter, which indicates that during this period, Mauser might not have had an agent in Valparaíso or Chile. On the other hand, Ludwig Loewe & Co. did have a Chilean agent in the form of the German trading house Vorwerk & Co., and it was through Vorwerk that Loewe began to pressure Chile into purchasing Mauser rifles (Sater and Herwig 1999, p. 133). It was not only Vorwerk that was actively lobbying for Mauser; in a reversal of his earlier praise of the Mannlicher rifle,

Körner was now gravitating to the Mauser camp. It would be right to question why this occurred.

From the arguments presented, it is clear that the pace of Mauser's technological innovation and the rapid acceptance of Mauser rifles by numerous nations undoubtedly played a role in swaying Körner's thinking. However, it has been acknowledged in Sater and Herwig's *The Grand Illusion: The Prussianization of the Chilean Army* (1999)—which incidentally builds much of its arguments concerning Mauser on the earlier *Deutsche Militärhilfe an Sudamerika: Militär- und Rüstungsinteressen in Argentinien, Bolivien und Chile vor 1914* (Schaefer 1974)—that the Chilean army was at the cusp of a new era during which German armaments would prevail. It has to be remembered that Körner, following his outstanding performance in the 1891 revolution, was in the perfect position to finally Prussianize the Chilean army. As such, it seems logical that he acquired everything Prussian, including weapons. Equally, these events should be seen in the wider context of imperialist competitions played between the major European powers. In this light, Körner's actions can be argued as German patriotism (Sater and Herwig 1999; Schaefer 1974). It has also been argued that Körner's intentions were not entirely pure. In 1881, while still in Germany, Körner had attained the rank of captain (Nunn 1970, p. 303). It has been proposed that because he lacked noble credentials, influential family ties, or wealth, Körner had thus reached the limits of his promotions in the German military (Sater and Herwig 1999, p. 32). For this reason, it would seem obvious why Körner, when approached by the Chileans in 1885 (who offered 12,000 marks per year and a promotion to lieutenant-colonel), would have jumped at the opportunity. It would appear that money was not the major consideration in his decision. A short while after Körner was offered his Chilean position, he was offered a similar role in the Japanese army for 2,000 British pounds (approximately 40,000 marks) per year. Körner declined this second offer because he claimed that Chile's proficiency in the War of the Pacific had impressed him (Donoso 1947, p. 372). It has also been pointed out that German armament firms were actively providing bribes to Chileans. More disturbingly, Körner's efforts in acquiring Mauser rifles for Chile have been argued as being instrumental in establishing this practice (Sater and Herwig 1999, pp. 176–202). Apart from Mauser, Körner is also identified as having obediently served the interests of the armaments behemoth Krupp. In January 1894, it was Körner who took over when Krupp fell out with its representatives in Chile—Schuchard, Grisar & Co.—ironically because of the embezzlement of 2.45 million marks (Sater and Herwig 1999, pp. 142–143). (This fact concerning the role played by bribes and the importance of influence will become clearer as this book progresses.) While bribes and influence can be seen as tools to secure a deal, a pretext for the deal was still necessary, and it was political tensions between neighboring countries that provided this pretext. In the late nineteenth century, political tensions in South America abounded and European arms merchants were exceptionally skilled at manipulating these for their own advantage (Sater and Herwig 1999, pp. 132–175). It would appear that a provisional answer to the question why Chile and Körner would abandon Mannlicher in favor of Mauser is arguably a combination of all the factors discussed.

The Chilean Trials of 1892

On 31 December 1892, Georg Luger—who was at that time employed by Ludwig Loewe & Co., and who would later become famous for his design of the parabellum pistol of 1908—wrote a long letter to Waffenfabrik Mauser in Oberndorf. His communique was in reply to an earlier Mauser dispatch written on 29 December. Luger began his letter by stating that to reach an agreement with Chile regarding the purchases of new Mauser rifles, the ability to ensure an extremely fast delivery schedule was paramount. This was because Chile feared a war beginning with Argentina no later than 1894. Luger then argued that everything necessary needed to be put in place for the first 5,000 rifles to be delivered in July 1893, with the remainder of the 60,000 rifles to be delivered in the following four months. To achieve this deadline, Luger argued that any technological advances that might impede production should be excluded

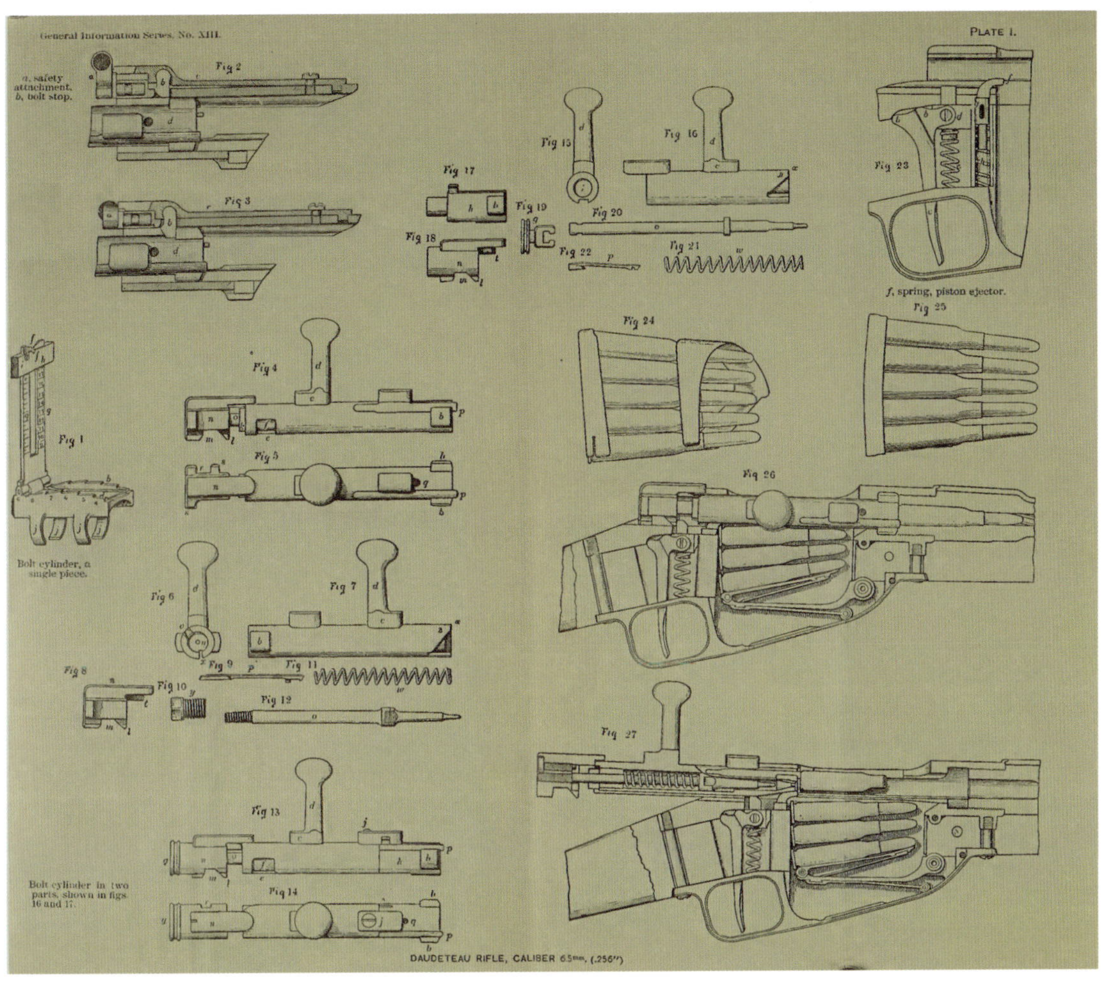

Daudeteau rifle in 6.5 mm caliber.
Unknown author. 1894. *Notes on the Year's Naval Progress*. Washington, DC: Government Printing Office.

from these proposed rifles. Luger identified the new interrupted-lug connection between the firing pin and cocking piece and the new safety lever as being innovations that were impeding current rapid production. Luger condescendingly stated that these innovations would not be appreciated by people who wanted only rifles that were reliable and could shoot accurately. Referring to the Chilean rifle trials of 1892, Luger stated that Mauser's practice of constantly introducing new innovations into its trial rifles was highly detrimental. He argued that competitors such as Steyr were presenting rifles that were complete and tested, while Mauser was constantly introducing innovations that were developed by studying and watching its competitors' rifles. He stated that while he appreciated new innovations, Mauser's products were conceptually identical to other designs. He then proceeded to argue that the new firing-pin and cocking-piece connection was somewhat similar to those in rifles such as Lebel, Schmidt, and Krag-Jorgensen but was especially similar, if not identical, to the Daudeteau. More evident was Mauser's ring connector for the handguard, which was, in Luger's opinion, a direct copy of the Daudeteau. Luger concluded this comparison by asserting that he could not present these as innovations, since Mauser's trial competitors would immediately identify them as theirs and subsequently defame Mauser. For this reason, Luger wrote that while public exposure was impossible, private disclosure was possible.

Thus, for public display, the sole 7 mm rifle that had started a long-term trial was the only option. This single 7 mm rifle was apparently very important because Luger stated that he kept it close, even at night, to prevent mishap (Luger 1892).

In relation to their Steyr competition in the trials, Luger stated that they were willing to start deliveries in February 1893 and complete the total order in three months. Luger then detailed that because of the superstitions of the very religious Chileans, who had gained their latest victories with the Mannlicher, they would probably come to an agreement with Steyr. According to Luger, Steyr agent August Schriever had even stated that neither for love nor money would he forgo a deal with Chile, even if he had to give them a new 6.5 mm Mannlicher for every old 8 mm Mannlicher. Bemoaning the fact that Mauser had not personally attended the trials, Luger argued that he recognized the danger that the 6.5 mm Mannlicher posed. As such, he had done everything in his power to discredit it by falsely stating (and even contrary to his own beliefs) that when compared to the 7.65 × 53 mm, the 6.5 mm trajectory was heavily affected by wind and weather. For these reasons, Luger argued, the Mauser 7 mm caliber was attracting special attention as the only acceptable solution for a reduction in caliber. Steyr had then simply countered this argument by proposing that he was willing to supply the Mannlicher in 7 mm caliber. To reduce the threat posed by the 6.5 mm Mannlicher, Luger stated that Loewe had presented the Beaumont rifle at the trials only in case Chile decided on the 6.5 mm caliber. However, because of a trial stipulation that only the caliber that the manufacturer regarded as the most suitable be tested, this Beaumont rifle was in 7 mm caliber. Another reason for presenting the 7 mm Beaumont in the trials was the unreliability of a second batch of 6.5 mm powder, which had produced numerous misfires. Luger then informed Mauser that Mr. Edouard de Beaumont was urgently seeking a number of drawings of his rifle so that he could write the instruction manual. Luger warned that Loewe had neither rifles nor other parts for the Beaumont, so it was urgently requesting that Mauser compile the necessary information, even if in copy form, and send it directly to Luger in Brussels or to Beaumont in Maastricht. He further advised that the only thing Loewe could contribute was a drawing of the bolt. In any case, he noted that the only other required drawing would be a detailed longitudinal section and images that depicted the operation and assembly of the important components. Luger ended the letter by asking that these drawings be urgently completed, since Mauser was the only one that could accomplish this (Luger 1892).

The content of Luger's letter deserves further context. As mentioned, Argentina's initial Mauser contract included Clause 18, which precluded delivery to other South American nations. Soon after signing this contract, Argentina ran into financial difficulties and had to renegotiate. New contracts were subsequently signed on 4 and 20 November 1891. In these amended versions of the contract, which halved the total number of rifles and carbines, Clause 18 was slightly altered to stipulate that while prohibition was still valid, it was now subject to financial performance by the Argentine government. Likewise, on 27 March 1893, Argentina signed a further amended contract for 55,000 rifles and 5,000 carbines. Importantly, in this 1893 contract, Ludwig Loewe & Co. undertook "not to deliver small calibre system Mauser weapons to any South American powers or private individuals before 5 November 1893" (Webster 2003, pp. 47–49, 246–261). This renegotiation, apart from severely damaging Argentina's credibility, also placed the sustainability of future Argentine orders in doubt. In an effort to expand and importantly develop and sustain its South American business, Loewe thus considered Chile the only viable option. In 1892, Krupp's representative in Europe, Schinzinger, purposefully informed the Chilean military attaché in Berlin, Col. Boonen Rivera, that despite facing difficulties, Argentina was still purchasing significant quantities of small arms. To panic the Chileans into a purchase, the Chilean *chargé d'affaires* in Berlin, Galo Irarrázaval, then visited the Loewe factory in Moabit (Martinickenfelde), Berlin, to confirm the accuracy of Schinzinger's information. Here Irarrázaval succeeded in physically seeing the Argentine rifles, complete with national crest, crated and ready for shipping. This visit in summer 1892 was accomplished on the pretext that Chile wanted to replace its Mannlichers with Mausers.

At the Loewe factory, Director Max Kosegarten proposed that a large Chilean order of 100,000 rifles was immediately deliverable, but only if the Argentine order was shipped. To sweeten the deal, Kosegarten offered to sell Chile's Mannlichers through its representatives and offered a new Mauser—including a bayonet and packaging—for 82.5 francs per rifle. Although the Chilean ambassador in Paris, Bulnes, eventually saw through the ruse being played and subsequently declined Kosegarten's offer, he did consequently urge his government in Santiago to come to an urgent resolution as to Chile's rifle question. In response to this request, the Chilean government established a Comisión Militar (European Weapons Commission) to be headquartered in Paris. This commission was directed by Körner's rival, Gen. Estanislao del Canto Arteaga, and also included Cols. Baeza and Boonen Rivera, Lt. Col. Vial, and Irarrázaval (Schaefer 1974, pp. 40–42). It was this European Weapons Commission that did the initial testing to determine the choice of Chile's new rifle. These trials were then followed in 1893 by further tests in Santiago. Before the later trials are discussed, it is necessary to detail developments that occurred immediately after the first trials.

On 30 January 1893, Augusto Matte Pérez, as newly appointed Chilean ambassador in Paris, wrote to Chilean minister of war Francisco Antonio Pinto Cruz. In his letter, Matte stated that he had forwarded a copy of the final report by the Chilean Weapons Commission that detailed its choice of Chile's new *armamento menor* (small arm)—the Spanish Mauser—to the minister in Santiago on 20 January 1893. Matte then proceeded to detail a meeting that he had held with the director of Ludwig Loewe & Co., Alexis Riese, on 22 January in Matte's Paris office. During this meeting, which was convened to establish the price and delivery schedules of Spanish Mausers to Chile, Riese had informed Matte that delivery of the Spanish Mauser could not start until September 1893. This

Undated image of Georg Luger, who is at the center of the image, while his son is second from the right in the back row. The carbine held by the seated gentleman on the right is in all probability a Chilean Model 1895. Likewise, the rifle second from the left is either a Spanish Model 1893 or a Chilean Model 1895. *Image with the permission of Jon Speed and Geoffrey Sturgess* Speed, J. 2007. *The Mauser Archive*. Cobourg, ON: Collector Grade. Notes: Date uncertain but is undoubtedly after 1894–95. Permission obtained from Jon Speed to use image.

was because the Spanish Mauser as presented at the Chilean trials had been manufactured only in very limited quantities. Thus, Riese stated that Loewe still had to retool its factory for the Spanish Mauser's mass manufacture, which could be accomplished only by June 1893. Importantly, Riese identified the new rotating extractor as the main reason for these delays. As an interim solution, Riese offered the Chileans a 7 mm rifle that was identical to the Spanish Mauser, except that it had an extractor of Argentine Model 1891 specification. This so-called *modelo mixto* (mixed model) could be delivered as early as July 1893. Matte then informed the war minister that before he could consider Riese's proposal, he would first have to ask the Weapons Commission what impact this proposal would have (Matte Pérez 1893b).

On 24 January 1893, Matte wrote to the Weapons Commission and requested that it assess whether the extractor change would alter its ranking and final choice of the Spanish Mauser. Importantly, in this letter the Mauser in question was identified as the 7 mm Spanish Mauser Model 1892 (Matte Pérez 1893c). The Military Commission, comprising Gen. Canto, Col. Boonen Rivera, and Lt. Col. Vial, replied to Matte's request the same day. After stating that the members understood the context of the request, Canto offered the first opinion, stating that the Mannlicher was an excellent rifle and that the 8 mm caliber was being used by most European nations and Chile. Thus, for him, the essential question facing the commission was whether to abandon the 8 mm caliber and adopt the 6.5 mm caliber. Canto then argued that while there were three 6.5 mm rifles in the trials—namely, Mannlicher, Daudeteau, and Beaumont—the 7 mm Spanish Model had delivered the best results. He then stated that despite the trials having been completed, the commission lacked the time needed to adequately assess all the rifles entered into them. Canto also mentioned that the Argentine Mauser used in the trials had repeatedly underperformed when compared to the four rifles above, since it often double-loaded from the magazine. He then stated that if the Chileans could not receive an identical Mauser as tested by the commission, it should not choose an inferior substitute, since it was the tested Mauser's extractor that had largely contributed to its success in the trials. As such, Canto recommended that Chile should procure the 8 mm Mannlicher, since it could later be converted to 6.5 mm caliber and meet the specification advised by the minister of war on 24 August 1892. Next to offer their opinions were Col. Boonen Rivera and Lt. Col. Vial, who argued that it was the ballistic characteristics of 7 mm caliber that allowed the Mauser to win the trials. In this light, Boonen Rivera and Vial argued that despite Mauser not being able to deliver a rifle identical to that tested in the trials, Chile should nevertheless procure the 7 mm Mauser with an Argentine extractor; that is, as a mixed model (Canto et al. 1893).

Returning to the 30 January 1893 letter by Matte to the minister of war, Matte stated that since the Weapons Commission had voted two to one to accept Riese's mixed model, he had resumed negotiations with Riese and had finalized an agreement. This agreement stated that Loewe would deliver Mauser rifles to Chile under the following conditions:

- 10,000 mixed-model Mauser 7 mm rifles with bayonets would be delivered in July 1893. This would be followed by a further 10,000 in August, for a total of 20,000 mixed-model Mausers.
- 5,000 full Spanish Mauser 7 mm rifles, as tested by the Weapons Commission, would be delivered in September 1893. This would be followed by 10,000 per month up to a total of 40,000 of this full specification.
- 5,000 mixed-model Mauser 7 mm carbines would be delivered in September 1893.

Matte then reported that Loewe had finally agreed on a price of 78.75 francs per mixed-model rifle, 81 francs for a full Spanish model rifle, and 72.25 francs per carbine—all packaged and shipped from Hamburg. It was reported by Matte that Loewe had initially quoted eighty-two francs per mixed-model rifle and eighty-six francs per full Spanish model rifle. The Chileans rejected this offer, arguing that they should not pay more that the Argentines and Spanish had agreed to; these figures were known to the Chileans through private inquiries. Because of these arguments, Loewe dropped its prices significantly. The ambassador then instructed that to secure the initial agreement,

Loewe required the immediate agreement of the Chilean government to its proposal by 1 February 1893, which was later extended to 15 February. Matte informed that according to information obtained from Loewe and other reliable sources, Argentina was executing an order with Loewe for 50,000 rifles and 10,000 carbines. Matte stated that as of 21 January 1893, 40,000 rifles had been completed and the remaining 10,000 would be complete in February. He then noted that according to his sources, Argentina, despite its current financial difficulties, was actively seeking to exercise its option to extend the provisions of this contract and acquire a further 50,000 rifles and 10,000 carbines. Matte then advised the minister that if Argentina failed to extend their contract, Chile could capitalize on this development by increasing the quantities and decreasing its delivery schedule; that is, 15,000 mixed-model Mausers a month earlier in June 1893, and 10,000 in July. To end his letter, Matte informed the minister that, as a supplement to his earlier letter of 20 January, he had now included additional important information that was alluded to in the Weapons Commission report. This information concerned detailed proposals by Daudeteau and Mannlicher, focusing on the 6.5 mm Dutch Mannlicher. Matte concluded by stating that in response to the minister's instruction of 9 December 1892, Mauser, Mannlicher, and Daudeteau, as the manufacturers being considered by the Weapons Commission, had been instructed to send examples of their weapons, along with 2,000 rounds of ammunition, to Chile (Matte Pérez 1893b).

No further information can be found to illuminate how these initial discussions progressed between Loewe and Chile. On 29 April 1893, Matte wrote to Isidoro Errázuriz as the newly appointed Chilean minister of war. In this letter, Matte informed the new minister that since he had previously communicated via private letter to former Minister Pinto Cruz, Argentina had agreed with Loewe to exercise their right to purchase a further 60,000 Mausers (Matte Pérez 1893a). Article 6 of this contract, signed on 27 March 1893, obligated Loewe not to supply small-caliber-system Mauser weapons to any South American powers of private individuals before 5 November 1893. From this fact and the tone of Matte's letter, it is clear that Chile could not contract for Mausers before 5 November 1893. While it is not known if Chile knew of the Article 6 prohibition, it can be assumed that the above negotiation ceased for the time being.

The Chilean Trials of 1893

Partly in response to Luger's concern about Mauser not sending an appropriate representative to the 1892 Chilean trials, on 30 April 1893 Paul Mauser's nephew—Paul Mauser II—arrived in Santiago, Chile (Mauser II 1893a). At this point, it is also worth clarifying that Paul Mauser II was the son of the older Mauser brother, Heinrich. In their early years, Wilhelm and Paul Mauser received assistance and support from Heinrich, who had died in 1874. Born in 1860, Paul Mauser II worked for his two uncles and was comprehensively trained in all aspects of their business. Paul Mauser II later became the foreman of Mauser's lower works on 5 November 1893. In 1907, he became a board member and, in 1909, the technical director of Waffenfabrik Mauser (Seel 1986, p. 59; Unknown author 1938, p. 100).

Reporting on his journey, arrival, and progress to date, Mauser II wrote a letter to Ludwig Loewe & Co. on 5 May 1893. In this communication, he stated that on 1 May he had written to the trading houses of Vorwerk & Co. and Saavedra Bernard & Co. in Valparaíso, and that on 2 May he had met with Körner. At this meeting, he was informed that Loewe's Steyr competitor, in the form of August Schriever & Co. and physically represented by a Mr. Visscher, had not yet arrived in Santiago. Körner had also advised Mauser II that Mr. Errázuriz was the new Chilean minister of war. Mr. Saavedra, as Mr. Bernard's partner in Saavedra Bernard & Co., was also at this meeting, and he had told Mauser II that because border negotiations with Argentina had reached a delicate stage, their chances of securing a large contract had subsequently diminished. Mauser II then wrote that he was due to meet the new war minister the following Monday, but that he had met with the Chilean president in the interim. At this meeting, the president and

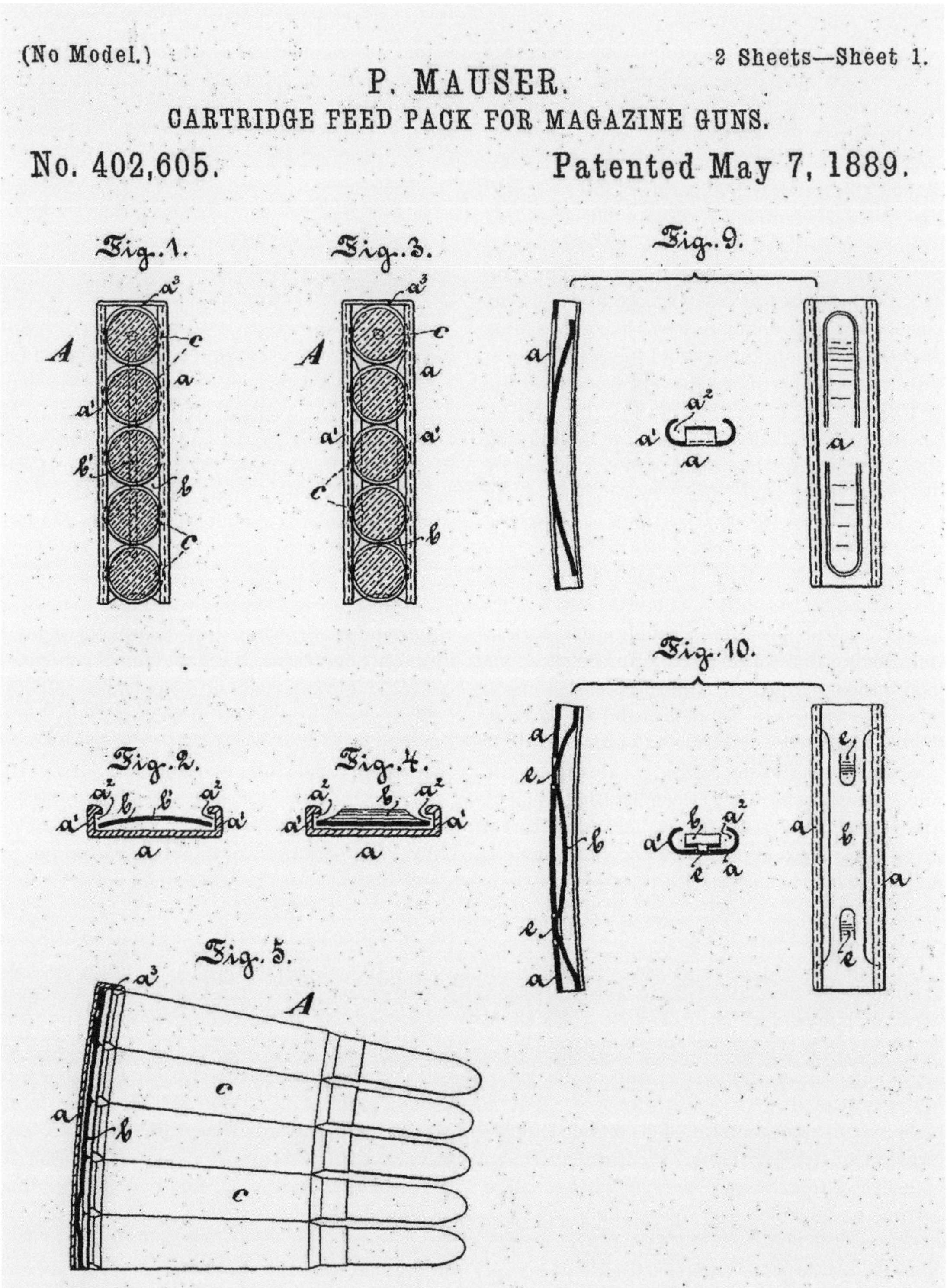

Paul Mauser was meticulous in protecting his inventions, and as such he initially patented his work in most European countries, then later also in the US. Above are the US patents relevant to the Belgian Model 1889.
Mauser, P. 1889. USA Patent No. 402605. US Patent Office.

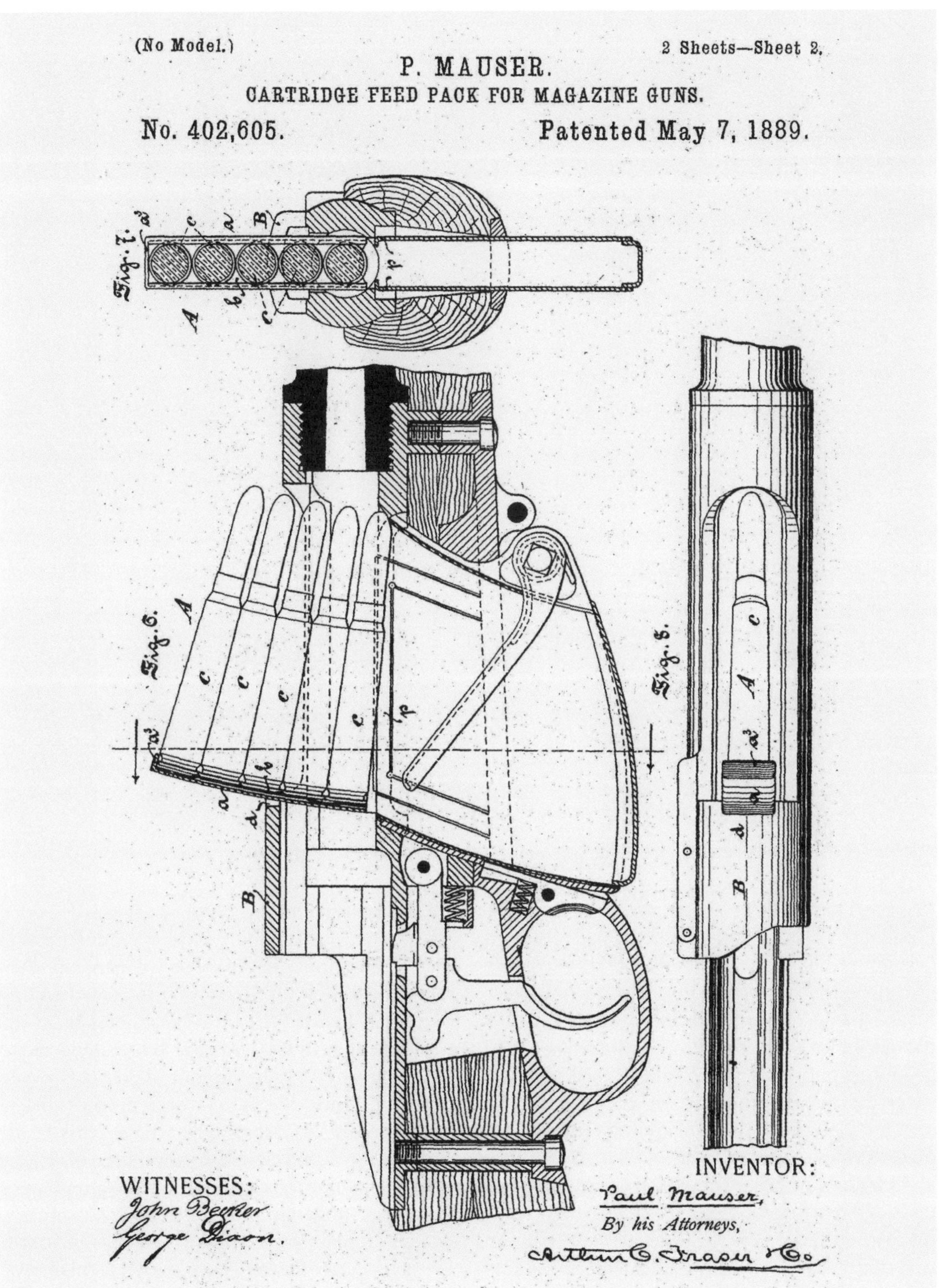

Mauser, P. 1889. USA Patent No. 402605. US Patent Office.

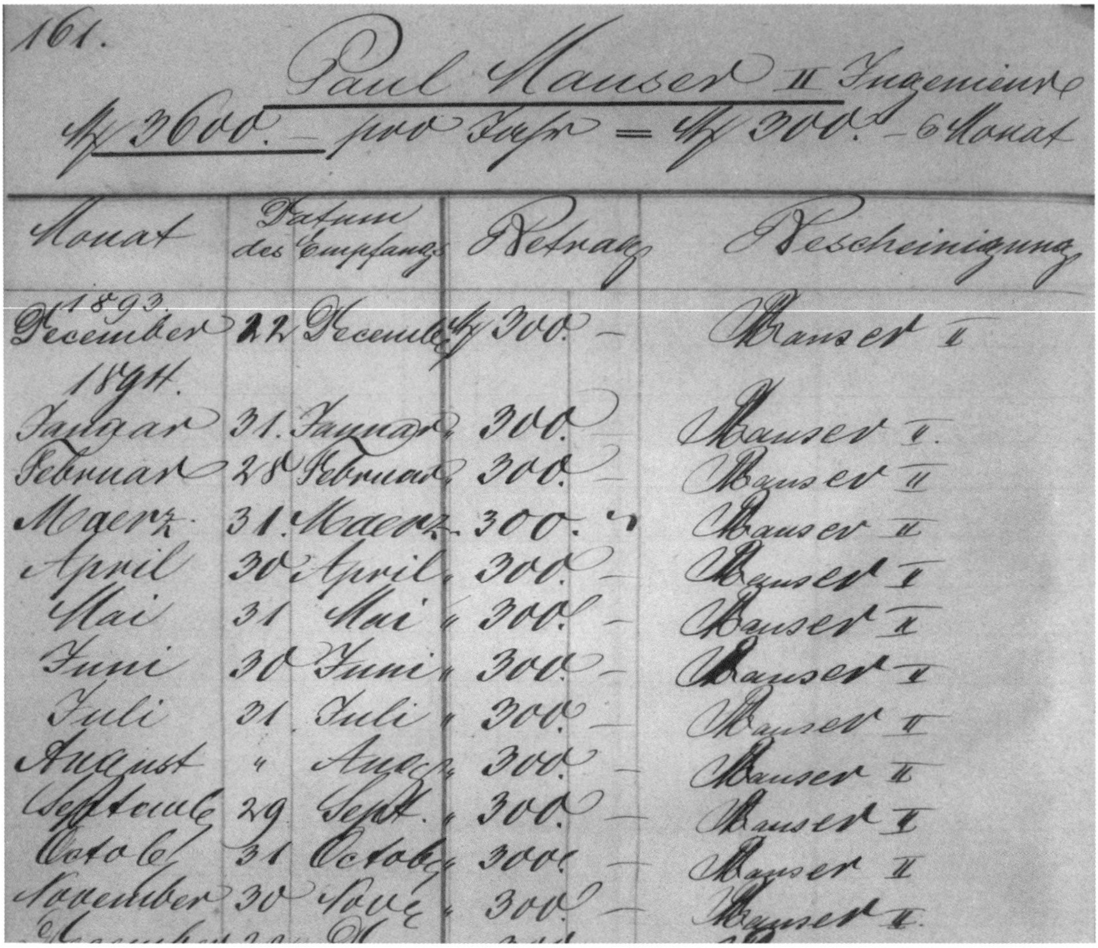

161. Paul Mauser II Ingenieur

M 3600.— pro Jahr = M 300.— Monat

Monat	Datum des Empfangs	Betrag	Bescheinigung
1893 December	22 December	M 300.—	Mauser II
1894 Januar	31. Januar	300.—	Mauser II
Februar	28 Februar	300.—	Mauser II
Maerz	31. Maerz	300.—	Mauser II
April	30 April	300.—	Mauser II
Mai	31 Mai	300.—	Mauser II
Juni	30 Juni	300.—	Mauser II
Juli	31 Juli	300.—	Mauser II
August	"	August	300.—	Mauser II
September	29 Sept.	300.—	Mauser II
October	31 October	300.—	Mauser II
November	30 Nov.	300.—	Mauser II

Paul Mauser II's salary of 300 marks per month as recorded in the Mauser salary register book. *Archive Jon Speed*

Mauser II had discussed the 7 mm caliber, and the president had stated that because he had promised to resolve Chile's financial difficulties, the prospect of concluding a weapons purchase was unlikely. Mauser II ended the letter by informing Loewe that the dates for the continuation of the trials would be known only early the following week. He also wrote that the commission, which was yet to be appointed, would both shoot and experiment with Loewe's rifles (Mauser II 1893a).

On 11 May 1893, Mauser II again wrote to Ludwig Loewe & Co. This letter provided some much-needed clarity as to the details of the Chilean rifle trials. Mauser II opened his letter by stating that he had indeed met with Minister Errázuriz on 10 May. During this audience, Mauser II was asked by Errázuriz how long he was planning to stay in Chile. Mauser II replied that the purpose of his visit was to continue the rifle trials begun in Paris and that the duration of his visit would depend on when these trials took place. Also during this meeting Mauser II handed the minister a letter from the Chilean envoy in Paris. Mauser II then reported to Loewe that he was sure the date of the trials would be soon, since the Schriever representative—Mr. Visshera or Fisher (presumably this is the Mr. Visscher mentioned in the letter of 5 May 1893)—had now arrived in Valparaíso after having departed Antwerp on 24 March on the steamship *Totmes* of steamship company Kosmos (Mauser II 1893b). Mauser II would have known of this arrival through his contacts at Vorwerk & Co., which at some point had acquired a partial ownership in Kosmos, which in turn had the rights to ship all arms shipments to Chile (Sater and Herwig 1999, p. 141; Schaefer 1974, p. 48). Mauser II continued his letter by affirming that while Körner had initially favored the Mannlicher due to its straight-pull action, he was now gravitating toward the Mauser system. This was because Mannlicher appeared to have departed from this action and had instead adopted the *mouvement combine* (combined motion), which was arguably the cocking of the firing pin on the opening of the bolt, or cock-on-open system; Körner thus saw no great advantage of the Mannlicher over the Mauser. Körner stated that what system Mannlicher presented would not be known until the arrival of the Steyr/Schriever agent. Mauser II then wrote that he had only one 7 mm rifle with 700–800 rounds of ammunition at his disposal. He informed Loewe that Körner had stated this would be sufficient because no endurance tests would be undertaken during the trials. Despite this assurance, and in an effort to ensure their victory in the trials, Mauser II then stated that he would like to telegram Saavedra Bernard & Co. and request a further five rifles in 7 mm caliber and one in 6.5 mm caliber with 500 rounds of ammunition. Mauser II concluded his letter by declaring that he would forward Loewe a copy of a document he had received from Körner describing the Mannlicher rifle that was overwritten with the phrase *Mémoire relatif aux fusils Mannl* (Mauser II 1893b).

On 17 May 1893, Mauser II again wrote to Ludwig Loewe & Co. and informed them that he had nothing new to report. He stated that he had traveled to Valparaíso, visited the business of Vorwerk, and met with its directors, Mr. Fischer and Mr. Neubauer. Both these gentlemen had extended their warmest welcome and had inquired as to the current state of Mauser II's progress in Chile, following which Mauser proceeded to offer a detailed account of the events to date. In turn, Fischer and Neubauer promised to do everything possible to advance Mauser's cause and placed themselves at his disposal in this regard. During this visit, the captain of the steamship *Totmes* also made an appearance, advising Mauser II that the Schriever agent, Visscher (again, presumably the Visscher, Visshera, or Fisher who is mentioned in letters dated 5 and 11 May 1893), who had arrived from Liège, had three rifles of different designs and a large quantity of ammunition in his possession. The Schriever agent had apparently been informing people that he was in Chile simply to conclude a contract. He was likewise quoted as having stated that Loewe's products were inferior, and that this had been demonstrated at the first round of tests. As such, he reportedly said that nothing other than a Mannlicher rifle had any chance in the trials. It was also revealed that the Schriever agent had expressed the view to a fellow passenger—Dr. Plate—that Gen. Canto was strongly in favor of the Mannlicher (Mauser II 1893c). In fact, Canto was in favor either of the Mannlicher or the Marga (Sater and Herwig, 1999, p. 145). Mauser II then stated that he had just returned from Körner, who had informed him that he would no longer wait for the Schriever agent to present himself and would thus start the trials. A statement about the inclusion of the brochure "Mannlicher-Gewehre von August Schriever in Liège" concluded the letter.

Mauser II again wrote a short letter to Loewe on Friday, 19 May 1893. In this correspondence, he stated that Körner had decided that subject to the preparatory work having been completed, the trials would take place the following Monday. Mauser II went on to write that their competitor had still not arrived in Santiago, and it was thus possible that the trials would be conducted without them. Mauser II also informed Loewe that Vorwerk had informed him that the Schriever agent Visscher had presented himself to them as the Mannlicher agent without him being aware that Vorwerk represented Mauser (Mauser II 1893d).

In a long letter written on 16 June 1893, Mauser II wrote that the trials had been completed and that a report based on the results was being prepared. This report had still to be signed by all members of the commission and, as such, had yet to be submitted to the ministry of war. Despite neither Mauser II nor Körner having seen this draft report, they were reliably informed that the commission was tending toward the Mannlicher. This was justified in the introduction to the provisional report by an argument that stated that when compared to the Mauser, the Mannlicher had been deemed easier to handle, having a superior insertion method for its cartridges and requiring slightly less pressure to close the bolt. Mauser II informed Ludwig Loewe & Co. that none of these

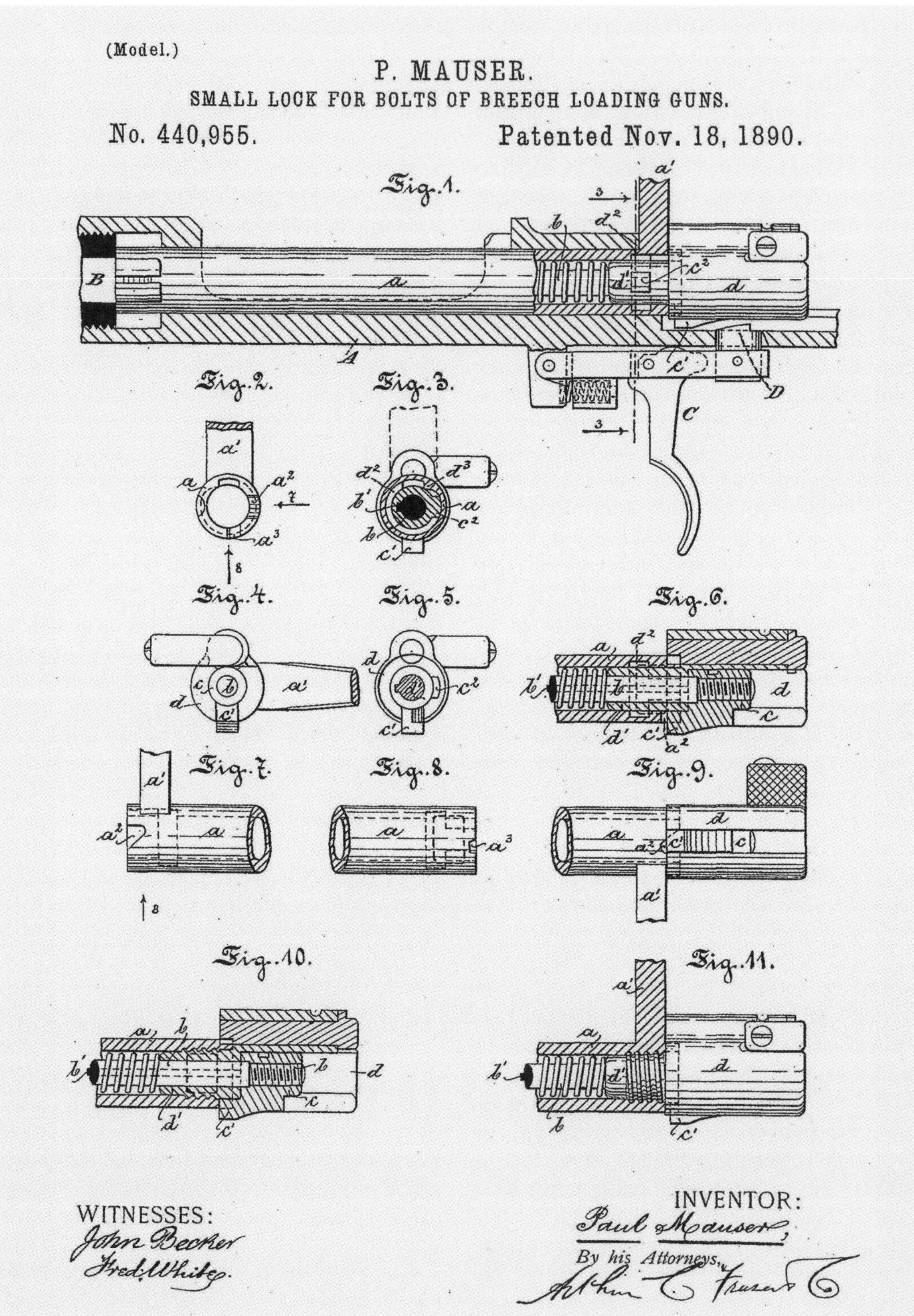

The Belgian Model 1889 breech mechanism as patented in the US in 1890.
Mauser, P. 1890. US Patent No. 440955. US Patent Office.

aspects had been mentioned during the trials, and despite the Mauser's superior performance in the trials, their subsequent appearance now suggested that Mauser's competitors had been busy skewing the recommendations of the report. Mauser II proposed that this was being done through the involvement of former German officer Herrn von Bischofshausen and the author of the report, Señor E. Gatica Lira, "Comandante del Batallón ingenieros militares." The draft report was at that stage signed by only four members of the commission's colonels: Aníbal Frías, C. Alberto Noroa, E. Gatica, and José Manuel Ortuza. According to Mauser II, this provisional outcome, which largely sided with the Mannlicher, was a result of Mauser's opposition having had longer and better-established connections in the Chilean officer corps. Opposing the Mannlicher was commission member Maj. Betzold, who stated that nothing during the trials had been found that could justify the comments contained in the draft report's introduction. To the contrary, Betzold argued, the trials had shown the Mauser to be superior. Two other members of the commission—Gen. Körner and Col. Vincente Palacios—had yet to sign the draft report. Once they had a copy of the final report, Mauser II relayed, they would lodge a complaint. He stated that they had every reason to believe that the report would not reach the ministry of war in its current form. Mauser II then described a further visit he made to Körner on 14 June, where Körner had informed him that despite the report not being finalized, their competitor had already submitted an offer to the ministry of war. Körner dutifully supplied this information to Mauser II, who then disclosed it both to Vorwerk and Saavedra Bernard in a meeting held on 15 June in Valparaíso. The same day about noon, the results of this meeting were then telegraphed to Loewe. While the exact contents of this telegram are not known, Mauser II alluded to them in the next portion of the letter. The Schriever agent was apparently offering to purchase all of Chile's existing rifles and carbines and then subsequently reequip Chile with new rifles and carbines with bayonets for seventy-nine francs each. Included in this deal were 40,000 rifles composed of Gras, Comblain, Remington, Beaumont, Bornmiller, Suider, etc., which the Schriever agent was offering to buy at four francs each. For Chile's stock of 20,000 Minie and muzzle-loading arms he was offering one franc each. There was some doubt whether Chile's newly acquired Mannlichers both in 8 and 11 mm would be included. In the event that Chile retained its approximately 30,000 8 mm Mannlichers, Mauser II estimated an order of 50,000–75,000 was still feasible. Mauser II also informed Loewe that the Beaumont rifle—with a new firing spring—and the carbine had now arrived and were in Körner's possession. Mauser II reported in the letter's postscript that the reserve firing spring in the Beaumont action had been poorly received by the Chileans and would thus never be accepted (Mauser II 1893e).

The Chilean trials of 1893 were conducted using the following: one Mauser "Argentine model" in 7.65 mm (0.301") caliber that used a 213-grain projectile; one Mauser "Spanish model" in 7 mm (0.276") caliber that used a 173-grain projectile; one Mauser in 6.5 mm (0.256") caliber that used a 162-grain projectile; four Daudeteau rifles in 6.5 mm (0.256") caliber, with three using 154- and one using 139-grain projectiles; one Beaumont in 6.5 mm (0.256") caliber with 156.5-grain projectiles; and one Mannlicher in 6.5 mm (0.256") caliber using 156-grain projectiles. Despite the prevalence of 6.5 mm rifles, the commission officially decided that the 7 mm Mauser was the most suitable rifle for the Chilean army, and its 7 mm caliber was an expedient choice while awaiting the reduction of caliber to 5 mm (Unknown author 1893).

However, in an odd twist of fate, it was neither the Mauser nor the Mannlicher that won the trials; rather, it appears to have been the Daudeteau, which recorded better scores in terms of projectile velocity, projectile penetration force, speed of firing, flatter projectile trajectory, accuracy, and resistance to wear. As examples of the Daudeteau's superiority: it is recorded as having fired thirty-seven shots in a minute, while Mannlicher could manage only twenty-four, and the 7 mm Mauser achieved twenty-eight; the Daudeteau also came first in the accuracy tests at 250 m, second after a Mauser at 500 m and third after the Mannlicher at 1,000 m; likewise, after two wear resistance tests of 950 and 3,000 shots, the Daudeteau emerged in first place, followed by the Mannlicher in second and a Mauser in third (Serrano 1894).

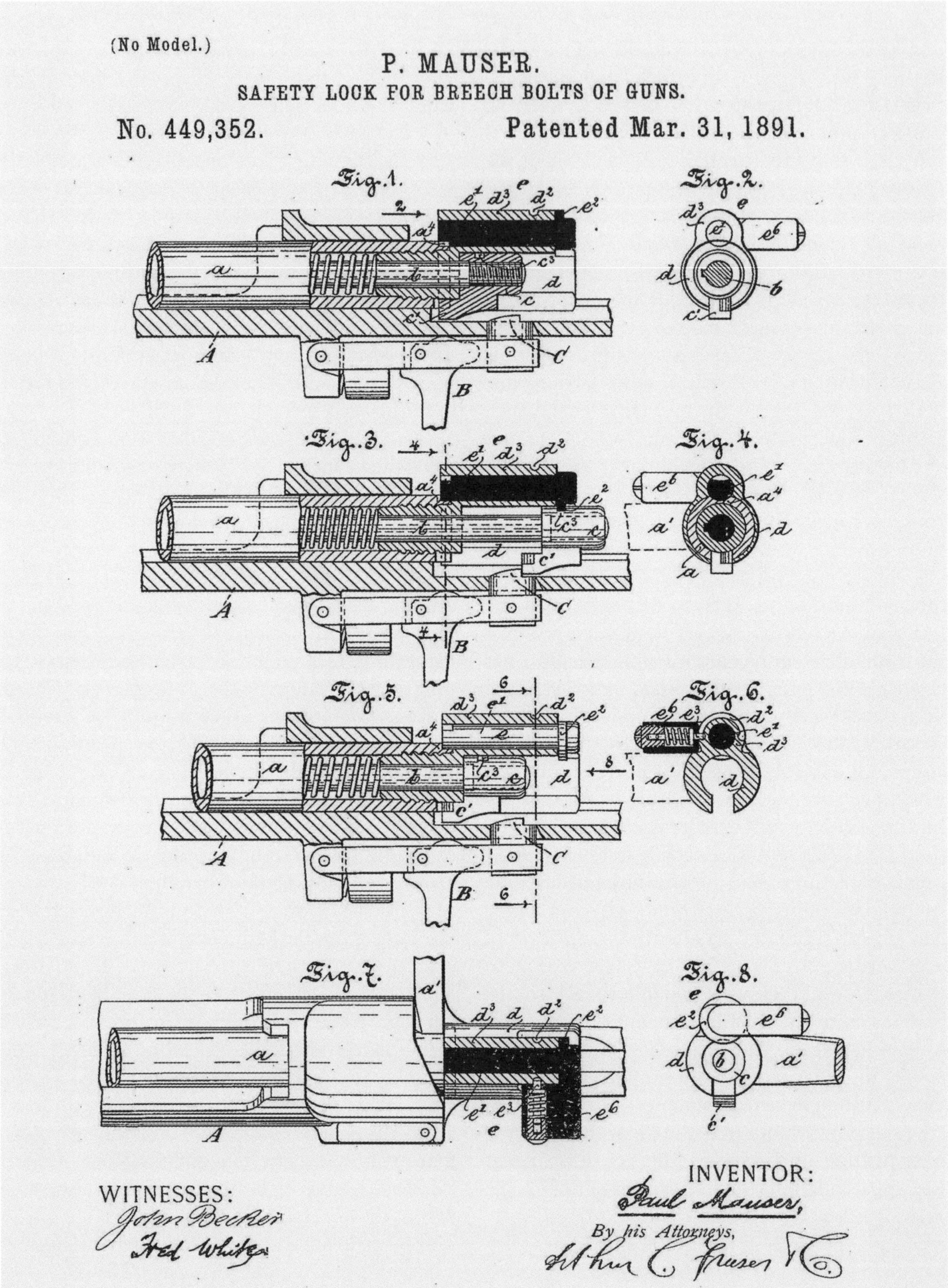

(No Model.)

P. MAUSER.

SAFETY LOCK FOR BREECH BOLTS OF GUNS.

No. 449,352. Patented Mar. 31, 1891.

Fig. 1. Fig. 2. Fig. 3. Fig. 4. Fig. 5. Fig. 6. Fig. 7. Fig. 8.

WITNESSES:
John Becker
Fred White

INVENTOR:
Paul Mauser,
By his Attorneys,
Arthur C. Fraser & Co.

The Belgian Model 1889 safety as patented in the US in early 1891.
Mauser, P. 1891. US Patent No. 449352. US Patent Office.

The Prelude to Chile's First Contract with Loewe in 1894

Körner carefully played his hand to action his desire for Mauser rifles. This he did in stages, the first being the establishment of his power base in Chile, which he achieved by gaining control of the army's general staff—having the support of President Jorge Montt and removing francophone war minister Luis Arteaga in September 1892. It should also be mentioned that in addition to military and political support, Körner undoubtedly realized that he still required a pretext for the purchase of arms. This he established by becoming a vocal supporter of the unofficial *Kriegspartei* (War Party) movement, which proposed that the growing tensions with Argentina could be resolved only by military might. Despite this domestic backing, the procurement of arms was still carried out in Europe by the Chilean Weapons Commission, headquartered in Paris and headed by Körner's francophile opponent, Canto. To achieve control over the Weapons Commission, in April 1894 Körner organized a two-year study trip to Europe with the aim of usurping control of the commission and thus ultimately purchasing German rather than French arms (Schaefer 1974, pp. 43–44).

Once in Europe, Körner soon learned from his colleagues and the armaments firms that it was not only Argentina that was buying arms, but also Peru and Bolivia. This changed his initial belief that Argentina was Chile's primary potential enemy. Körner subsequently maneuvered to turn this situation into an order for armaments. He thus requested permission from his government that he, as Weapons Commission vice president, be allowed to buy arms to counter this perceived threat. Having been given authority to do so, he purchased mountain and field artillery on 24 July 1894 from none other than Krupp (Schaefer 1974, pp. 44, 49).

Following the second round of Santiago tests and the finalization of the related report, Körner returned to Chile and proceeded to finalize his Mauser procurement plans. Evidently armed with these two reports—one from the first Paris trials of 1892, and one from the Santiago trials of 1893—Chilean president Montt convened a meeting of his senior army leadership on 23 November 1894, with the aim of finally deciding on Chile's new rifles and carbines. While the first report, written by Canto, confirmed the choice of the Mannlicher, Körner's second report oddly favored the 7.65 mm caliber Mauser. This confirms that Paul Mauser II was correct in his prediction in the 16 June letter that the report would not reach the ministry of war in its current form. The result of this meeting was the choice of the Mauser in 7.65 mm caliber. The justification for this choice appears to have been that while the Mannlicher was available only from Steyr-Werke, the Mauser was the overwhelming choice of the army and could be bought either from Loewe in Berlin or FN in Brussels. It was also decided that considering the constraints of Chilean finances at that time, only 50,000 rifles and 10,000 carbines could be purchased in a production period of seven months (Schaefer 1974, p. 45).

An initial decision to favor FN over other manufacturers such as Loewe and Steyr did not materialize from nothing. In the months leading up to the decision of 23 November 1894, significant interactions had already occurred between FN and the Weapons Commission.

On 4 October 1894, Canto wrote to Director of FN Jules Chantraine, the stated purpose of which was to reply to an earlier FN request for his proposed specifications and information concerning Chile's new rifle. Canto was clear in explaining that if FN did decide to proceed with his proposals and build prototypes, then he was bound by an agreement with Körner that it would then be reviewed by both of them. Canto's specifications were listed as follows:

- General conditions listed the proposed rifle as being the Chilean Model 1894, with a repetition mechanism, a five-round magazine, and a bayonet. Further, the rifle would have a magazine cut-off, a device to prevent double-loading, and a safety lock. The total weight of the unloaded rifle without the bayonet would be 3.6 kg.
- Special conditions specified that the stock would be of one-piece walnut construction

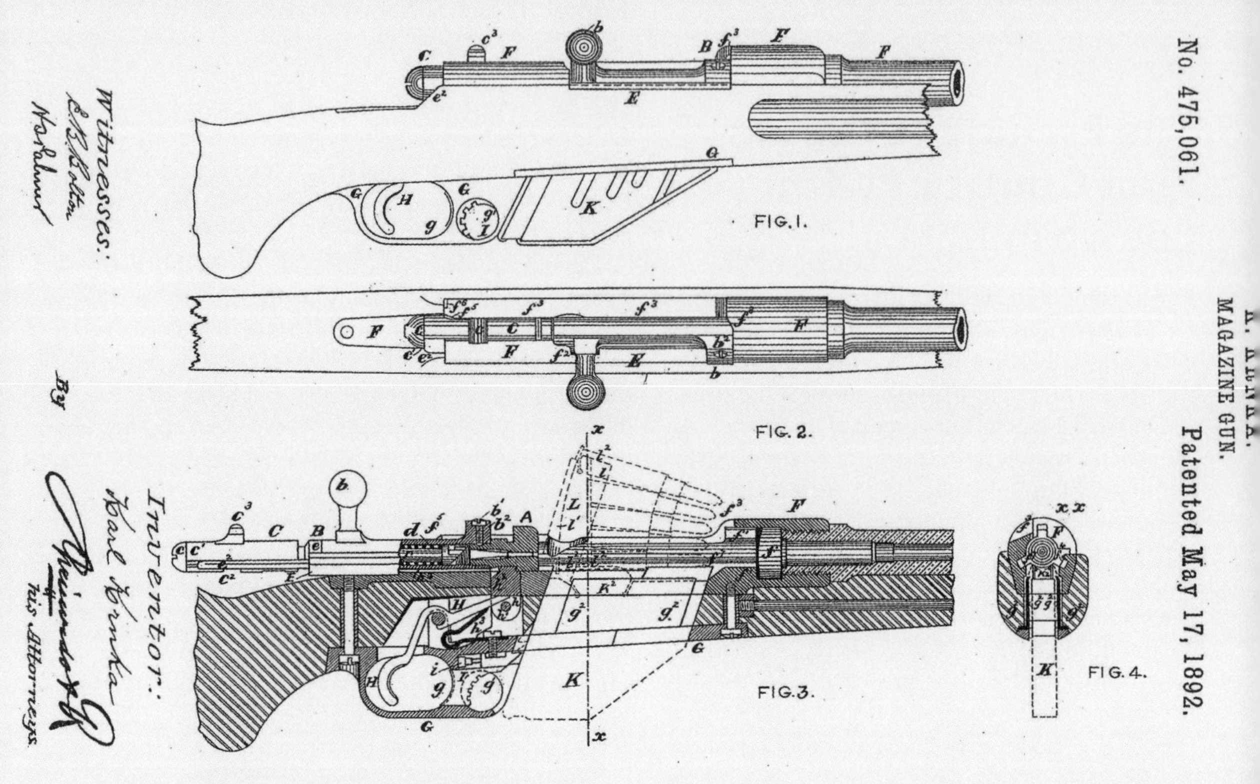

Karl Krnka rifle as patented in the US in 1892.
Krnka, K. 1892. US Patent No. 475061. US Patent Office.

with a protective handguard identical to that of the Brazilian Model 1894.

- The barrel requirements were for a 6.5 mm caliber rifled barrel without a barrel sleeve according to either the Daudeteau, Mannlicher, or Mauser type. The sights were specified as similar to those of the Belgian Model 1889 and were to be graduated from 50 m to 2,000 m in 50 m intervals. The velocity of the 6.5 mm projectile was listed as having to be 720 m/s measured at 25 m from the muzzle. Likewise, the projectile had to penetrate 15 cm into fir wood planks at a range of 2,000 m, and the cartridge would develop a maximum chamber pressure of 2,500 kg/cm^2.
- The receiver and bolt were listed as having to be a combination of the Brazilian Model 1894 and the Mannlicher Model 1892. The bolt had to have a one-piece design that included the locking lugs; that is, no removable bolt head. The extractor was to have been strong like that of the Spanish model (presumably the Model 1893), but without its overall dimensions and without a physical projection from the bolt face. The bolt handle was to be placed along the centerline of the bolt body, with the bolt closure and firing-pin spring similar to the Mannlicher. Additionally, the safety was to have been similar to the Beaumont.
- The magazine was specified as having to be like the Brazilian Model 1894, with the same arrangement of cartridges, follower, and follower spring. The magazine was listed as having required a cut-off on the right side of the rifle that had an arrangement similar to the Engh or Bergman. The device to prevent double-loading was to have produced the same results as that of the Daudeteau. The ejector was to have been of solid construction similar to that of the Belgian Model 1889 and would eject spent cartridges without affecting surrounding shooters.

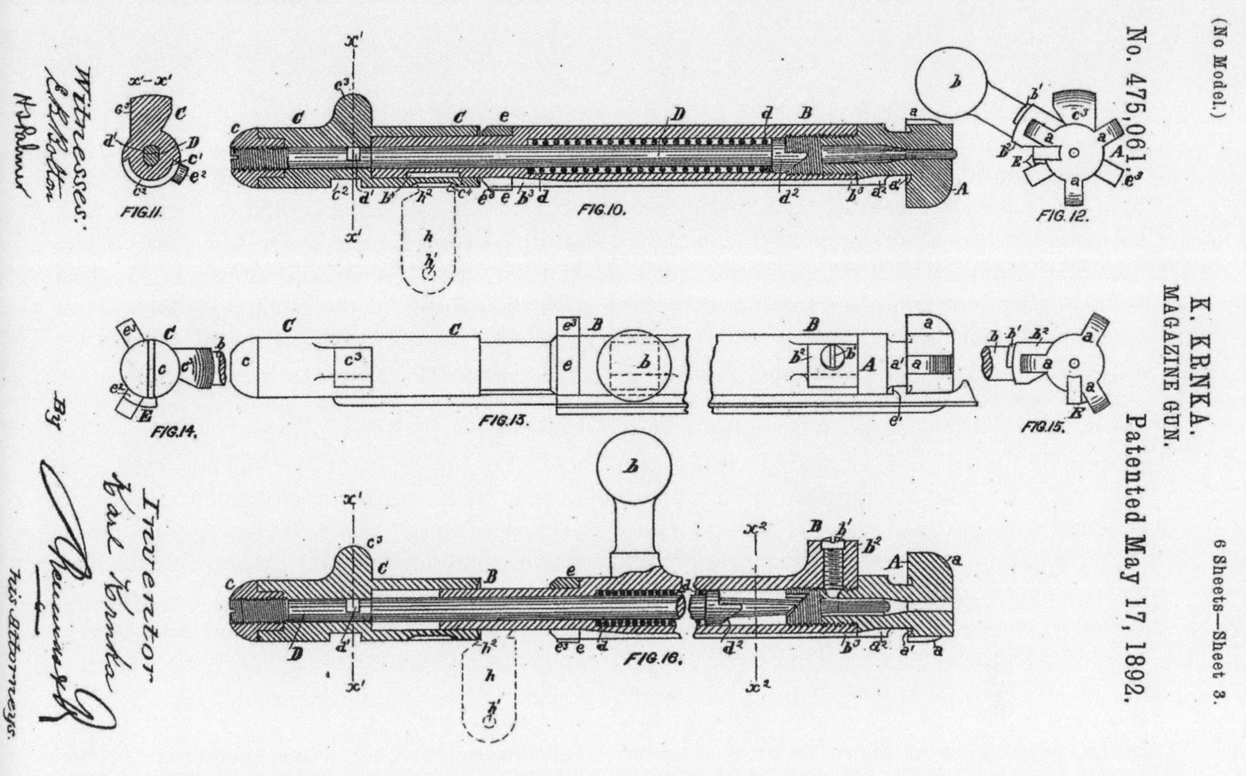

Krnka, K. 1892. US Patent No. 475061. US Patent Office.

- The required trigger mechanism was to have been similar to that of the Mannlicher, while the bayonet was to have been according to the Brazilian pattern, but with a metal sheath.
- The cartridge was specified as having been of rimless design, with a projectile having a nickel steel jacket with all the latest improvements (Canto 1894b).

On 31 October 1894, Chantraine replied to Canto's letter of 4 October. In this reply, the FN director offered some remarkable insights into events that transpired before the letter of 4 October. Interestingly, he mentioned that FN had made an earlier proposal to the Chilean government via Canto on 19 May 1893. Chantraine continued his letter by stating that he was grateful that Canto and Körner, as representatives of the Chilean government, had verbally accepted this FN proposal during a meeting with him that had taken place the previous Wednesday, 24 October. This reply likewise alludes to the fact that it was Körner who had signing authority over final acceptance of this proposal, and that Canto's specification letter of 4 October was in response to a requirement of Article 1 of FN's letter of 19 May. Chantraine's letter of 31 October continued by stating that to satisfy Article 2 of the earlier proposal, FN needed to know the minimum number of rifles and ammunition required by Chile. After this was made known, FN could submit a provisional contract to Chile detailing prices and supply schedules. Chantraine then emphasized the necessity of concluding the contract as quickly as possible, because under the terms of the earlier proposal, FN still had to supply prototype rifles and consequently also the terms of manufacture. He then pointed out that even if Körner did physically sign the proposal, it would still not be legally binding, since that contractual responsibility was the sole prerogative of the Chilean government and was likewise still subject to the final testing and approval of the rifles. Chantraine concluded by informing Canto that despite these outstanding obligations, the construction of three prototype rifles was proceeding well (Chantraine 1894b).

Canto dutifully replied to Chantraine's letter of 31 October on 9 November 1894. In this letter, he stated that he had submitted FN's requests via the Chilean embassy in Paris for his government's further actions and comment. Canto was careful to point out that in his submissions to the Chilean government, he had clearly stated that his dealings with FN were exclusively intended to further Chile's search for a new rifle, and that he had in no way committed Chile to any contractual obligations, since these were the sole preserve of the Chilean government. Canto then said that during his next visit to Chile, he would be very happy to present to his government the prototype rifles that were currently being built by FN, but only if they met his expectations (Canto 1894a).

Interestingly, in a letter written by Körner to Augusto Matte on 6 November 1894, the FN prototype rifles are explicitly mentioned as ten "*fusiles modelo del Canto*" (Canto model rifles) that were being tested in Herstal by Canto, along with Luger rifles (Körner 1894a). Furthermore, a later newspaper clipping confirmed that Chile did do a deal with FN in 1894. This article states that Chile contracted for 50,000 rifles and twenty-five million cartridges, having paid 1.2 million francs in advance. The delivery of these items was supposed to have started in December 1894, but the article is clear that nothing had been delivered as of May 1895 (Unknown author 1895).

While nothing seems to have materialized from these initial interactions with FN, the Chilean Weapons Commission was also actively courting other manufacturers for the supply of rifles and carbines. On 13 March 1894, the commission received an offer letter from the Société Française des Munitions de Chasse, de Tir et de Guerre (French Company for Hunting, Shooting and War Ammunition) proposing the supply of Lebel Model 1886 rifles with the modifications of 1893, including a bayonet and a scabbard, for sixty-two francs each. Model 1890 cavalry carbines including a bayonet were offered at fifty-nine francs each. Smokeless ammunition, with jacketed projectiles and chargers for the rifle and carbine, were also offered at 135 and 150 francs, respectively (Société Française des Munitions de Chasse 1894). This offer was nevertheless recommended for rejection by Canto and Körner on 31 October 1894. Writing from Halle, Germany, Körner informed Minister of War Santiago Aldunate that he had met with Canto to consider the proposal by the Société Française des Munitions de Chasse, de Tir et de Guerre. In justifying their joint decision to reject the Lebel, Körner wrote that Lebel was inferior when compared to modern weapons such as the Spanish Mauser and the Mannlicher. Moreover, Körner argued, it was substandard when compared to other rifles being studied, such as the Luger. Körner then argued that both he and Canto proposed that if Chile did accept the Lebel, which would dramatically increase the number of antiquated weapons in Chile's arsenal, then Chile would be better served to purchase more-antiquated weapons than Chile already had, such as the Mannlicher. Körner concluded by noting that despite these facts, the prices offered for the Lebel were comparable to more-superior weapons (Körner 1894c).

Apart from mainstream manufacturers, the Chilean Weapons Commission was also studying obscure rifles such as those produced by Karl Krnka and its unique 5 mm Hebler-Krnka munition. In a letter to the Chilean minister of war dated 11 September 1894, the Chilean embassy in Paris informed him that despite the scarcity of this rifle, a copy of it had been acquired and tested, along with 1,000 rounds of ammunition, in Holland. While the results of the test were excellent, the tremendous difficulties in manufacturing both the rifle and its ammunition, and their exorbitantly high price, led the embassy to decide that Krnka's benefits were in no way realistic when compared to the 6.5 mm caliber (Vega 1894). While no more information can be found on this subject, it is proposed that the rifle tested could have been similar to that patented on 17 May 1892 in US Patent 475,061.

With the Chilean Weapons Commission having conducted two rounds of official trials by 1893 and extensive testing of numerous rifles throughout 1894, the final impetus for Chilean commitment to purchase its new rifles came in the form of a telegram to the Chilean embassy in Paris on 25 November 1894. This telegram from the Chilean government and its military leaders communicated to the embassy that they were, in consultation with the Weapons Commission, to acquire 50,000 rifles and 10,000 carbines chambered for the 7.65 mm Argentine cartridge, without slings. Additionally, they were to acquire eighteen million smokeless cartridges and 3,000 swords. The embassy was tasked to immediately sign a contract, with the only provisos being that the payments were divided into four equal amounts: one each in July and November 1895, and one each in July and November 1896. The telegram stated that the embassy should try the manufacturer in Liège. Price did not seem of concern, since the communique informed the embassy that it was at liberty to advise the total price after signing the contract. The telegram concluded by stating that the international situation for Chile was unchanged (Canto et al. 1894; Matte Pérez 1894b).

In response to this telegram, the Chilean embassy immediately contacted the Weapons Commission and requested that it urgently respond to the government's requests, which it did on 4 December 1894, having convened an extraordinary meeting attended by Matte, Canto, Körner, and Vial. In the minutes of this meeting, Matte quoted Canto's response that the 7.65 mm Mauser specified in the telegram could not be considered a viable option, since it was still under development and was subject to fundamental changes. Considering these constraints and the urgency expressed in the telegram, these changes would delay finalization, acceptance, and delivery. As such, Canto argued that to rush an imperfect rifle into production would be detrimental to the members of the Chilean army, and that such a rifle could not assure its position at the forefront of modern weapons development. Körner's opinion was that regardless of the final rifle chosen and no matter what the diplomatic emergency, the outcome should rather be dictated by efficient configuration and operation. To achieve this, he proposed:

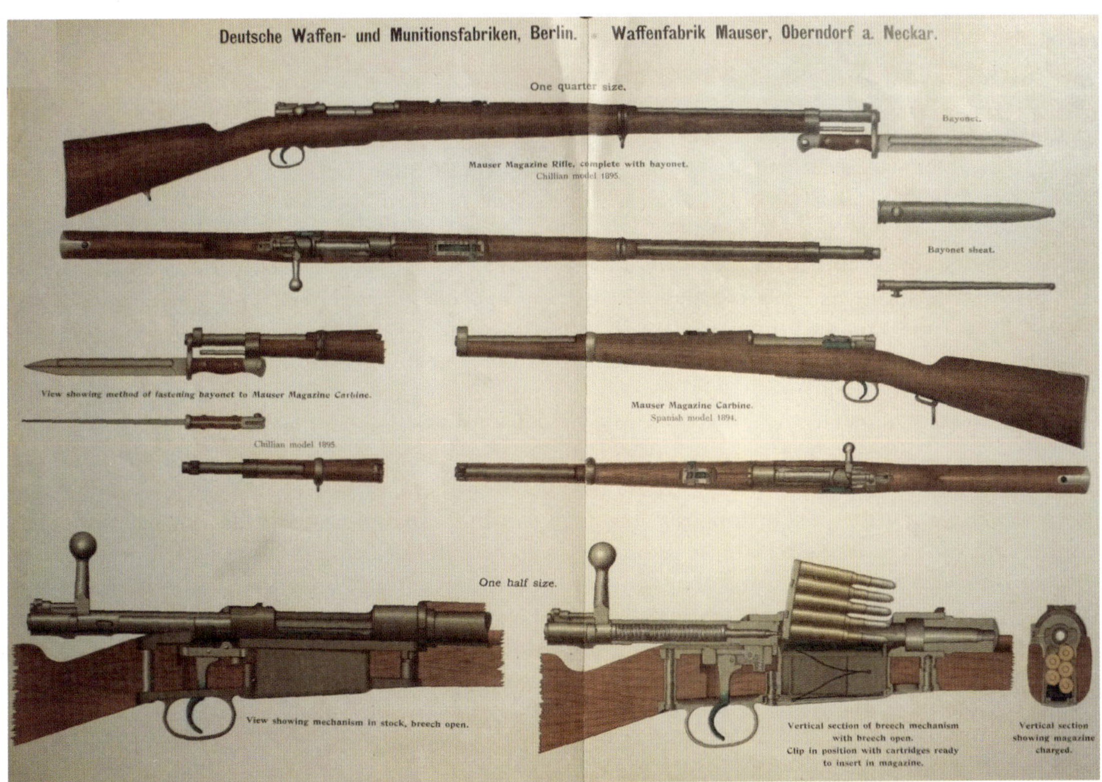

Chilean Model 1895 rifle and carbine together with a Spanish Model 1894 carbine.
Unknown author. 1897b. "The Mauser Magazine Rifle Calibre 7mm Model 1893–95 and Its Ammunition." In *The Mauser Magazine Rifle*. Edited by W. Mauser. Berlin: H. S. Herman.

- that the Chilean 7.65 mm Mauser have a bolt mechanism that worked even with an empty magazine,
- that the bolt mechanism be equipped with a Luger extractor,
- that the Mauser have ballistics at least equal to that of the 7.65 mm Argentine cartridge, and
- that the Chilean government delegate sole responsibility for the choice of final caliber and rifle specification to the Weapons Commission.

Longitudinal sections through the Chilean Model 1895. Unknown author. 1897b. "The Mauser Magazine Rifle Calibre 7mm Model 1893–95 and Its Ammunition." In *The Mauser Magazine Rifle*. Edited by W. Mauser. Berlin: H. S. Herman.

Col. Vial then identified that he considered the observations of his leaders perfectly justified, and therefore he accepted the model proposed by his government and the proposals of Gen. Körner. The insistence by Körner on a Luger extractor was then identified as problematic, since one of the approached manufacturers had stated that it could not commit to this inclusion under the deadlines proposed. Thus, the ambassador had asked the Weapons Commission to consider if the Luger extractor was of paramount importance, to which the reply was that none of the proposed improvements should in any way slow production. Finally, the ambassador, having spoken in favor of the initial telegram of 25 November 1894, stated that his office had contacted FN, Loewe, and Steyr and requested that they identify under which conditions they were willing to manufacture the required rifles and carbines as outlined in the telegram and the accepted amendments as proposed by Körner (Canto et al. 1894).

Subsequently, Matte informed the minister of war on developments in a long and detailed letter dated 6 December 1894. Matte started the letter by reiterating the conclusions reached in his meeting with the Weapons Commission two days earlier. Matte then informed the minister that despite the Chilean government's wish that he and the Weapons Commission preferably deal with FN, they had seen fit to also involve Loewe and Steyr, a decision that was taken to ensure the best interests of Chile. Matte stated that they had already met with all three manufacturers and had already received their initial proposals. From these, it had become clear that the Chileans' proposed schedule of delivery, the required quantities, and the payment constraints were problematic. Matte stated that initial deliveries by February 1895 were thus impossible. All three manufacturers and the Weapons Commission had affirmed that it was materially impossible to start deliveries within three months following the submission of the design and dimension tables. Matte did affirm that the completion of the entire order of rifles, carbines, and eighteen million rounds of ammunition was entirely feasible by September 1896. Although the terms of payment had not yet been discussed, Matte then argued that it was prudent to inform the minister that the Chileans' current requirement for four equal payments was all but impossible, and a completely unusual practice in these types of matters. Matte informed the minister that in the context of recent German, Spanish, Brazilian, and Argentine contracts, the requirement was always for up-front monetary guarantees, bills of exchange, and a cash payment before any deliveries started. Next, Matte, having consulted with Canto and Körner, argued that the monitoring of production and the reception of the rifles, carbines, and ammunition required special attention, the implementation of which could not be delayed.

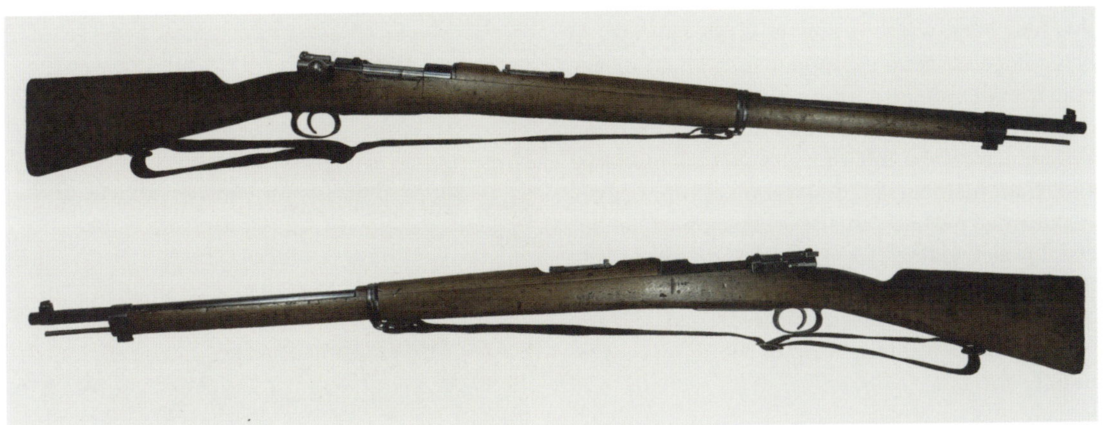

A left- and right-hand view of the Chilean Model 1895 rifle. *Author*

In this regard, Matte then informed the minister that Gens. Canto and Körner were best placed to inform as to the best practices adopted by nations in recent years to ensure complete suitability for its intended purpose. He then illustrated this point by stating that the German Empire had rejected 12 percent of their recent acquisitions. If Chile was not to instigate a rigorous process of verification, inspection, and reception, they too could reasonably expect a similar defect rate (i.e., 7,200 rifles and carbines unfit for their intended purpose and the waste of approximately 500,000 francs). Matte then argued that nations such as Argentina had a reception commission composed of around thirty officers and technical experts to ensure that their 120,000 rifles and carbines were fit for purpose. This same number was likewise adopted by Spain, which had received even fewer rifles than Argentina, but the example of Argentina was praised as a model of industriousness that had honored Argentina through its considerable work in a relatively short period for 120,000 rifles. All the reception commissions were then identified as being organized into sections, with the Argentine and Spanish having five sections each comprising at least six officers and numerous gunsmiths. Matte then proposed that it was inconceivable that Chile could do without a similar reception commission comprising three sections, and suggested it be staffed and resourced according to the dictates of Canto and Körner. Accordingly, it was proposed that the first of these sections would monitor the manufacture and reception of the rifles and carbines, the second would monitor the manufacture and reception of the ammunition, and the third would double-check the rifles, carbines, and ammunition once they were received. The first section would be headed by Col. Roberto Goni, assisted by Capt. Luis Cabrera, Capt. Don MacLean, and Sgt. Maj. Agustín Prieto; the second section would be headed by Lt. Col. Juan Vial, assisted by Capt. Carlos Briones Luco, 2nd Lt. Julio de Canto, and Sgt. Maj. Tobías Barros Merino; and the third would be headed by Gens. Canto and Körner, assisted by Capt. Luis Goni, Capt. Luis Vial Infante, and Master Gunsmith Erhalt. Matte then wrote that while Chile already had six gunsmiths in Europe, an additional six were required. He then asked the minister to urgently identify suitable Chilean candidates of the highest quality and urgently dispatch them to Europe. Matte concluded his letter by affirming that the provisional contract had already been drafted by Lt. Col. Juan Vial, while the *cahier de charges* (specifications) had been written by Körner. As to the choice of the final caliber of Chile's new rifles and carbines, Matte stated that

The complete action and rear sight to a Chilean Model 1895 rifle. *Author*

this had been written into the draft contract as being dependent on personnel already in Europe. Specifically, an article contained in the draft contract delegated this decision to Gens. Canto and Körner, Col. Roberto Goni, and Lt. Col. Juan Vial as current members of the Weapons Commission. According to Matte, this specification of caliber was due eight days after signing the contract (Matte Pérez 1894b). In the two weeks following this letter of 6 December 1894, events proceeded at a frantic pace, ultimately culminating in the signing of an initial contract.

Chile Buys the Mauser Chileno Modelo 1895

The generally accepted history surrounding these two weeks is that Ludwig Loewe & Co. initially offered rifles and bayonets at the stock price of eighty-two francs and 155 francs per 1,000 rounds of ammunition. In an effort to gain market share, FN offered a Mauser rifle for sixty-eight francs and 135 francs per 1,000 rounds of ammunition. Considering the very competitive pricing offered by the Belgian firm, the Chilean government in Santiago instructed the Chilean Weapons Commission in Europe to consider its offer and to enter into negotiations to procure 7.65 mm Mausers. Having received news of the Chilean government's intention from its agents in Santiago, Steyr attempted to derail the Mauser decision by immediately countering the initial offers by Loewe and FN. This offer specified a delivery period of just five months for all 60,000 units and a spreading of the total amount payable into four semiannual payments. The Chileans promptly took this offer to Loewe and argued that if it did not want them to change their decision to purchase Mauser rifles in 7.65 mm caliber, then Loewe would have to offer better conditions in terms of price and mode of payment. On 5 December 1894, Loewe reduced its initial price per rifle with equipment to seventy-five francs, which was still seven francs higher than that of FN. To decisively beat Loewe's latest offer and that of FN, weapons dealer August Schriever countered with an offer for the latest Mannlicher with all its accessories for only sixty-nine francs each. Loewe,

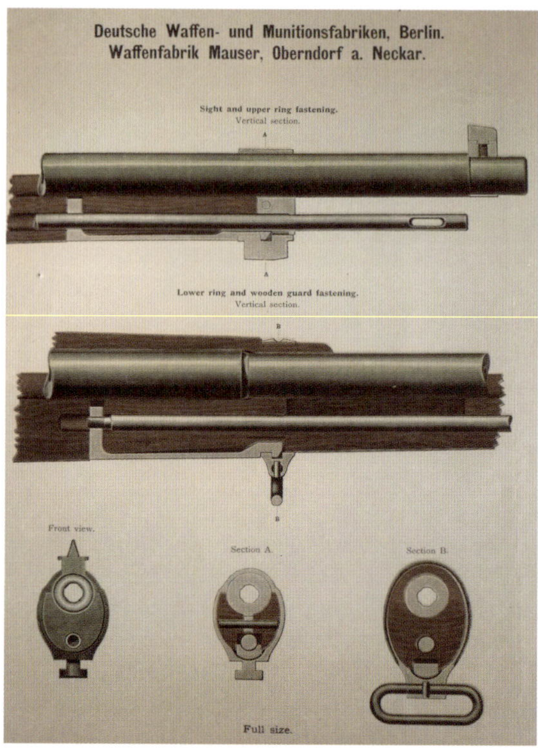

Longitudinal and cross sections through the front portions of the Chilean Model 1895, showing the barrel bands and cleaning-rod retaining mechanism.
Unknown author. 1897b. "The Mauser Magazine Rifle Calibre 7mm Model 1893–95 and Its Ammunition." In *The Mauser Magazine Rifle*. Edited by W. Mauser. Berlin: H. S. Herman.

through the direct involvement of Director Riese, then concluded the negotiations. Riese's efforts in this regard were threefold. First, he told the Chileans that FN had a license to manufacture only the Model 1889 and not the Model 1891. Second, he dropped Loewe's price to equal that of FN; that is, sixty-eight francs (Schaefer 1974, pp. 45–46). In dropping the price, Riese importantly stated that Loewe was about to freely market the Model 1893 in 7 mm caliber, which would make the Model 1891 and the newest Mannlicher obsolete. Third, he added that Loewe would not hesitate to sue FN for patent violation if it attempted to produce its own version of the Model 1893 (Sater and Herwig 1999, p. 145).

In this last regard, Director Edmund Groncki of the Waffenfabrik Mauser wrote a terse letter to FN on 11 December 1894 in which he informed them that Mauser had been reliably informed that

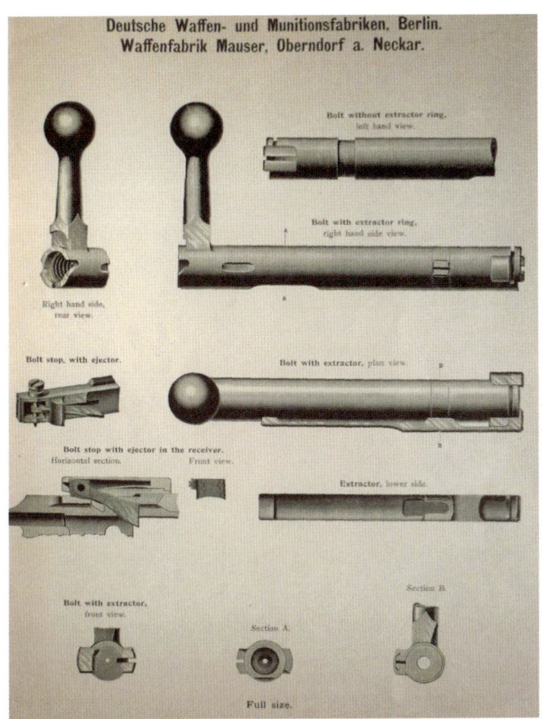

Details of the bolt and ejection mechanism to the Chilean Model 1895.
Unknown author. 1897b. "The Mauser Magazine Rifle Calibre 7mm Model 1893–95 and Its Ammunition." In *The Mauser Magazine Rifle*. Edited by W. Mauser. Berlin: H. S. Herman.

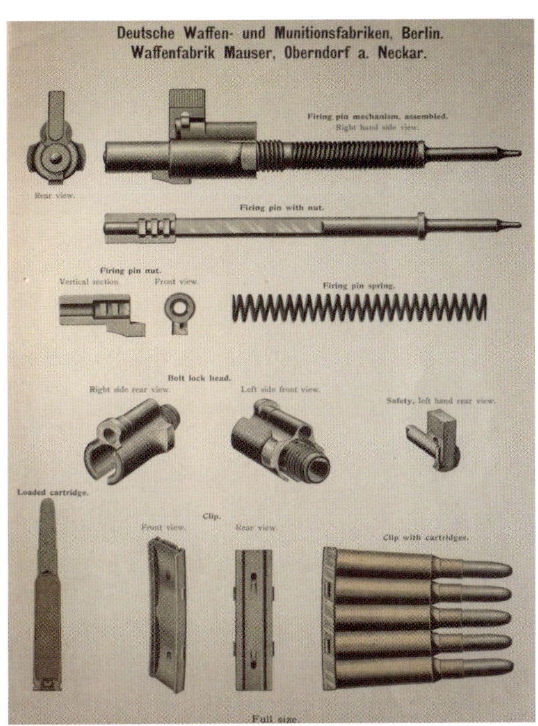

Details of the bolt and ammunition to the Chilean Model 1895.
Unknown author. 1897b. "The Mauser Magazine Rifle Calibre 7mm Model 1893–95 and Its Ammunition." In *The Mauser Magazine Rifle*. Edited by W. Mauser. Berlin: H. S. Herman.

FN was manufacturing rifles that contained parts that were subject to patents owned by Mauser. Specifically, Groncki named Belgian Patent 9,436 and supplementary patents 98,339; 99,373; 99,067; 103,102; and 105,890. Groncki then informed FN that it was not entitled to exploit these patents, since they were the property of Mauser. He likewise stated that FN had three days to comply with a request to cease production, after which legal action would be initiated (Groncki 1894). This letter appears to have been freely shared with the Chileans, and its importance is emphasized by there being Spanish, German, and French versions of it in the Chilean National Archives.

Painfully aware that the Chileans must have known about Groncki's letter, FN Director Chantraine wrote to the Chileans on 14 December 1894. In this letter, Chantraine stated that despite false allegations raised by its German competitors concerning inferior manufacturing and materials, FN had nevertheless supplied delivery terms and prices that were recognized by the Chileans as being the most advantageous—that is, sixty-eight francs for a rifle with a bayonet, sling, and muzzle cover; sixty-three francs for a carbine without a bayonet, but with a sling and muzzle cover; and 135 or 129 francs per 1,000 rounds of ammunition. In effect, Chantraine argued that FN had offered the Chileans exactly what they had specified. Notwithstanding this and despite everything being in order for the signing of a contract, its German competitor had now posed the patent question. This, in Chantraine's opinion, was devoid of any foundation and, despite its serious appearance, should be treated only with humor. He then explained that under the terms of a 26 November 1891 agreement between FN and the holder of Waffenfabrik Mauser's privileges in Belgium, Alex Résimont, FN had permission to employ all the privileges that had been agreed, or that would be agreed in Belgium as they related to improving the Belgian Model 1889. Chantraine

A section of the Chilean Dragones Calvary Regiment at the Pan-American Exposition in Buffalo, New York, in 1901, armed with Chilean Model 1895 carbines.
Budge, E. 1901. *Chile at the Pan-American Exposition: Brief Notes on Chile and General Catalogue of Chile Exhibits.* Buffalo, NY: Commission of Chile to the Pan-American Exposition.

argued that not only did FN hold a license to produce the Model 1889, but it was also entitled to produce it for export, including all its subsequent improvements—as long as it was a majority Model 1889 system. In exchange for this right, FN was to have paid 2.50 francs per rifle in royalties and was precluded from doing business with Turkey. If FN did decide to export to Germany, Austria, Spain, Italy, England, Russia, or the US, prior negotiation with Waffenfabrik Mauser was necessary. Having sent the Chileans a copy of the 26 November 1891 agreement, Chantraine then asked if given such an irrefutable agreement, Waffenfabrik Mauser's letter of 11 December 1894 was just a distraction. He pointed out that Waffenfabrik Mauser had used these very same tactics against FN when it was negotiating with Brazil in June 1894, and that despite these threats, the Brazilian government had seen fit to order 50,000 rifles and twenty-five million rounds of ammunition. Chantraine then argued that regardless of all the fuss being created by Waffenfabrik Mauser, its claim to the listed patents was invalid, since under Article 23 of Belgian Patent Law, if the owner of a patent did not use it in Belgium within a year of its being granted, it could be expropriated by royal decree. Considering that none of the six patents listed by Waffenfabrik Mauser had yet been employed in Belgium, this, according to Chantraine, was a distinct option. The FN director concluded by stating that having been informed by the Chileans during a meeting on 11 December 1894 of Loewe's decision to drop its prices to equal that of FN, he and his board were willing to offer improved pricing of sixty-three francs per rifle, fifty-eight per carbine, and 127 francs per 1,000 rounds of ammunition (Chantraine 1894a).

This last offer by FN was futile, since the Chilean government had already decided on 12 December 1894 to sign a contract with Loewe. On 21 December 1894, Ambassador Matte wrote a lengthy and comprehensive letter to his government summarizing the events directly before and during this eventual signing with Loewe. Matte opened the

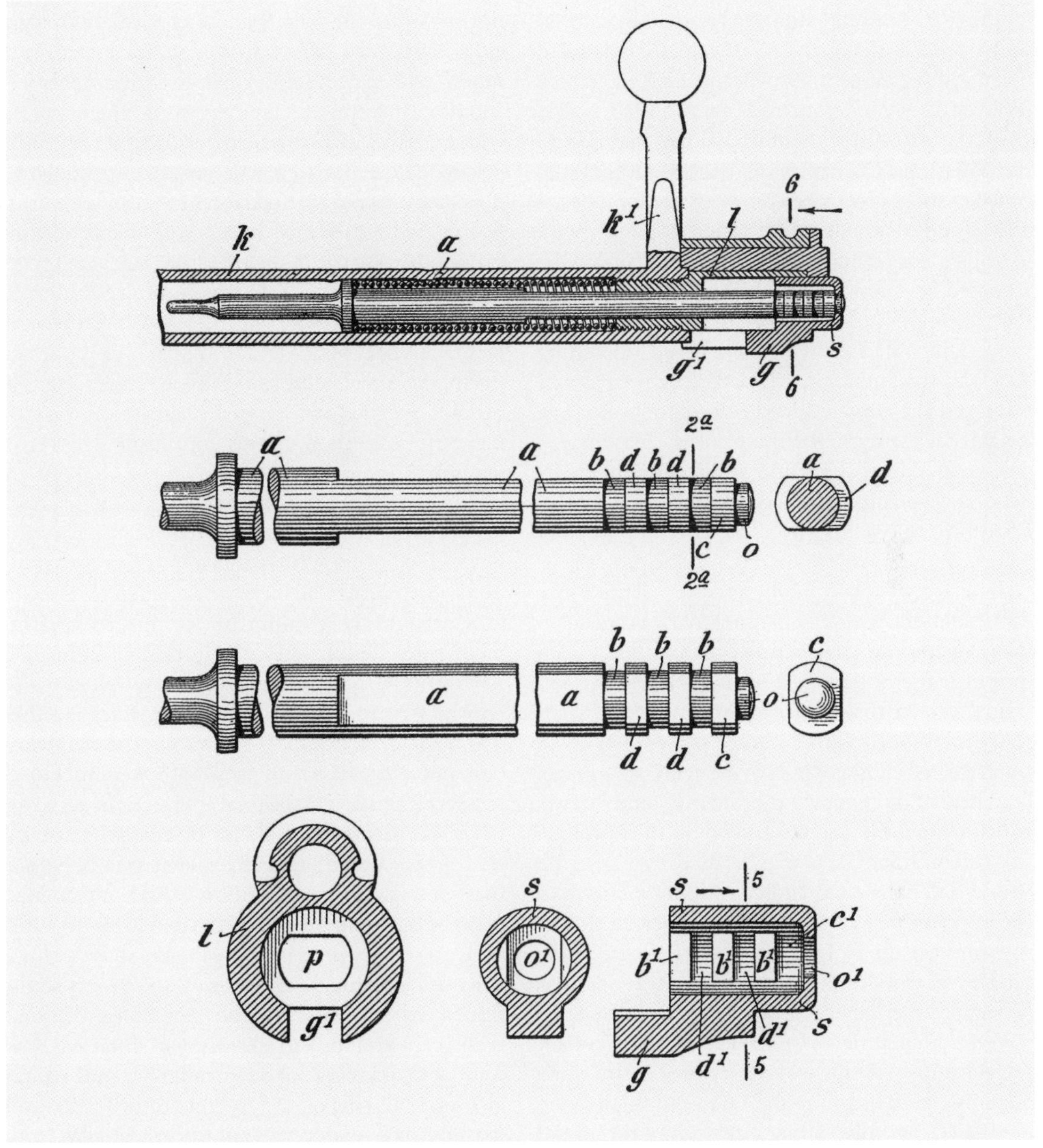

German patent 70114 as granted on 15 January 1893, depicting the interrupted-lug connection between the firing pin and the cocking piece.
Mauser, P. 1893a. Germany Patent No. 70114. Kaiserliche Patentamt.

letter by stating that Steyr had been eliminated at the onset because its offers were based on rifles and carbines not relevant to the Chilean specification. Matte then stated that because FN was offering a better price of sixty-eight francs per rifle or carbine and Loewe's offer was two francs higher, it was initially decided to proceed with the FN offer. Matte then confirmed that it was indeed the dispute surrounding the patents that had altered this initial decision. Interestingly, Matte stated that having consulted the Weapons Commission on this matter, both Gen. Canto and Körner were still in favor of continuing negotiations with FN, while Matte, Col. Goni, and Lt. Col. Vial thought it unwise to commit Chile to a contract that could be disrupted by legal disputes. Matte then detailed that this disagreement soon disappeared when they received a copy of Groncki's letter of 11 December 1894. In this context, Matte explained that he and the Weapons Commission proposed that the contract should be shared between FN and Loewe. This would ensure that if FN failed to comply with its contractual obligations, these could simply be assumed by Loewe. The Chileans also proposed that Loewe should commit to the FN price of sixty-eight francs per rifles or carbine, including slings, bayonets, and muzzle covers; likewise, it was proposed that this reduced price should include freight, packaging, and dispatch from Hamburg, as well as all of the gauges and verification materials necessary for reception. These reception extras, according to Matte, would be worth more than 60,000 francs, or more than one franc per rifle or carbine. Loewe subsequently accepted all the above conditions but could not consent to the proposal to split the contract. In Loewe's opinion, this would diminish the importance of the negotiation and thus threaten to withdraw entirely. Matte then stated that faced with a choice between FN—as the preferred choice of the government in Santiago, but one that did not own the patents—and Loewe, which owned the patents and could thus provide the rifle and carbines as specified by Chile, he would defer the final choice of manufacturer to the minister of war. Matte communicated this to the minister on 11 December 1894, who replied on 12 December 1894 that the contract should be signed with Loewe, as long as it respected the payment schedule as specified by the Chilean government. Empowered by the minister's response, Matte summoned Loewe to finalize the contract. Crucially, before concluding the initial contract for 50,000 rifles and 10,000 carbines, Chile proposed several important amendments over the draft contract. The first of these proposals was that Chile would have the right to acquire a further 60,000 identical rifles, carbines, or both within four years of signing the initial contract, pay the same price, and receive priority supply conditions. The reasoning behind this inclusion was that Matte and the members of the Weapons Commission feared that in an "international emergency," an initial order of 60,000 rifles and carbines would not be sufficient. Likewise, they foresaw that in such an event Chile would have to "scurry" to manufacturers, urgently seeking armaments—a situation these manufacturers would then exploit with arguably inappropriate products at very high prices. Matte reported that because of their ongoing, persistent determination to achieve this proposal, Loewe had reluctantly agreed. The second of the proposals was that in the event of *force majeure* at the Loewe factories, Chile would have the right to produce the contracted rifles and carbines in a factory in Santiago. Matte was proud to report to the minister that because of the wide interpretation of *force majeure* in European legislation, Loewe had agreed to include this condition. The third proposed inclusion that Loewe also agreed to include was that in the event of technical disputes between the reception staff and Loewe, these would be resolved by the Chilean Weapons Commission. The fourth proposal, likewise accepted by Loewe, was essentially a compromise agreed on the payment schedule, stipulating that Chile would pay only the remaining third of the value of the contract in the first half of 1896. Because this was a major concession by Loewe, the company demanded that this and proposal 5 were included in a secret portion of the final contract. (In agreeing to proposal 4, Loewe feared that if news spread that it was willing to deliver armaments before they were paid for, its business would suffer, since everybody would demand this concession.) Fifth and last of the agreed proposals was that the final price for a rifle or carbine would be sixty-eight francs, which would include the sling, bayonet with scabbard, and a muzzle cover. Likewise, the total contract value of 4.08 million francs would also include packaging, freight from Berlin, and loading onto a ship in Hamburg, along with all the gauges and verification materials necessary for reception. Because of reasons identical to proposal 4, Loewe equally insisted that the concession to include 60,000 francs of free reception materials was also to be kept secret. Matte then proudly stated that through both his and the Weapons Commission's tough negotiation skills, they had achieved the very best price possible when placed within the context of other nations: Turkey, 80 francs; Belgium, 79 francs; Spain, 82.50 francs; Argentina, 77 francs; the Netherlands, 78.50

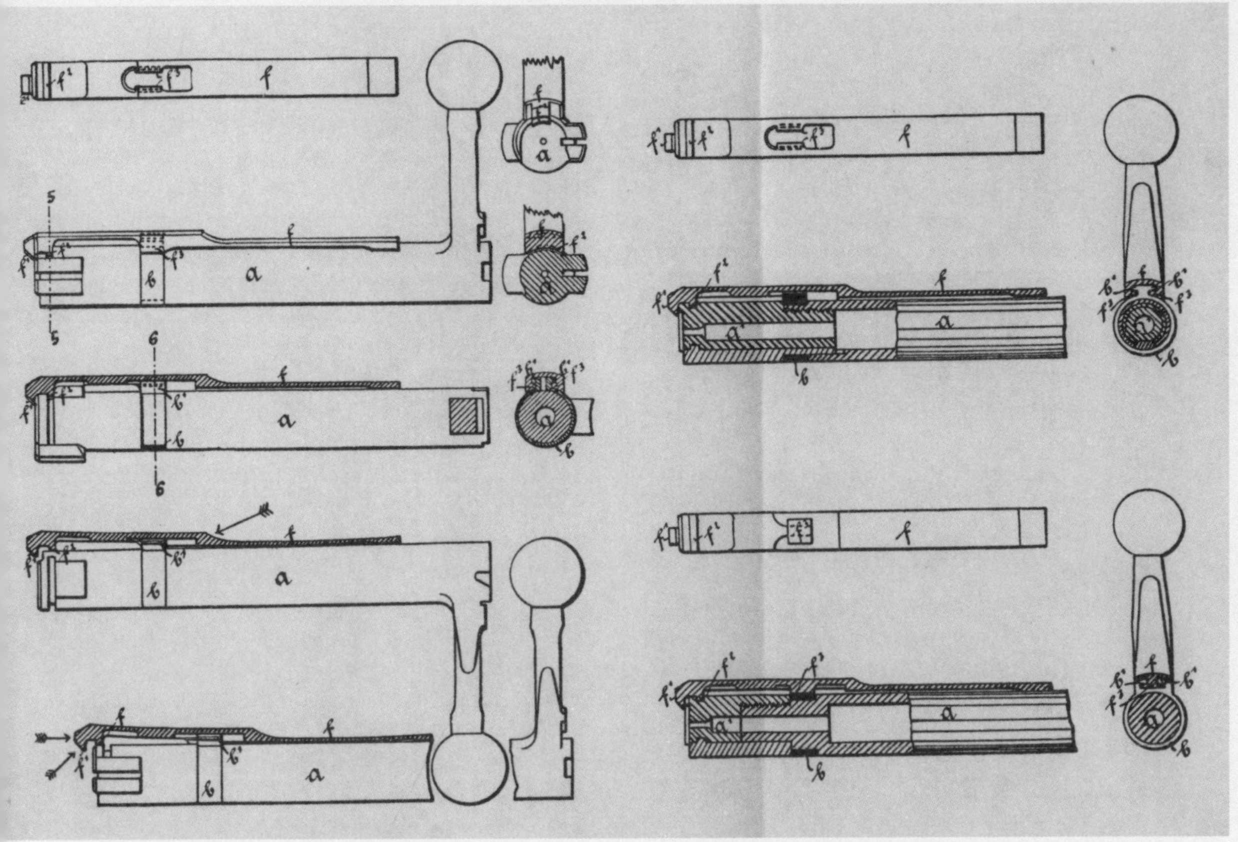

German patent 65225 as granted on 16 February 1892, showing the Mauser rotating-claw extractor and its associated collar. Mauser, P. 1892c. Germany Patent No. 65225. Kaiserliche Patentamt.

francs; and Brazil, 82 francs from Loewe and 69.50 francs from FN. Subsequently, on 14 December 1894, Matte informed the minister of war that they had concluded a "deal" with Loewe and that details would follow shortly. Consequently, on 17 December 1894, Matte again cabled the minister and informed him that they had signed a contract with Loewe that stipulated the first delivery in May 1895 and the last in October 1895, with two-thirds of the payment in 1895 and the remaining third in the first half of 1896. Matte also stated in his letter that this contract would comprise two distinct parts—one public and the other secret—the latter specifying the deferred payment and "free" reception materials. On 18 December 1894, Minister of War Carlos Rivera Jofré replied with his acceptance and congratulations to Matte and the Weapons Commission. As stated, Chile had eight days after the signing of the contract to decide the caliber of their new rifles and carbines. As such, Matte summonsed the Weapons Commission—comprising Canto, Körner, Goni, and Vial—to a meeting, where it was decided that the caliber would be 7 mm, rather than the 7.65 mm Argentine. This decision to set the caliber at 7 mm was then communicated to the minister of war on 17 December 1894, to which he replied on 19 December 1894 with his acceptance (Matte Pérez 1894a).

Chile's Initial Contract with Loewe for 50,000 Rifles and 10,000 Carbines

In Matte's letter of 21 December 1894, he stated that the first contract with Loewe was signed on 16 December 1894 (Matte Pérez 1894a). This date is confirmed in a later letter written by the Loewe Company to Matte (Ludwig Loewe & Cie 1895l). This date is also frequently recorded as 15 December 1894, in a ledger that appears to have been the master accounting ledger of the Chilean embassy in Paris during that period (Legación de Chile en Paris 1892). This earlier date is also confirmed in another letter from the Loewe Company to Matte (Ludwig Loewe & Cie 1895m). At the time of writing, the author has been unable to obtain a copy of the December 1894 contract or the *cahier de charges*. This is arguably because they have been lost or are stored in a unique location in the Chilean Archives because of their secret portion. Nevertheless, it is partially clear from previous discussion as to the exact conditions this contract included. Likewise, the accounting ledger offers some fascinating insights and contradictions. First, the ledger documented that on 15 February and 15 May 1895, Loewe first delivered to the Chilean Weapons Commission two prototype rifles and then two carbines, respectively. Both these deliveries were accompanied by their respective "tables of dimensions and tolerances." It also recorded that subsequent deliveries would comprise 5,000 rifles in May 1895; 7,000 rifles in June; 10,000 rifles in July; 12,000 rifles and 2,000 carbines in August; 15,000 rifles and 4,000 carbines in September; and 1,000 rifles and 4,000 carbines in October. This would provide a total of 50,000 rifles and 10,000 carbines. The ledger furthermore recorded that the payment schedule would be 10 percent of the total on 1 January 1895, 25 percent of the total after the delivery of the first 10,000 rifles, and the remaining 65 percent following final delivery (Legación de Chile en Paris 1892, p. 5). This last fact contradicts Matte's communication to the minister on 21 December 1894 that a third of the payment should have been deferred to the first half of 1896. Alternatively, the first 10 percent payment was listed as having been due on signing of the contract (Legación de Chile en Paris 1892, p. 78). Subsequently, under a heading of "costs to the Embassy during the month of January 1895," a payment of 163,200 pesos was recorded as having been paid, or as being due to Loewe for the initial 10 percent value of the contract (Legación de Chile en Paris 1892, p. 7). Equally, the 25 percent requirement of 408,000 pesos was recorded under the heading "costs to the embassy during the month of June 1895" (Legación de Chile en Paris 1892, p. 8), as was the 65 percent requirement (1,060,800 pesos) recorded under the heading "costs to the embassy during the month of October 1895" (Legación de Chile en Paris 1892, p. 9). Later in the ledger, the date of the 10 percent payment was recorded as 15 February 1895, while the 25 percent payment was recorded as having been 20 July 1895 (Legación de Chile en Paris 1892, p. 78). The ledger stated that the initial contract also included two large orders of rifle and carbine spare parts and 3,000 screwdrivers: the first portion of spare parts was worth 33,657.50 francs (table 1), the second was worth 29,461.80 francs (table 2), and the screwdrivers were listed as being worth 3,000 francs (Legación de Chile en Paris 1892, p. 15). Further interesting facts concerning

Table 1

CASE NO.	NUMBER OF COMPONENTS	COMPONENTS (ASSUMEDLY ALL FOR RIFLES?)
6001, 6002, 6003, 6004, 6005	500	Cajas (Stocks)
6006, 6007	1000	Guarda-manos (Handguards)
6008, 6009	500	Cañónes (Barrels)
6010	1500	Muelles del elevador (Follower spring)
6011	500	Cerrojos (Bolts)
6011	750	Abrazadera superior (Upper/front barrel band)
6011	500	Porta seguro (Bolt sleeve/shroud)
6011	100	Guarda-monte (Trigger guard)
6011	1000	Palanca del disparador (Sear)

CASE NO.	NUMBER OF COMPONENTS	COMPONENTS (ASSUMEDLY ALL FOR RIFLES?)
6011	1000	Cabeza del percutor (Cocking piece)
6011	1500	Baquetas (Cleaning rod)
6011	1000	Percutores (Firing pins)
6011	500	Disparadores (Triggers)
6012	100	Cajón del mecanismos (Receivers)
6012	500	Abrazadera inferiores (Lower/rear barrel bands)
6012	1000	Muelles de la abrazadera superior (Upper/front barrel band springs)
6012	250	Cantoneras (Butt plates)
6012	1000	Muelles de la abrazadera inferior (Lower/rear barrel band spring)
6012	1500	Tapa bocas (Muzzle cover)
6012	1000	Chapas de alza (Rear sight ladder)
6012	750	Muelles del alza (Rear sight leaf spring)
6012	500	Bases de la anilla inferior (Lower/rear sling swivel bases)
6012	750	Anillos del punto (Front sight bases)
6012	1000	Correderas (Rear sight ladder slides)
6012	1500	Muelles del pestillo (Magazine floorplate catch springs)
6012	1500	Muelles del disparador (Sear springs)
6012	1000	Muelles del percutor (Firing-pin springs)
6012	1500	Ejes del disparador, del pestillo (Trigger and magazine floorplate catch pins)
6012	250	Tubos del tornillo inferior (Stock pillar to the lower/back trigger guard screw)
6012	2500	Muelles del diente de la corredera (Rear sight slide catch springs)
6012	2500	Pasadores (ejes) diente de la corredera (Rear sight slide catch pins)
6012	2500	Ejes de alza (Rear sight pins)
6012	500	Arandela del guarda-mano (Handguard retaining rings)
6012	1000	Porta expulsores (Ejector boxes)
6012	1000	Muelles del porta expulsores (Ejector box springs)
6012	1500	Expulsores (Ejectors)
6012	1500	Dientes de la corredera (Rear sight slide catches)
6012	1000	Tornillos del anillo del punto (Front sight base screws)
6013	500	Pies del alza (Rear sight bases/barrel sleeves)
6013	1000	Elevadores (Followers)
6013	1000	Extractores (Extractors)
6013	500	Muelles del porta expulsores (Ejector box springs)
6013	500	Escudetes (Stock nose caps)
6013	1500	Tornillos inferior (Lower/back trigger guard screws)
6013	2000	Tornillos de la cantonera (Butt plate screws)
6013	1500	Tornillos superior (Upper/front trigger guard screws)
6013	1000	Seguros (Safeties)
6013	1500	Topes de la corredera (Rear sight ladder slide stop screw)

CASE NO.	NUMBER OF COMPONENTS	COMPONENTS (ASSUMEDLY ALL FOR RIFLES?)
6013	1000	Pestillos del depósito (Magazine floorplate catches)
6013	1500	Tornillos del porta expulsor (Ejector box screws)
6013	1500	Tornillos del muelle del alza (Rear sight leaf spring screws)
6013	1500	Pasadores (ejes) del escudete (Stock nose cap pins)
6013	800	Fondos del depósito (Magazine floorplates)
6013	1500	Puntos de mira (Front sights)
13 cases total		Total value: 33,675.50 francs

Table 2

CASE NO.	NUMBER OF COMPONENTS	DESCRIPTION (AS RECEIVED BY THE CHILEAN COMMISSION MILITARY)
6014	400 for carbines	Guarda-manos (Handguards)
6015	400 for rifles	Guarda-manos (Handguards)
6016 - 6017	200 for rifles	Cajas (Stocks)
6020	600 for rifles	Muelles del elevador (Follower springs)
6020	600 for carbines	Muelles del elevador (Follower springs)
6021	300 for carbines	Abrazaderas superior (Upper/front barrel band)
6021	400 for carbines	Fondo del depósito (Magazine floorplate)
6021	400 for carbines	Cabezas del percutor (Cocking piece)
6021	400 for carbines	Palancas del disparador (Sear)
6021	400 for carbines	Percutores (Firing pin)
6021	200 for carbines	Base de la anilla inferior con anilla (montada) (Lower/rear sling swivel base with ring [mounted])
6021	300 for carbines	Protecciones del punto de mira (Protection for front sight)
6021	40 for carbines	Guarda montes (Trigger guard)
6021	200 for carbines	Muelle del porta expulsor (Ejector spring)
6021	600 for carbines	Tapa bocas (Muzzle cover)
6021	1000 for carbines	Muelles del diente de la corredera (Spring to rear sight slide catch)
6021	400 for carbines	Pestillos del depósito (Magazine floorplate catch)
6021	200 for carbines	Escudetes (Stock nose cap)
6021	40 for carbines	Cajónes del mecanismo (Receiver)
6021	600 for carbines	Baquetas (Cleaning rod)
6021	400 for carbines	Elevadors (Follower)
6021	400 for carbines	Muelles de la abrazadera inferior (Lower/rear barrel band spring)
6021	200 for carbines	Porta seguros (Bolt sleeve/shroud)
6021	200 for carbines	Disparadores (Trigger)
6021	400 for carbines	Muelles de la abrazadera superior (Upper/front barrel band spring)
6021	300 for carbines	Anillos del punto (Front sight base)
6021	200 for carbines	Lominas

CASE NO.	NUMBER OF COMPONENTS	DESCRIPTION (AS RECEIVED BY THE CHILEAN COMMISSION MILITARY)
6021	100 for carbines	Cantoneras (Butt plate)
6021	200 for carbines	Abrazaderas inferior (montada) (Lower/rear barrel band [mounted])
6021	200 for carbines	Arandelas del guardamano (Handguard retaining ring)
6021	400 for carbines	Seguros (Safety)
6021	400 for carbines	Tornillos del anillo del punto (Front sight base screw)
6021	1000 for carbines	Ejes del alza (Rear sight pin)
6021	600 for carbines	Tornillos del muelle del alza (Rear sight leaf spring screws)
6021	1000 for carbines	Pasadores del diente de la corredera (Rear sight slide catch pins)
6021	1200 for carbines	Pasadores pestillo y ejes del disparador (Trigger shaft and sear pins)
6021	600 for carbines	Diente de la corredera (Rear sight slide catch)
6021	600 for carbines	Tornillos del porta expulsor (Ejector box screws)
6021	400 for carbines	Tornillos a la cantoneras (Butt plate screws)
6021	800 for carbines	Tornillos bases de la anilla inferior (Screws to lower/rear sling swivel bases)
6021	300 for carbines	Muelles del alza (Rear sight leaf spring)
6021	600 for carbines	Puntos de mira (Front sights)
6021	100 for carbines	Tubos del tornillo inferior (Stock pillar to the lower/back trigger guard screw)
6021	200 for carbines	Expulsores (Ejectors)
6021	600 for carbines	Pasadores del escudete (Stock nose cap pins)
6021	200 for carbines	Pies del alza (Rear sight bases/barrel sleeves)
6021	600 for carbines	Extractores (Extractors)
6021	400 for carbines	Correderas (Rear sight ladder slides)
6021	600 for carbines	Pasadores de la protecciones (Pins to front sight protector)
6021	400 for carbines	Chapas de alza (Rear sight ladder)
6021	600 for carbines	Muelles del disparador (Sear springs)
6021	600 for carbines	Muelles del pestillo (Magazine floorplate catch springs)
6021	600 for carbines	Tornillos superior (Upper/front trigger guard screws)
6021	600 for carbines	Topes de la corredera (Rear sight ladder slide stop screw)
6021	400 for carbines	Porta expulsores (Ejector boxes)
6021	400 for carbines	Muelles del porta expulsores (Ejector box springs)
6021	400 for carbines	Expulsores (Ejectors)
6021	400 for carbines	Muelles del percutor (Firing-pin springs)
6021	600 for carbines	Tornillos inferior (Lower/back trigger guard screws)
6021	6200 for carbines	Aparatos por baquetas madera (Appliance for wooden cleaning rod)
6022	40 for rifles	Cajón del mecanismos (Receivers)
6022	600 for rifles	Baquetas (Cleaning rod)
6022	300 for rifles	Abrazaderas superior (Upper/front barrel band)
6022	600 for rifles	Fondos del depósito (Magazine floorplates)
6022	200 for rifles	Pies del alza (Rear sight bases/barrel sleeves)

CASE NO.	NUMBER OF COMPONENTS	DESCRIPTION (AS RECEIVED BY THE CHILEAN COMMISSION MILITARY)
6022	200 for rifles	Base de la anilla inferior con anilla (montada) (Lower/rear sling swivel base with ring [mounted])
6022	40 for rifles	Palanca del disparador (Sear)
6022	400 for rifles	Percutores (Firing pin)
6022	400 for rifles	Chapas de alza (Rear sight ladder)
6022	300 for rifles	Muelles del alza (Rear sight leaf spring)
6022	200 for rifles	Cerrojos (con anillo parta extractor) (Bolts with the extractor collar)
6022	100 for rifles	Cantoneras (Butt plate)
6022	40 for rifles	Guarda montes (Trigger guard)
6022	400 for rifles	Cabezas del percutor (Cocking piece)
6022	200 for rifles	Arandelas del guardamano (Handguard retaining ring)
6022	400 for rifles	Seguros (Safety)
6022	400 for rifles	Muelles de la abrazadera inferior (Lower/rear barrel band spring)
6022	400 for rifles	Muelles de la abrazadera superior (Upper/front barrel band spring)
6022	200 for rifles	Porta seguros (Bolt sleeve/shroud)
6022	400 for rifles	Elevadors (Follower)
6022	400 for rifles	Correderas (Rear sight ladder slides)
6022	400 for rifles	Pestillos del depósito (Magazine floorplate catch)
6022	200 for rifles	Escudetes (Stock nose cap)
6022	1000 for rifles	Muelles del diente de la corredera (Spring to rear sight slide catch)
6022	600 for rifles	Diente de la corredera (Rear sight slide catch)
6022	1000 for rifles	Ejes del alza (Rear sight pin)
6022	300 for rifles	Muelles del percutor (Firing-pin springs)
6022	200 for rifles	Disparadores (Trigger)
6022	200 for rifles	Muelle del porta expulsor (Ejector spring)
6022	200 for rifles	Abrazaderas inferior (montada) (Lower/rear barrel band [mounted])
6022	400 for rifles	Tornillos del anillo del punto (Front sight base screw)
6022	600 for rifles	Puntos de mira (Front sights)
6022	600 for rifles	Tornillos del porta expulsor (Ejector box screws)
6022	100 for rifles	Tubos del tornillo inferior (Stock pillar to the lower/back trigger guard screw)
6022	200 for rifles	Expulsores (Ejectors)
6022	600 for rifles	Pasadores pestillo y ejes del disparador (Trigger shaft and sear pins)
6022	800 for rifles	Tornillos bases de la anilla inferior (Screws to lower/rear sling swivel bases)
6022	600 for rifles	Pasadores del escudete (Stock nose cap pins)
6022	600 for rifles	Muelles del pestillo (Magazine floorplate catch springs)
6022	600 for rifles	Tornillos superior (Upper/front trigger guard screws)
6022	400 for rifles	Porta expulsores (Ejector boxes)
6022	400 for rifles	Muelles del porta expulsores (Ejector box springs)
6022	400 for rifles	Expulsores (Ejectors)
6022	600 for rifles	Tapa bocas (Muzzle cover)

CASE NO.	NUMBER OF COMPONENTS	DESCRIPTION (AS RECEIVED BY THE CHILEAN COMMISSION MILITARY)
6022	1000 for rifles	Pasadores del diente de la corredera (Rear sight slide catch pins)
6022	600 for rifles	Muelles del disparador (Sear springs)
6022	600 for rifles	Tornillos inferior (Lower/back trigger guard screws)
6022	600 for rifles	Topes de la corredera (Rear sight ladder slide stop screw)
6022	600 for rifles	Tornillos del muelle del alza (Rear sight leaf spring screws)
6022	1100 for rifles	Extractores (Extractors)
6022	400 for rifles	Muelles del percutor (Firing-pin springs)
6023	200 for carbines	Cañónes (Barrels)
6024	200 for rifles	Cañónes (Barrels)
6025 - 6032	4000 for rifles	Baquetas madera por fusil (Wooden cleaning rod)
17 cases total		Total 29,461.80 francs
		Note: crates 6018 and 6019 are not part of the order.

Chile's payment for this first contract emerge when a letter written to Matte from Director Riese of the Loewe Company is considered. In this letter, dated 1 December 1895, Riese thanked Matte for his letter of 29 November 1895, in which he stated that an amount of 1,338,061.80 francs was available for payment to Loewe. Riese then affirmed that this amount was composed of 1,305,600 francs—representing 32 percent of value of the rifles and carbines—29,461.80 francs for the spare parts, and 3,000 francs for the screwdrivers. Riese then asked Matte to pay this amount to the Credit Lyonnais in Paris for forwarding to Loewe's bankers, Born & Busse, in Berlin (Riese 1895a).

The ledger also recorded the quantities, shipping dates, ship names, and other details of the rifles and carbines; these are given in table 3, which equally includes these details for all subsequent orders. While previous discussion noted that Loewe paid for the packing and transportation of the rifles and carbines to Hamburg, table 3 shows that the embassy then paid for the shipping and insurance to the port of Valparaíso in Chile. A further fascinating insight offered by the ledger is that starting on 16 August 1894, and then often repeated, there was reference to the Chilean embassy having paid "Schwartz" for the shipping and insurance (Legación de Chile en Paris 1892, p. 8). It was initially assumed by the author that "Schwartz" was a gentleman in the employ of the Kosmos shipping line. On further investigation, it was revealed that "Schwartz"—translated as the German word "black"—was not a gentleman, but rather a direct reference to the black funnel used by the Kosmos line from 1872 to 1921 ("Deutsche Dampfschifffahrts-Gesellschaft Kosmos—DDG Kosmos").

Table 3

NUMBER OF CASES	SHIP	DATE SHIPPED FROM HAMBURG	VALUE IN FRANCS	NUMBER OF RIFLES	NUMBER OF CARBINES	GRAND TOTAL	NOTES
200	*Menes*	27 June 1895	340,000	5000	0	5000	Start of first contract. Payment of freight and insurance to Schwartz for 200 cases of rifles on the ***Menes*** for 2,189.50 pesos.
200	*Tanis*	6 July 1895	340,000	5000	0	10,000	Payment of freight and insurance to Schwartz for 200 cases of rifles on the ***Tanis*** for 2,291.76 pesos.

NUMBER OF CASES	SHIP	DATE SHIPPED FROM HAMBURG	VALUE IN FRANCS	NUMBER OF RIFLES	NUMBER OF CARBINES	GRAND TOTAL	NOTES
200	***Isis***	20 July 1895	340,000	5000	0	15,000	Loewe letter of 2 August 1895 to Ambassador Augusto Matte indicating the receipt by the Chilean Military Commission of 5,000 rifles on 16 July 1895 and shipped onboard ***Isis***. Payment of freight and insurance to Schwartz for 200 cases of rifles on the ***Isis*** for 2,229.02 pesos.
140	***Volumnia***	27 July 1895	238,000	3500	0	18,500	Loewe letter of 2 August 1895 to Ambassador Augusto Matte indicating the receipt by the Chilean Military Commission of 3,500 rifles on 23 July 1895 and shipped onboard ***Volumnia***.
140	***Totmes***	8 August 1895	238,000	3500	0	22,000	Loewe letter of 2 August 1895 to Ambassador Augusto Matte indicating the receipt by the Chilean Military Commission of 3,500 rifles on 29 and 30 July 1895 and shipped on the ***Totmes***. This shipment by ***Totmes*** also included the 3,000 screwdrivers.
50	***Albdos***	17 August 1895	85,000	1250	0	23,250	
218	***Luxor***	31 August 1895	370,600	5250	200	28,700	Payment of freight and insurance to Schwartz for 210 cases of rifles, 8 crates of carbines, 13 crates of spare parts, and numerous other goods on the ***Luxor*** for 3,332.97 pesos.
120	***Glenely***	5 September 1895	204,000	2700	300	31,700	Payment of freight and insurance to Schwartz for 108 cases of rifles and 12 cases of carbines on the ***Glenely*** for 1,737.97 pesos.
220	***Hathor***	14 September 1895	374,000	5500	0	37,200	Loewe letter of 4 September 1895 to Ambassador Augusto Matte indicating the receipt by the Chilean Military Commission of 14,700 rifles and 500 carbines. Payment of freight and insurance to Schwartz for 312 cases of rifles, 20 cases of carbines, and 2 cases of other goods on the ***Hathor*** for 3,512.27 pesos.

NUMBER OF CASES	SHIP	DATE SHIPPED FROM HAMBURG	VALUE IN FRANCS	NUMBER OF RIFLES	NUMBER OF CARBINES	GRAND TOTAL	NOTES
112	***Hathor***	14 September 1895	190,400	2300	500	40,000	
200	***Hispania***	28 September 1895	340,000	3600	1400	45,000	Payment of freight and insurance to Schwartz for 244 cases of rifles and 64 cases of carbines on the ***Hispania*** and ***Pentaur*** for 3,205.68 pesos.
108	***Pentaur***	30 September 1895	183,600	2500	200	47,700	
132	***Delia***	5 October 1895	224,400	2700	600	51,000	Loewe letter of 15 October 1895 to Ambassador Augusto Matte indicating the receipt by the Chilean Military Commission of 11,100 rifles and 2,700 carbines. Payment of freight and insurance to Schwartz for 108 cases of rifles and 24 cases of carbines on the ***Delia*** for 1,803.91 pesos.
132	***Ramses***	14 October 1895	224,400	1800	1500	54,300	Payment of freight and insurance to Schwartz for 72 cases of rifles and 60 cases of carbines on the ***Ramses*** for 1,335.68 pesos.
136	***Desdemona***	19 October 1895	231,200	1600	1800	57,700	Payment of freight and insurance to Schwartz for 64 cases of rifles and 72 cases of carbines on the ***Desdemona*** for 1,827.14 pesos.
116	***Herodot***	26 October 1895	197,200	900	2000	60,600	Approximate end of first contract and start of second contract. Payment of freight and insurance to Schwartz 36 cases of rifles, 80 cases of carbines, and 17 cases of spare parts on the ***Herodot*** for 1,189.96 pesos.
108	***Banda***	3 November 1895	183,600	1200	1500	63,300	Loewe letter of 5 November 1895 to Ambassador Augusto Matte indicating the receipt by the Chilean Military Commission of 5,500 rifles and 6,800 carbines. Payment of freight and insurance to Schwartz for 48 cases of rifles and 60 cases of carbines on the ***Banda*** for 1,401.32 pesos; this amount also included a further charge to the 17 cases of spare parts shipped earlier on the ***Herodot***.

NUMBER OF CASES	SHIP	DATE SHIPPED FROM HAMBURG	VALUE IN FRANCS	NUMBER OF RIFLES	NUMBER OF CARBINES	GRAND TOTAL	NOTES
202	***Memphis***	Approximately November/ December 1895	343,400	5050	0	68,350	Payment for freight and insurance to Schwartz for 202 cases of rifles and 10 cases of spare parts on the ***Memphis*** for 2,326.05 pesos.
48	***Valeria***	Approximately November/ December 1895	81,600	600	600	69,550	Payment for freight and insurance to Schwartz for 24 cases of rifles, 24 cases of carbines, and 1 case of tools/instruments on the ***Valeria***.
32	***Modestia***	Approximately November/ December 1895	54,400	800	0	70,350	Loewe letter of 4 December 1895 to Ambassador Augusto Matte indicating the receipt by the Chilean Military Commission of 6,450 rifles and 600 carbines during November 1895.
48	***Tanis***	Approximately December 1895 / January 1896	81,600	200	1000	71,550	
64	***Modestia***	Approximately December 1895 / January 1896	108,800	600	1000	73,150	Payment of freight and insurance to Schwartz for 56 cases of rifles, 40 cases of carbines, and 6 cases of machinery on the ***Modestia*** for 1,546.38 pesos.
82	***Tanis***	Approximately December 1895 / January 1896	139,400	1250	800	75,200	Payment of freight and insurance to Schwartz for 58 cases of rifles and 72 cases of carbines on the ***Tanis*** for 1,737.26 pesos.
214	***Volumnia***	Approximately December 1895 / January 1896	363,800	3150	2200	80,550	Unsighted Loewe letter of 4 January 1896 supposedly indicating the receipt by the Chilean Military Commission of 3800 rifles and 4,200 carbines during December 1895.
80	***Albdos***	Approximately January/ February 1896	136,000	1000	1000	82,550	
230	***Luxor***	Approximately January/ February 1896	391,000	4050	1700	88,300	Unsighted Loewe letter of 31 January 1896 supposedly indicating the receipt by the Chilean Military Commission of 6,450 rifles and 3,500 carbines during January 1896.

NUMBER OF CASES	SHIP	DATE SHIPPED FROM HAMBURG	VALUE IN FRANCS	NUMBER OF RIFLES	NUMBER OF CARBINES	GRAND TOTAL	NOTES
68	*Hathor*	Approximately January/ February 1896	115,600	0	1700	90,000	End of second contract. Unsighted Loewe letter of 15 February 1896 supposedly indicating the receipt by the Chilean Military Commission of 1,700 carbines during February 1896.
160	*Karnak*	Approximately mid-1896	272,000	0	4000	94,000	Start of third contract. Payment of freight and insurance to Schwartz for 160 cases of carbines on the ***Karnak*** for 3,512.71 pesos.
160	*Luxor*	Approximately mid-1896	272,000	0	4000	98,000	
80	*Denderah*	Approximately mid-1896	136,000	0	2000	100,000	End of third contract. Payment of freight and insurance to Schwartz for 80 cases of carbines on the ***Denderah*** for 1,744.82 pesos.
80	*Neko*	16 June 1898	136,000	2000	0	102,000	Start of fourth contract.
320	*Memphis*	19 July 1898	544,000	8000	0	110,000	End of fourth contract.
			7,480,000	80,000	30,000		

It has been identified that a bagged cleaning set containing a screwdriver, bore jag, chamber jag, and brush with a grease container was issued for every 100 rifles or carbines bought by the Chileans (Boado y Castro 1896a, p. 20). From illustrations of these Chilean components, it can be concluded that they were identical to those supplied to Argentina. It has also been argued that in the case of Argentina, their cleaning kits were initially manufactured by Loewe for the Model 1891, and then later by August Fonson & Co. of Liège for the Model 1909 (Webster 2003, pp. 87, 164). Webster also states that for the Argentine Model 1891, Fonson supplied the rifle slings, ammunition pouches, and bayonet frogs, while August Loh Sohne of Berlin supplied the carbine slings and action covers (Webster 2003, pp. 85–87). In the arguments presented, it is clear that the Loewe contract with Chile included supply of the slings and muzzle covers. It would therefore be logical to assume that Chile's accounting processes would not mention the supply or pricing of these. In October 1895, the ledger does mention a few instances where August Loh Sohne supplied 2,500 pieces of "equipment" to the value of 30,625 pesos. In August 1896, it likewise recorded a further, smaller order for 2,286 pesos that mentioned "knives" and "equipment" (Legación de Chile en Paris 1892, pp. 23, 43). As to August Fonson, the ledger appears to have made no mention of him.

In mid-September 1894, Eugene Schuchard of Bonn made overtures to August Fonson & Co. concerning initial negotiations with Chile. As identified later in the section that details ammunition contracts, Schuchard appears to have been an independent representative of Ludwig Loewe & Co. August Fonson then wrote to Ludwig Loewe & Co. on 24 September 1894. In this letter, August Fonson stated that following a meeting among himself, Ludwig Loewe & Co., and their representative, A. van Makkelenberg, it had subsequently been agreed that Chile and all other countries—including Brazil and Spain—were to be included for a period of two years into their prior agreement of 18 September 1894 (Fonson 1894b). Subsequently, on 29 September 1894, Makkelenberg wrote to Director Riese of Loewe

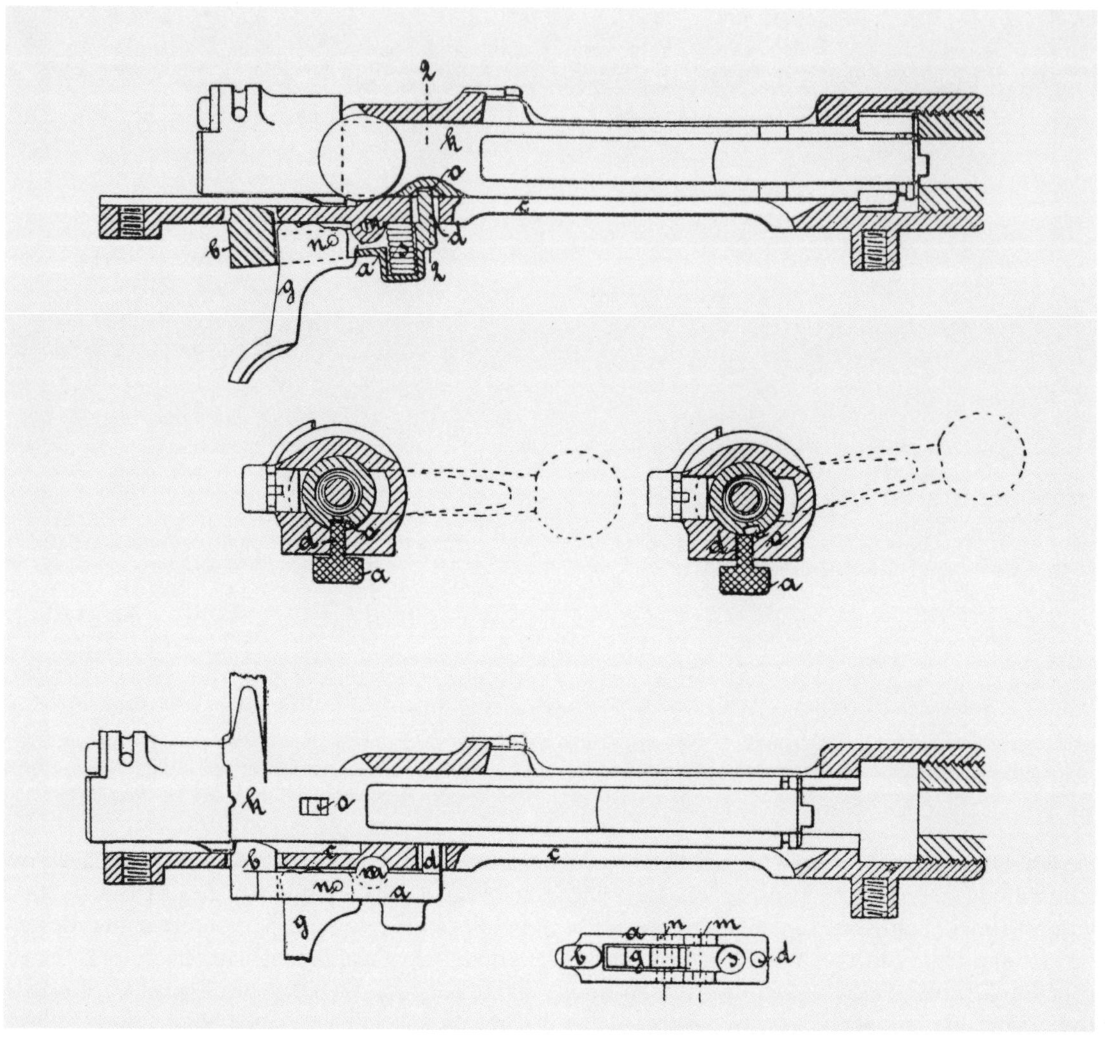

German patent 67343 as granted on 1 April 1892, for the trigger system as used on all Model 1893 types.
Mauser, P. 1892a. Germany Patent No. 67343. Kaiserliche Patentamt.

Company and restated Fonson's earlier statement, while further specifying that in exchange for Ludwig Loewe & Co. directing business toward August Fonson & Co., Fonson would pay a commission of 5 percent. In terms of Schuchard's offer of including Fonson in their Chile dealings, Makkelenberg had written to him and offered him a further 2 percent commission (Makkelenberg 1894). In a letter of 12 October, Fonson again wrote to Loewe and argued that it was understood that Loewe would use its influence over the respective weapons commissions, delegates, and government officials to obtain orders that would benefit August Fonson & Co. Fonson likewise argued that if his company was expected to pay a 5 percent commission, then it would be reasonable that any of his competitors who likewise benefited from Loewe's intervention would also have to pay this amount (Fonson 1894a). On 15 October 1894, Ludwig Loewe & Co. replied to Fonson's letter of 12 October and agreed that all was in order (Ludwig Loewe & Cie 1894).

Despite history having documented an agreement between Loewe and August Fonson, it still cannot be determined exactly who supplied the extras for Chile's rifles and carbines.

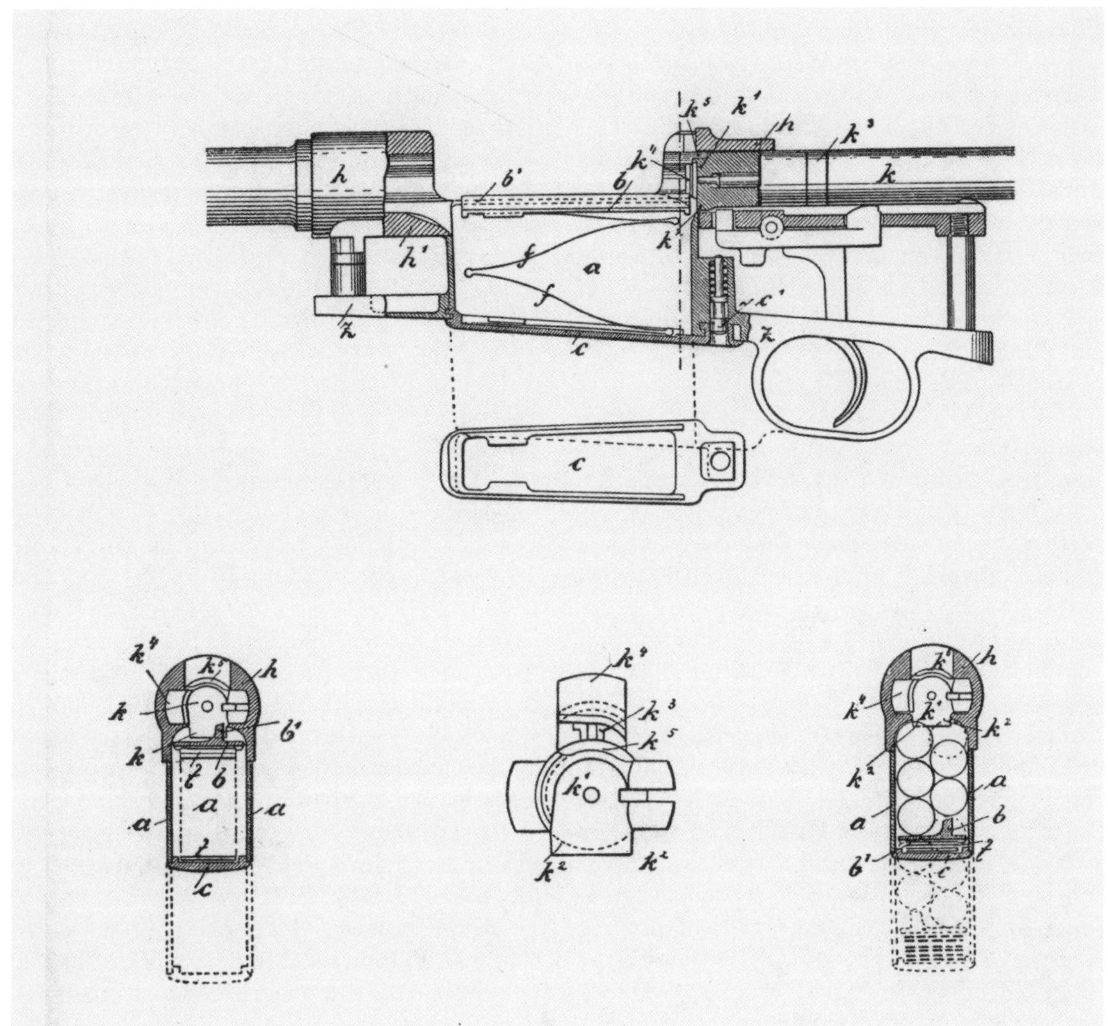

German patent 74162, which was granted on 8 June 1893 and depicts Mauser's integrated five-round magazine arrangement. Mauser, P. 1893b. Germany Patent No. 74162. Kaiserliche Patentamt.

Argentina's Contract with Loewe and Its Effect on Chile

It has been identified that Chile's decision to purchase Mausers in December 1894 was in some way restricted by the 1890 Argentina contract (Webster 2003, p. 105). This important point deserves further clarification. As already stated, in signing its initial 1890 contract with Ludwig Loewe & Co., Argentina saw fit to include Article 18, which prohibited the delivery of "system Mauser 1889 weapons" to other South American powers until three-quarters of the ordered weapons had been delivered (i.e., 78,000 rifles and 12,000 carbines). Because of financial difficulties, Argentina then had to renegotiate this contract soon after it was signed. On 4 November 1891, it signed a supplementary contract for 25,000 rifles. This supplementary contract also clarified the status of the remaining 75,000 rifles and 20,000 carbines of the initial contract. Article 7 stipulated that Argentina committed not to purchase the remaining 95,000 "Mauser system repeaters" from another manufacturer until 1 January 1895. Loewe, in turn, undertook to manufacture these weapons, but only until 1 January 1895. Article 13 of the supplementary contract also clarified that the restrictions placed on Loewe by Article 18 of the initial contract now allowed delivery of "Mauser system weapons" to other South American powers only once three-quarters of the reduced order for 25,000 rifles had been delivered. On 20 November 1891, a supplement added a further 25,000 rifles and 10,000 carbines to the amended contract order of 25,000 rifles; that is, Argentina would have ordered 60,000 in total. Article 18 of the initial contract and Article 13 of the amended contract were redefined in Article 4 of the supplement, since it stated that Loewe could not deliver "system Mauser weapons" to South American powers or private individuals until all of the 60,000 rifles and carbines had been delivered to Argentina. It likewise stipulated that this prohibition was subject to timely payment (Webster 2003, pp. 241–252). The delivery of these 60,000 rifles and carbines was subsequently completed on 3 May 1893. Importantly, delivery was satisfied only when the rifles and carbines had been inspected by the Acceptance Commission, officially accepted, sealed in their seaworthy packaging at Loewe's factory in Moabit, Berlin, and then shipped from an agreed European port (Webster 2003, pp. 104–105). On 27 March 1893, Argentina contracted for the delivery of the remaining 55,000 rifles and 5,000 carbines. In Article 6 of this supplementary contract, the original definition of Article 18 of the 1890 contract was once again changed. It now stated that under the penalties originally stated, Loewe undertook not to deliver "small caliber system Mauser weapons" to South American powers or private individuals before 5 November 1893. It was further stated in Article 9 that all provision of the original contract would not be altered or deleted by this contract and would thus remain in force (Webster 2003, pp. 259–261). It is curious that while the March 1893 contract stipulated a delivery schedule that spanned from 20 May to 31 December 1893 (Webster 2003, p. 259), the actual deliveries took place only from 11 December 1893 to the final supply of the last 5,000 carbines on 10 January 1895 (Webster 2003, p. 106). This is even more puzzling considering that the delivery schedules for the first 60,000 rifles and carbines had been satisfied (Webster 2003, pp. 106, 247, 251). Loewe could have been freed from the restrictions imposed by Article 6 of the March 1893 contract, which stipulated an end date of 5 November 1893. However, as stated in Article 9 of the March 1893 contract, the three-quarter rule under Article 18 of the original 1890 contract would still have been valid. Accordingly, the rifle component of this three-quarter rule—86,000 units—was satisfied by 11 May 1894 (Webster 2003, p. 106). The carbine three-quarter component was satisfied only on 10 January 1895 (Webster 2003, p. 106). While the original 1890 contract had originally specified 20,000 carbines, renegotiation had resulted in an actual need for only 15,000 carbines. Considering that the carbines were delivered in two batches—10 August 1893 and 10 January 1895—the three-quarter rule could have been satisfied only on 10 January 1895. As such, unless Loewe was prepared to pay a fine, it could not have sold Mausers to Chile before 10 January 1895. Interestingly, Loewe was so enticed by the Chilean market and its promised profits that it was prepared to pay the 500,000 franc fine (Schaefer 1974, p. 41). It has even been proposed that it was Chilean profits that allowed Loewe to take over FN (Sater and Herwig 1999, p. 146).

Having received this initial contract worth 4.08 million francs (3.2 million marks), Ludwig Loewe & Co., despite tough negotiations, managed to keep its factories busy well into the foreseeable future. Loewe importantly realized that having now hooked the Chileans, it could make up for any loss of immediate profits by simply increasing its prices on any further contracts (Schaefer 1974, p. 46). It did not have to wait long for this to eventuate. On 2 July 1895, the Chilean government instructed its representative in Paris, Augusto Matte, to purchase a further 20,000 rifles and 10,000 carbines. This contract was duly ratified by Ludwig Loewe & Co. on 4 July 1895. This was followed by a further order for 10,000 rifles in September 1895. Despite the Chileans again inviting FN to submit bids for both these orders, Loewe again used the threat of legal action to eventually win the second contract worth 2.04 million francs (Schaefer 1974, p. 49).

The Second and Third Contracts with Loewe for 30,000 Rifles and 10,000 Carbines

As with the December 1894 contract, FN was again requested to submit a bid for a further Chilean contract during summer 1895. On 2 July 1895, FN Director Chantraine forwarded a copy of a letter to Ambassador Matte that he had previously handed to Gen. Canto. In this letter, FN offered to supply a rifle with bayonet and 1,000 rounds of ammunition in stripper clips for 189 francs. Delivery of these could commence in November 1895 at a rate of 7,000–10,000 rifles per month. Chantraine also noted that while an influenza epidemic and some unexpected manufacturing setbacks had slightly delayed the delivery of the Brazilian order, FN was now able to manufacture a fully interchangeable rifle of the highest quality for the Chileans. He likewise reiterated that his board was extremely confident that the outstanding issue of the Mauser license could not stop manufacture of any proposed Chilean rifles, since it would ultimately be settled through the award of monetary damages (Chantraine 1895). In response to this letter, on 5 July 1895 a request was made that FN supply Chile with a detailed breakdown of prices, certificates attesting to the quality of fabrication of the Brazilian order, and ministerial statements concerning Mauser patents, lapses, or agreements. Likewise, the Chileans insisted that any delivery should start in October 1895 (Legrand 1895). On the same day, FN replied that its initial offer of 189 francs would constitute sixty-four francs for a rifle with bayonet and 125 francs for 1,000 rounds of ammunition in stripper clips. On Chile's request for certificates and statements, FN responded that these could be supplied by the following Wednesday, 10 July 1895 (Fabrique Nationale d'Armes de Guerra 1895). Despite FN's willingness to provide proof that the issue of the Mauser license would in no way affect delivery and having offered a better price, Chile again chose Ludwig Loewe & Co.

In early July 1895, Chile signed a second contract with Loewe for the supply of a further 20,000 rifles and 10,000 carbines. Like the first contract, the exact date of this second contract is alternatively recorded, having been either 4 July 1895 in Loewe correspondence (Ludwig Loewe & Cie 1895d, 1895m), or 11 June 1895 in the ledger (Legación de Chile en Paris 1892, pp. 15, 78). These initial ledger records of 11 June are then contradicted in the ledger by a date of 4 July 1895 (Legación de Chile en Paris 1892, p. 43). It is therefore reasoned that the exact date of this second contract was indeed 4 July 1895.

The second appearance of conflicting dates can best be described by a system whereby numerous copies of a contract were exchanged for original signature between Ludwig Loewe & Co., the Weapons Commission, the Chilean embassy in Paris, and the Chilean government in Santiago. This process is partly described in a letter that the Loewe Company sent to the Chilean embassy on 12 July 1895, stating that having received four copies

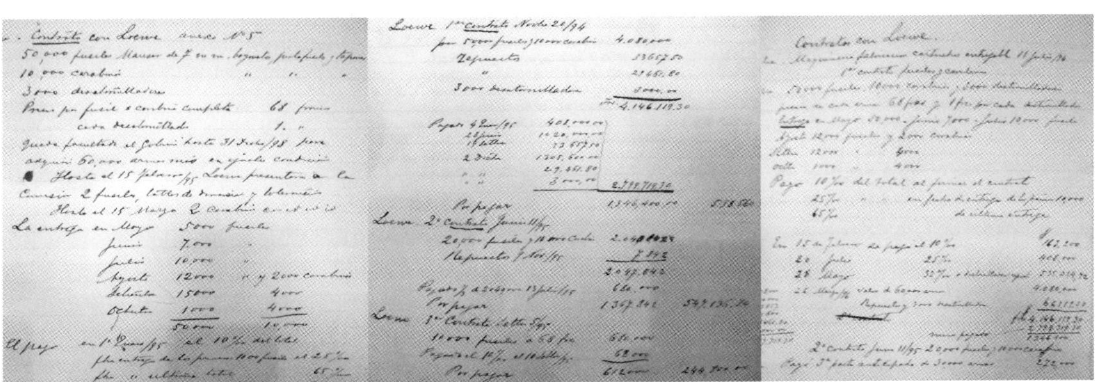

Pages from the master accounting ledger showing some of the contractual specifics of Chile's first and second contracts with Loewe.
Legación de Chile en Paris. 1892. *Legación de Chile en Paris, 1892–1898*. Vol. 2088. Archivo Nacional de Chile, Santiago.

1906 photographs of a mounted machine gun section armed with the carbine version of the Chilean Model 1895. Note the ammunition pouches unique to these and other cavalry troops. *Julio Morandé and the Ejército de Chile*

of the second contract that was signed in Paris on 4 July 1895, Loewe was returning two copies bearing its second signature to the Chilean embassy. In a later letter—again written by Ludwig Loewe & Co.—to Matte on 7 September 1895, concerning the third contract, the company stated that it was honored to submit to Matte copies of the recently signed contract. Additionally, the Loewe Company wrote that it had handed the third signed copy of this contract to the Weapons Commission in Berlin and looked forward to receiving the fourth countersigned contract back from Matte (Ludwig Loewe & Cie 1895j). From these two sources, it is reasonable to assume that each of the contracts between Loewe and Chile was completed in quadruple: two copies for the embassy in Paris and one copy each for the Weapons Commission and Loewe.

Payment for these 30,000 rifles and carbines was stipulated at one-third upon signing the contract and the remaining two-thirds after final delivery (Legación de Chile en Paris 1892, p. 19). The total value of the second contract was recorded as 2.04 million francs, and the initial one-third payment of 680,000 francs was to have been made on 13 July 1895 (Legación de Chile en Paris, 1892, p. 15). This initial payment is then later described as having been an advance payment of 272,000 pesos (Legación de Chile en Paris 1892, p. 78), therefore implying that the exchange rate at that time between the peso and the franc was 1:2.5. Likewise, it can be deduced that the price in this second contract was the same as the first; that is, sixty-eight francs (27.2 pesos) per rifle or carbine.

The delivery schedule of this second contract was 7,000 rifles and 3,000 carbines in November 1895, 7,000 rifles and 3,000 carbines in December 1895, and 6,000 rifles and 4,000 carbines in January 1896 (Legación de Chile en Paris 1892, p. 19).

Shortly before signing its second contract with Loewe, Chile proposed altering the design of the receiver-locking mechanism and gas-venting abilities of the design that had been contracted in December 1894. On 23 June 1895, Ambassador Matte wrote to Ludwig Loewe & Co. and pointed out that two rifles had suffered catastrophic failure during reception. In response to this, both Matte and the members of the Weapons Commission had expressed their desire that the current design be changed. The Chileans also requested that this proposed modification be adaptable to rifles and carbines that had already been received. Director Riese responded to this request on 20 July 1895, stating that the two rifles in question—number 2496, tested on 17 June, and number 8383, tested on 22 June—were the first rifles to experience such a catastrophic failure. Riese then stated that rifle 2496 had failed on the first proofing shot, while number 8383 failed after the fifth proofing shot. In both cases, the cartridge case had ruptured and had then blown gas and molten brass back into the mechanism. In both cases the chamber had not ruptured, but gas venting had resulted in an expanded magazine, split stock, and damage to the bolt stop. The extractor was also broken on rifle number 2496. Riese then affirmed that following a Loewe technical report into this matter, these failures had been identified as being the direct

Infantry on maneuvers in 1923, armed with what appears to be Chilean Model 1895 rifles. Note the ammunition pouches as issued to the infantry. *Ejército de Chile*

result of defective cartridges that were overloaded and that had brass that was too soft. The Loewe director then stated that considering 7,000 rifles had already been received without issue, Matte and the Weapons Commission should abandon any notion of changing an already excellent design, especially when such changes would result in considerable time delays (Riese 1895b).

A third contract with Loewe for 10,000 rifles was signed on 5 September 1895, and in this instance both Loewe Company communications with Matte and the ledger are in agreement as to the date (Legación de Chile en Paris 1892, pp. 15, 78; Ludwig Loewe & Cie 1895j). The ledger also identified the cost as sixty-eight francs per rifle or carbine and that a 10 percent advance payment of 68,000 francs was required by 10 September 1895 (Legación de Chile en Paris 1892, p. 15). This amount is then later requoted as having been 27,200 pesos, thus confirming the quoted exchange rate of 1:2.5 (Legación de Chile en Paris 1892, p. 78). Ludwig Loewe & Co., via letter, subsequently confirmed receipt of a cheque to the value of 68,000 francs for this 10 percent advance payment, together with the required countersigned fourth copy of the contract on 12 September 1895 (Ludwig Loewe & Cie 1895h).

It is possible that by September 1895, Chile had contracted with Loewe to buy 80,000 rifles and 20,000 carbines. Despite this, further weapons purchases were still to happen as long as the border issue with Argentina remained unresolved.

A Fourth Contract with Deutsche Waffen und Munitionsfabriken for 10,000 Rifles

In late 1897, the Chilean Weapons Commission informed Santiago that Argentina had concluded a contract with newly amalgamated DWM to procure a mammoth sixty million cartridges. This news added fuel to the already burning fire that was the growing border tensions with Argentina. The Chilean president responded in early 1898 by summoning the members of his cabinet to special sessions to urgently discuss these matters. Körner, as head of the newly formed National Defense Council, was also invited to these sessions. Supported by Minister of War Patricio Larraín, Körner proposed that Chile should purchase

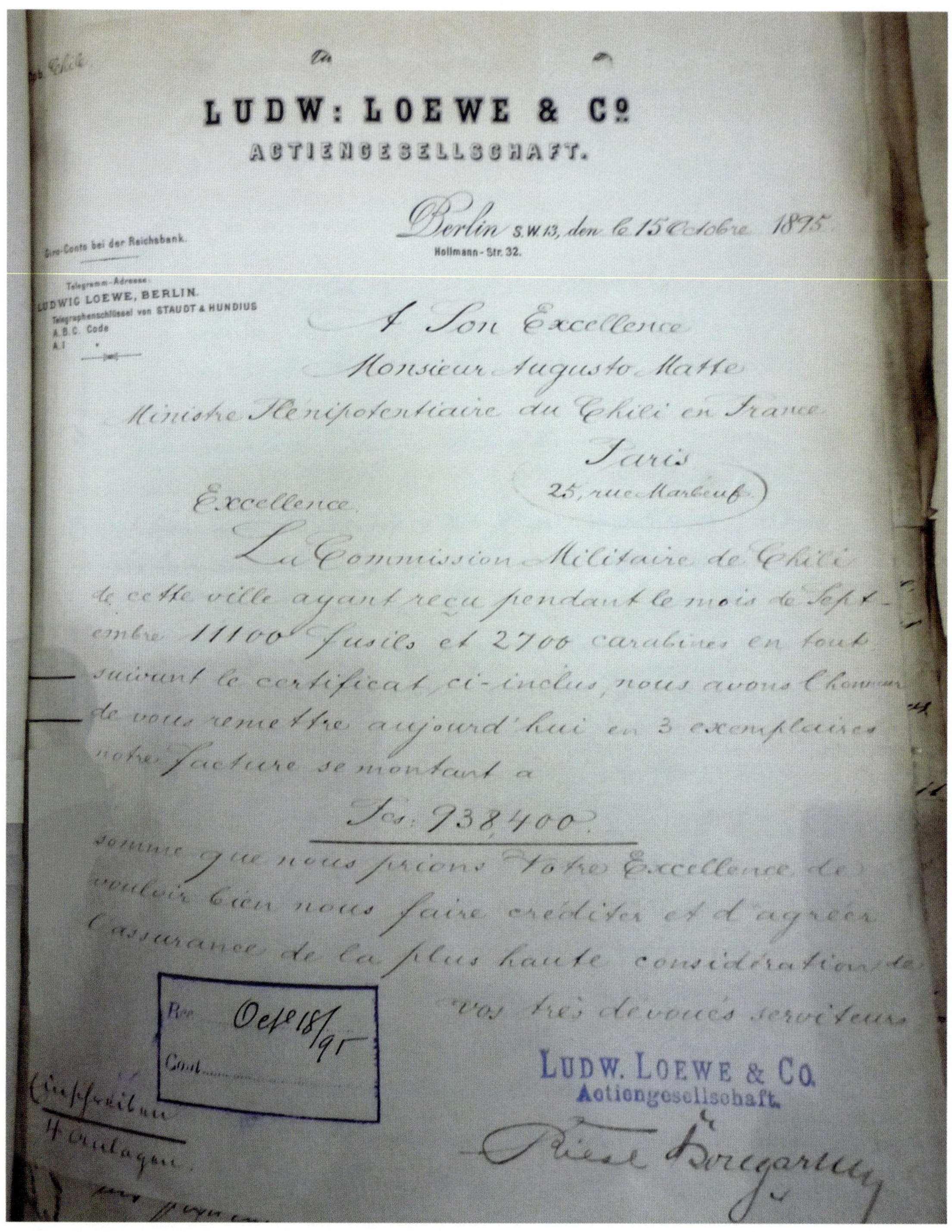

LUDW: LOEWE & Co.
ACTIENGESELLSCHAFT.

Giro-Conto bei der Reichsbank.

Telegramm-Adresse:
LUDWIG LOEWE, BERLIN.
Telegraphenschlüssel von STAUDT & HUNDIUS
A.B.C. Code
A.1

Berlin S.W.13, den le 15 Octobre 1895
Hollmann-Str. 32.

A Son Excellence
Monsieur Augusto Matte
Ministre Plenipotentiaire du Chili en France
Paris
25, rue Marbeuf

Excellence

La Commission Militaire de Chili de cette ville ayant reçu pendant le mois de Septembre 11100 fusils et 2700 carabines en tout suivant le certificat ci-inclus, nous avons l'honneur de vous remettre aujourd'hui en 3 exemplaires notre facture se montant a

Fcs: 938400.

somme que nous prions Votre Excellence de vouloir bien nous faire créditer et d'agréer l'assurance de la plus haute considération de vos très dévoués serviteurs

LUDW. LOEWE & Co.
Actiengesellschaft.

Rec Oct 18/95
Cont......

A Loewe bill to the Chilean ambassador Augusto Matte to the value of 938,400 francs. Issued on 15 October 1895, the bill is for the delivery of 11,100 Chilean Model 1895 rifles and 2,700 carbines and is signed by Loewe director Riese.
Ludwig Loewe & Cie. 1895g. "La commission militaire du Chili de cette ville ayant reçu pendant le mois de septembre 11,100 fusils et 2700 carabines." Legación de Chile en Francia e Inglaterra, vol. 400. Letter in Archivo Nacional de Chile, Santiago.

weapons and equipment for an army of 150,000 men. So that the contingency of war with Argentina could be prepared, the cabinet duly accepted this proposal while still conducting negotiations with Argentina. To action this dictate, the Chilean Weapons Commission entered into negotiations with DWM for the purchase of 40,000 rifles and additional machinery for the manufacture of small-arms ammunition (Schaefer 1974, pp. 62–63).

Because of a deteriorating Chilean economy driven by declining nitrate prices and agricultural failures, nothing came of the proposal for 40,000 additional rifles. To make matters worse, both German and British banks became increasingly reluctant to extend Chile loans for weapons purchases until the border issue with Argentina was resolved. In an effort to sustain its weapons purchases, Chile then asked Germany for assistance, particularly for the procurement of warships (Schaefer 1974, pp. 62–66).

On 18 January 1898, Larraín instructed the embassy in Berlin to acquire a further 10,000 Mauser rifles and ten million rounds of ammunition (Legación de Chile en Paris 1892, p. 121). Following this instruction, arguably one of the very first concessions offered by the Germans was a subsequent contract for 10,000 rifles with DWM signed on 30 January 1898. Because this contract is in the possession of the author, it is included in translated form and reveals some interesting insights into the nature of these documents:

> Contract concluded and signed by Colonel Don Vicente Palacios Chairman of the Military Commission of Chile, duly authorized by Ramón Barros-Luco Plenipotentiary Ministry of Chile in France acting on behalf of the Government of Chile on the one hand, and Deutsche Waffen und Munitionsfabriken on the other hand, have agreed the following:
>
> **Article 1:** The Government of Chile entrusts the Deutsche Waffen und Munitionsfabriken to deliver 10,000 7 mm Mauser rifles Chilean Model of 1895 for the same price and under the same conditions agreed for weapons that have been matter of the contracts of 15 December 1894 and others.
>
> **Article 2:** Payment of the specified rifles will be effected in the following manner: 10% of the total value of the signing of the contract, 45% on delivery of weapons, and at the option of the Minister of Chile, the remaining 45% will be paid within six months after final delivery, in which case Chile shall pay an additional, 5% annual interest, calculated from the date of the final delivery to the final cash payment.
>
> **Article 3:** Delivery of the 10,000 rifles will begin two months after the date of signing the contract and be completed two months later; i.e., on 31 May 1898.
>
> **Article 4:** It is understood that all the provisions contained in the contract of 15 December 1894 and *cahier des charges* annexure will remain in force in this contract, which should be considered as supplemental.
>
> Made in identical quadruple copies in Paris on 30 January 1898.
>
> Signed for Chile by Vicente Palacios and Ramón Barros-Luco
>
> Signed for the Deutsche Waffen und Munitionsfabriken by Paul Gontard
>
> (Legación de Chile en Francia 1893)

On 17 and 23 June 1898, the ledger recorded that a telegram was received stating that 2,000 rifles had been shipped on the *Neko* (Legación de Chile en Paris 1892, pp. 126, 153). The ledger also recorded the shipment of a further 8,000 rifles on 19 July 1898 on the *Memphis* (Legación de Chile en Paris 1892, p. 129). It is proposed that these 10,000 rifles were those bought under the contract of 30 January 1898.

Despite this initial success, the Kaiser and the German government became increasingly resistant to further weapons purchases, since the Kaiser was personally irritated by the continued presence of the Chilean Weapons Commission in Paris. Only when the Weapons Commission was transferred to Berlin in summer 1898 did the Germans become more amenable, allowing the completion of existing contracts. These included a colossal order of Krupp cannons and 90,000 kg (198,416 lbs.) of smokeless powder from Rottweil, in Cologne. After these were delivered in August 1898, Germany then prevented further weapons sales until the border issue with Argentina was resolved (Schaefer 1974, pp. 62–66).

It is clear that by the end of May 1898, Chile could have had 90,000 Mauser rifles and 20,000 carbines, for a total of 110,000.

It is generally accepted that these 110,000 rifles and carbines—known by their receiver inscription as the Mauser Chileno Modelo 1895 (Chilean Mauser Model 1895)—existed in eleven sequential blocks, each comprising 10,000 serial numbers. Following standard Mauser practice, each of these blocks is distinguished by an alphabetical serial prefix that corresponds either to "A," "B," "C," "D," "E," "F," "G," "H," "K," "L," or "M." It is not known why alphabetical prefixes "I" or "J" were not used, but this is likely due to how these letters were reinterpreted in the evolving Spanish language during that period.

In December 1894, Chile initially ordered 50,000 rifles and 10,000 carbines; these 60,000 would presumably have composed the six alphabetical prefixes from "A" to "F." From table 3, it is clear that this contract was shipped to Chile. Chile's second order was contracted in July 1895 and was for 20,000 rifles and 10,000 carbines; these would have reasonably composed the three alphabetical prefixes "G," "H," and "K." Again from table 3, it is clear that this contract was shipped to Chile. The third order, in September 1895, was for 10,000 rifles and would plausibly have been delimited in the one alphabetical prefix "L." Since the only remaining serial prefix is "M," it would be rational to assume that this comprised the 10,000 rifles from the January 1898 contract, but contradictions are always evident in history.

Estimating the Number of Mauser Chileno Modelo 1895s

When consulting the accounting ledger, a further Loewe contract becomes evident. Not only does the ledger specify that this contract dated 23 May 1896 was for 10,000 carbines, but it also provides a shipping indication on 7 August 1896, identifying the three lots of case numbers 801–960, 961–1040, and 1121–1200, and total value of 680,000 francs (Legación de Chile en Paris 1892, p. 63). Shipment and insurance of these carbines are then confirmed through the recording of payments to Schwartz that mirror the numbers of the cases and lots and that also list ship names (Legación de Chile en Paris 1892, pp. 59, 60, 62). Curiously, the ledger has also recorded that only 612,000 francs—or 90 percent of the value—of the 10,000 carbines needed to be paid (Legación de Chile en Paris 1892, p. 63). If indeed these last facts are correct, then by the end of May 1898, Chile could have had 90,000 Mauser rifles and 30,000 carbines, for a total of 120,000. This total of 120,000 does not fit the known reality of eleven alphabetical blocks.

Later in the ledger, under the heading "Section Confidential—1898," the Chilean embassy in Paris has recorded a summary concerning Chile's total number of artillery and small arms. The total number of Mauser rifles is listed as 90,000 and that of carbines as 32,000. Remarkably, right next to the total of 90,000, the word "error!" is written faintly in red (Legación de Chile en Paris 1892, p. 127). Still later in the ledger, a further page reveals more extraordinary facts as to the actual number of Mauser rifles and carbines that were physically present in Chile. On the right-hand side of the page, under the heading "Actual Inventory, 22 December 1899," the total number of Mauser rifles is listed as 85,390, of which 50,000 were new and 35,390 were used. Of the 50,000 new rifles, 10,100 were in Valparaíso (Legación de Chile en Paris 1892, p. 180). Likewise, the total number of Mauser carbines is listed as 24,559, of which 15,000 were new and 9,559 were used (Legación de Chile en Paris 1892, p. 181). Thus, it is highly likely that as of 22 December 1899, 109,949 Mauser rifles and carbines were present in Chile.

To contextualize these numbers even further, the ledger likewise recorded that as of 12 October 1898, a total of 17,660 Mausers rifles had been issued to the infantry; 2,460 Mauser rifles, to the engineers; 500 Mauser rifles, to the coastal artillery; 8,020 Mauser carbines, to the cavalry; 6,980 Mauser carbines; to the artillery; and 180 carbines had been

" 22 A D. del P. y M. ordena remitir por G. M. [illegible] 12 Octbre

	Garrison	Unit	No.	Quantity	Arm
Infantería	Santiago	por Buin	N 1	1900	Mauser
	Valparaíso	Maipo	2	2880	"
	Santiago	Yungay	3	2400	"
	Iquique	Rancagua	4	1600	Mannlicher
	Concepción	Carampangue	5	1960	Mauser
	Lautaro	Chacabuco	6	1440	"
	Antofagasta	Esmeralda	7	1960	Mannlicher
	Talca	Valdivia	8	2880	Mauser
	Chillán	Pudeto	9	2400	"
	Los Angeles	Lautaro	10	1800	"
Caballería	Angol	~~Tacna~~ Granaderos	N 1	900 carb.	Mauser
	Santiago	~~Arica~~ Cazadores	2	960	"
	Iquique	~~Art. Costa~~ Húsares	3	960	"
	Temuco	~~Chorrillos~~ Carabineros	4	900	"
	[illegible]	~~Miraflores~~ Lanceros	5	1600	"
	Curicó	Dragones	6	1800	"
	Angol	Guías	7	900	"
Artillería	Santiago	Tacna	N 1	1280	" "
	Copiapó	Arica	2	1280	" "
	Santiago	Art. Costa	3	1600	" "
	Cauquenes	Chorrillos	4	1280	" "
	Traiguén	Miraflores	5	1540	" "
Ingenieros	Iquique	Cía Atacama		640	rifles Mannlicher
	Concepción	Concepción		640	" Mauser
	Angol	Arauco		540	" "
	Santiago	Santiago		640	" "
Art. Costa	Talcahuano	Talcahuano		500	" "
Magallanes	Infantería			630	" Mannlicher
	Ingenieros			90	" "
	Caballería			90	carabinas Mauser
	Artillería			"	" "

Mannlicher and Mauser rifles and carbines as issued to the Chilean infantry, cavalry, artillery, and engineers in 1898. The ten infantry battalions are Buin, Maipo, Yungay, Rancagua, Carampangue, Chacabuco, Esmeralda, Valdivia, Pudeto, and Lautaro. The seven cavalry battalions are Granaderos del General Bulnes, Cazadores del General Baquedano, Husares, Carabineros, Lanceros, Dragones, and Guías. The five artillery battalions are Tacna, Arica, Campana, Chorrillos and Miraflores. Last, the four engineering battalions are Atacama, Santiago, Concepción, and Arauco.
Legación de Chile en Paris. 1892. Legación de Chile en Paris, 1892–1898, vol. 2088. Archivo Nacional de Chile, Santiago.

miscellaneously issued (Legación de Chile en Paris 1892, p. 134).

From the contracts listed above, there are only four—December 1894, July 1895, May 1896, and January 1898—for which both contractual specifics and shipping confirmation are available (table 3). As will also become evident, these four contracts had associated spare-parts orders. Likewise, considering that the May 1896 contract required only 90 percent of the total value to be paid, it can be assumed that the other 10 percent had already been received by Ludwig Loewe & Co. for something else. Therefore, it is proposed that the May 1896 contract replaced or amended that of September 1895; this contention is also later supported when spare-parts purchases are discussed. It has been identified that on 12 September 1895, Loewe received a 10 percent payment for this contract. Furthermore, two irrefutable facts cannot be ignored. The first is the actual inventory numbers of 22 December 1899: 85,390 Mauser rifles and 24,559 carbines. The second is the eleven known sequential blocks. These discrepancies can best be explained by the fact that while the ledger's recording of the facts concerning the first two contracts (December 1894 and July 1895) is impeccable, the same cannot be said for any subsequent contracts. In the context of this argument, it is feasible that while the ultimate number of approximately 110,000 is not in doubt, it is possible that some of the purchases that recorded rifles were in fact carbines.

The conclusion is that there is compelling reason to believe that by the end of 1899, Chile had approximately 85,000 Mauser rifles and 25,000 carbines at its disposal.

Accounting for the Boer Rifles in Chile

Despite Argentina and Chile having conceded to mediation of their border dispute in late 1898, tensions and provocations nevertheless continued. In March 1901, Chile's constant refusal to hold the agreed plebiscite in Tacna and Arica resulted in the Peruvians recalling their diplomats from Santiago. This recall and the Peruvian call for the vote to be held were supported by the Argentine press. These events, coupled with border violations and further arms purchases by Argentina, resulted in the establishment by the Chilean congress of a special committee to deal with national defense. In July 1901, this resulted in two Chilean defense bills that authorized further expenditure on weapons. To take action on these, the military council, under the chairmanship of Körner, met in November 1901 and decided to purchase further artillery and small arms. Receiving this news, German armaments manufacturers reacted with delight. Using tactics similar to those it had previously employed, in 1901 DWM attempted to entice the Chileans into buying its new Model 1898. Again, the Chileans were invited to view Loewe's supposedly secret order books. Here, both Körner and the Chilean envoy in Berlin, Ramon Subercaseaux, sighted the enormity of Argentina's long-arm procurements. Again, the Chileans were more than convinced that the Argentines were plotting war, and subsequently signed a weapons contract on 21 December 1901 for 3.8 million marks. This included 100 Maxim machine guns and seventeen million cartridges. Shortly before this contract, Chile had also agreed to purchase 4.25 million cartridges and 5,800 blockaded Mauser rifles initially intended for the Boer Republics in South Africa (Schaefer 1974, pp. 72–73, 238).

This last paragraph is very interesting for numerous reasons. The first of these concerns the rifles destined for the Boer Republics, which were eventually bought by the Chileans. It has been argued that the Zuid-Afrikaansche Republiek (South African Republic, or simply ZAR) had 4,000, and the Oranje Vrystaat (Orange Free State, or simply OVS) had 1,000 rifles blockaded by the British. These rifles, with turned-down bolt handles, squared bolt face, and no third safety lug behind the bolt handle, were eventually returned to Germany and sold to Chile (Ball 2011, pp. 432, 442; Bester 2003, pp. 222, 231–232). It has been proposed that the 4,000 ZAR rifles had serial numbers C0001 to C4000, while those of the OVS started at serial number 7901 and ended at 8900 (Ball 2011, pp. 432, 442). This would mean that the historical record acknowledges only 5,000 blockaded rifles. It is therefore curious why Schaefer would report 5,800 Boer rifles. This discrepancy is best answered by the acknowledgment that the exact number of Mausers purchased by the OVS is unclear. It is also an irrefutable fact that Chilean OVS Mausers with serial numbers below 7901 have been observed (Bester 2003, pp. 231–232). A further interesting fact is that Chilean literature also records 500 "Boer Mauser" receivers as having been purchased as part of a spare-parts order in 1910 (Pinto Concha et al. 1911, p. 9).

When these Boer rifles are included, it can be inferred that by the end of 1901, Chile had acquired a total of approximately 115,800 Mausers. Of this total, approximately 110,000 were "true" Mauser Chileno Modelo 1895, comprising approximately 85,000 rifles, 25,000 carbines, and a further 5,800 Mauser Model 1893 rifles originally intended for the Boers.

Spare Parts for the Mauser Chileno Modelo 1895

Chile's first contract with Loewe on 15 December 1894 also included two large orders of spare parts. After Chile signed its second contract with Loewe on 4 July 1895, it saw fit to further extend these initial spare-parts orders, which were officially quantified only on 28 May 1895. According to a letter from Loewe director Riese to Ambassador Matte on 29 July 1895, the Weapons Commission then extended the initial spare-parts order on 26 July 1895. Riese informed Matte that Ludwig Loewe & Co. would now provide spare parts for 90,000 weapons on time and in proportion to the deliveries of complete rifles and carbines (Ludwig Loewe & Cie 1895e). In an earlier letter of 12 July 1895, Loewe confirmed that any spare parts ordered under the second contract would be provided under the same conditions and at the same prices as the initial contract (Ludwig Loewe & Cie 1895k). These eventual spare parts have been listed in tables 1 and 2.

Table 3 shows that on 31 August 1895, thirteen crates of spare parts were shipped to Chile onboard the *Luxor*, seventeen cases of spare parts were shipped to Chile onboard the *Herodot* on 26 October 1895, and ten cases of spare parts were later shipped onboard the *Memphis*.

On 17 September 1895, the Loewe Company wrote to Matte, specifying it had dispatched thirteen crates of Mauser spare parts to the value of 33,654.50 francs on 27 August 1895, and thus attached an invoice for payment (Ludwig Loewe & Cie 1895a). This amount was subsequently paid by check on 23 September 1895 (Ludwig Loewe & Cie 1895f). Equally, it has already been mentioned that on 1 December 1895, Loewe director Riese instructed Ambassador Matte that the amount of 29,461.80 francs for spare parts should be paid to its bankers.

Table 4

CASE NO.	NUMBER OF COMPONENTS	DESCRIPTION (AS RECEIVED BY THE CHILEAN COMISIÓN MILITAR)
6053	160	Cañónes (Barrels)
6054	160	Cañónes (Barrels)
6055	160	Cañónes (Barrels)
6056	160	Cañónes (Barrels)
6057	160	Cañónes (Barrels)
6063	1500	Puntos de mira (Front sights)
6063	1750	Anillos del punto (Front sight base)
6063	800	Pies del alza (Rear sight bases / barrel sleeves)
6063	1800	Muelles del alza (Rear sight leaf spring)
6063	900	Chapas de alza (Rear sight ladder)
6063	1000	Diente de la corredera (Rear sight slide catch)

CASE NO.	NUMBER OF COMPONENTS	DESCRIPTION (AS RECEIVED BY THE CHILEAN COMISIÓN MILITAR)
6063	900	Correderas (Rear sight ladder slides)
6063	200	Cerrojos con anillo parta extractor (bolts with the extractor collar)
6063	200	Seguros (Safety)
6063	600	Cabezas del percutor (Cocking piece)
6063	20	Guarda montes (Trigger guard)
6063	800	Elevadors (Follower)
6063	600	Pestillos del depósito (Magazine floorplate catch)
6063	100	Tubos del tornillo inferior (Stock pillar to the lower/back trigger guard screw)
6063	300	Escudetes (Stock nose cap)
6063	400	Abrazaderas superior (Upper/front barrel band)
6063	600	Tornillos inferior (Lower/back trigger guard screws)
6063	600	Tornillos superior (Upper/front trigger guard screws)
6063	600	Tornillos del porta expulsor (Ejector box screws)
6063	600	Tornillos del muelle del alza (Rear sight leaf spring screws)
6063	300	Pasadores del escudete (Stock nose cap pins)
6063	500	Pasadores pestillo y ejes del disparador (Trigger shaft and sear pins)
6063	1000	Ejes del alza (Rear sight pin)
6063	1000	Pasadores del diente de la corredera (Rear sight slide catch pins)
6063	600	Muelles del percutor (Firing-pin springs)
6063	600	Muelles del pestillo (Magazine floorplate catch springs)
6063	600	Muelles del disparador (Sear springs)
6063	800	Muelles del diente de la corredera (spring to rear sight slide catch)
6063	1000	Tapa bocas (Muzzle cover)
6068	100	Cajas (Stocks)
6068	125	Guarda-manos (Handguards)
6069	100	Cajas (Stocks)
6069	125	Guarda-manos (Handguards)
6070	100	Cajas (Stocks)
6070	125	Guarda-manos (Handguards)
6071	100	Cajas (Stocks)
6071	125	Guarda-manos (Handguards)
6072	100	Cajas (Stocks)
6072	125	Guarda-manos (Handguards)
6073	100	Cajas (Stocks)
6073	125	Guarda-manos (Handguards)
6074	100	Cajas (Stocks)
6074	125	Guarda-manos (Handguards)
6075	100	Cajas (Stocks)
6075	125	Guarda-manos (Handguards)

CASE NO.	NUMBER OF COMPONENTS	DESCRIPTION (AS RECEIVED BY THE CHILEAN COMISIÓN MILITAR)
6076	140	Cajón del mecanismos (Receivers)
6076	400	Porta seguros (Bolt sleeve/shroud)
6076	2600	Percutores (Firing pin)
6076	1000	Extractores (Extractors)
6076	400	Porta expulsores (Ejector boxes)
6076	600	Muelles del porta expulsores (Ejector box springs)
6076	600	Expulsores (Ejectors)
6076	300	Disparadores (Trigger)
6076	400	Palancas del disparador (Sear)
6076	900	Fondos del depósito (Magazine floorplates)
6076	1000	Muelles del elevador (Follower springs)
6076	500	Muelles de la abrazadera superior (Upper/front barrel band spring)
6076	500	Muelles de la abrazadera inferior (Lower/rear barrel band spring)
6076	400	Abrazaderas inferior (montada) (Lower/rear barrel band [mounted])
6076	300	Bases de la anilla inferior con anilla (Lower/rear sling swivel bases with swivel)
6076	150	Cantoneras (Butt plate)
6076	1000	Baquetas (Cleaning rod)
6076	300	Arandelas del guardamano (Handguard retaining ring)
6076	600	Topes de la corredera (Rear sight ladder slide stop screw)
6076	500	Tornillos del anillo del punto (Front sight base screw)
6076	800	Tornillos de la cantoneras y bases de la anilla inferior; 4 piezas (Screws for butt plate and rear sling swivel base; four pieces)
6076	2000	Aparatos por bayonetas de madera (Appliance for fitting wooden bayonet?)
		Total price rifle spares: 38,753.80 francs

Table 5

CASE NO.	NUMBER OF COMPONENTS	DESCRIPTION (AS RECEIVED BY THE CHILEAN COMISIÓN MILITAR)
6051	150	Cañónes (Barrels)
6052	150	Cañónes (Barrels)
6058	100	Cajas (Stocks)
6058	120	Guarda-manos (Handguards)
6059	100	Cajas (Stocks)
6059	120	Guarda-manos (Handguards)
6060	100	Cajas (Stocks)
6060	120	Guarda-manos (Handguards)
6061	100	Cajas (Stocks)
6061	120	Guarda-manos (Handguards)

CASE NO.	NUMBER OF COMPONENTS	DESCRIPTION (AS RECEIVED BY THE CHILEAN COMISIÓN MILITAR)
6062	100	Cajas (Stocks)
6062	120	Guarda-manos (Handguards)
6064	700	Puntos de mira (Front sights)
6064	450	Anillos del punto (Front sight base)
6064	600	Pasadores de la protecciones (Pins to front sight protector)
6064	300	Pies del alza (Rear sight bases/barrel sleeves)
6064	450	Muelles del alza (Rear sight leaf spring)
6064	400	Chapas de alza (Rear sight ladder)
6064	700	Diente de la corredera (Rear sight slide catch)
6064	600	Correderas (Rear sight ladder slides)
6064	400	Seguros (Safety)
6064	1800	Percutores (Firing pin)
6064	600	Cabezas del percutor (Cocking piece)
6064	900	Expulsores (Ejectors)
6064	600	Elevadors (Follower)
6064	600	Pestillos del depósito (Magazine floorplate catch)
6064	150	Tubos del tornillo inferior (Stock pillar to the lower/back trigger guard screw)
6064	300	Escudetes (Stock nose cap)
6064	450	Abrazaderas superior (Upper/front barrel band)
6064	700	Tornillos inferior (Lower/back trigger guard screws)
6064	700	Tornillos superior (Upper/front trigger guard screws)
6064	700	Tornillos del porta expulsor (Ejector box screws)
6064	700	Tornillos del muelle del alza (Rear sight leaf spring screws)
6064	700	Topes de la corredera (Rear sight ladder slide stop screw)
6064	800	Tornillos del anillo del punto (Front sight base screw)
6064	800	Tornillos a la cantoneras; 2 piezas (Butt plate screws; pairs)
6064	1800	Tornillos bases de la anilla inferior; 2 piezas (Screws to lower/rear sling swivel bases; pairs)
6064	700	Pasadores del escudete (Stock nose cap pins)
6064	1200	Pasadores pestillo y ejes del disparador; 2 piezas (Trigger shaft and sear pins; pairs)
6064	1500	Ejes del alza (Rear sight pin)
6064	1500	Pasadores del diente de la corredera (Rear sight slide catch pins)
6064	800	Muelles del percutor (Firing-pin springs)
6064	1200	Muelles del pestillo (Magazine floorplate catch springs)
6064	1200	Muelles del disparador (Sear springs)
6064	1200	Muelles del diente de la corredera (Spring to rear sight slide catch)
6065	300	Cerrojos con anillo parta extractor (Bolts with the extractor collar)
6065	900	Extractores (Extractors)
6065	400	Porta expulsores (Ejector boxes)

CASE NO.	NUMBER OF COMPONENTS	DESCRIPTION (AS RECEIVED BY THE CHILEAN COMISIÓN MILITAR)
6065	900	Muelles del porta expulsores (Ejector box springs)
6065	300	Disparadores (Trigger)
6065	600	Palancas del disparador (Sear)
6065	80	Guarda montes (Trigger guard)
6065	600	Muelles de la abrazadera superior (Upper/front barrel band spring)
6065	600	Muelles de la abrazadera inferior (Lower/rear barrel band spring)
6065	700	Baquetas (Cleaning rod)
6066	2000	Baquetas madera con aparato para limpiar fusil (Rifle wooden cleaning rod with cleaning device)
6067	2300	Baquetas madera con aparato para limpiar carabina (Carbine wooden cleaning rod with cleaning device)
6077	170	Cajón del mecanismos (Receivers)
6077	300	Porta seguros (Bolt sleeve/shroud)
6077	600	Fondos del depósito (Magazine floorplates)
6077	900	Muelles del elevador (Follower springs)
6077	300	Abrazaderas inferior (montada) (Lower/rear barrel band [mounted])
6077	300	Bases de la anilla inferior con anilla (Lower/rear sling swivel bases with swivel)
6077	300	Lomines?
6077	150	Cantoneras (Butt plate)
6077	300	Arandelas del guardamano (Handguard retaining ring)
6077	1000	Tapa bocas (Muzzle cover)
6077	2200	Aparatos por bayonetas de madera (Appliance for fitting wooden bayonet?)
		Total price carbine spares: 27,113.90 francs

Table 6

PIEZAS (PIECE)	FUSIL (RIFLE PRICE IN PESOS)	CARABINA (CARBINE PRICES IN PESOS)
Cañones (barrels)	11.28	10.71
Punto de mira (front sight)	0.2	0.2
Protección del punto de mira (front sight protector)	0	0.76
Pasador del punto de mira (pin for the protector)	0	0.15
Anilo del punto (front sight screw)	0.33	0.33
Pie de alza (rear sight bases / barrel sleeve)	0.8	0.8
Muelle del alza (rear sight leaf spring)	0.41	0.41
Chapa del alza (rear sight ladder)	0.65	0.65
Diente de la corredera (Rear sight slide catch)	0.05	0.05
Corredera (Rear sight ladder slide)	0.3	0.3
Cajones del mecanismo (Receiver)	8.24	8.24

PIEZAS (PIECE)	FUSIL (RIFLE PRICE IN PESOS)	CARABINA (CARBINE PRICES IN PESOS)
Cerrojos con anillo porta-extractor (Bolts with the extractor collar)	5.16	5.16
Porta seguro (Bolt sleeve/shroud)	1.48	1.48
Seguro (Safety)	0.6	0.6
Percutor (Firing pin)	1.09	1.09
Cabeza del percutor (Cocking piece)	0.74	0.74
Extractor (Extractors)	0.23	0.23
Porta expulsor (Ejector box)	0.99	0.99
Muelle del porta expulsor (Ejector spring)	0.69	0.69
Expulsores (Ejectors)	0.16	0.16
Disparador (Trigger)	0.14	0.14
Palanca del disparador (Sear)	0.64	0.64
Guarda monte (Trigger guard)	5.07	5.07
Fondo del depósito (Magazine floorplate)	0.83	0.83
Elevador (Follower)	0.56	0.56
Muelle del elevador (Follower springs)	0.2	0.2
Pestillo del depósito (Magazine floorplate catch)	0.16	0.16
Tubo del tornillo del guarda monte (Stock pillar to the lower/back trigger guard screw)	0.12	0.12
Escudete (Stock nose cap)	0.37	0.37
Abrazadera superior (Upper/front barrel band)	0.71	0.71
Abrazadera inferior montada para el fusil (Lower/rear barrel bands for rifle)	0.96	0.96
Muelle de la abrazadera superior (Upper/front barrel band springs)	0.54	0.54
Muelle de la abrazadera inferior (Lower/rear barrel band spring)	0.56	0.56
Base de la anilla con anilla (Lower/rear sling swivel bases with the swivel)	0.43	0.43
Cantonera (Butt plate)	0.74	0.74
Baqueta (Cleaning rod)	0.79	0.79
Plancha de sosten de la base de la annila inferior (Carbine saddle ring and sling swivel)	0	0.23
Arandela del guardamano (Handguard retaining ring)	0.38	0.38
Caja (Stock)	11.93	11.94
Guardamano (Handguard)	0.88	0.88
Tornillo inferior del guarda monte (Lower/back trigger guard screw)	0.12	0.12
Tornillo superior del guarda monte (Upper/front trigger guard screw)	0.11	0.11
Tornillo del porta expulsor (Ejector box screw)	0.11	0.11
Tornillo del muelle del alza (Rear sight leaf spring screw)	0.06	0.06
Tornillo del anillo del punto (Front sight base screw)	0.03	0.03
Tornillo de la cantonera y base de la anilla; 4 piezas (Butt plate and rear sling swivel screws; four pieces)	0.22	0
Tornillo de la cantonera; 2 piezas (Butt plate screws; two pieces)	0.22	0.22

PIEZAS (PIECE)	FUSIL (RIFLE PRICE IN PESOS)	CARABINA (CARBINE PRICES IN PESOS)
Tornillo de la base de la anilla; 2 piezas (Rear sling swivel screws; two pieces)	0	0.05
Tope de la corredera (Rear sight ladder slide stop screw)	0.03	0.03
Pasador del escudete (Stock nose cap pin)	0.03	0.03
Pasador del pestillo y ejes del disparador (Trigger shaft and sear pins)	0.03	0.03
Eje del alza (Rear sight pin)	0.03	0.03
Pasadores del diente de la corredera (Rear sight slide catch pin)	0.03	0.03
Muelle del percutor (Firing-pin spring)	0.2	0.2
Muelle del pestillo (Magazine floorplate catch spring)	0.08	0.08
Muelle del disparador (Sear spring)	0.03	0.03
Muelle del diente de la corredera (Rear sight slide catch spring)	0.08	0.08
Tapa boca (Muzzle cover)	0.4	0.4
Baqueta con aparato para limpiar fusiles y carabinas (Cleaning rod with apparatus to clean rifles and carbines)	0.22	0.1
Bayoneta sin vaina (Bayonet without scabbard)	0.5	0.5
Vaina de bayoneta (Bayonet scabbard)	2.5	2.5
Porta-fusil y carabina (Sling for rifle and carbine)	1.5	1.5

Again in 1896, the ledger made mention of two large spare-parts orders for rifles (table 4) and carbines (table 5) to the value of 38,753.80 and 27,113.90 francs, respectively, with a contract date of 15 May 1896 (Legación de Chile en Paris 1892, pp. 57–58). These spares were contained in a total of twenty-seven crates numbered 6051–6077 that were shipped onboard the *Banda*, apparently on 15 August 1896 (Legación de Chile en Paris 1892, pp. 69–71).

To contextualize the reader as to the value of individual spare parts, on 27 December 1895 the Chilean minister of war decreed the price (table 6) of Model 1895 spare parts when used as replacements due the culpable negligence of members of the army (Boado y Castro 1896a, pp. 44–47).

In 1898, Chile contracted with DWM twice for the supply of spare parts, and both these contracts are in the author's possession. The first contract was relatively small and was dated 24 March 1898. It reads as follows:

Contract signed by Colonel Don Vicente Palacios, as chairman of the Military Commission of Chile, duly authorized by Mr. Don Ramón Barros-Luco, as ambassador of Chile in France who is acting on behalf of the Government of Chile on the one hand, and Deutsche Waffen und Munitionsfabriken on the other hand, have agreed the following:

The Government of Chile entrusts the Deutsche Waffen und Munitionsfabriken to deliver

- 2,000 Extractors at 0.23 francs each for a subtotal of 460 francs,
- 2,000 Firing pins at 1.09 francs each for a subtotal of 2,180 francs,
- 2,000 Rear sight ladder slides at 0.30 francs for a subtotal of 600 francs,
- 2,000 Rear sight slide catches at 0.05 francs each for a subtotal of 100 francs,
- 2,000 Real sight leaf springs at 0.41 francs each for a subtotal of 820 francs,

Table 7

QUANTITY	PART
2,672	Caja (Stock)
738	Guardamano (Handguard)
736	Cañones (Barrels)
3,552	Percutor (Firing pin)
448	Cabeza del percutor (Cocking piece)
352	Disparador (Trigger)
352	Palanca del disparador (Sear)
368	Guarda monte (Trigger guard)
5,040	Baqueta (Cleaning rod)
512	Cerrojos con anillo porta-extractor (Bolts with the extractor collar)
416	Porta seguro (Bolt sleeve/shroud)
336	Abrazadera superior (Upper/front barrel band)
352	Chapa del alza (Rear sight ladder)
3,312	Corredera (Rear sight ladder slide)
320	Abrazadera superior (Upper/front barrel band)
736	Muelle del percutor (Firing-pin spring)
1,424	Muelle del alza (Rear sight leaf spring)
320	Muelle de la abrazadera inferior (Lower/rear barrel band spring)
320	Muelle de la abrazadera superior (Upper/front barrel band springs)
368	Arandela del guardamano (Handguard retaining ring)
624	Expulsores (Ejectors)
320	Base de la anilla inferior (Lower/rear sling swivel base)
368	Anilo del punto (Front sight screw)
200	Muelle del porta expulsor (Ejector spring)
2,000	Cajones del mecanismo (Receiver)
560	Muelle del elevador (Follower springs)
384	Muelle del disparador (Sear spring)
944	Mecanismos de retirada (retenido) y expulsión (porta-expulsor) (Complete ejector boxes?)
336	Muelle del pestillo (Magazine floorplate catch spring)
736	Ejes del disparador (Trigger to sear pin)
10,304	Diente de la corredera (Rear sight slide catch)
2,112	Muelle del diente de la corredera (Rear sight slide catch spring)
432	Eje del alza (Rear sight pin)
1,520	Diente de la corredera (Rear sight slide catch)
368	Tornillo del anillo del punto (Front sight base screw)
384	Pasador del pestillo (Sear pin)
320	Tubo del tornillo del guarda monte (Stock pillar to the lower/back trigger guard screw)
336	Cantonera (Butt plate)
336	Pie de alza (Rear sight bases/barrel sleeves)

QUANTITY	PART
432	Elevador (Follower)
848	Extractor (Extractors)
464	Seguro (Safety)
464	Tornillo inferior (Lower/back trigger guard screw)
398	Tornillo superior (Upper/front trigger guard screw)
464	Fondo del depósito (Magazine floorplate)
1,360	Tornillo de la cantonera (Butt plate screw)
320	Escudete (Stock nose cap)
3,072	Tornillo corredera (Rear sight ladder screw)
1,040	Punto de mira (Front sight)
352	Pestillo del depósito (Magazine floorplate catch)
5,120	Tornillo del porta expulsor (Ejector box screw)
11,648	Baqueta con aparato para limpiar fusiles (Cleaning rod with apparatus to clean rifles)
11,341	Piezas de bronce para bayonetas de madera; aparatos para bayonetas de madera (Apparatus for fitting wooden bayonets?)
320	Pasador del escudete (Stock nose cap pin)
848	Tornillo del muelle del alza (Rear sight leaf spring screw)
	Total price for rifle parts: 79,058.48 Francs

- 1,000 Front sights at 0.20 francs each for a subtotal of 200 francs.
  Total: 4,360 francs.

Delivery and payment of these parts will be made in the same way and for the same rifles as contracted for on 30 January 1898, with the Deutsche Waffen und Munitionsfabriken.

Concluded in Paris, in identical quadruple copies on 24 March 1898.

Signed for Chile by Vicente Palacios and Ramón Barros-Luco

Signed for the Deutsche Waffen und Munitionsfabriken by Paul Gontard

(Legación de Chile en Francia 1893)

The second, much-larger contract was dated 5 December 1898—the rifle contents of this are listed in table 7, while those for the carbines are listed in table 8—which were delivered on 28 February 1899 and were worth 79,058.48 and 16,475.68 francs, respectively (Legación de Chile en Paris 1892, p. 179):

Contract signed by Colonel Don Vicente Palacios, as chairman of the Military Commission of Chile, duly authorized by Mr. Don Ramón Barros-Luco, as ambassador of Chile in France who is acting on behalf of the Government of Chile on the one hand, and Deutsche Waffen und Munitionsfabriken on the other hand, have agreed the following:

Article 1: The Government of Chile entrusts the Deutsche Waffen und Munitionsfabriken to deliver spare parts for rifles and carbines, Mauser 7 mm Chilean Model 1895 as per their respective prices in the attached lists, and under identical conditions that have been agreed for weapons, which have been the subject of the contracts of 15 December 1894 and others.

Article 2: The payment of the mentioned spare parts shall be effected upon completion of the reception and surrender of the certificate of receipt to the Military Commission and after confirmation of arrival in Hamburg.

Article 3: Delivery of the spare parts will begin two months after the date of this contract and will terminate on 28 February 1899.

Article 4: It is understood by all parties that all the provisions contained in the contract of 15 December 1894 and the supplementary *cahier des charges* annexure will remain in force for this contract.

Made in identical quadruple in Paris on 5 December 1898.

Signed for Chile by Vicente Palacios and Ramón Barros-Luco
Signed for the Deutsche Waffen und Munitionsfabriken by Director Riese
(Legación de Chile en Francia 1893)

Before dealing with a large and very complicated spare-parts order in 1910, it is worth mentioning that Chile appears to have bought or ordered 500 extractors and extractor collars for their Model 1895s in 1930. This order is detailed in the Mauser Werke Order or Offer Book on 7 March 1930 and was facilitated through the Schweizerische Industrie Gesellschaft (Swiss Industrial Company, or simply SIG). In communicating this information to the author in 2016, Jon Speed stated that this extractor order was in addition to an earlier order by Chile—again through SIG—for 500 bolt bodies. Likewise, on 1 April 1930 the Hamburg trading firm of H. Fölsch & Co. signaled its intention to procure rifle and carbine stocks for the Chileans. In a note at the bottom of the entry in the Mauser Offer Book, it is explained that 10,000 rifle stocks were purchased and that carbine stocks had been ordered. A clearer understanding both of SIG and H. Fölsch & Co. will emerge in the later chapter that deals with the Chilean Modelo 1935.

OEWG Spare Parts

Despite Chile awarding its Mauser rifle, carbine, and associated spare part orders to Loewe and then later DWM, OEWG and Austria nevertheless gained a further opportunity at redemption in 1910. Chile decided it needed more rifles, carbines, ammunition, and spare parts because the simmering Tacna and Arica question had again reached a crisis point.

Despite limited business success, Austria still had impeccable contracts with the Chilean government and military. In 1910, these contacts resulted in the award to OEWG of a contract for 20,000 Mauser rifle barrels and 6,000 carbine barrels to a value of 670,000 marks (Schaefer 1974, p. 166). Another source cites the total number of carbine barrels as 6,500 (Ortmeier 2006, p. 59). In addition to the barrels, Chile's Weapons Commission—now in Berlin—also called for the supply of Mauser spare parts, including bolts, firing pins, receivers, 20,000 stocks with handguards, and 30,000 rear sights to adapt existing Mausers to the ballistic characteristics of the newer spitzer munition (Sater and Herwig 1999, pp. 151–152).

On 9 November 1909, the Chilean Dirección del Material de Guerra (War Material Department) informed Col. Eduardo Gormaz—who replaced Gen. Canto on the Chilean Weapons Commission in Europe—of the urgent need to acquire 46,000 rifle and 12,000 carbine barrels to transform weapons currently issued, and to meet current repair requirements for the adoption of spitzer munition (Unknown author 1912b).

On 10 March 1910, the Chilean minister of war issued a decree authorizing the purchase of Mauser spare parts and instructed its representatives in Europe to request prices from OEWG, because it was authorized to manufacture Mauser rifles. Subsequently, on 29 March 1910 the Weapons Commission received a telegram from the minister requesting it to approach both DWM and OEWG and request spare-parts prices for rifle barrels and sights to accommodate the new spitzer munition, as well as the carbine *cañón alargado* (elongated carbine barrels) that also had a new sight to accommodate the new ammunition. Apparently this lengthening of carbine barrels was necessary to allow the efficient operation of the new spitzer, or

Bala P munition. Having received Minister Aníbal Rodríguez's request, the Weapons Commission duly approached DWM and OEWG and immediately telegrammed the quoted prices to Santiago on 28 April 1910. This telegram was then followed up with a detailed explanation by mail. In this letter, the Weapons Commission argued that despite OEWG offering more-advantageous pricing, this alone could not preclude DWM from being awarded the contract, since the primary intention of the purchase was to satisfy the fundamental requirements of a *fusil moderno* (modern rifle). Having considered the telegrammed information, on 30 April 1910 Minister Rodríguez then asked the Weapons Commission what type of sights were being proposed by DWM and OEWG. To this, the commission replied that OEWG could supply "curved" or "straight" sights for the quoted prices, while DWM could supply only curved. Afterward, on 8 May 1910, the war minister again telegrammed the Weapons Commission and instructed them to purchase spare parts and barrels only with straight or "vertical" sights, as long as the amount of 455,860 marks was not exceeded. The Weapons Commission replied on 10 May 1910 that the allocated amount was insufficient, and that 990,660 marks was needed. Significantly, the commission also advised that the elongated carbine barrels would mean that any stocks ordered—originally numbered at 2,000—would also have to be lengthened to accommodate a bayonet. This fact had also been advised on 3 April 1910, and then later on 21 June 1910. In reply to the telegram of 10 May 1910, the minister replied that the Weapons Commission should continue negotiations for the rifle and carbine barrels, as well as for all the other spare parts, so the Weapons Commission received no instruction regarding its concerns. Only much later, on 29 May 1911, was this matter finally clarified through the issue of Supreme Decree 1,392–G5, which stated that an equal number of stocks should be bought to accommodate the elongated carbine barrels (Pinto Concha et al. 1911, pp. 3–9).

At this point, it should be acknowledged that the straight or vertical sight mandated by the Chileans was the generic rear sight traditionally associated with the Mauser Model 1893 family. Indeed, this sight design was already present on all existing Mauser Chileno Modelo 1895s. On the other hand, the curved sight refers to the tangent rear sight type, which had a curved base (i.e., a sight based on tangents of the angles of elevation).

On 4 June 1910, the Weapons Commission contracted with OEWG for the supply of the requested spare parts and delivered to OEWG one rifle and carbine Mauser Chileno Modelo 1895 (Unknown author 1912d). Article 4 of this contract stated that this rifle and carbine had been placed at OEWG's disposal as prototypes, which would ensure authentic and correct manufacture of the spare parts. Similarly, it also stated that a prototype rifle sight calibrated for the spitzer munition would be made available. As to the carbine sight, this was to be calculated and designed by OEWG to suit the spitzer ammunition. In a later communication to the new Chilean war minister on 2 October 1911, the Weapons Commission confirmed that the rifle and carbine given to OEWG had also been used to manufacture the jigs and gauges that were used to manufacture the spare parts (Pinto Concha et al. 1911, pp. 7–8). To ensure that OEWG's jigs and gauges were identical to those used earlier by Loewe, the directors of OEWG procured an identical set from DWM that was delivered on 27 June 1910. Later, to prove the accuracy of the OEWG jigs and gauges, previously marked defective parts were then measured both by the OEWG and DWM jigs, with both sets producing identical results (Pinto Concha et al. 1911, p. 11). On 6 June 1910, the rifle and carbine in unissued condition were sent from Chile to Europe onboard the ship *Thuringa*; these were received by the Weapons Commission on 19 July 1910 (Unknown author 1912b).

The first batch of OEWG-manufactured spare parts left Hamburg on 5 November 1910 onboard the ship *Polynesia* and arrived in Valparaíso on 21 December 1910, while the last batch left Hamburg on 22 April 1911 (Pinto Concha et al. 1911, p. 7).

Even the award of a relatively small contract to OEWG did not sit well with DWM, which then did everything in its power to discredit OEWG, a process that used political and media pressures. In particular, Gen. Jorge Boonen Rivera resorted to unscrupulous means.

As inspector general of the Chilean army, Boonen Rivera could have become aware of the OEWG purchase when, on 9 August 1910, the ministry of war forwarded a copy of the OEWG contract—which included 20,000 rifles and 6,000 carbine barrels—to the Dirección del Material de Guerra (Unknown author 1912b). However, a year would have to pass before he decided to actively condemn the OEWG purchase.

On 23 September 1911, Master Gunsmith Baldomero García wrote to his superior, director of the Fábricas y Maestranzas del Ejército (Factories and Arsenals of the Army, or simply FAMAE), and informed him that there were tolerance problems both with the OEWG-manufactured barrels and receivers. García wrote that the OEWG barrels had a "thinned" threaded portion that screwed into the receiver. When these OEWG barrels were fitted to forty existing Loewe and DWM receivers, only 20 percent could be used, and these were generally in poor condition. García also noted that when the OEWG barrels were fitted to OEWG receivers, of which 2,000 had been received, only 80 percent could be deemed acceptable (Unknown author 1912b).

García's note was duly forwarded to the War Ministry on 29 September 1911 by the director of war material. Following this, it was decided that the Comisión de Experiencias (Review Commission)—being the standing body within the Dirección del Material (Directorate of Material)—was to be convened to officially examine the issue and then report its findings on 100 of the OEWG-produced barrels. The Comisión de Experiencias then conducted the required tests on eighty rifle and twenty carbine barrels that were randomly chosen. Using measuring devices originally supplied by Loewe, it was found that of the eighty rifle barrels, only fourteen were within tolerance, while the remaining sixty-six (82.5%) were defective when the threaded portion that screwed into the receiver was measured. Of the twenty carbine barrels, 50 percent had identical issues. The Comisión de Experiencias then reported that after using OEWG parts that were within tolerance, it had put together three rifle and two carbine barrels, receivers, and complete bolts. When a "normal" chamber gauge was inserted into the chamber, none of the rifles or carbines would allow the bolt to close. When these rifles and carbines were then disassembled and remeasured, it was found that the threaded portions of all the barrels were in excess of the maximum tolerance. When OEWG barrels were fitted to used Loewe or DWM receivers, it was found that the barrels were "loose." It was then reported that a rifle was constructed using Loewe and DWM parts, but with the barrel, receiver, and bolt having been made by OEWG. This rifle was then subjected to a firing test that comprised five rounds from the Union Cartridge Company, followed by ten of the standard *Bala P* (spitzer) rounds manufactured in Chile, and then a final five blank rounds. Once the firing was complete, the rifle was disassembled and the barrel was remeasured, which confirmed that the threaded portion had "lengthened." The chamber was also measured by using a special set of six calibrators that each measured different parts, which again confirmed that the chamber had lengthened, leading the Comisión de Experiencias to determine that the barrel steel was of inferior quality. The report concluded with the statement that the commission had not tested the resistance of the bore, since it lacked both the Nobel powder and the pressure-testing apparatus necessary to generate in excess of 5,000 atmospheres. This report was signed on 5 October 1911 by Comisión de Experiencias' president Lt. Col. Manuel A. Delano and its two members: Capt. M. Grove and B. García (Unknown author 1912b).

Obviously sensing the potential dangers inherent in the García note of 23 September 1911, acting minister of war Enrique Zañartu telegrammed the Weapons Commission and asked for the names of the reception committee for the OEWG spare parts. To this, Gen. Pinto Concha, as head of the Weapons Commission, replied that the committee comprised Altamirano, Bennett, Medina, and Quintiliano Barbosa. When the appointed minister of war Alejandro Huneeus returned to the War Ministry, he telegrammed the Weapons Commission on 2 October 1911, asking for the source of the templates and gauges that were used during the manufacture of the OEWG spare parts. To this, Pinto replied on 4 October 1911 that these had been derived from the rifle and carbine that Chile had provided to OEWG. On 7 October 1911, Huneeus telegrammed the Weapons Commission and asked if the plans and technical information sent on 28 July 1910 by the Dirección del Material had been used in the manufacture of the OEWG spare parts. To this, Pinto replied that the sent information had arrived only on 27 September 1910 (Unknown author 1912c).

The Comisión de Experiencias' report was then forwarded to the Ministry of War on 6 October 1911, accompanied by a note written by Boonen Riviera. It was in this communication that Boonen Riviera slandered not only OEWG, but also his fellow officers in the Chilean army. Boonen Rivera's letter, after first outlining the course of events described above, then attacked the Weapons Commission in Europe for contracting with an "unknown and strange" factory that he had every reason to distrust. Had the Weapons Commission instead contracted with DWM, as he had instructed them to do, Chile would not be facing a scenario where it might have to litigate against OEWG and abandon its existing relationships with DWM. He then proceeded to discredit the Weapons Commission's claim that DWM had been excluded because they would not manufacture the straight or vertical sights as mandated, by arguing that these could have been purchased from numerous other factories in England, France, or Belgium. In concluding his letter, Boonen Rivera then accused the Weapons Commission of being negligent in their duties by not properly overseeing and receiving the spare parts. This negligence, he charged, had thus resulted in a real financial "scam" that had severely jeopardized the security of Chile (Unknown author 1912b).

On 10 October 1911, Minister Huneeus telegrammed the Weapons Commission, asking if any anomalies had been found during the proof firing of the OEWG barrels. To this, Pinto replied on 12 October that the OEWG barrels had been found to far exceed the requirements stipulated in the previously mandated Loewe *cahier des charges*, in terms of yield strength and elongation. Pinto reported that proofing shots had been successfully undertaken at 5,800 atmospheres (Unknown author 1912c).

The Comisión de Experiencias produced a further report on 11 October 1911, which addressed the need to test the barrels in excess of 5,000 atmospheres. To produce the required pressures, the commission reported that it had loaded its own ammunition by using the maximum capacity of "Reinsdorf" powder and an earlier round-tipped bullet (i.e., 173 grains). Five shots of this ammunition were then fired in two rifles. The first of these rifles was identical to that used in the first report—that is, constructed from Loewe and DWM parts—but the barrel, receiver, and bolt had been made by OEWG; the second rifle was made exclusively from Loewe and DWM parts. Interestingly, the commission claimed that the OEWG parts used were ones that were in excess of normal dimensions, because as identified in the first report, if they were within tolerance, then the rifle's bolt would not be able to close on a normal chamber gauge. After firing, it was reported that, as expected, the threaded portion of the barrel and the chamber of the OEWG rifle were elongated, while the Loewe/DWM rifle was fine. Further, the OEWG rifle suffered three bolt and two extractor failures, rendering it inoperable. These failures thus demonstrated that the materials used in the OEWG parts were inferior, since they could not withstand the required proofing pressures of 5,000 atmospheres. On the same day that the second report was published, both the ministers of war and foreign affairs were witness to a further demonstration, in which two shots were fired from the two previously used rifles. The only difference this time was that the Loewe/DWM rifle had been modified to fire the *Bala P* round. The two shots in question were one manufactured by Hirtenberg and the other by Karlsruhe; that is, DWM. Once again, the Loewe/DWN rifle was fine, while the OEWG example suffered a broken bolt and extractor. The Comisión de Experiencias noted that while the ammunition from DWM had performed flawlessly, that from Hirtenberg had split in both rifles; this indicated that its brass was less ductile because of poor annealing. The report not only damned the OEWG spare parts (stating that they were manufactured form inferior steels) but also vilified the Hirtenberg ammunition. Like the first report, it was signed by Delano, Grove, and García (Unknown author 1912b).

On 13 October 1911, Minister Huneeus again telegrammed the Weapons Commission to ask if the *cahier des charges* was part of the OEWG contract and if it had been used when the spare parts had been received. Col. Altamirano replied on 14 October 1911 that the *cahier des charges* was the same as that used in the Loewe contract of 15 December 1894, and that it had been used during reception to inform on any defects. Also on

13 October 1911, Huneeus communicated to the Weapons Commission that the rifle barrels were 80 percent, and those for the carbine 50 percent—useless. As such, he requested that the Weapons Commission urgently report on the reception of the OEWG spare parts (Unknown author 1912c).

Since issue of the OEWG spare parts had thus developed into a serious matter, the Chilean cabinet was convened on 13 October 1911 to decide a solution. The next day, the War Ministry was issued a decree that required a full investigation and the allocation of blame. This decree—number 2,286 of 14 October 1911—had six main points, with the main thrust being that the spare parts supplied by OEWG did not meet the requirements of the contract of 4 June 1910, despite the Chilean treasury having paid 572,163 marks for them. Because Chile could thus not modernize, fully repair, or service its existing Mauser rifles or carbines, national security had also been seriously compromised. While calling for those responsible to be quickly identified and prosecuted, the decree also called for litigation to be instituted against OEWG to recover monies paid. In a further decree—number 7,772 of 16 October 1911—the War Ministry ordered that any received OEWG spare parts be kept in their original packaging and not be used under any circumstances (Unknown author 1912c).

Despite this very clear instruction, Boonen Riviera saw fit to convene a further ad hoc committee to investigate the OEWG spare parts. This committee comprised himself, Col. Eduardo Gormaz, and Capts. Carlos Novoa and Juan Gamboa, as well as Master Gunsmith Baldomero García. The findings of the group were in total agreement with the two prior reports by the Comisión de Experiencias. Furthermore, in a shameless push to rectify the situation, the committee recommended that Chile buy sufficient quantities of DWM spare parts to keep 50,000 rifles and carbines serviceable into the foreseeable future (Unknown author 1912c).

In response to the growing furor surrounding the OEWG spare-parts purchase, on 3 November 1911 the government of Chile dissolved the Weapons Commission. When asked why this had been done, Minister Huneeus replied that it was to ensure the soundest principles of good governance. Huneeus stated that before 25 July 1902, the Weapons Commission had operated under the oversight and final authority of the Chilean embassy. After this date, it had become an independent authority that was able to contract at will, and this scenario was no longer tenable because it countered the concepts of proper administration (Unknown author 1911).

It would be reasonable to conclude that OEWG had been totally discredited, but this was not the case.

Assisted by its Valparaíso agent, Arturo Medina, Steyr then demanded that Santiago establish a special military commission to investigate the charges (Sater and Herwig 1999, pp. 152–153). The Austrian ambassador in Santiago, Johann Baron von Styrcea, subsequently contacted Chilean Foreign Minister Rodríguez and agreed that a strict and scrupulous examination would be conducted. To ensure the integrity of the commission, OEWG and the ambassador insisted that two senior OEWG engineers—Maximilian Rechl and Hugo Lipowsky, who were in Lima at that time—attend these tests. Starting its work on 11 November 1911, the special commission later reported that the OEWG barrels were, in reality, of impeccable quality and superior to those originally supplied by Loewe (Schaefer 1974, pp. 169–170). Rechl reported that having fired 4,000 rounds through randomly selected rifles and carbines, the barrels were found to be of the highest quality. Explaining the earlier findings of inferiority, Rechl concluded that the fault lay not with the barrels, but with the propellant that was used. Supposedly lacking the proper propellant, the earlier committees had improvised the use of an unsuitable propellant that had exerted too-much pressure and had subsequently damaged the barrels. This error, caused by inept technical personnel, had thus caused the earlier findings. Former minister of war Huneeus was not so diplomatic in his contentions that the two earlier commissions had deliberately sabotaged the OEWG barrels to redirect the order to DWM. Going one step further, journalist Joaquín Díaz identified two former DWM employees at the Fábrica de Cartuchos as having provided the improvised propellant (Sater and Herwig 1999, p. 153).

At some point during December 1911, the former Weapons Commission published its report. This report was divided into two parts: the first was its response to charges being bought against the

Weapons Commission on 24 November 1911, and the second was a detailed dismissal of Comisión de Experiencias' reports of 5 and 11 October 1911, and Boonen Rivera's letter of 6 October 1911.

The report opened by quoting a telegram of 19 December 1911, in which Huneeus sheepishly informed the Chilean ambassador in Berlin about the outcome of the latest tests: "Steyr spare parts tests finished and have given satisfactory results. Advise Commission members—Huneeus" (Pinto Concha et al. 1911, p. 1). Then the authors of the report systematically established the unfounded nature of the accusations made against the Weapons Commission. Equally, they openly demanded the restoration of their honor, which had been damaged through slander and prejudice. Not stopping there, the report also accused Boonen Rivera of blatantly lying in his letter that accompanied the first report of the Comisión de Experiencias. On the first charge—that the Weapons Commission had independently and without consultation contracted with OEWG for spare parts—the commission stated that it knew that this charge was driven by Boonen Riviera. It then demonstrated that this charge was baseless by quoting official communication with the war minister. Specifically, the commission firmly established that it was Minister Rodríguez who had instructed them to ask for prices from OEWG, that this same minister had been informed at all times during the course of this negotiation, and that the minister had absolute knowledge that DWM was unable to manufacture the specified sight and had therefore given the order to purchase only the specified sight.

The second charge stated that the Weapons Commission had been negligent in its reception of the spare parts. To this, the commission replied that again, it knew that charge was driven by Boonen Riviera and was in fact debunked by his own recorded statement. This was proven by the commission stating that Boonen Rivera had acknowledged receipt of the OEWG contract in his letter of 6 October 1911. Specifically, he had stated that on 9 August 1910, the ministry of war had forwarded a copy of the OEWG contract to the Dirección del Material de Guerra. Using this defense, the commission then argued that having received the contract, Boonen Riviera would have also received the *cahier des charges*. This, the commission argued, clearly stated in its first article that OEWG provided the commission only with spare parts that had been approved after performing necessary controls and checks, and they had been marked with an official stamp of acceptance in the presence of a Chilean officer. This same *cahier des charges* also specified that special steels be used that were also subject to strict quality assurance by OEWG before manufacture started. The third charge offered that the ordered carbine stocks and existing carbine stocks were too short to accommodate the lengthened carbine barrels contracted for by the commission. The commission replied that this charge was incomprehensible, since it had been clearly instructed by the war minister on 29 March 1910 to procure lengthened barrels. While the commission had subsequently informed the war minister on 3 April and 21 June 1911 that this procurement would cause problems with the carbine stocks, a response regarding this issue was received only on 29 May 1911, by which time the spare parts had already been delivered (Pinto Concha et al. 1911, pp. 3–9).

The second part of the Weapons Commission report was divided into six sections. The first five discredited the Comisión de Experiencias' report of 5 October 1911, while the last addressed that of 11 October 1911. The first of these dismissed the claim that 82.5 percent of rifles and 50 percent of carbine barrels were defective. The Weapons Commission stated that having inspected more than 5,000 barrels, it had not encountered even one that was outside tolerances. It was then reasoned that the only scenario under which this significant mismatch could have occurred was if either the gauges and calibrators, or the plans of the rifle and carbine that they had used, were themselves defective or incorrect. This was not the case, since their comparison between the plans sent by the Dirección del Material on 28 July 1910 and those produced by OEWG proved them to be identical. Likewise, both these sets of plans were also compared to a set received from DWM, and this too proved that all three sets were identical. As for the gauges and calibrators actually used during reception, these too were an exact match when compared to a set forwarded from DWM to OEWG on 27 June 1910. As to a further possible explanation for the high failure rate experienced in Chile, the Weapons Commission also proposed that OEWG may have forwarded parts to Chile that had not been officially received. This, the Weapons Commission then argued, was impossible, since each received part had been stamped with the symbol found on all Model 1895 parts in the presence of the reception officer. Likewise, to distinguish OEWG parts from those manufactured by Loewe or DWM, OEWG had also insisted that its parts bear a unique OEWG factory stamp. As a last resort to settle this matter, the Weapons Commission and the Chilean embassy had engaged the German Oficina Central de Ensayos Técnicos (Central Office for Technical Trials) to verify several parts that were deemed defective. While still awaiting the outcome of this process, the Weapons Commission was confident that the German office would fully verify their findings (Pinto Concha et al. 1911, pp. 10–12).

The second of the Weapons Commission's dismissals of Comisión de Experiencias' first report concerned the contention that the three rifles and carbines assembled using OEWG barrels, receivers, and bolts would not allow the action to easily close on a normal chamber gauge. This, it was argued, was incorrect, since the Comisión de Experiencias had erred fundamentally by dramatically over-torquing the barrels into the receivers. The third dismissal related to the accusation that once these three OEWG rifles and carbines were disassembled, the threaded portion of the barrel was then outside the maximum tolerance. This, the Weapons Commission responded, was again a direct result of the over-torquing. The fourth dismissed charge concerned the contention that new OEWG barrels were loose when fitted to Loewe or DWM receivers. This, the commission stated, was a direct result of the used Loewe or DWM parts being outside acceptable tolerances. It would therefore be logical to find that any new OEWG barrels would be loose when placed into these defective parts. The fifth dismissal related to the defects found in the OEWG parts after they were subject to the twenty test shots. This was dismissed on numerous grounds, including that the test cartridges had developed abnormally high pressures that were totally inconsistent with the proofing requirements of the *cahier des charges*, and that the test probes used to measure the expansion of the chamber were not those specified by Loewe, DWM, or OEWG (Pinto Concha et al. 1911, pp. 12–18).

The last of the dismissals related to the Comisión de Experiencias report of 11 October 1911. Here the Weapons Commission pointed out that while the OEWG rifle had fired eight shots, the Loewe/DWM rifle had fired only three, and that it was during the last three shots that the OEWG rifle was damaged. It was well known to the Weapons Commission that the Mauser Model 1893 design had poor gas-venting abilities in the event of a cartridge failure, and that this fact had already resulted in a proposal to redesign the locking mechanism of the Model 1895 in June–July 1895. The commission likewise stated that it was well known that a split cartridge could easily be caused if the ammunition was preheated before firing. This condition would be enormously aggravated if the ammunition in question was then also overloaded. While the *cahier des charges* specified only that two proofing rounds of 5,500 atmospheres be fired, the commission stated that firing eight at this abnormally high pressure would undoubtedly cause a failure. As such, they concluded that the second round of tests had deliberately been sabotaged. The Weapons Commission concluded its extensive report by firmly declaring that it would not tolerate Boonen Rivera defaming its honor through the use of whimsical findings and slander (Pinto Concha et al. 1911, pp. 18–24).

When copies of this report arrived in Santiago, it caused a political tsunami that resulted in its contents being kept confidential. Nevertheless, the Chilean press was aware of the existence of twelve copies of the report and subsequently requested its release. In firmly denying this request, War Minister Alejandro Rosselot argued that he could not authorize its publication, since it was inconceivable that the prestige of the country, army, and government could be damaged through the vanity and caprice of two or three generals (Unknown author 1912a). Likewise, Gen. Boonen Rivera also had to further explain the accusations that he had made in his letter of 6 October 1911. In reply to earlier questioning by Minister Ismael Valdés Vergara, Boonen Rivera stated that his use of the word "scam" was poorly chosen, which had then been interpreted by others incorrectly because he was referring to OEWG and not his fellow officers. He likewise stated that he had every reason to distrust OEWG because he had prior knowledge that the Mannlichers bought during 1889–1891 were received under similar circumstances as later OEWG spare parts, and these had also been subsequently deemed to be outside tolerance limits. Boonen Rivera concluded by stating that despite the final report having exonerated the OEWG spare parts, they were still, in his opinion, of inferior quality when compared to those of Loewe or DWM (Unknown author 1912e).

While the issue of the barrels had been resolved in OEWG's favor, the same could not be said for new or existing carbine stocks, which could not accommodate a bayonet and the OEWG-lengthened barrels. As a result, the ministry of war had to contract with OEWG to supervise and train the employees of the Santiago arsenal in their subsequent modification (Sater and Herwig 1999, p. 153).

7 × 57 mm Ammunition and Associated Contracts

By purchasing the Mauser Chileno Modelo 1895, Chile also sought to purchase significant amounts of 7 × 57 mm ammunition and the machinery for its domestic manufacture.

On 1 September 1893, the Chilean minister of war concluded an agreement in Santiago with Loewe representative Schuchard for the purchase of machinery for the manufacture of small-arms munitions in the Chilean capital (Bulnes 1894). On 15 September 1893, in Supreme Decree No. 1, the Chilean government duly authorized this agreement (Körner 1894b). Subsequently, on 15 November 1893 the Chilean ambassador in Paris ratified the contract with Loewe in Berlin:

> Contract between the High Government of Chile, represented by His Excellency Gonzalo Bulnes Minister Plenipotentiary in Berlin, and the House of Ludwig Loewe & Co., Aktiengesellschaft, Berlin, the following was concluded in accordance with offers of 15 June and 24 July this year, submitted to the High Government of Chile by Mr. Eugene Schuchard, representing the house of Ludwig Loewe & Co.
>
> **Article 1:** The House of Ludwig Loewe & Co. is committed to provide the machines and accessories as detailed in the lists annexed to this contract.
>
> **Article 2:** The House of Ludwig Loewe & Co. undertakes to introduce during the construction of the machines all enhancements subsequently invented, which seem useful and agreed with the representatives of the High Government of Chile.
>
> **Article 3:** Materials used in the construction of these machines must be of the highest quality, and the performance of the work must be done with the greatest care.
>
> **Article 4:** The High Government of Chile reserves the right to monitor the manufacturing of machines and accessories during their construction.
>
> **Article 5:** The reception of the machines, etc., will be made in Berlin, seven months after the ratification of this agreement by the House of Ludwig Loewe & Co., which is nevertheless committed to apply all their care, to carry out the order before that date. The machines, etc., will be delivered packed ready to be shipped to Chile.
>
> **Article 6:** The House of Ludwig Loewe & Co. agrees, as soon as reception is made on the part of the High Government of Chile, to perform—on behalf of and according to the instructions that Government—shipping of the machines, etc., to a Chilean port, within the limitations of *force majeure*.
>
> **Article 7:** The fixed price for the machines and accessories is 215,830 marks—two hundred fifteen thousand eight hundred and thirty marks—not including packaging, that will be 3%—three percent—of the total value of the order. The above price includes all the merchandise taken from the Berlin factory, and

all the accessories, details, and all inclusions in the attached list. Payment will be made in Berlin, by the Minister of Chile to Ludwig Loewe & Co. in the following way: a quarter of the total amount will be paid immediately after signature by Ludwig Loewe & Co., and the three-quarters remaining, after presentation of the certificate of receipt on the part of the reception committee, designated by the High Government of Chile.

Article 8: The High Government of Chile shall have the right to send two craftsmen, to be instructed in the use of machines for the manufacture of cartridges, as well as in the composition of guns of war, costs of this will be for the House of Ludwig Loewe & Co., in Berlin.

Agreed—in three identical copies—in Berlin on 15 November 1893.

Signed: Gonzalo Bulnes
Signed: Alexis Riese
(Ministerio de Guerra 1893)

Before signing this contract, Ludwig Loewe & Co. cautioned Ambassador Bulnes on 11 November 1893 that it did not specify what caliber/cartridges were to be manufactured. Considering that the type of machinery and its associated tooling varied according to the caliber/cartridge being manufactured, Loewe advised that the Chileans should thus reserve the right to specify this information within two months after signing (Ludwig Loewe & Cie 1893).

Having been cautioned by Loewe, Bulnes subsequently informed the minister of war on 23 December 1893 that this provision had been agreed upon with Loewe. Bulnes then argued that it was essential that the minister of war urgently decide this matter and inform him accordingly (Bulnes 1893).

Arguably in response to this request, on 5 January 1894 Körner advised the minister of war that Chile already had antique machinery that could produce ammunition for small arms that were currently in use. He therefore cautioned that the true meaning of the 15 September 1893 decree was that the new machinery should be adaptable to numerous calibers from 6.5 to 11 mm. Because Chile was still in the process of procuring new rifles and carbines in an unknown caliber/cartridge configuration, the decision concerning this was still to be made (Körner 1894b). Considering that the Chilean government could not advise what it did not know, no information was forthcoming.

Chile's munitions-manufacturing contract with Loewe was suitable mostly for the manufacture of coins, medals, and general pressings, rather than ammunition. To resolve this quandary, Ambassador Bulnes subsequently involved Boonen Rivera, who through further discussions with Loewe established that Loewe was only willing to supply the machines and dies for one caliber/cartridge combination. This did not suit Chile, since they required the ability to manufacture numerous calibers/cartridges. It was under these circumstances that Körner found himself when he arrived in Europe. Following Körner's involvement, Loewe then relented and, despite a loss of several thousand marks, agreed that it was bound by the original contract and would include all the machinery necessary to manufacture numerous calibers/cartridges. Bulnes even reported to his government that this goodwill on behalf of Loewe was in a direct hope that they would be awarded the pending rifle and carbine contract. Körner's solution was to sign a supplementary contract with Loewe, specifying an extensive list of specialized machines and dies for the manufacture of numerous calibers/cartridges. On 27 October 1894, Ambassador Bulnes telegrammed the Chilean war minister, informing him of Körner's proposed solution, and requested urgent authorization to do this (Bulnes 1894).

The minister's authorization was duly sent, and the supplementary contract was initially signed on 27 December 1894, which was then further amended two days later. It reads as follows:

Agreed between the High Government of Chile, represented by His Excellency the Minister Plenipotentiary Gonzalo Bulnes in Berlin, on the one hand, and the House of Ludwig Loewe & Co., Berlin Aktiengesellschaft, on the other hand, the following supplementary to the contract of 15 November 1893:

Article 1: The House of Ludwig Loewe & Co. is discharged from the delivery of the following

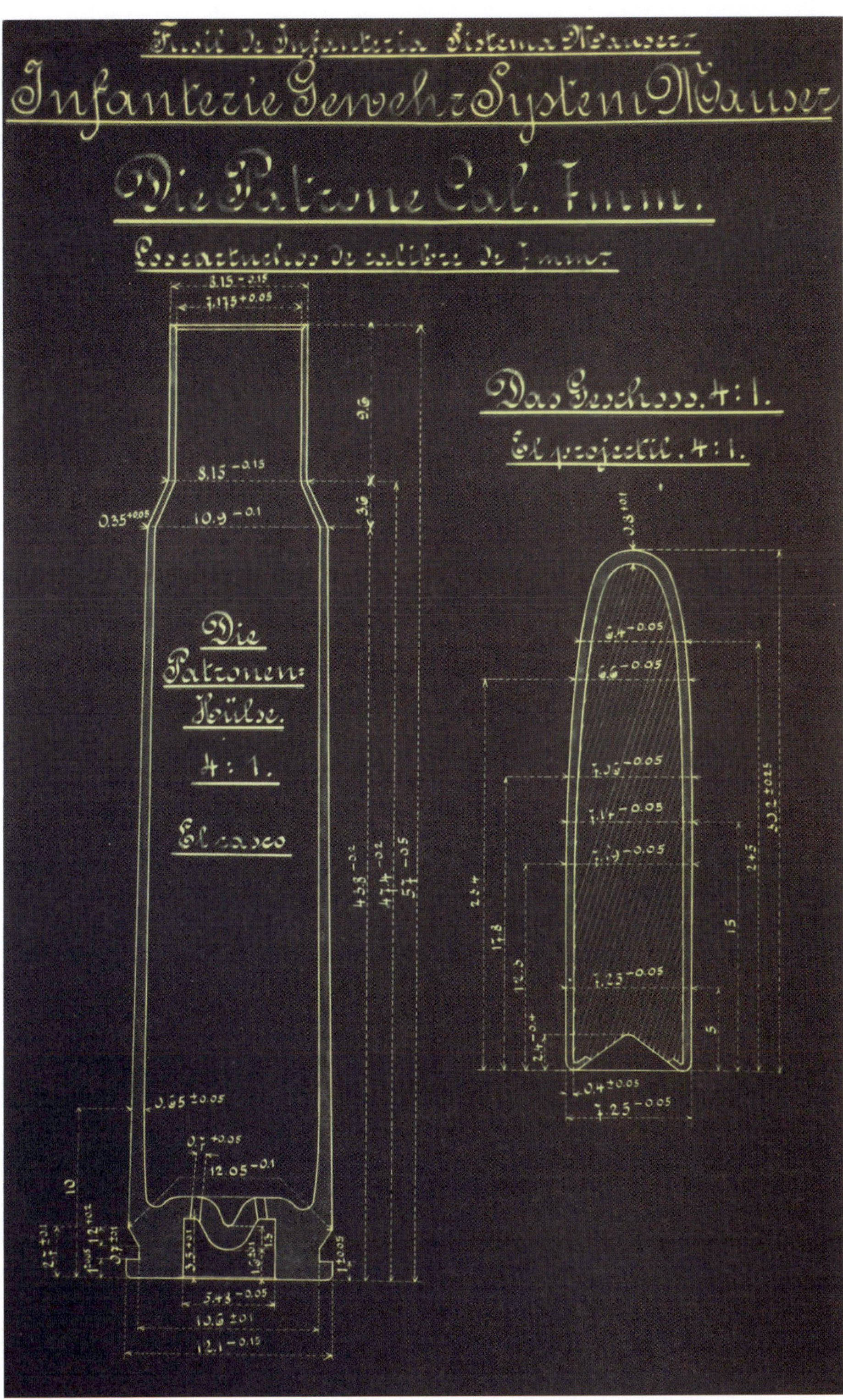

The oval projectile 7 × 57 mm cartridge as specified in 1893, which was the same as initially adopted by the Chileans for their new Model 1895. *Archive Jon Speed*

machines for manufacturing of chargers listed under "G" in the Annex of the contract of 15 November 1893; namely:

- A stamping flywheel press with reference;
- A special machine to turn the steel sheet;
- Special rounding machine for the steel sheet;
- A special machine for tightening the walls;
- A polishing drum,
- and the delivery of tools and templates for the manufacturing of the listed chargers under the "J" Annex.

The total amount of machinery: 13,385 marks
Tools and Templates: 5,265 marks

18,650 marks

Article 2: The House of Ludwig Loewe & Co. engages below to provide extra objects in addition to the Annex for the production of 11 mm Gras and 8 mm Mannlicher cartridges:

For the Gras 11 mm cartridge:
- Cartridge-manufacturing tools: 2,050 marks
- Projectile envelope–manufacturing tools: 1,160 marks
- Priming tools: 1,500 marks
- Loading tools: 900 marks
- One set of working templates, with verification instruments
- Two caliber review templates, with 1 set verification instruments: 5,500 marks

For the 8 mm Mannlicher cartridge:
- Cartridge-manufacturing tools: 2,050 marks
- Two drilling machines for primer holes: 2,500 marks
- Projectile envelope–manufacturing tools: 800 marks
- Lead core tools: 150 marks
- Assembly tools: 250 marks
- Priming tools: 900 marks
- Loading tools: 1,250 marks
- One set of working templates, with verification instruments
- Two caliber review templates, with 1 set verification instruments: 5,500 marks

---

24,510 marks

The House of Ludwig Loewe & Co. will also provide the tools for the manufacture of 7 mm Mauser cartridges. The costs are included in the total amount of 215,830 marks of the contract of 15 November 1893, so for these tools, there will be no extra price to pay.

Article 3: The tools for making 11 mm Gras and Mannlicher 8 mm cartridges above is specified as 24,510 marks, while the machines for manufacturing the above named chargers, according to Article 1, amount to 18,650 marks. Accordingly, the provisions of Article 2 therefore result in a deficit of 5,860 marks, the payment of which the House of Ludwig Loewe & Co. waives as a special demonstration of its kindness. As such, the modified provisions, as above, will be provided at the original contract cost of 215,830 marks.

Article 4: His Excellency Gonzalo Bulnes, on behalf of High Government of Chile, and the House of Ludwig Loewe & Co., also agree to procure the machines and tools necessary for the manufacture of chargers for the 7 mm Mauser and 8 mm Mannlicher:

Machines:
- Two flywheel machines, Mod III: 3,300 marks
- Two presses, Mod. II: 1,310 marks
- One polishing drum: 285 marks

Tools for the 7 mm Mauser charger:
- One set of tools for manufacture: 3,550 marks
- One set of review templates, with verification instruments: 400 marks
- Tools for the 8 mm Mannlicher charger:
- One set of tools for manufacture: 2,250 marks
- One set of review templates, with verification instruments: 350 marks

---

11,445 marks

- 3% for packaging: 343.35 marks

Total: 11,788.35 marks

As the order for the rifle and carbines adopted by the Chilean Commission was given to the gentlemen of Ludwig Loewe & Co., they will further waive the payment of the sum of 11,788.35 marks. The capacity of the facility to manufacture chargers will be at least 4,000 Mannlicher chargers, or, 3,000 Mauser chargers.

Article 5: In addition, the High Government of Chile orders from the House of Ludwig Loewe & Co. the following machines and apparatuses:

- A machine to adjust the rear sight upward: 850 marks
- A machine to align the barrel: 380 marks
- Two vices with wrenches, to screw the barrel to the receiver: 720 marks
- Two sets of measuring devices for the alignment machine: 240 marks
- An emery polishing machine for barrels: 2,500 marks
- Twelve cleaning apparatus: 216 marks
- Two devices to adjust front sights (with scales): 376 marks
- Twelve devices to adjust front sights (without scales): 1,056 marks
- Twelve jigs, for soldering the rear sight sleeve to the barrel: 48 marks
- Fifty supports for bluing of barrels: 285 marks
- Four rotary metal wire brushes: 440 marks
- One hundred kilograms of metal wire brushes: 450 marks
- One hundred and fifty kilograms of abrasive in three various grades: 157.5 marks
- One hundred long-barrel cleaning rods with rotating sleeves: 1,530 marks
- A soldering machine for rear and front sights: 948 marks
- Six barrel chamber reamers: 156 marks
- A split tapping die for barrel threading: 145 marks
- Three taps to adjust the receiver's barrel threads: 72 marks
- Six taps for the receiver's trigger guard screws: 58.5 marks
- Twelve taps for the rear and front sight threads: 54 marks
- Twelve drill bits to drill holes to front and rear sights: 8.4 marks
- A protractor to measure the height of a steel chamber gauge: 57 marks
- Twelve steel chamber gauges (max 3.1 mm): 90 marks
- Twelve steel chamber gauges (max 3.0 mm): 90 marks
- Twenty-four small files to cut the aperture in the rear sight: 64.8 marks
- Three gas appliances with rubber bladders for soldering: 60 marks
- A extractor fan for these three gas appliances: 200 marks
- An annealing furnace: 3,100 marks
- A vertical drilling machine No: 21 Mod. 1: 2,020 marks
- A tempering furnace with ventilator, Mod. 2: 300 marks
- A machine to sharpen tools, with several emery discs: 800 marks
- A revolver turret machine, No: 32, Mod 2 with clamping, advance, and a set of tools: 2,500 marks

---

20,584.20 marks
Prices are net, taken in Berlin and include packaging.

Article 6: Delivery of all items in the contract of 15 November 1893 and those in this supplement will be four months from the date of signing of this supplementary contract. The dimensional tables and tolerances required for the manufacture of cartridges for Mauser, Mannlicher, and Grass, and chargers for Mauser and Mannlicher, are annexed to this contract and are used as the basis for the execution of the above agreement.

Article 7: The provisions of the main contract of 15 November 1893, provided that they are not affected by this supplementary contract, will remain in force.

This supplementary contract was executed in three identical copies and signed by both the contracting parties.

Berlin, 27 December 1894

Signed: Gonzalo Bulnes
Signed: Ludwig Loewe & Co.

Additional Article.
Everything that relates to the Gras rifle cartridges is hereby removed from the contract. The House of Ludwig Loewe & Co. will deduct from the total price: Twenty Thousand, Five Hundred and Eighty-Four marks, Twenty pfennigs (20,584.20 marks), the sum of the Eleven Thousand, One Hundred and Ten marks, representing the value of the Gras items, in Article 2. It is admitted that the House of Ludwig Loewe & Co. will not provide the tools, templates, and instruments in the abovementioned Article 2. The High Government of Chile will therefore pay to the House of Ludwig Loewe & Co. only the sum of Nine Thousand, Four Hundred and Seventy-Four marks, Twenty pfennigs (9,474.20 marks).

Signed in triplicate.

Berlin, 29 December 1894.

Signed: Gonzalo Bulnes
Signed: Alexis Riese
(Ministerio de Guerra 1894)

It was reported in 1896 that even after having installed this modern machinery, only 12,000–13,000 cartridges per day were being produced in Santiago, despite the fact that the facility had a daily capacity of 25,000 rounds and had hired a master gunsmith to oversee its functioning (Donoso et al. 1982, p. 214).

Despite having what appeared to be a credible ability to domestically manufacture ammunition, Chile then proceeded to procure forty million rounds of 7 × 57 mm ammunition from Keller & Co. of Hirtenberg, in Austria.

In line with the negotiations surrounding the specification and procurement of Chile's new rifles and carbines, the Weapons Commission was also engaged in negotiations with munitions manufacturers. From the onset, the Weapons Commission demanded a cartridge that had a brass case and a hardened, round-nosed, nickel-plated, steel-jacketed projectile that was loaded with a smokeless "Froisdorf" propellant. Considering Keller & Co. had offered a better price than both FN and Loewe, the Weapons Commission decided to determine if Keller had the means to meet the supply schedule. When it was satisfactorily shown that Keller could supply Froisdorf propellant and that it had the ability to manufacture 500,000 cartridges a day, the Weapons Commission proceeded to enter into preliminary negotiations with them and subsequently demanded a two-franc reduction in price over the initial offer of 132 francs per 1,000. In these negotiations, August Schriever acted on behalf of Keller & Co.; as such, numerous offers and counter-demands were made. Despite these protracted dealings, the Chileans eventually attained the requested price reduction. Thus, on 18 December 1894, the Chileans signed a contract with Keller & Co. for eighteen million 7 × 57 mm cartridges (Matte Pérez 1894a).

While a copy of this contract is not in the author's possession, most of the important details are known: the price included the cost of packing and freight to Antwerp or Hamburg, and the cost of loading onto a ship; payment of one-third of the total price would be delayed until the first half of 1896; to mobilize domestic demand, the Chileans had the right to request the supply of the cartridge components for manufacture in their Santiago factory; after the start of the contract, the Chileans had the right to procure an equal number of cartridges at the same price and under the same conditions; Chile had the right to advance the agreed-on delivery schedule on short notice; the costs related to equipment and tooling for the experimentation of raw materials, elements, and finished cartridges was to be made by Keller & Co.; the Weapons Commission would resolve all disagreements that might arise concerning technical matters; in the event that the Chileans did exercise their right to purchase more cartridges and in the interim the price of raw materials such as copper or lead had risen sharply, Keller would receive a corresponding increase; and the Chileans were to have paid 5 percent of the contract value up front (Matte Pérez 1894a). This 5 percent payment (46,800 pesos) was then subsequently recorded in the Chilean embassy ledger on 15 February 1895 (Legación de Chile en Paris 1892, p. 7). Later in the

Noviembre 23 Cuadro recepcion, embarque y pago cartuchos Mauser con Keller y Cia

Facturas	Cajones	Vapor	Salida de Hamburgo	Munición
Agosto 5	3000	Fotheran	Agosto 10	4.500,000
" "	333⅓	Abydos	" 24	500,000
" 14	2266⅔	"	" "	3.400,000
" 31	2800	Luxor	Setbre 7	4.200,000
" "	733⅓	Glenely	" 14	1.100,000
Setbre 17	466⅔	"	" "	700 000
" "	2000	Pentaur	Octbre 5	3.000,000
" "	400	Ramses	" 19	600,000
Octubre 8	4200	"	" "	6.300,000
" 26	2600	Herodot	Novbre 2	3.900,000
Novbre 6	1800	Neko	16	2.700,000
	20.600			30.900,000

18.000,000 según contrato 18 Diciembre de 1894

Fin del 1er contrato por 18,000000 – 12 millones pagados del 2o contrato hay pagados hasta Novbre 2/95: un tercio del total de 15.000,000 y 1/3 de la cantidad entregada.

The shipping details of the first 30.9 million rounds of 7 × 57 mm ammunition for Chile, which were agreed to under the first two contracts with Keller & Co. on 18 December 1894 and 27 July 1895. The first column indicates the invoice date; the second, the number of cases; and the third, the ship name, while the fourth is the departure date and last is the number of rounds in each shipment. Each case contained 1,500 rounds of ammunition.
Legación de Chile en Paris. 1892. Legación de Chile en Paris, 1892–1898, vol. 2088. Archivo Nacional de Chile, Santiago.

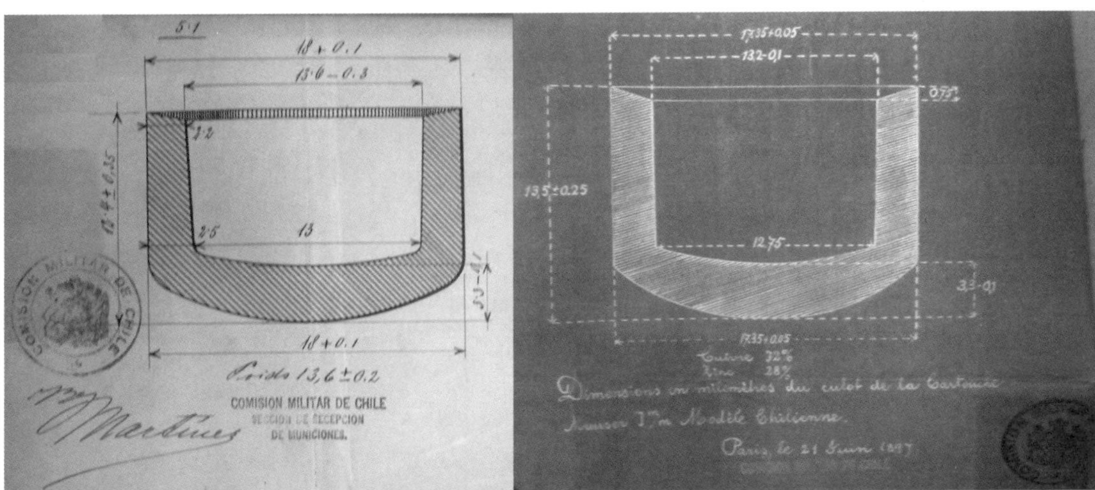

Drawings of the *culot* (blank) used to manufacture the cartridge cases for the Chilean 7 × 57 mm ammunition bought from Keller & Co. The image on the left is supposedly of the original version, while on the right is a later improved version, which bears the date 21 June 1897 and specifies a metallurgy of 72 percent copper and 28 percent zinc.
Comisión Militar de Chile Sección de Recepción de Municiones. 1896. *Culot*. Legación de Chile en Francia, 1893–1898, vol. 373.
Technical drawing in Archivo Nacional de Chile, Santiago.
Keller & Co. and Comisión Militar de Chile. 1898. "Cahier des charges pour la reception des cartpuches cal 7mm Mauser Modele Chilien 1896." Legación de Chile en Francia, 1893–1898, vol. 373. Specification in Archivo Nacional de Chile, Santiago.

ledger, the total price of the contract was recorded as having been 93,600 British pounds, or 936,000 pesos (Legación de Chile en Paris 1892, p. 106).

Subsequently, on 27 July 1895 the Chileans signed a second contract with Keller & Co. for a further fifteen million 7 × 57 mm cartridges. This was then followed by third and fourth orders—also with Keller—on 5 November 1895 and 14 May 1896, for seven million and ten million cartridges, respectively. The total value of the second order was quoted as having been 76,200 British pounds; the third, as 34,946 pounds; and the fourth, as 50,400 pounds (Legación de Chile en Paris 1892, pp. 106–107).

The 27 July 1895 date on the second contract is confirmed in a letter that Keller & Co. wrote to the Chilean embassy in Paris on 10 August 1895 (Keller & Co, 1895c). However, in a letter that Keller wrote on 28 September 1895, there is mention of a firm order from the Chileans on that same day for a further seven million rounds of ammunition to be executed under the same terms and conditions as the previous order for 15 million (Keller & Co. 1895d). Similarly, in a letter of 8 November 1895, Keller wrote that its representative, a Mr. Mandl, had just returned from Paris with a new contract for a further ammunition purchase (Keller & Co. 1895b). As to the date of the fourth contract, this is disputed when the actual contract is referenced:

> Contract between Mr. Augusto Matte, Envoy Extraordinaire and Ministry Plenipotentiary of Chile in France, acting on behalf of the Government of Chile, on the one hand, and Keller & Co., of Hirtenberg, Austria, on the other hand; the following was agreed:
>
> **Article 1:** Under the contract between the parties on 5 November 1895, the Minister of Chile commands Keller & Co. to provide 10 million rounds Mauser Model Chilean with reinforced cartridge and projectile walls, lubricated, with chargers and loaded with Froisdorf smokeless powder, in accordance with the new conditions as indicated by the Military Commission in the *cahier de charges*, and to its satisfaction. Delivery will begin five weeks after the date of signature of this agreement, being 7 May 1896.
>
> **Article 2:** The agreed price is One Hundred and Twenty-Six francs (126) per one thousand cartridges, which will have reinforced cartridge and projectile walls, lubricated, with chargers, packed and then placed onboard a ship either in Antwerp or Hamburg.
>
> **Article 3:** Delivery, which will begin as indicated in Article 1 and shall be complete by 7 July 1896.
>
> **Article 4:** Payment will be as follows:
> - One third (1/3) on signing of this contract,
> - One third (1/3) after final quantities have been placed onboard and are ready for shipping,
> - One third (1/3) and balance, four months after the signing date, with annual interest of 5% from the date of the final delivery. However the Government of Chile can forestall the payment of all or part of this last third at their convenience, and interest will not be charged for amounts paid in advance.
>
> **Article 5:** Conditions for the control and reception of the ammunition by the Military Commission and all other terms of the previous contract will remain in force. In relation to the new conditions relating of the reinforced cartridge and projectile walls, new alloy for the casings and lubrication will be introduced by the Military Commission in the *cahier de charges*, which are annexed to this contract.
>
> **Article 6:** The Government of Chile reserves the right until 31 December 1896 to extend this order by up to 30 million cartridges, and Keller & Co. is committed to provide all the quantities that might be commissioned. It is understood, however, that if notice is given before 15 June 1896 to provide up to 10 million additional cartridges, Keller & Co. are committed to deliver them within a period of one and a half months from 7 July 1896 to 22 August 1896. If the command was for 20 million cartridges, they will have to deliver these in the period of two months ending on 7 September 1896. In the event of any additional orders, payments will be made on the same basis as those referred to in Article 4.

Concluded in Paris, in quadruplicate, on 2 April 1896.

Signed: Augusto Matte
Signed: Keller & Co.
(Legación de Chile en Francia 1893)

On 12 February 1898, Chilean ambassador Palacios concluded a contract worth 36,000 francs with Keller & Co., comprising machinery to weigh powder, load it into cartridges, and then cap it with a projectile. This machinery had a maximum capacity of 500,000 cartridges in a ten-hour working shift. Later, on 6 April 1898, Chile signed a fifth contract with Keller & Co. for the supply of ten million 7 × 57 mm Mauser cartridges. On 5 July 1898, Keller wrote to the Chilean embassy in Paris, confirming receipt of a check in the amount of 289,333.33 francs representing 23.3 percent of the contract value (Keller & Co. 1898). From this it can be deduced that the price paid per 1,000 cartridges was approximately 124 francs.

This fifth contract appeared not to be the last signed during 1898, since the ledger reports a total of thirty million Mauser cartridges were procured from Keller & Co. during that year. It would further appear that of these thirty million cartridges, twenty million were to be in stripper clips, while the remaining ten million were to be loose (Legación de Chile en Paris 1892, pp. 140–141).

Published years later, a 1924 Chilean naming-and-classification manual confirms the existence of all the above 7 × 57 mm ammunition either as "Cartridges Mauser M.95," "Cartridges Mauser M.96," or "Cartridges Mauser M.98." It can reasonably be deduced that the numerals correspond to the year of manufacture and that they are of Keller manufacture. This reference likewise makes mention of the existence of "Cartridges Mauser M.02" and "Cartridges Mauser M.02 Machinegun" (Dirección del Material de Guerra 1924, pp. 44–45), which are in all probability those cartridges that were purchased in 1901, along with the Maxim machine guns. It is important to recognize that these M.02 cartridges were bought from DWM and not Keller & Co. (Schaefer 1974, pp. 72–73, 238).

It is interesting to note that in 1894 the powder magazine at the Santiago factory exploded, supposedly because it was still using paraffin lamps for lighting. Despite this setback, it was recorded that in 1899 the factory, under the supervision of German technical staff, could fabricate 150,000 rounds of 7 × 57 mm ammunition per day (Sater and Herwig 1999, p. 127).

As well as purchasing spare parts from OEWG in 1910, Chile also decided to procure a further thirty million rounds of 7 × 57 mm ammunition.

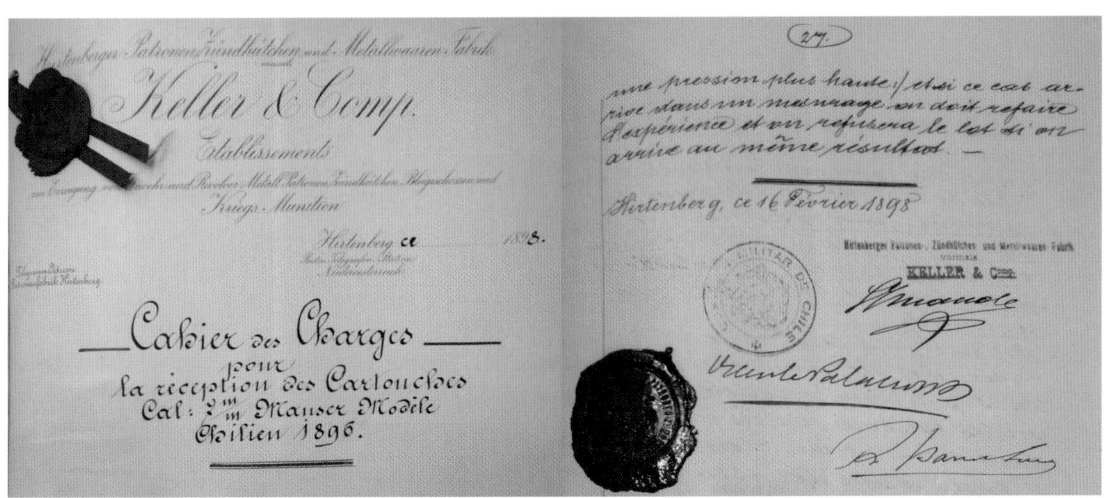
Keller & Comp.
Etablissements
Kriegs-Munition
Hirtenberg ce 1898.
Cahier des Charges
pour
la réception des Cartouches
Cal: 7 m/m Mauser Modèle
Chilien 1896.

(27)
une pression plus haute; et si ce cas arrive dans un mesurage on doit refaire l'expérience et on refusera le lot si on arrive au même résultat. —
Hirtenberg, ce 16 Février 1898
KELLER & Cie

Cover and last pages of the "Cahier des charges," or specification for Chile's ammunition purchase of 1898 from Keller & Co. Keller & Co. and Comisión Militar de Chile. 1898. "Cahier des charges pour la reception des cartpuches cal 7mm Mauser Modele Chilien 1896." Legación de Chile en Francia, 1893–1898, vol. 373. Specification in Archivo Nacional de Chile, Santiago.

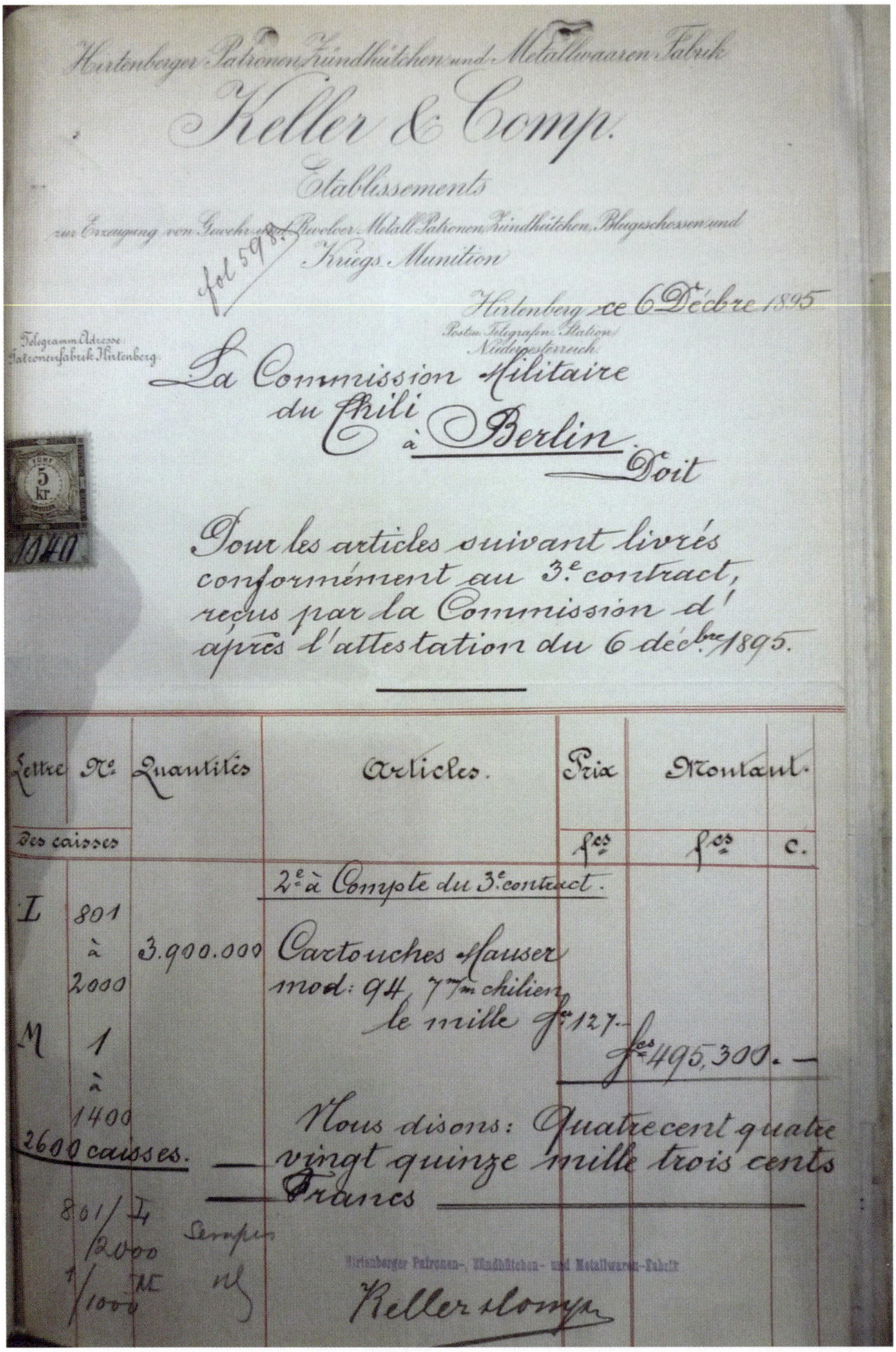

Hirtenberger Patronen-Zündhütchen- und Metallwaaren-Fabrik

Keller & Comp.

Etablissements

zur Erzeugung von Gewehr- und Revolver-Metall-Patronen, Zündhütchen, Bleigeschossen und Kriegs-Munition

fol 598

Hirtenberg, ce 6 Décbre 1895

Postu. Telegrafen-Station Niederösterreich.

Telegramm-Adresse: Patronenfabrik Hirtenberg

La Commission Militaire du Chili à Berlin

Doit

Pour les articles suivant livrés conformément au 3.e contract, reçus par la Commission d'après l'attestation du 6 déc.bre 1895.

Lettre	N.o	Quantités	Articles.	Prix	Montant	
des caisses				f.cs	f.cs	c.
			2.e à Compte du 3.e contract.			
I	801 à 2000	3.900.000	Cartouches Mauser mod: 94, 7m/m chilien le mille f.cs 127.-		f.cs 495,300.–	
M	1 à 1400					
2600 caisses.		—	Nous disons: Quatrecent quatre vingt quinze mille trois cents Francs			

801/I /2000
1/1000 M
Serapis

Hirtenberger Patronen-, Zündhütchen- und Metallwaren-Fabrik

Keller & Comp.

Delivery confirmation and invoice for 3.9 million 7 × 57 mm Mauser cartridges procured under the third contract with Keller & Co. It is interesting to note that this was for Model 1894 cartridges shipped onboard the *Serapis* of the Kosmos shipping line.
Keller & Co. 1895a. "La Commission Militaire du Chili a Berlin: Pour les articles suivant livres conformerment au 3 contrat." Legación de Chile en Francia e Inglaterra, vol. 400. Delivery confirmation in Archivo Nacional de Chile, Santiago.

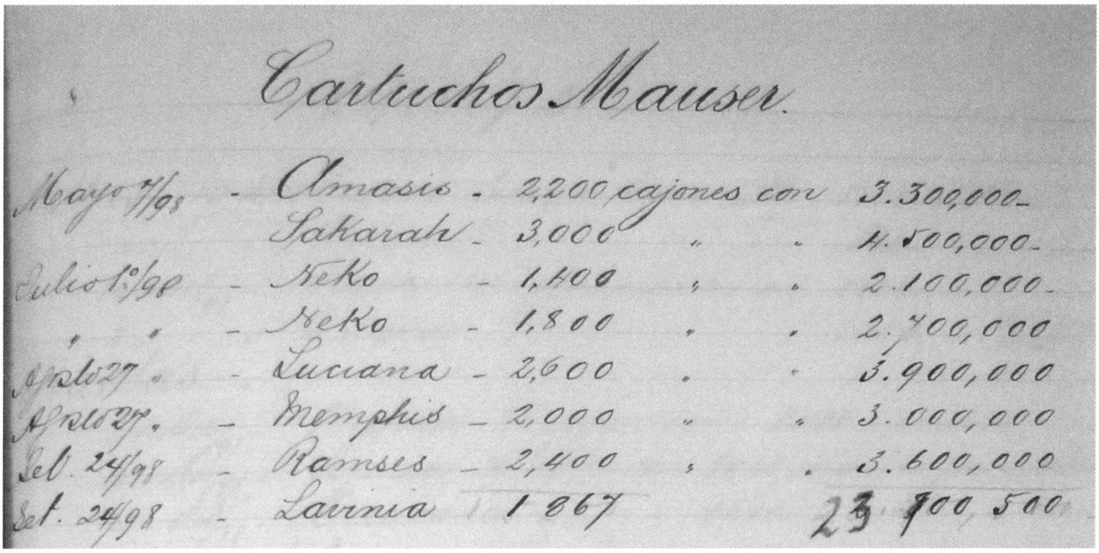

Cartuchos Mauser.

Mayo 7/98	Amasis	2,200	cajones con	3.300,000
	Sakarah	3,000	"	4.500,000
Julio 1°/98	Neko	1,400	"	2.100,000
" "	Neko	1,800	"	2.700,000
Abril 27	Luciana	2,600	"	3.900,000
Abril 27	Memphis	2,000	"	3.000,000
Set. 24/98	Ramses	2,400	"	3.600,000
Set. 24/98	Lavinia	1867		23.900,500

Shipping details of 7 × 57 mm Mauser cartridges to Chile during 1898. The ships involved were the *Amasis*, *Sakkarah*, *Neko*, *Luciana*, *Memphis*, *Ramses*, and *Lavinia*.
Legación de Chile en Paris. 1892. Legación de Chile en Paris, 1892 1898, vol. 2088. Archivo Nacional de Chile, Santiago.

As with the spare parts, the Austrian company Keller & Co. offered the best price and quality (Schaefer 1974, p. 166). Through its entrenched network of sympathizers, DWM soon learned of the Chileans' predisposition to Keller & Co., and the prices that had been agreed on. By leveraging its Chilean contacts to the fullest, DWM subsequently managed to overturn the provisional award and start a new tender process. To win support for the DWM cause, in early 1911 Gen. Boonen Rivera declared that the ammunition that Chile had originally bought in 1895 was totally unsafe and had to be discarded (Schaefer 1974, p. 167).

In an attempt to sidestep developing shenanigans, Minister of War León Luco decided to transfer the decision on whose ammunition to purchase to the Chilean Weapons Commission in Europe (Schaefer 1974, p. 167). The Weapons Commission, under the leadership of Gen. Pinto Concha, then tested various types of ammunition and, on the basis of quality, price, and delivery times, subsequently chose Keller & Co. from a field of seven that included DWM. On 30 June 1911, Concha informed Santiago that he had purchased thirty million rounds of 7 × 57 mm ammunition at 150 francs per 1,000 (Sater and Herwig 1999, p. 157). On 4 July 1911, Santiago received confirmation of the Keller & Co. order (Sater and Herwig 1999, p. 159). To add further insult to injury, the Austrians also offered a delivery period that was three months shorter than their German competition (Schaefer 1974, p. 167).

On receiving news of this purchase, Boonen Rivera sprang into action and declared that the Weapons Commission had exceeded its authority in purchasing the ammunition, since the required technical tests had not been conducted to confirm the inclusion of Rottweil propellant. Simplistically, this would mean that only DWM could supply the ammunition. Nevertheless, while Pulverfabrik Rottweil supplied propellant to DWM, Keller & Co. was supplied by Vereinigten Rheinischen-Westfälische Pulverfabriken. Both these propellant manufacturers, under the directorship of Emil Müller, offered identical products (Schaefer 1974, pp. 167–168). Despite this fact, Keller & Co. and the various Chilean factions demanded special tests to ascertain the supremacy either of Keller or DWM ammunition. Considering that the contract had already been awarded to Keller & Co., this request was peculiar. As with the spare parts, a predictable series of events subsequently unfolded. Keller consented to the Dirección del Material de Guerra conducting the tests; not surprisingly, it found that the DWM ammunition was superior. After obligatory protests, further tests were held both in Chile and Austria, which found the Austrian ammunition to be superior. And in a further bizarre turn of events, the Chilean minister of war—refusing to accept the later findings—then signed a further contract for thirty million 7 × 57 mm cartridges with DWM for 4.488 million francs (Sater and Herwig 1999, pp. 158–159). The end result was that Chile now had sixty million rounds of ammunition and had spent approximately nine million francs.

The 1924 Chilean naming-and-classification manual lists what is assumed to be the Keller & Co. ammunition from this period as "Cartridges Mauser P.M.98/10," "Cartridges Mauser P.M.98/11," "Cartridges Mauser P.M.98/12," "Cartridges Mauser P.M.12 Hirtenberg," and "Cartridges Mauser P.M.12 Hirtenberg Machinegun." Likewise, the DWM-manufactured ammunition is denoted as "Cartridges Mauser P.M.12 Karlsruhe" or "Cartridges Mauser P.M.12 Karlsruhe Machinegun" (Dirección del Material de Guerra 1924, pp. 44–45).

Following the scandals of 1910–1912, Chile appears to have lost its appetite for foreign-manufactured ammunition. In the naming-and-classification manual, any entries that subsequently appear indicated only domestic manufacture: "Cartridges Mauser P.M.12 Santiago 1913," "Cartridges Mauser P.M.12 Santiago 1914," "Cartridges Mauser P.M.12 Santiago 1917," "Cartridges Mauser P.M.12 Santiago 1918," and "Cartridges Mauser P.M.12 Santiago 1923" (Dirección del Material de Guerra, 1924, pp. 44–45).

In addition to these "Cartridges of War," the naming-and-classification manual also referenced the existence of unspecified manufacturer "Cartridges Blank-firing for rifle and carbine Mauser" and "Cartridges Practice Cal. 7 mm" (Dirección del Material de Guerra 1924, p. 47). The blank cartridges were described as having had an ordinary cartridge case that was filled with 0.8 grams of smokeless powder and loaded with a red-painted, wooden projectile, while the practice cartridges comprised a nickel-plated cartridge case that had a permanently affixed "projectile." A Chilean soldier could easily discern these practice rounds because they had three indents perpendicular to the length of the case, had a missing primer, and were much lighter than the "Cartridges of War" (Boado y Castro 1896a, pp. 18–19).

The 7 × 57 mm ammunition procured between 1894 and 1902 was described as having a round-nosed, steel-jacketed projectile with a flat base, with a weight of 11.2 grams or 173 grains. The powder was described as a smokeless Froisdorf type and had a load weight of 2.5 grams or 38.58 grains. This load would produce an average pressure of 3,136 atmospheres for an average velocity of 699 m/s when measured at 25 m from the rifle's muzzle. The first two million rounds of 7 × 57 mm ammunition bought from Keller & Co. in 1894 contained a different type of Froisdorf powder; these were loaded with 2.35 grams of powder to achieve the stated velocity of 700 m/s, but at the same pressure (Boado y Castro 1896a, pp. 36–41). The overall length of the loaded ammunition was 78 mm, while the length of the projectile was quoted as having been 30.8 mm (Boado y Castro 1896a, p. 44).

The "P" ammunition bought from 1910 onward was described as having a spitzer projectile with a steel jacket that was cupronickel coated, was 29.8 mm long, and weighed 9 grams or 139 grains. The powder was referenced as having been a Rottweil type with a load weight of 3.15 grams (48.61 grains), which could propel the projectile to 860 m/s in the rifle barrel when measured at 25 m from the muzzle; for the extended carbine, this velocity was 820 m/s. The overall length of the loaded ammunition was 78 mm (Boado y Castro 1915, pp. 39–41).

Ammunition Pouches and Slings

Two different types of ammunition pouches were purchased for the Modelo 1895: one for mounted troops and one for regular infantry. For mounted troops, the pouch was similar to that of the German model of 1888. Constructed from leather and with brass fittings, it was equipped with two leather straps, with the first being slung over the left shoulder, allowing the pouch proper to be mounted on the right hip or lower back. The second leather strap was fastened around the waist and

The Chilean Model 1895's sling. *Author*

prevented the pouch from rocking uncontrollably. Both straps had large, oval, brass buckles to allow length adjustment and were dyed black like the pouch. The straps were fastened to the pouch via two pronounced brass swivels that were riveted to the pouch. The pouch proper was also constructed of leather and had a perforated grill that was riveted to the interior, allowing fifty rounds of 7 × 57 mm ammunition in stripper clips to be carried. The pouch was closed with a large, flap-like lid that was buttoned to its underside (Kruck 2000, p. 21).

The pouch for regular infantry also followed the German example of 1888. Two of these black-leather pouches were carried against the upper waist through the use of a leather belt and suspenders. The rectangular leather pouch had two large leather loops to allow the belt to pass through and a brass eyelet in the middle to allow the suspender to be attached. Each pouch allowed the carrying of fifty rounds of 7 × 57 mm ammunition in stripper clips and was closed with a leather lid that was fastened to two corresponding brass buttons at the short sides (Kruck 2000, p. 22).

Both types of pouches were used well into the mid-twentieth century both by the Chilean army and navy.

The black-leather sling for the Modelo 1895 was marked by having a large, square buckle and an additional protective leather flap at the button end that prevented the button from marring the stock. The buckle was looped onto one end of the sling and was secured by three parallel rows of stitching. Like the buckle, the button was initially constructed from brass, and then later from steel that was blued. Observed slings were measured as having been 33 mm wide and 1,090 mm long; it is unknown if there was any difference between the sling intended for rifles and those for carbines.

Difference between the Spanish Model 1893 and the Chilean Model 1895

Before describing the Mauser Chileno Modelo 1895 in detail, it is useful to first describe the major differences between it and the Spanish Model 1893. One of the most obvious differences between the two is that the Spanish Model 1893 has a squared protrusion to the lower bolt face. Likewise, the extractor groove, running parallel to and just behind the bolt face of the 1893 model, has its wall cut on the upper portion to allow the removal of the extractor. In the Chilean 1895, the bolt face is fully cylindrical, and it does not have the extractor groove cut. Because of the squared bolt face of the 1893, the receiver was correspondingly cut to accommodate it; this is also not present in the 1895. In the 1895, the union between the bolt ball and its stem is filleted or rounded, while in the 1893 it is sharp or perpendicular. As for the receiver, the 1895 has the rectangular safety lug that was positioned a few microns behind the closed bolt handle. Apart from the Serbian Model 1899 and the later Mauser *Tankgewehr* (Tank rifle) M1918, this feature is apparently unique to the Modelo 1895 and is not evident on the Model 1893. Because of the inclusion of the safety lug, the rear tang dimensions of 1895 receivers are different from those of the 1893, and, as such, the stocks of the 1895 and 1893 are correspondingly also different to accommodate this. Differences between the firing pins are also evident, with the 1895 having a less dramatic taper to the base of its tip compared to the Model 1893. A further minor difference relates to the recess for the rear trigger guard screw. On the Model 1893, the screw is concentrically recessed. On the 1895, while still recessed, it is nonconcentric and extended toward the rear of the trigger guard tang. Importantly, the guide ridge that runs the length of the magazine follower is chamfered at the rear on the 1895, allowing the bolt to close on an empty magazine. This chamfer is not evident in the

1893. Another small and often-overlooked detail relates to the 1893's cleaning rod, which is a two-piece design comprising the main rod and a smaller pinned and replaceable threaded section. On the 1895, the cleaning rod is a single-piece design, with the threads being tapped directly onto the main rod. The last notable difference relates to the lower or rear barrel band. On the 1893, the sling loop is secured to the band itself with a screw and locking nut, while on the 1895, these two components are pinned (Boado y Castro 1897, pp. 39–40).

Crests, Inscriptions, Cartouches, and Proofmarks

A modern observer would be hard-pressed not to notice the numerous symbols and inscriptions that are evident on the Mauser Chileno Modelo 1895.

Depending either on Loewe, DWM, or OEWG manufacture, the following wording is inscribed on the left-hand side of the receiver rail of all true Model 1895s:

"MAUSER CHILENO MODELO 1895"
"MANUFACTURA LOEWE BERLIN"

"MAUSER CHILENO MODELO 1895"
"DEUTSCHE WAFFEN-UND MUNITIONS-FABRIKEN"
"BERLIN"

"MAUSER CHILENO MODELO 1895"
"STEYR"

The most commonly encountered receivers are those manufactured by Loewe, and it is generally accepted that these included serial number prefixes "A" through "H." Less commonly encountered are receivers manufactured by DWM, and it is generally accepted that these constituted serial number prefixes "H," "K," "L," and "M." Receivers manufactured by OEWG are scarce, and because these were spare parts they can theoretically be present in any of the serial number prefixes.

The Boer rifles acquired by Chile in 1901 are inscribed with the following on the left outer surface of the receiver rail:

"DEUTSCHE WAFFEN-UND MUNITIONS-FABRIKEN"
"BERLIN"

Finally, all Modelo 1895s had the Chilean coat of arms rolled-stamped (crested) onto the top portion of the receiver ring.

While no direct information can be found as to the exact meaning of the numerous proof and acceptance marks present on "true" Model 1895s, similar common practices by Spain and Argentina are very insightful.

Common Mauser practice of the period dictated that numerous inspection stages and subsequent certification and final acceptance were involved in the manufacture of small arms. For Chile, this process has already been identified as having been crucial to assuring that high-quality components and finished rifles and carbines were delivered.

For the Argentines, the inspection and certification of their Mausers involved a multiphase process including the use of three distinct groups of stamps that took the form of graphic symbols. The first process involved the individual inspection of every component after it was manufactured. Once each of these individual parts had been verified as compliant with the technical specification; a Mauser factory employee—under the supervision of a member of the Argentine Commission—then officially accepted it by marking it with the first set of stamps. The second phase involved the complete assembly of the unblued rifle or carbine, after which it was subject to an overpressure proof firing. If all major components—barrel, receiver, stock, and bolt—successfully passed a subsequent inspection, a second individual stamp was then applied to these parts. The position of these stamps is important, since their placement appears to be common both among the Argentines and the Spanish: the top of the barrel was marked just ahead of the receiver ring, the bolt handle was marked on the ball, the receiver's forward ring was stamped on the left side near the serial number, and the stock was marked just below its serial number. Stage 3 involved the placement of serial numbers on certain parts before

Model 1895 receiver rail inscription indicating Loewe manufacture. *Author*

Model 1895 receiver rail inscription indicating DWM manufacture. *Author*

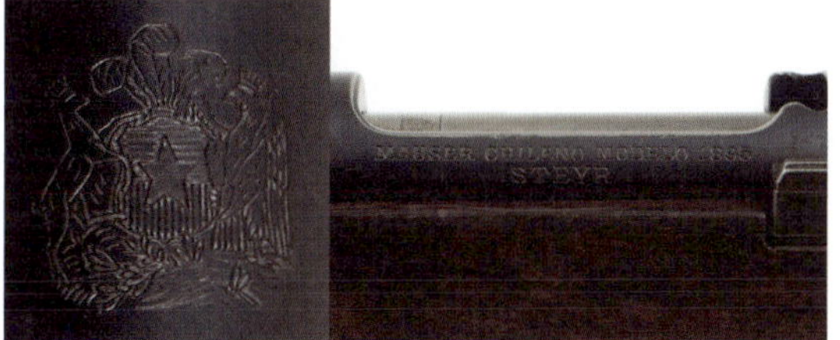

Forward ring crest and side rail inscription on a Chilean Model 1895 receiver that indicates Steyr manufacture. *Pedro Bello*

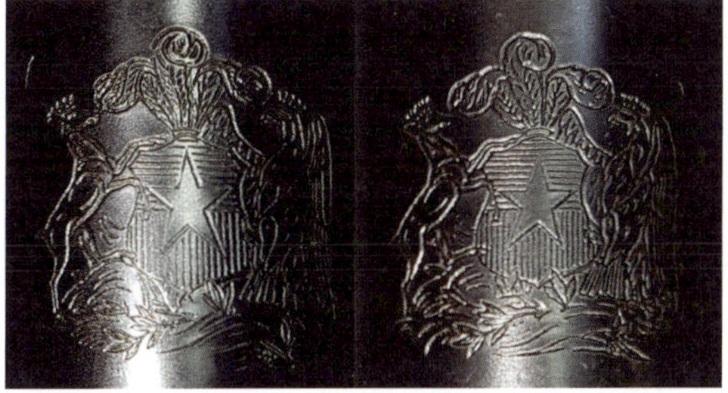

On the left is the crest present on the receiver ring from a "D"-prefix rifle manufactured by Loewe, while the crest on the right is from a DWM-manufactured "M"-prefix rifle. The reader should note the very subtle differences in the design. *Author*

they were blued, while stage 4 involved the sighting-in of the rifle. Once this last stage was successfully completed, a small witness line was placed on the front sight. Only after a further test firing of a random selection and further inspection was the final stage completed and the final acceptance mark applied: the Argentine coat of arms placed on the rear butt of the stock (Webster 2003, p. 69).

For the Spanish, the acceptance of their rifles entailed a similar process. As with the Argentines, each part manufactured for their rifles and carbines was subject to inspection and certification by the placement of various stamps. Departing slightly from the Argentines, the Spanish then fully assembled the barrel and sight components. Following an inspection to check the functioning and alignment of the sights, marks were stamped on the rear sight ladder, its slider, and rear sight sleeve base. Likewise, the small witness line was applied to the foot of the front sight blade. The next stage involved the overpressure proof firing of the fully assembled rifle. Having passed a subsequent inspection, the four crucial components were then marked: the barrel just ahead of the torque shoulder, the bolt body on the ball, the receiver just before the serial number, and the stock below its serial number. Following this step, the rifle was then completely reassembled and inspected. If no deficiencies were found, then a mark was applied to the stock just behind the tang of the trigger guard. The rifle or carbine then appeared to have been test fired to determine its accuracy. After this was successfully completed, a further mark was then applied to the stock just behind the base of the rear sling swivel. Only once all these inspections had been completed and the unit was ready for shipment was the Spanish coat of arms applied to the butt of the stock. Unfortunately, it is not known when the serial numbers, receiver crest, or side rail model description were added. It can be assumed that these were added after overpressure proof firing (Boado y Castro 1896c, pp. 175–176).

On Chilean 1895 rifles, individual parts have either one or more symbolic verification marks. It would be fair to assume that the presence of more than one symbolic mark indicates that the part in question was subject to further verification past the first stage after initial manufacture. It would also be logical to assume that there would be no overlap between the symbols used between stages, in particular between the initial post-manufacturing stage and all subsequent ones.

It is noteworthy that many of these parts, in particular the complex ones, also had small letters stamped onto their surfaces. Good examples of these are to be found on the left and right flanks to the lower portions of the receiver and the inside surfaces of the stock. At this point, it must be stressed that these letters have nothing to do with the verification process and final inspection that was undertaken by the Chileans. These letters can be reasoned as having been evidence of internal manufacturer processes, whereby groups of Mauser employees, having performed certain manufacturing and machining tasks, would then mark that process as having been executed by them. Officially abandoned in 1899, this process was supposedly intimately tied to Loewe's *Kontraktur-System* (Contractor System). In this system, a master artisan—having employed his own workmen—would deliver a certain number of components at an agreed-on price, with payment being made only on parts that were within tolerances (Matscoss and Schlesinger 1930, pp. 42–43).

In the case of the Mauser Chileno Modelo 1895, the first of their processes would have been the inspection and verification of individually manufactured parts. If the above argument is considered—that is, the presence of only one symbol stamped on an individual part—then for the rifles, the following first-stage marks can be argued as having been applied:

- A crossed hammer and pick: upper and lower barrel bands, safety lever, and the bolt shroud
- A triangle containing a cycle: rear sight leaf spring, sear, ejector box, rear sight ladder and its slider and retaining catch(es), front sight base sleeve, and the rear base to the sling swivel
- A circle containing horizontal and vertical lines: magazine floorplate, trigger guard, butt plate, and the barrel
- A diamond containing diagonal lines that originate from the corners: handguard retaining ring, magazine follower, ejector box leaf spring, ejector, and the trigger
- A five-pointed star: the nose cap
- Female symbol containing a dot at the center of the circular head: front sight blade, extractor, trigger guard screws, handguard springs, butt plate screws, rear sling swivel screws, magazine floorplate release button, ball of the bayonet scabbard, and also on the scabbard throat insert
- Three intertwined circles or Krupp circles: handguard
- A stylized forward-sloping S: cleaning rod
- A large diamond comprising four smaller diamonds: cocking piece, firing pin, and trigger. It is important to note that on DWM triggers this symbol appears slightly different (i.e., a diamond containing a square).

Following this argument further, if any of these symbols were then present on any other parts with more than one stamp, it would be fair to assume that they too related to the first-stage verification. In this case they are also present on the following:

- The crossed hammer and pick symbol can also be found on the rear sight base, and the bolt body.
- The five-pointed star can also be found on the rear sight base, also sometimes seen with a five- or four-pointed star or a simple, but pronounced, circular punch mark.
- The three intertwined circles or Krupp circles can also be found on the bayonet blade.

As for the stock, the only symbol that is common to it and any other component is a circle containing a horizontal line with a point at its center; this is also found on the receiver to the left of the side rail inscription. In both configurations of the carbine, this circle containing a horizontal line with a point at its center is also found on the

Some of the myriad of acceptance marks and proofmarks found on the Chilean Model 1895. *Author*

baseplate that secured their rear swing swivel to the opposite side of the stock.

An anchor symbol is also evident on the right shoulder of the receiver's recoil lug. This anchor symbol is grouped with numerous internal manufacturing-process marks that have been described. It is thus proposed that the circle containing a horizontal line with a point at its center is the first-stage verification symbol of the receiver, and not the anchor.

It can be reasoned that the second phase of verification could have comprised either the assembly of the barrel and sights or the overpressure proof firing. It would be rational to assume that the proof firing was done as the second stage because the sights were not needed for this process. Similarly, the soldering of the sight base to the barrel could have obscured any defects, which would have resulted in wasted labor, time, and materials in the case of the barrel being rejected. While the specifics of this are unknown, the resulting verification marks are visible. An examination of existing Model 1895 rifles reveals that the proof-firing marks can be discerned in a manner similar to the Spanish: a shield symbol stamped below (Loewe) or to the right of the serial number (DWM) to the left side of the receiver ring, a six-pointed star or "Star of David" below the serial number on the left side of the stock, a circle with a dot at its center and with nine radiating spokes to its exterior on the ball of the bolt body, and two concentric circles connected with four spokes on the top of the barrel, just ahead of the torque shoulder. It is interesting to note that on some observed rifles, one of these four marks can also sometimes be found on the horizontal ledge of the stock, to the right of the receiver ring.

Likewise, the process of sighting-in the complete barrel can also be discerned from existing examples: the witness line can be discerned on the foot of the front sight blade, and five- and four-pointed stars and the circular punch mark can be found on the underside of the rear sight base sleeve. It is proposed that the next step involved the application of the serial numbers and subsequent bluing, but only once the destructive testing and alignment of the sights were complete and verified. This is a sensible conclusion because the integrity of the preceding two steps was totally dependent on certain individual components staying together. In the case of the Chilean 1895 rifles, the full serial number and alphabetic prefix can be found on the receiver, bolt body, barrel, stock, trigger guard, cross guard to the bayonet, sheath of the bayonet, and, curiously, the cleaning rod. The last two digits of the serial number can also be found on the rear sight ladder and its complete slider assembly, the magazine floorplate, the safety lever, and the bolt shroud.

Presumably, the rifle was then fully assembled and final quality inspections could take place. It would also be fair to deduce that no further symbols were stamped onto any metal surfaces after they were blued, since this would affect the integrity of the blued finish. Any further stamping could have been applied exclusively to the stock, the unblued bolt components, or the top of the rear sight ladder. Considering that all the stamps present on the bolt components and rear sight leaf can be described as having originated in preceding stages, the reasoning that any further stamps were exclusively applied to the stock is the only believable outcome.

Following the Spanish example, the final quality inspection can be witnessed through the occurrence of a spearhead, five-pointed star, and other symbols present on the wrist of the stock just behind the tang of the trigger guard. The five-pointed star symbol is often also observed on the underside of the rear sight base. The process of test firing for accuracy can equally be identified by the presence of a four-bladed propeller symbol evident on the stock just behind the base of the rear sling swivel. Only once all these steps had been completed and the rifle was ready for shipping was the final acceptance mark applied. In the case of Chile, a cartouche composed of the country's coat of arms with the date below was applied to the left of the butt of the stock. The bayonet was also stamped with a simplified Chilean coat of arms.

In the case of Loewe manufacture, the stock cartouche has the coat of arms contained within a circle, with the date below bounded by a rectangle. The year is indicated as "1895" and can be argued as referring to the model designation, as opposed to the year of contract, manufacture, or delivery. For DWM rifles, the stock cartouche is markedly different, in that the design of the coat of arms and the absence of the bounding circle are immediately apparent. Likewise, the year is represented either as "1898" or "1902" and lacks the rectangular outline. It is clear from the arguments presented that Chile concluded a contract with DWM in 1898. It is therefore proposed that the rifles with this date on the cartouche represent those rifles that were both manufactured and delivered to Chile during that year. For rifles containing a "1902"-dated cartouche, the explanation is unclear. By 1899, Chile had approximately 85,000 Mauser rifles and 25,000 carbines that had been manufactured and delivered. This would mean that all known eleven alphabetical serial number prefixes would have been used by 1899 and could have been composed of only the "1895"- or "1898"-dated cartouches. It is a well-known fact that rifles with the "L" and "M" prefix are commonly marked with the "1902"-dated cartouche. Following this logic, this would suggest that these rifles were manufactured or delivered in 1902. To compound the history of Chile's Mauser purchases even further, it has been documented that in addition to the already mentioned purchase of 100 Maxim machine guns and seventeen million cartridges, Chile also ordered 14,000 "Standard 7 mm Rifles" in 1901 (Schaefer 1974, p. 238). This important fact cannot be dismissed simply because it does not fit with the main sequence of purchases as already outlined. While further research is undoubtedly necessary, for the purposes of this book, Chile's "1902"-dated cartouche will remain a mystery.

It has to be remembered that the processes described applied only to rifles after initial manufacture and can reasonably not be applied to rifles that were remanufactured, were repaired, or had spare parts fitted in Chile. Numerous examples of 1895 rifles have been observed with stocks that have different final-acceptance cartouches. These examples have the Chilean coat of arms with the letter "M.F." or "M.E." below (i.e., as a substitute for the year). Many theories have been propagated as to the meaning of these letters and the origin of the stocks. Likewise, a few examples have been observed that have both the "1895" and "M.F." cartouches in the same position; that is, these examples appear to have been overstruck with a second cartouche.

On the left is the "1895" stock cartouche, while on the right is an "M.F." example as found on the Chilean Model 1895. *Author*

As detailed, it has been shown that Chile bought extensive amounts of spare parts—including numerous stocks—from Loewe, DWM, and OEWG. It is proposed that stocks with "M.F." and "M.E." cartouches are these spare parts. This theory is supported by the fact that on rifles that have these spare-parts stocks, a number of the second and third verification symbols are almost always not present. Further, in all the extensive original literature predating 1900 that the author has seen, the 1895 Mausers are often generically referred to as "Mauser Fusil." Thus, it is reasoned that "M.F." could have stood for "Mauser Fusil." Another fact already established is that OEWG-manufactured spare parts always had a unique OEWG factory stamp. This mark—comprising a small but distinct capital "OE" with "WG" below—has been observed by the author on numerous parts, but never on stocks. As such, it has already been argued that OEWG-made stocks had to be reworked to accommodate the lengthened carbine barrels. It is possible that during the remanufacture

FAMAE stock cartouche as evident on an M95-12-36. *Pedro Bello*

process, the originally applied OEWG mark could have been obliterated. In the context of the massive controversy surrounding the whole OEWG spare-parts affair, the last thing OEWG would have desired was for its remanufactured stocks to be confused with those of Loewe or DWM. It is entirely feasible that OEWG would have insisted on the unique and quick identification of its products. It is therefore proposed that "M.E."-marked stocks could have been those originally manufactured by OEWG in Steyr, Austria, and then remanufactured in Santiago, Chile.

Chilean 1895s have also been observed with a stock cartouche comprising a shield with a star at the center and the words "Chile" above and "FAMAE" below. Simply stated, these stocks were in all probability those remanufactured domestically by the Chilean state-controlled arms manufacturer, or FAMAE.

It has to be remembered that the cartouche on the butt of the stock was a symbolic indication that the rifle or carbine in question had been officially accepted as compliant with specifications and regulations and was thus fully functioning and fit for purpose.

Following this reasoning, and the fact that later replacements are clearly marked as FAMAE, then it would make a stronger argument to propose that "M.E." stands for Maestranza del Ejército (Army Armory) and that "M.F." indicates its latter evolution into the Maestranzas y Fábricas (Armories and Factories). This argument is reinforced even further when considering the origins of FAMAE (detailed in the next section).

Another point of importance is that barrels have been observed that were manufactured by Loewe, DWM, Steyr, and Schweizerische Industrie Gesellschaft: Loewe and DWM barrels are identified by their lack of a company acronym, Steyr barrels have the letters "OE" over "WG" stamped on the middle portion of the barrel, and Schweizerische Industrie Gesellschaft barrels are identified with the letters "S.J.G." contained within a rectangular border. (More information on the Schweizerische Industrie Gesellschaft's involvement with Chile can be found in chapter 3.)

Apart from receivers and barrels, other parts manufactured by OEWG and identified with the "OE" over "WG" stamp have been observed. Bolt bodies, bayonets, and rear sight ladders with complete sliders have been observed, the latter two being commonly encountered.

Fábricas y Maestranzas del Ejército and the Chilean M.95-12, M.95-12-36

Arguably the first attempt by the Chileans at domestic manufacture of small arms and associated ammunition was made in 1810, during the Chilean War of Independence. Having converted the Jesuit monastery of Loreto in Santiago into an army barracks, the former pottery facility of this monastery was then transformed into Maestranza del Ejército: a facility to store, repair, and manufacture small arms for the army. On 16 August 1861, a further facility, the Maestranza de Artillería (Artillery Armory), was also created, with a factory in Limache, Chile. In February 1875, the Maestranza de Artillería was moved to Santiago and became the Fábrica y Maestranza de Artillería (Artillery Factory and Armory). With the outbreak of the War of the Pacific, the Fábrica y Maestranza de Artillería was placed under the Dirección General de Maestranzas y Parque de Artillería on

Side views of a M95-12-36. *Pedro Bello*

Calle Blanco Encalada (Blanco Encalada Street). One of the first tasks of the Fábrica y Maestranza de Artillería was the manufacture of metallic small-arms cartridges. Following a large explosion on 29 January 1880, the facility was relocated to Avenida Pedro Montt (Pedro Montt Avenue), where the Fábrica de Cartuchos (Cartridge Factory) was subsequently built. After the War of the Pacific, the need for a larger central facility to store numerous existing and captured weapons became apparent. Thus, on the former site of the Fábrica y Maestranza de Artillería, a new Arsenales de Guerra (Arsenal of War) was constructed (Navarro et al. 1982, pp. 164–166).

On 4 November 1892, the Dirección General de Maestranzas y Parque de Artillería was organized to contain two distinct portions: the Parque and the Maestranza. The larger of the two sections—the Maestranza—incorporated numerous subsections; namely, a Fábrica de Cartuchos, a Taller de Armería (Gunsmithing Workshop), a Taller de Carpintería y Cerrajería (Carpentry and Locksmithing Workshop), and a Taller de Talabartería (Leather Workshop) (Donoso et al. 1982, p. 201).

Subsequently, in 1901, it was deemed necessary to totally separate the two portions of the Dirección General de Maestranzas y Parque de Artillería. From this point onward, the Parque—or newly named Arsenales de Guerra—would administer, store, and distribute weapons, while the Maestranzas—which became FAMAE—would repair and manufacture them (Navarro et al. 1982, p. 167).

It is within FAMAE that three conversions to the Mauser Chileno Modelo 1895 can be discerned: M.95-12, M.95-12-36, and M.95-61.

Conventional wisdom has it that the M.95-12 was a standard Model 1895 rifle or carbine upgraded with the newer rear sight ladder to accommodate the 7 × 57 mm "P" ammunition, with the "12" indicating official adaptation in 1912. It is often assumed that with the adoption of the "P" ammunition that the barrels, like the sights, were also upgraded, but this is not the case.

Likewise, the M.95-12-36 is often argued as a subsequent iteration of the M.95-12—that is, still chambered for 7 × 57 mm—which had undergone a further sight modification and was officially adopted in 1936. With a few exceptions, these examples comprise the extended carbine configuration and are identified by most examples having a tangent rear sight graduated to 1,400 m.

The M.95-61 was officially adopted in 1961 and is a Model 1895 rifle or carbine that has had its barrels rebored and rechambered to 7.62 × 51 NATO specification. These examples are identified by a prominent "7.62" with an "N" below stamped onto the rear bridge to the receiver. Less commonly encountered are examples that have the acronym "NATO" with the date "1961" below, also stamped onto the rear bridge to the receiver. To accommodate this transformation, the Chileans counterbored the chamber area on existing barrels, soldered a plug into the resulting counterbore, and then rebored the whole barrel to a 7.62 mm diameter. This arrangement was then rifled and rechambered to 7.62 × 51 mm.

But some discrepancies are immediately apparent with the generally accepted M.95-12 and M.95-12-36 designations. The most obvious relates to the M.95-12-36, which was supposedly the further replacement of an already replaced sight. It could be argued that if indeed this was correct, then why not simply call it an M.95-36?

In all the extensive original literature the author has surveyed concerning the original purchase of the Model 1895 by Chile, these are exclusively referenced either to *fusiles* (rifles) or *carabinas* (carbines). In DWM marketing material of 1897, the Chilean Model 1895 rifle and carbine are clearly illustrated, and the carbine is clearly a conventional carbine—not an extended one. Likewise, the first mention of extended carbine barrels appears in the OEWG spare-parts controversy as outlined. In this section, it has been clearly identified that these barrels would not allow the fitting of bayonets to existing or ordered carbine stocks. It has also been identified that Chile had to further contract with OEWG to supervise the training of its Santiago arsenal employees to modify carbine stocks to accommodate a bayonet and an extended barrel. All of this could indicate only that the M.95-12 was the extended carbine. Equally, this argument more appropriately addresses the M.95-12-36 as having been the extended carbine that had its 1912 specification sight replaced with a tangent sight in 1936.

Chilean "Navy" Mauser Chileno Modelo 1895

As mentioned, 500 Mausers were issued to the coastal artillery at Talcahuano to a regiment with the same name. It is with this small fact that the origins of the so-called Chilean navy's Mauser Chileno Modelo 1895 can be hypothesized.

The Chilean "navy" Model 1895s are primarily distinguished by the presence of a receiver crest that depicts a five-pointed star positioned with a larger fouled anchor that is the insignia of the Armada de Chile (Chilean navy). This crest is also sometimes observed as the final acceptance stamp on the left of the butt of the stock. Notably, the serial numbers of navy examples generally have no alphabetical prefixes, and it has been proposed that the total number was no more than 500 examples. Likewise, the vast majority of observed examples are of Loewe manufacture, while approximately one in six are DWM (see "Chilean Navy Mausers M1895," http://forums.gunboards.com, 2015).

A Chilean navy Model 1895 identified by the fouled anchor crest on the forward receiver ring. *Pedro Bello*

After the War of the Pacific, the Regimiento de Marina (Marine Regiment), a unit mobilized for the Chilean army in Antofagasta for the surveillance and defense of the coast, was reduced to the level of a battalion by a presidential decree of 11 September 1885. Its manpower was likewise reduced to 600 men, who were then divided into six companies. The Regimiento de Marina then served as a basis for the organization of the similarly sized Batallón de Artillería de Costa (Coastal Artillery Battalion), created on 7 December 1887 (Donoso et al. 1982, pp. 85–86).

On 16 June 1893, the Chilean army's 3rd Artillery Regiment was transferred to the Regimiento de Artillería de Costa to man the coastal forts not under the auspices of the ministry of the navy. The military plan of that time dictated that with this incorporation, the Regimiento de Artillería de Costa would consist of three batteries together with the command; the first two were in Valparaíso, while the third would be installed at Talcahuano (Donoso et al. 1982, pp. 200–201). A

A top view of the receiver and rear sight of a Chilean navy Model 1895, with markings on the rear receiver bridge indicating it was converted to 7.62 NATO. *Pedro Bello*

year prior to its transfer, the 3rd Artillery Regiment was based in Valparaíso and consisted of 261 men (Donoso et al. 1982, p. 195). Interestingly, in 1898, the Regimiento de Artillería de Costa, while still contained under the army's artillery regiments, was listed separately, and in addition to the five existing artillery regiments (Donoso et al. 1982, p. 199). It is important to note that the Regimiento de Artillería de Costa was an army regiment and was transferred to the Chilean navy only in early 1903 (Donoso et al. 1982, p. 201). When this happened on 8 April, the new Regimiento de Artillería de Marina (Naval Artillery Regiment) had 1,200 men and included the equipment, fortifications, and associated coastal artillery regiments of Valparaíso and Talcahuano, as well as the Brigada de Rifleros de la Armada (Naval Rifle Brigade). Along with these, and while fortification work continued at Talcahuano, the engineers assigned to this work were also included (Arellano and Goycoolea 2009, p. 381).

Being their major port, Valparaíso was of critical concern for the Chileans. Following the Spanish bombardment of Valparaíso on 31 March 1866, the Chileans increasingly devoted substantial resources to its fortification. An immediate solution was to take cannons from deactivated warships and install them in fortifications overlooking Valparaíso and its bay. In the 1880s, the coastal artillery was a shambles of different and antiquated cannons, consisting of some ancient muzzle-loading Spanish cannons along with Parrot, Rodman, and Armstrong examples (Sater and Herwig 1999, pp. 29–30, 36).

To remedy this situation, Rear Adm. Juan José Latorre was sent to Europe in 1888 to examine and then request proposals for modern cannons that would be allocated to coastal defense. Following this visit, the chiefs of the navy and the army established a committee that ultimately decided to purchase further Krupp cannons (Donoso et al. 1982, pp. 85–86). Initially, Chile purchased four Krupp L/22 210 mm cannons for Valparaíso in 1879 (Sater and Herwig 1999, p. 136). Then, in 1889, the Chileans bought ten L/40 280 mm cannons for 3.2 million marks (Sater and Herwig 1999, p. 137; Schaefer 1974, p. 34). This was followed by a further purchase in January 1892 of another two L/40 280 mm cannons and two 280 mm howitzers (Sater and Herwig 1999, p. 140). Chile lacked the expertise to effectively install the new Krupp cannons, and as such hired Prussian officer Gustav Adolf Karl Nicolaus Betzhold in 1899 to accomplish this task. Together with his assistant, Sgt. Maj. Alberto de la Cruz, Betzhold oversaw both the Krupp installation and the further fortification of the port of Valparaíso (Donoso et al. 1982, p. 86). While the majority of the 280 mm Krupp cannons were earmarked for Valparaíso, four were transported overland to Talcahuano, where they remained in storage and were installed only in 1898, into the Punta de Parra and Punta Larga fortifications (Arellano and Goycoolea 2009, pp. 381–382).

While it would make a very appealing story to argue that the newly installed Krupp artillery was manned by troops who furnished equally new Mauser rifles, this is simply not credible. This is primarily because the final-acceptance mark and receiver crest would undoubtedly indicate that these 500-odd rifles were procured by the navy and not the Chilean army. Likewise, Chilean artillery regiments were equipped with carbines, not rifles. Thus, a more probable narrative has to be constructed.

A few examples of navy 1895s have been observed that have what appear to be ship names present on their stocks—for example, *Blanco Encalada*, *Baquedano*, *Esmeralda*, and *Almirante Simpson*—which is worth exploring.

Throughout the 1890s, Chile purchased significant amounts of modern material for all branches of its armed forces, including the navy. In the context of growing tensions with Argentina, the Apostadero Naval (Naval Station) at Talcahuano was officially established by the Chilean Supreme Decree of 29 January 1895 (Mardones 1995, p. 5). In 1887, Chile had budgeted 3.13 million

British pounds to modernize its fleet. These monies commissioned the second-class battleship *Capitán Pratt* and the protected cruisers *Presidente Errazuriz* and *Presidente Pinto*, along with the torpedo boats *Lynch* and *Condell*. Interrupted by the Civil War of 1891, Chile then purchased the protected cruiser *Blanco Encalada* in late 1892. This first protected cruiser, *Esmeralda*, originally built in 1875, was then sold in 1894 and replaced by an identically named vessel and four torpedo boats in May 1895. In August 1895, a further protected cruiser, the *Ministro Zenteno*, was bought. The armored cruiser *O'Higgins*, along with six 140-ton torpedo boats, was acquired in 1895 (Scheina 1987, pp. 46–49). Likewise, the *Almirante Simpson*—an 800-ton torpedo gunboat—was delivered to Chile in 1896 (see "Chilean Navy, Torpedo Ships, Almirante Simpson," www.navypedia.org, 2015). The *Baquedano*, which was launched in July 1898, served as the Chilean navy's first training ship (Garcia-Huidobro Correa 1999, p. 1).

It is clear that certain of the so-called navy 1895 Mausers were indeed assigned to Chilean navy ships acquired during the 1890s. Likewise, it is also highly probable that a number of these rifles were also assigned to period facilities, such as Talcahuano Naval Station. It is also very probable that the Chilean navy's Brigada de Rifleros could have also been issued a number of these rifles.

The Mauser Chileno Modelo 1895 in Detail

Following the convention of the time, the rifle and carbine versions of the Mauser Chileno Modelo 1895 were described as having been divided into eleven main parts: barrel and sights, receiver, bolt, trigger mechanism, bolt stop and ejector, repetition mechanism, stock, handguard, stock fittings, cleaning rod, and bayonet. Modelo 1895s were purchased by Chile in two main types: *fusil* or *carabina*. Importantly, the *carabina* is further divided into either a conventional configuration (i.e., simply *carabina*) or the *Carabina Alargada* (Long or Extended Carbine), with the latter often referred to as a short rifle, or *Mosquetón*.

With a bayonet attached, the rifle had a total length of 1,484.5 mm and a weight of 4,450 g, while without the bayonet, the length was 1,236 mm and the weight was 4,075 g (Boado y Castro 1915, p. 39). The extended carbine with bayonet attached had a length of 1,305 mm and a weight of 4,050 g, while without the bayonet, the length was 1,055 mm and the weight was 3,650 g (Boado y Castro 1915, p. 40).

Barrels and Sights

Mauser Chileno Modelo 1895 barrels were typical of the Model 1893 type, in that they had a single torque shoulder and were of stepped-contour design. The overall length of the barrel for the rifle was 738 mm (Boado y Castro 1896a, p. 42; 1915, p. 39); for the extended carbine it was 556 mm (Boado y Castro 1915, p. 40), and for the carbine it was 464 mm (Ball 2011, p. 76). (This last figure of 464 mm does not appear to include the 16 mm threaded barrel shank, meaning that the carbine barrel was 480 mm.) All barrels were originally chambered for the 7 × 57 mm cartridge, having a twist rate on one turn in 220 mm and with four lands and grooves. The diameter of the rifle's bore when measured between the lands was 6.99 mm, and it was 7.25 mm when measured into the grooves, with each groove being 0.13 mm deep. Lands were 1.4 mm wide, with grooves being 3.9 mm wide (Boado y Castro 1915, p. 39). Other earlier sources have identified the rifle bore diameter as 7 mm, with corresponding groove depths of 0.125 mm (Boado y Castro 1896a, pp. 42–43). For the extended carbine, the barrel bore was also quoted as 7 mm exactly, with the depth of the grooves also correspondingly shallower at 0.125 mm deep (Boado y Castro 1915, p. 40). For the rifle, the twist of the barrel's lands and grooves was to the right (Unknown author 1897a, p. 2).

As for the front and rear sights, these too were similar to those of the Model 1893. The flat, rectangular rear sight ladder was mounted onto a tube that was soldered to the barrel. The tube contained a milled recess that allowed a flat leaf spring to be fitted. In addition to elevating the sight ladder, the leaf spring also had a rectangular protrusion at its head that allowed the sight slider to be locked in the forward position. The leaf spring

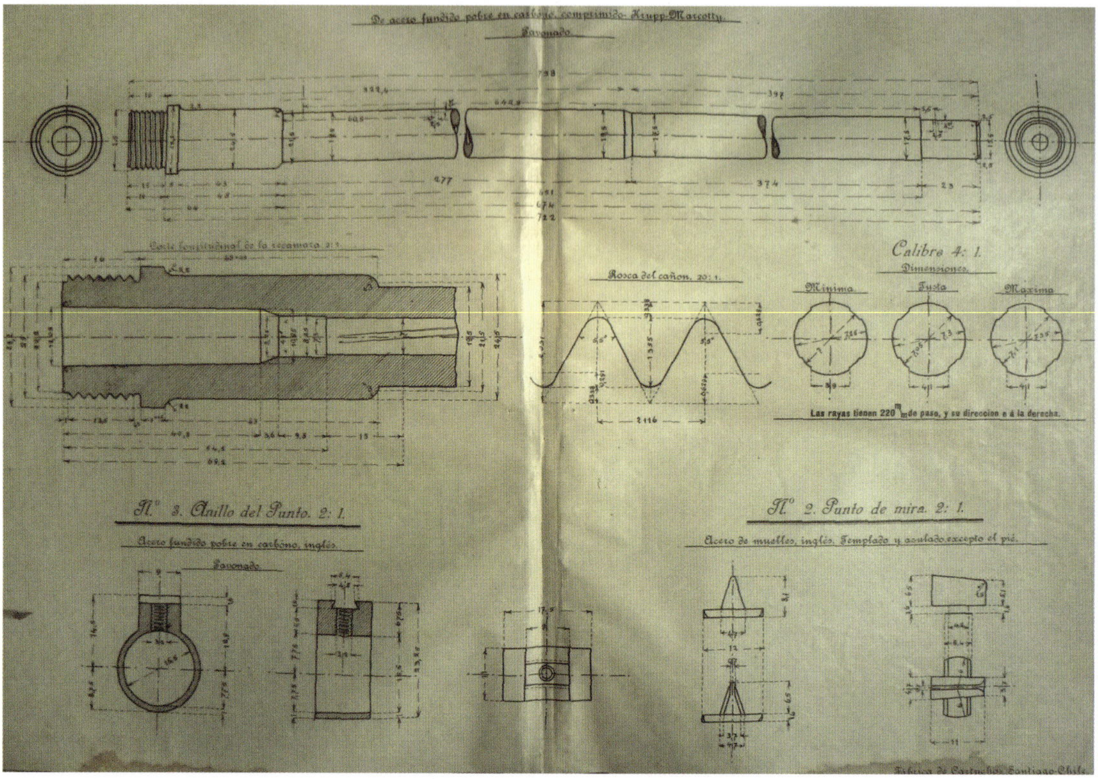

Technical drawing of the barrel and front sight to the rifle of the Chilean Model 1895.
Unknown author. 1897a. *Atlas del fusil Mauser 7mm Modelo Chileno 1895*. Berlin Ludwig Loewe.

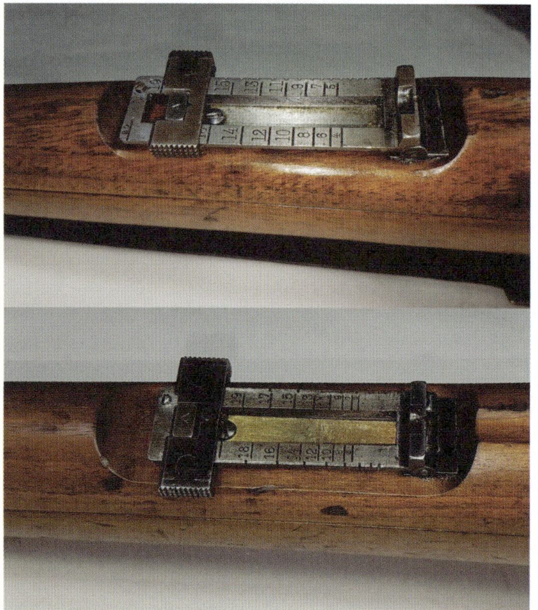

The original (top) and replacement (bottom) rear sights as fitted to the Chilean Model 1895. *Author*

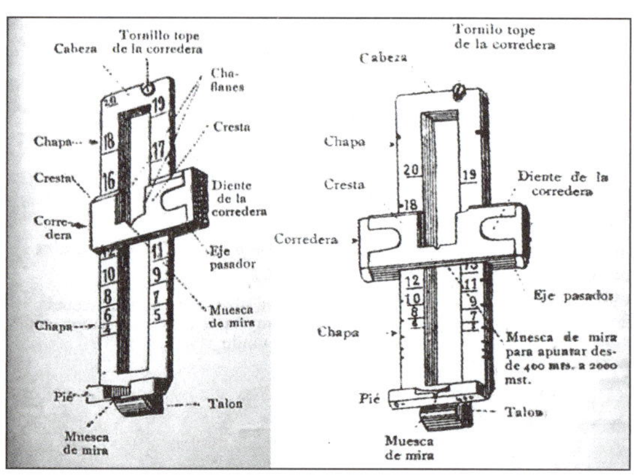

The two different Chilean Model 1895 rifle rear sights; the one on the left is the earlier example.
Boado y Castro, J. 1915. *Cartilla del fusil i la carabina Mauser Chilena Modelo 1895 por el Comandante Don José Boado i Castro i Corregida para el fusil transformado en 1912 por el Inspección de Fábricas i Maestranzas del Ejército*. Santiago, Chile: Imprenta de la Inspección de Fábricas i Maestranzas del Ejército.

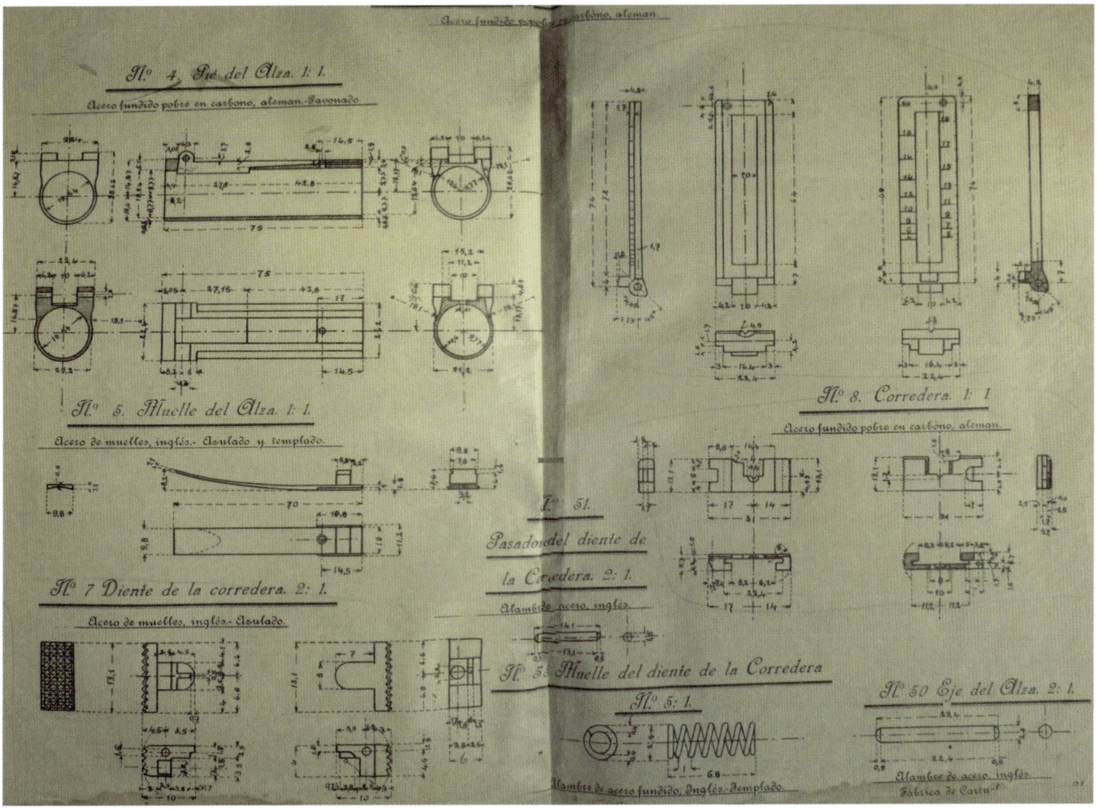

Rear sight to the rifle of the Chilean Model 1895.
Unknown author. 1897a. *Atlas del fusil Mauser 7mm Modelo Chileno 1895*. Berlin: Ludwig Loewe.

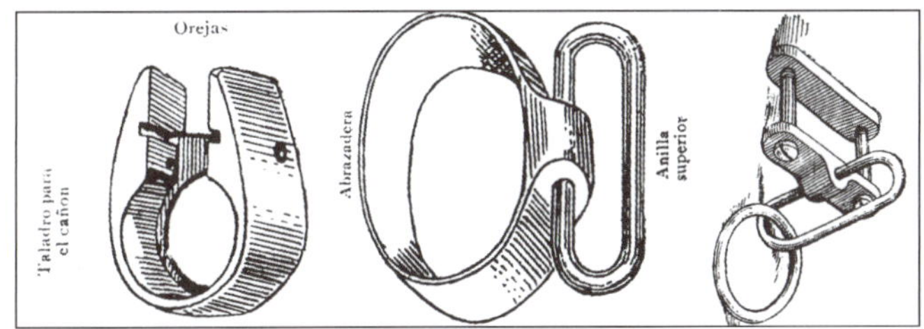

Details of the stock fittings and front sight protector unique to the carbine version of the Chilean Model 1895.
Boado y Castro, J. 1915. *Cartilla del fusil i la carabina Mauser Chilena Modelo 1895 por el Comandante Don José Boado i Castro i Corregida para el fusil transformado en 1912 por el Inspección de Fábricas i Maestranzas del Ejército*. Santiago, Chile: Imprenta de la Inspección de Fábricas i Maestranzas del Ejército.

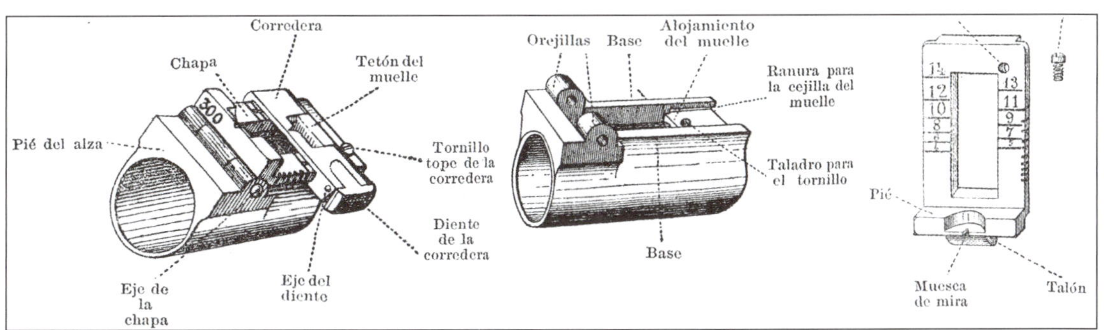

Spanish carbine rear sight, which was identical to that of the Chilean Model 1895 carbine rear sight.
Boado y Castro, J. 1896b. *Le fusil Mauser espagnol de 7 mill., Modèle 1893*. Paris: Imp. de Berger-Levrault.

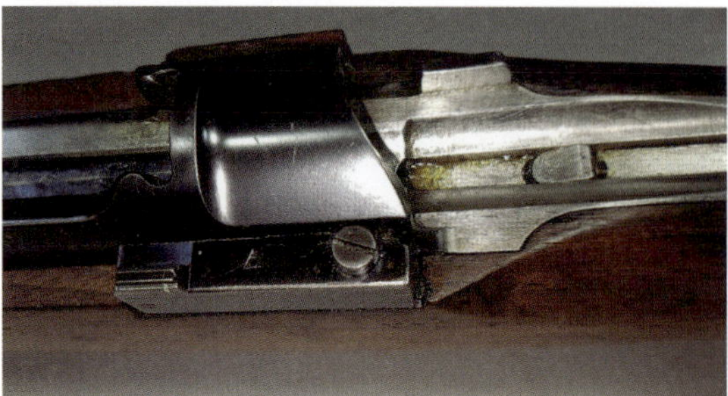

The rear safety lug to the Chilean Model 1895. *Author*

The guide rib to the receiver's left bolt way on the Chilean Model 1895. *Author*

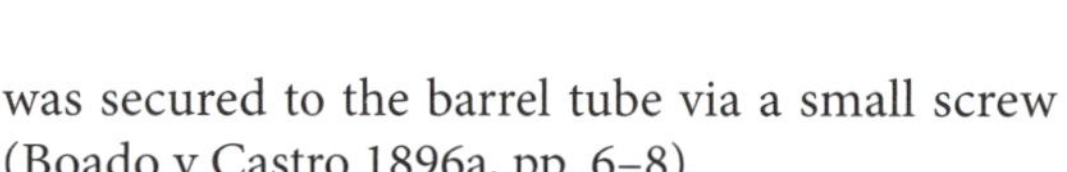

was secured to the barrel tube via a small screw (Boado y Castro 1896a, pp. 6–8).

Initially, the sight ladders were configured for lower-velocity, round-nosed ammunition. As such, these earlier sight ladders were longer than the second, later version, which were retrofitted after 1910 and were intended for "P" ammunition. A distinguishing feature between these types of sights was that the earlier sight had a single catch to the right of the sight slider, while the latter had two catches with one on either side. Further, the earlier rifle sight ladder had a battle setting calibrated to a maximum of 300 m, while the latter was to 400 m. These values are stamped on the rear of the respective sight, being either "300" or "0–400." For the rifle, the maximum distance indicated on the sight ladder was 2,000 m, while for both configurations of the carbine this distance was 1,400 m (Boado y Castro 1896a, pp. 6–8; 1915, pp. 6–8, 20).

As to the front sights, these were composed of a triangular blade slotted into the sight base that was in turn both soldered and screwed to the front step of the barrel. During reception and once sighted in, a small witness mark line was stamped onto the foot of the blade and corresponding upper face of the sight base. Both configurations of the carbine had an additional pinned protection sleeve that was fitted over the barrel and entire front sight assembly (Boado y Castro 1896a, p. 6; 1915, pp. 6, 20). Carbine front sight bases were distinguished from those of the rifle by having a small hole drilled near their front face to accommodate the pin for the protector.

Receiver

While it was the most important component of the Mauser Chileno Modelo 1895, the receiver is nevertheless scantly described in literature. Essentially, the receiver was the component that unified the major systems of the Model 1895: barrel, bolt, trigger mechanism, bolt stop and ejector, and repetition mechanism. Receivers for rifles and both configurations of carbines were identical. As mentioned, the Model 1895 is unique in that it had the safety lug positioned a few microns behind the closed bolt handle. As with the Model 1893, the Model 1895 also had the guide rib in the receiver's left bolt way.

At this point, it is important to note that in all the sources by José Boado y Castro that detail the Model 1895, the bolt face and receiver are always illustrated as those of the Model 1893.

Bolt

In the Chilean Model 1895, the complete bolt assembly acted as locking, extraction, firing, and safety mechanisms. The Model 1895 had a cock-on-closing system with two forward-locking lugs that engaged two shoulders on the inside of the receiver's forward ring. The left locking lug had a perpendicular cut to facilitate the receiver's guide rib and the ejector. As stated, the bolt face was round and lacked the square feeding shoulder of the Model 1893; it likewise allowed the base of the cartridge to be recessed and partly enclosed. The extractor is of a rotating-claw design and is fixed to the bolt body via an extractor collar positioned behind the locking lugs. The firing pin and its compression spring are contained in the hollow bolt body via the bolt shroud. Held under tension by the spring, the firing pin is actuated by the cocking piece, which is attached to the rear of the firing pin via an interrupted lug arrangement. The

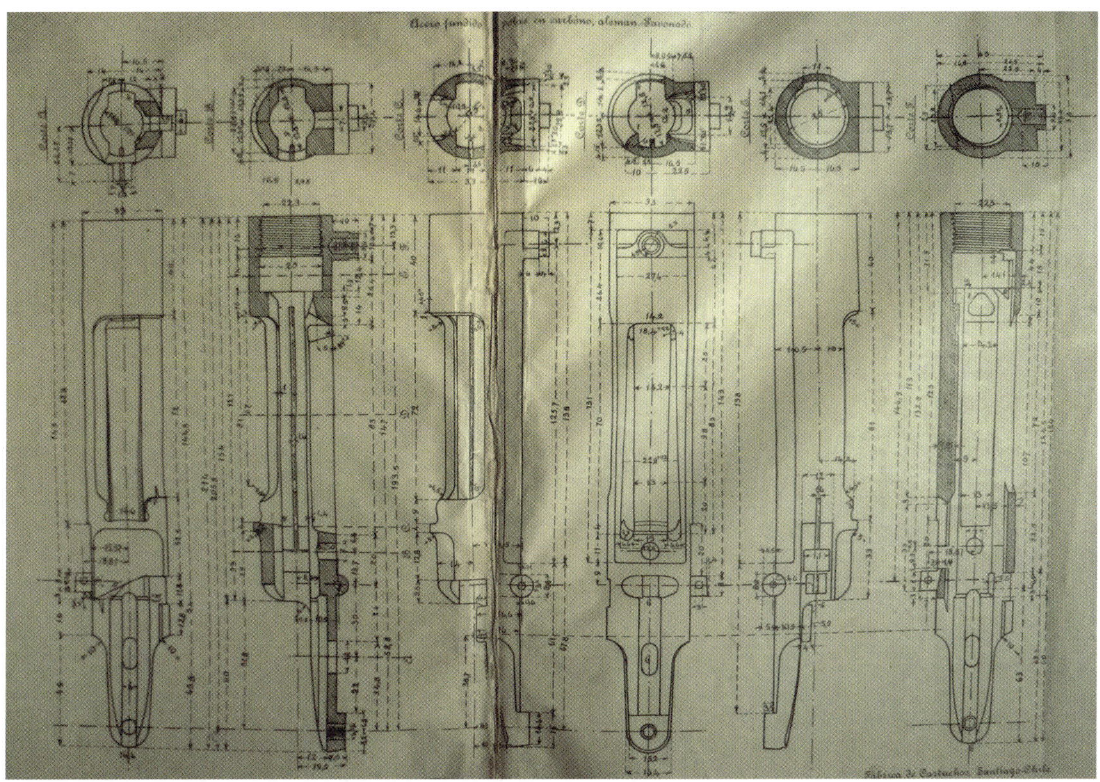

Technical drawing of the receiver of the Chilean Model 1895. Note the Fábrica de Cartuchos, Santiago, Chile, designation in the bottom right hand corner.
Unknown author. 1897a. *Atlas del fusil Mauser 7mm Modelo Chileno 1895*. Berlin Ludwig Loewe.

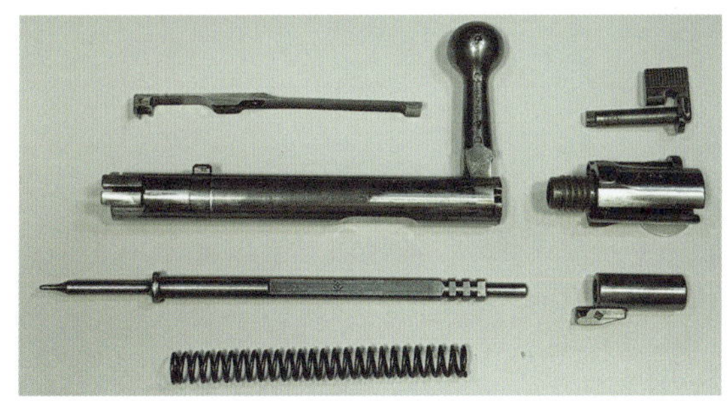

The complete bolt components for the rifle version of the Chilean Model 1895. *Author*

safety lever, which was accommodated in the bolt shroud, was a three-position design that allowed for firing, bolt disassembly, and safety. Disassembly and safe positions are accomplished by the safety lever engaging a notch in the cocking piece. In addition, the safe position also locks the bolt and thus prevents it from rotating (Boado y Castro 1896a, pp. 9–11; 1915, pp. 10–12). An important distinction is made between the bolt handles of Model 1895 rifles and both configurations of carbines, with the former being "straight" while the latter is "bent."

Arguably, the only deficiency in the design of the Model 93/95's bolt was its total lack of gas venting in the event of a cartridge failure. Furthermore, on Chilean 1895s, the bolt body, extractor, extractor collar, safety lever, bolt shroud, firing pin, and cocking piece were polished and left unblued.

Trigger Mechanism

In the Model 1895, a separate trigger and sear were pinned together to form the trigger mechanism. A further pin secured the whole trigger mechanism together with an internal compression spring to the underside of the receiver. When pulled, a raised surface (or cam) on the trigger is forced against

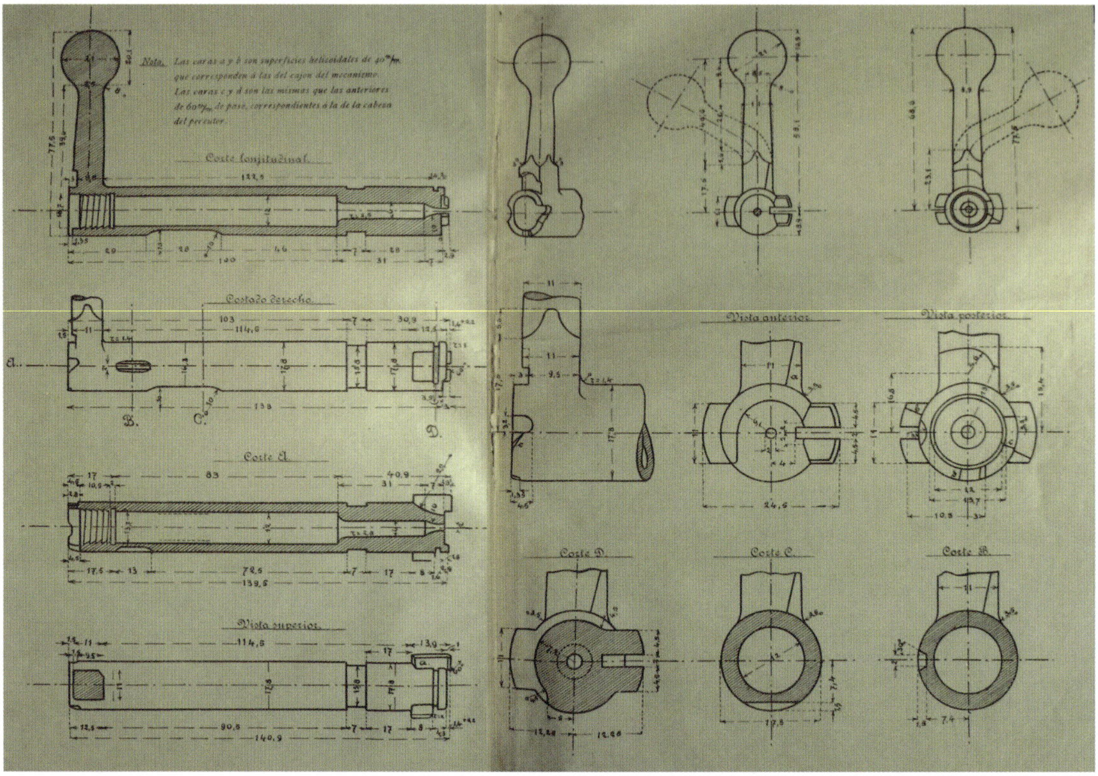

Technical specifics of the bolt proper to the Chilean Model 1895.
Unknown author. 1897a. *Atlas del fusil Mauser 7mm Modelo Chileno 1895*. Berlin Ludwig Loewe.

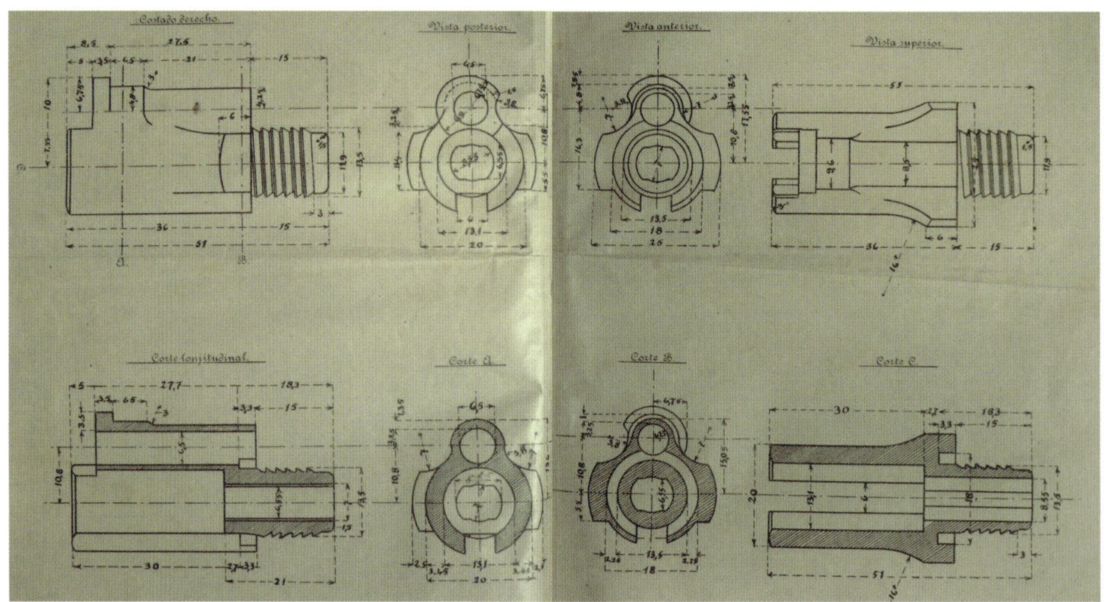

Bolt shroud to the Chilean Model 1895.
Unknown author. 1897a. *Atlas del fusil Mauser 7mm Modelo Chileno 1895*. Berlin Ludwig Loewe.

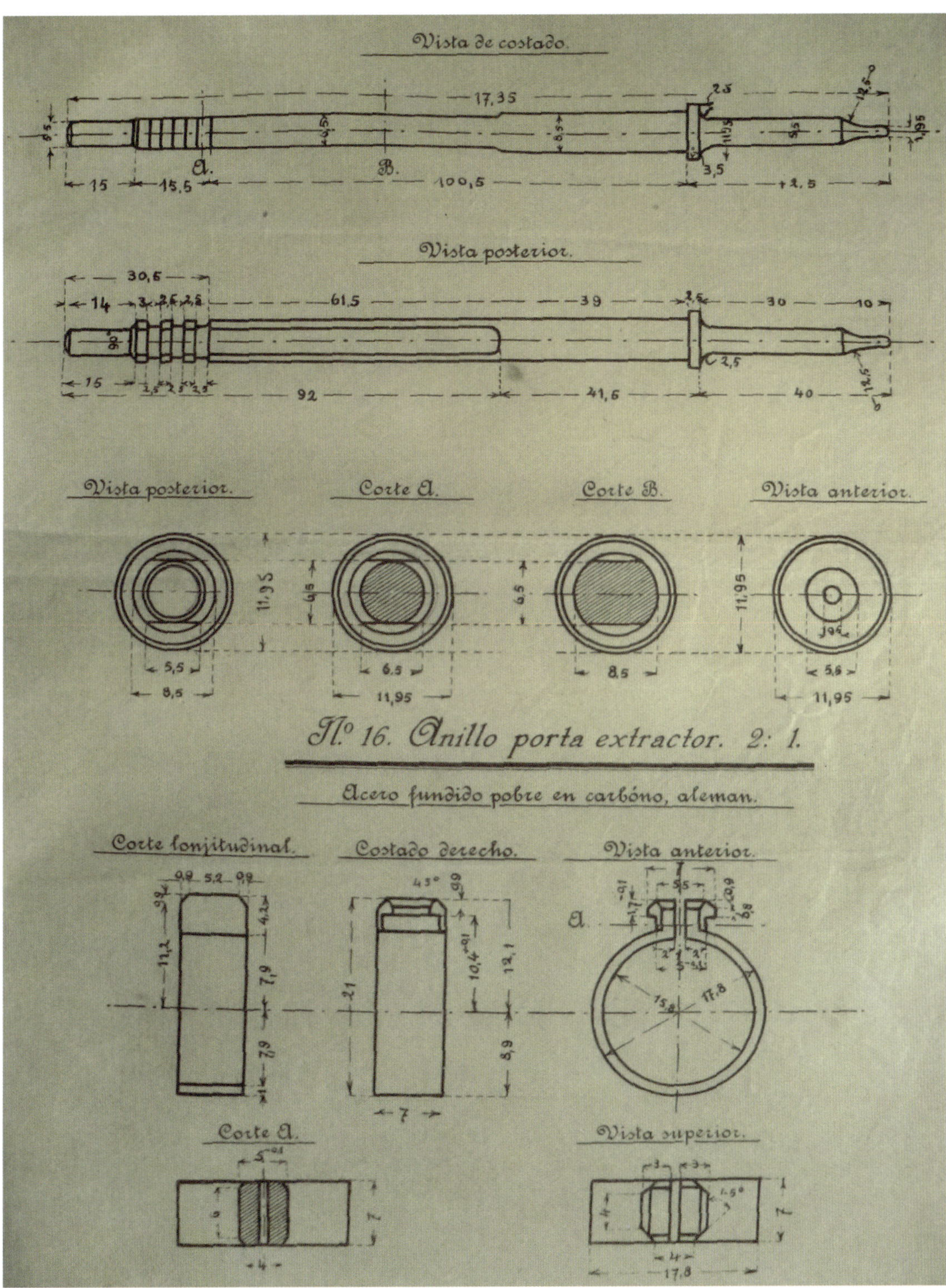

Firing pin and extractor collar to the Chilean Model 1895.
Unknown author. 1897a. *Atlas del fusil Mauser 7mm Modelo Chileno 1895*. Berlin Ludwig Loewe.

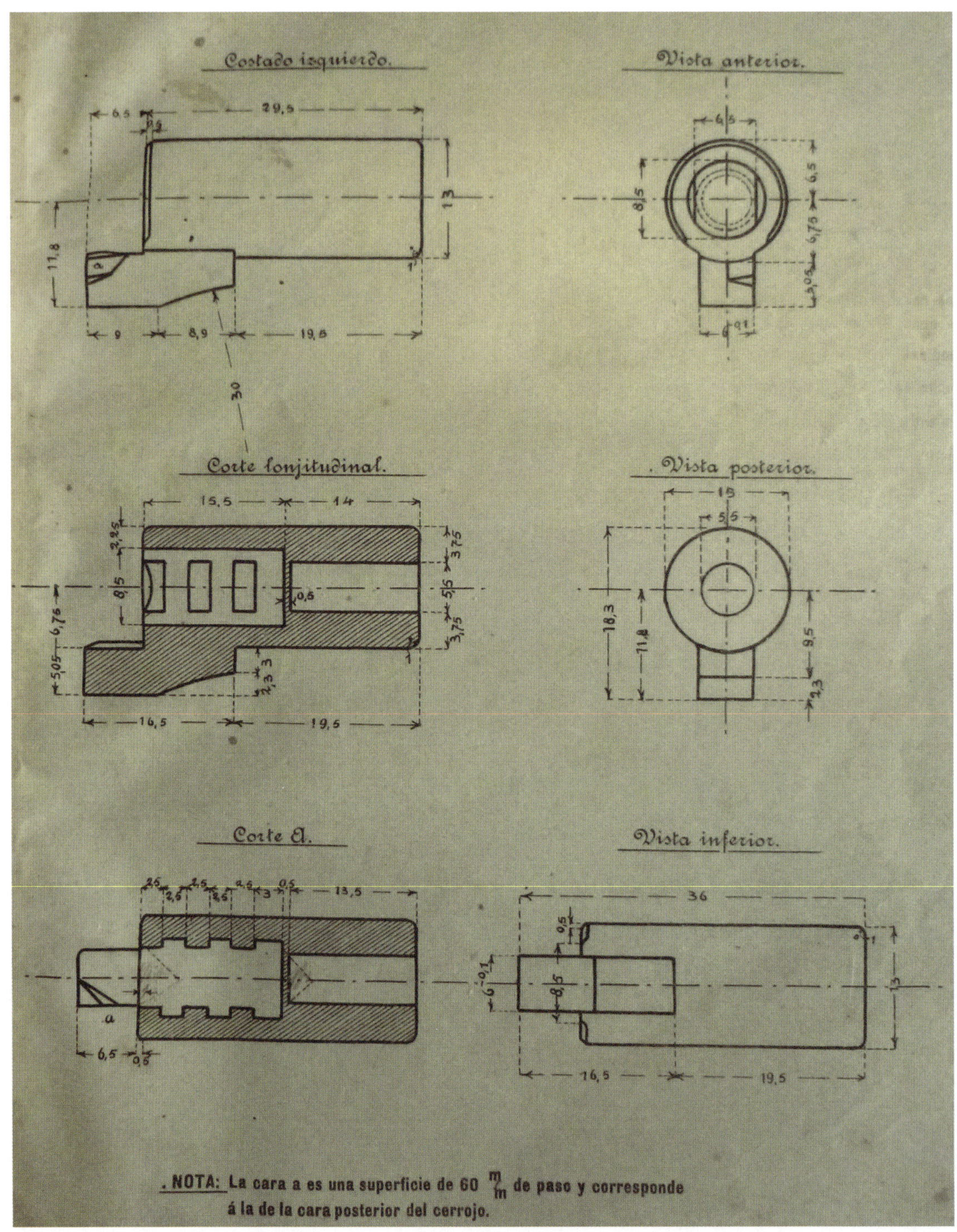

Cocking piece to the Chilean Model 1895.
Unknown author. 1897a. *Atlas del fusil Mauser 7mm Modelo Chileno 1895*. Berlin Ludwig Loewe.

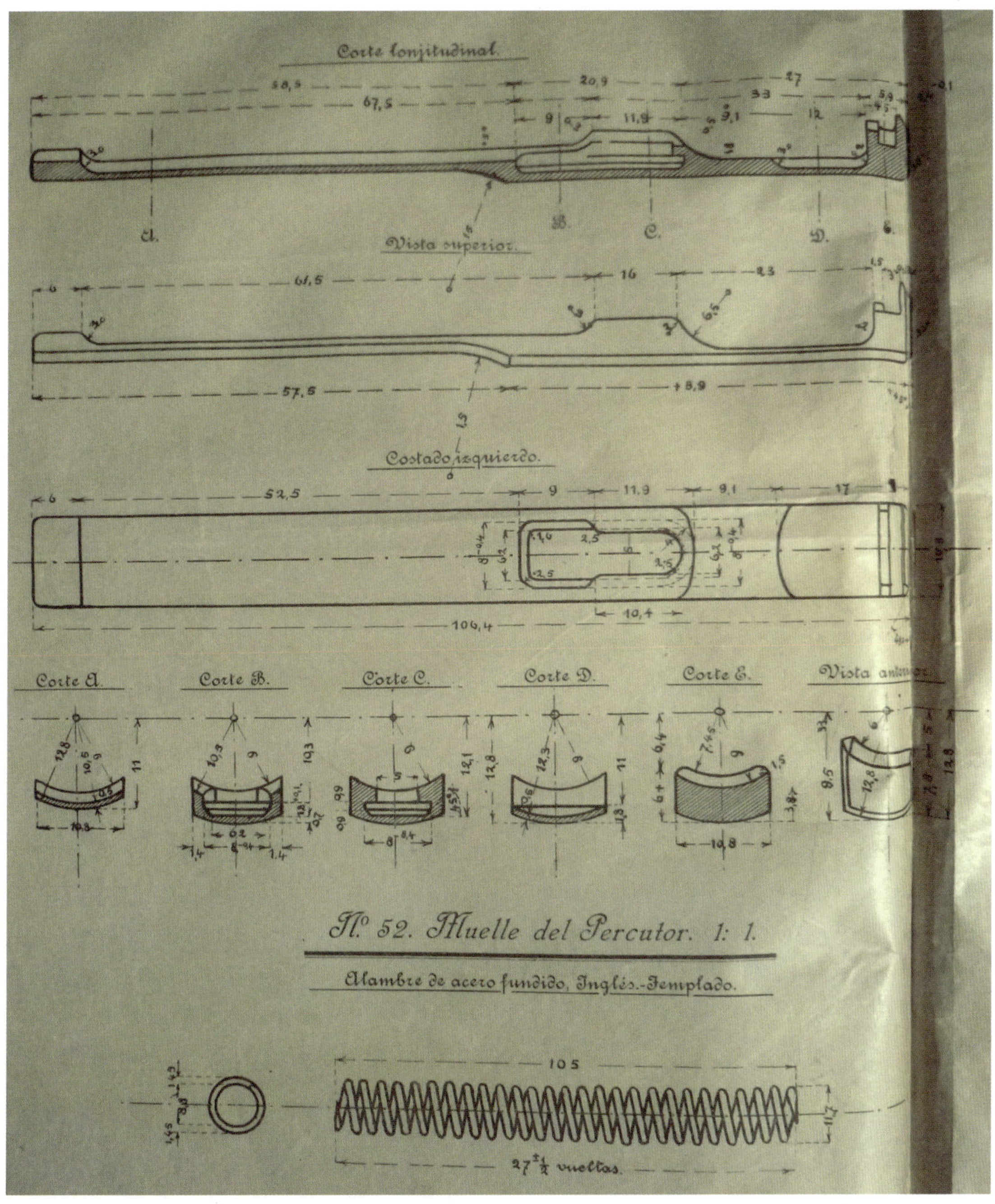

Extractor and firing pin spring to the Chilean Model 1895.
Unknown author. 1897a. *Atlas del fusil Mauser 7mm Modelo Chileno 1895*. Berlin Ludwig Loewe.

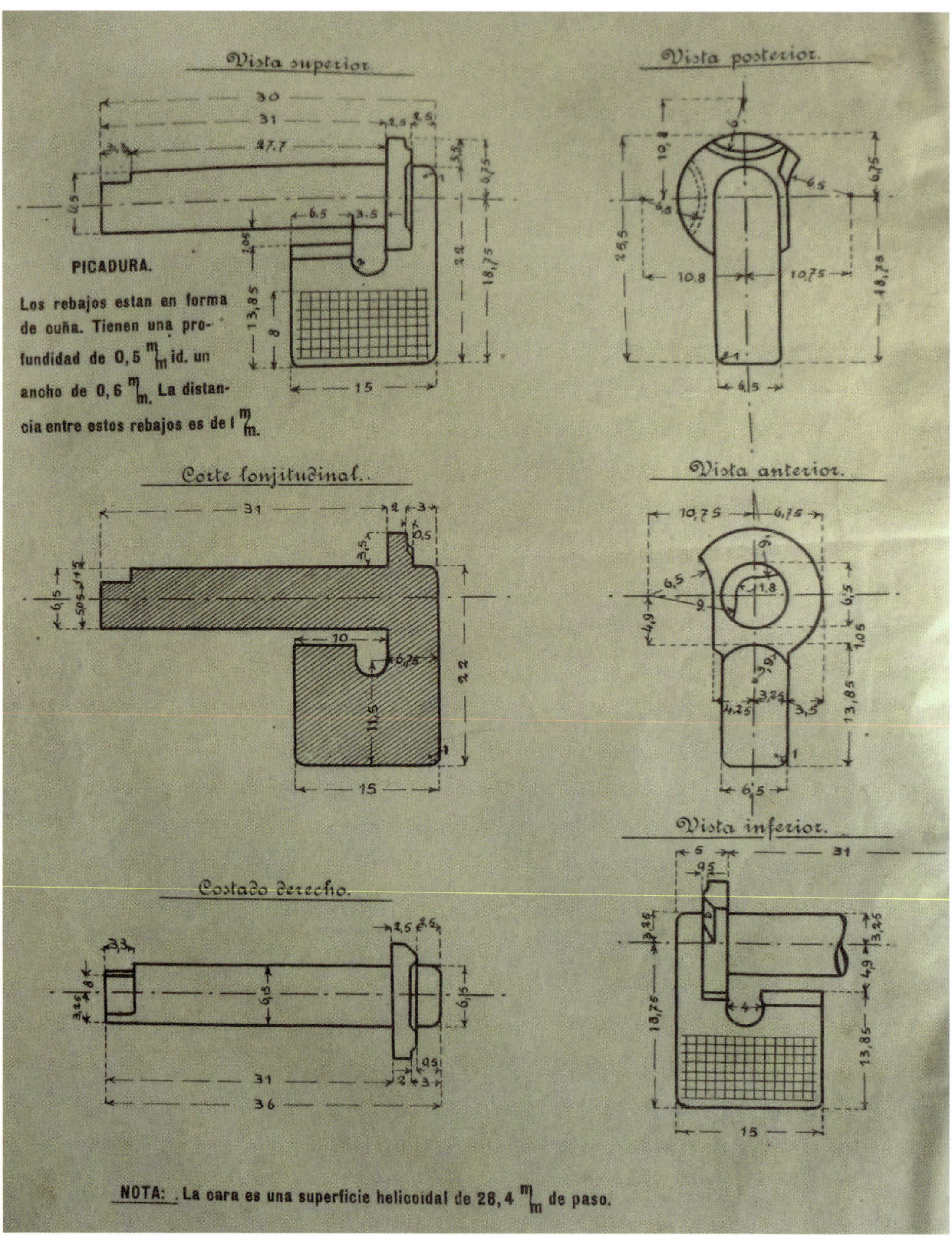

Safety lever to the Chilean Model 1895.
Unknown author. 1897a. *Atlas del fusil Mauser 7mm Modelo Chileno 1895*. Berlin Ludwig Loewe.

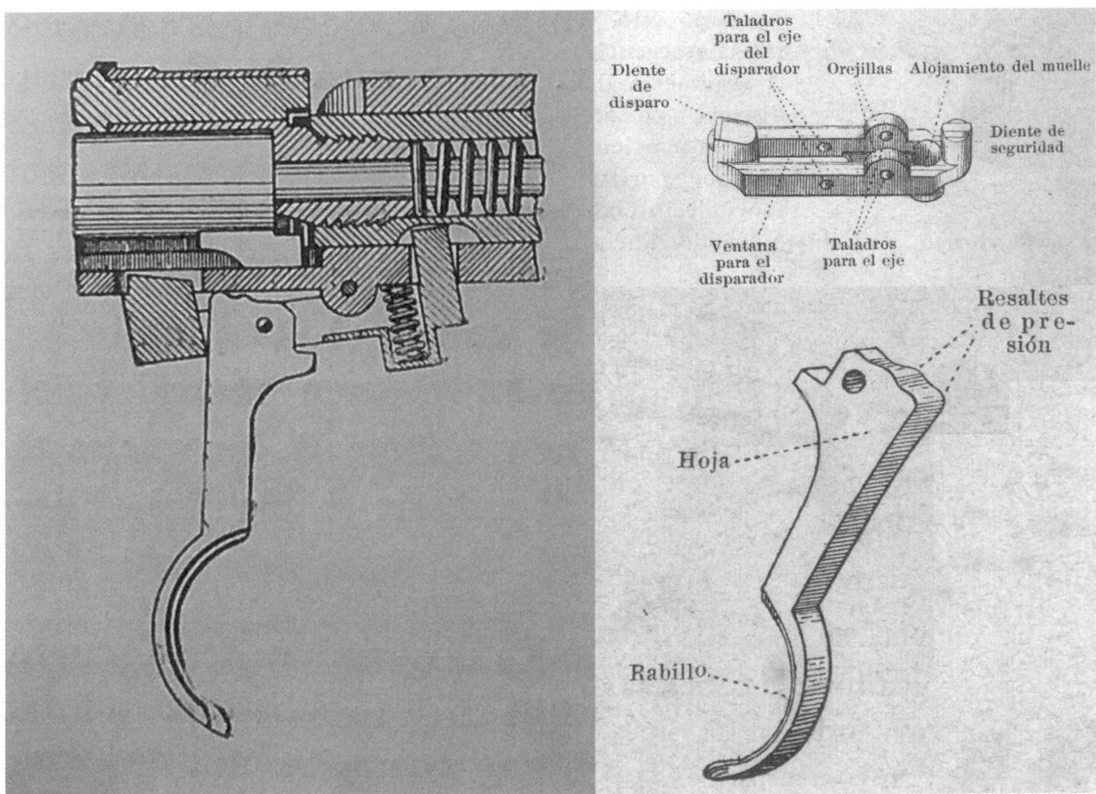

Sections through, sear and trigger proper of the trigger mechanism of the Chilean Model 1895.
Boado y Castro, J. 1915. *Cartilla del fusil i la carabina Mauser Chilena Modelo 1895 por el Comandante Don José Boado i Castro i Corregida para el fusil transformado en 1912 por el Inspección de Fábricas i Maestranzas del Ejército*. Santiago, Chile: Imprenta de la Inspección de Fábricas i Maestranzas del Ejército.
Boado y Castro, J. 1896b. *Le fusil Mauser español de 7 mill., Modèle 1893*. Paris: Imp. de Berger-Levrault.

the underside of the receiver, lowering the sear proper and thus disengaging the cocking piece. The two-stage trigger, apart from initiating the firing sequence, also serves as a secondary safety device. At the front of the sear, a pronounced lug is raised when the trigger is pulled. This lug recesses into a small groove machined to the underside of the bolt body. In the event that the bolt was not properly closed, the lug could not engage with the groove, and firing could not occur (Boado y Castro 1896a, pp. 11–12; 1915, pp. 12–13).

Bolt Stop and Ejector

As with the trigger mechanism, the bolt stop and ejector were hallmarked by clever engineering. Attached by a small screw to the rear left portion of the receiver and kept flush via the action of an integrated leaf spring, the bolt stop served the dual function of preventing the bolt from disengaging from the receiver and, when pivoted outward to the left, allowing the removal of the bolt. The leaf spring likewise served to project the ejector into the receiver. When the bolt was pulled reward after firing, the ejector, which rotated on the shaft of the screw and, having passed through the cut in the left locking lug of the bolt body, then expelled the empty case by hitting its base (Boado y Castro 1896a, pp. 12–13; 1915, pp. 13–14).

Repetition Mechanism

For the Chileans, the repetition mechanism comprised the trigger guard with its integrated five-round staggered magazine. Secured to the underside of the receiver, the trigger guard was fixed via two guard screws. The longer of these two guard screws was supported in the stock by

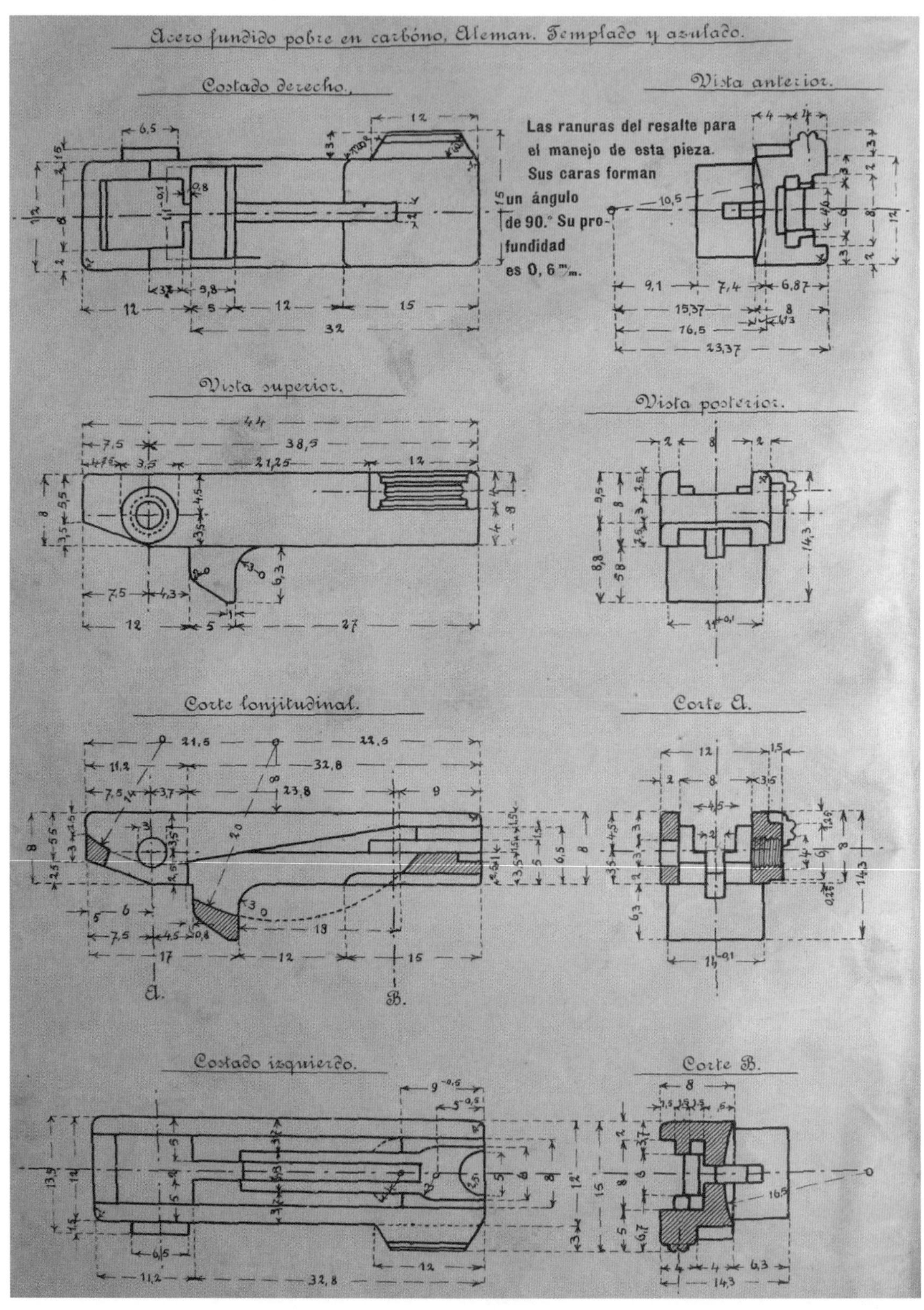

Ejector box to the Chilean Model 1895.
Unknown author. 1897a. *Atlas del fusil Mauser 7mm Modelo Chileno 1895*. Berlin: Ludwig Loewe.

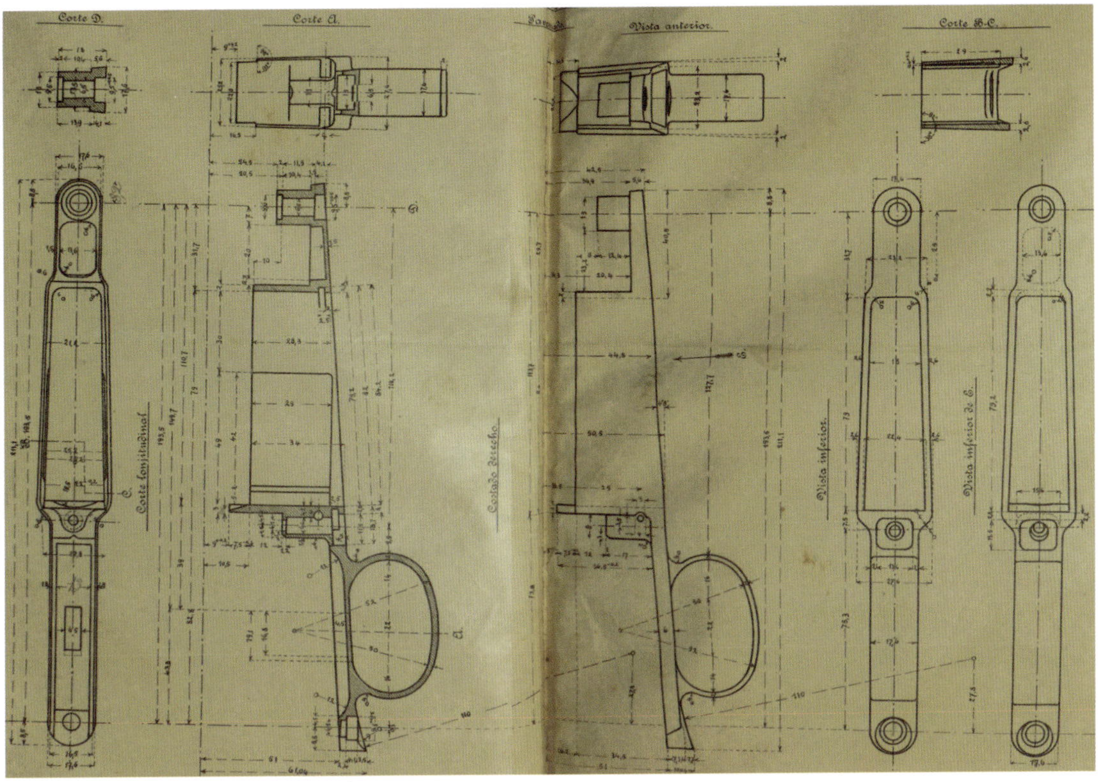

Trigger guard to the Chilean Model 1895.
Unknown author. 1897a. *Atlas del fusil Mauser 7mm Modelo Chileno 1895*. Berlin: Ludwig Loewe.

a tubular stock pillar and screwed into the rear tang of the receiver. The shorter of the two was screwed directly to a threaded hole in the middle of the receiver's recoil lug. A magazine floorplate closed the bottom of the magazine by clipping into recesses cut into the bottom of the trigger guard. The floorplate was secured via a small, spring-loaded button pinned into the trigger guard. A leaf spring actuated the magazine follower and was fixed into milled slots on the top side of the floorplate and the underside of the follower (Boado y Castro 1896a, pp. 13–14; 1915, pp. 14–15).

Stock

Arguably, the components that most dramatically differentiate the visual appearance of the rifle from the two configurations of carbines were the length of their walnut stocks and the placement of the rear sling swivel and its base. For the rifle, the length of the stock with the butt plate and without the nose cap was 1,142.3 mm (Unknown author 1897a, p. 17).

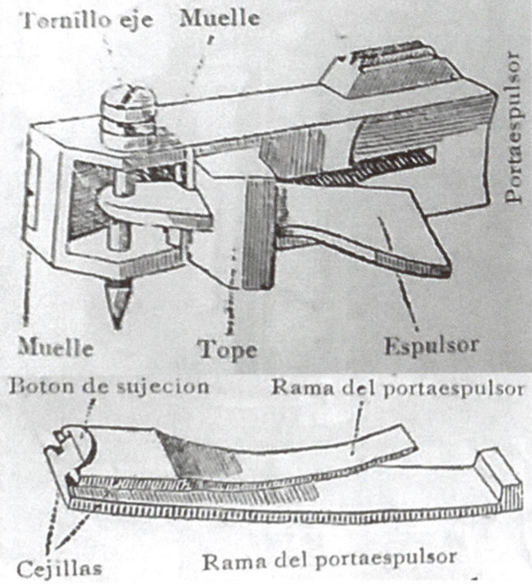

Complete bolt stop mechanism for the Chilean Model 1895.
Boado y Castro, J. 1915. *Cartilla del fusil i la carabina Mauser Chilena Modelo 1895 por el Comandante Don José Boado i Castro i Corregida para el fusil transformado en 1912 por el Inspección de Fábricas i Maestranzas del Ejército*. Santiago, Chile: Imprenta de la Inspección de Fábricas i Maestranzas del Ejército.

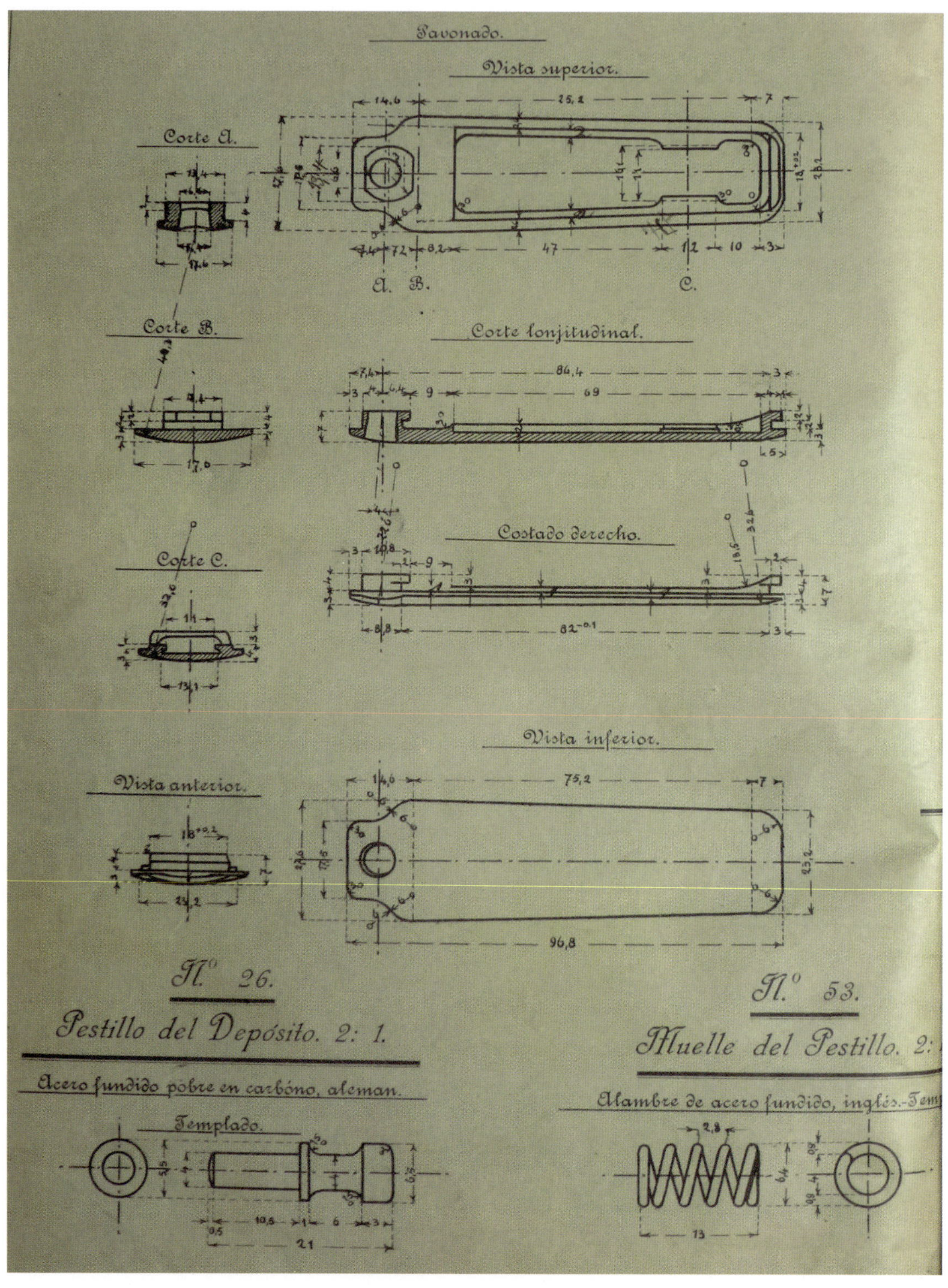

The magazine floorplate and its retention mechanism for the Chilean Model 1895.
Unknown author. 1897a. *Atlas del fusil Mauser 7mm Modelo Chileno 1895*. Berlin: Ludwig Loewe.

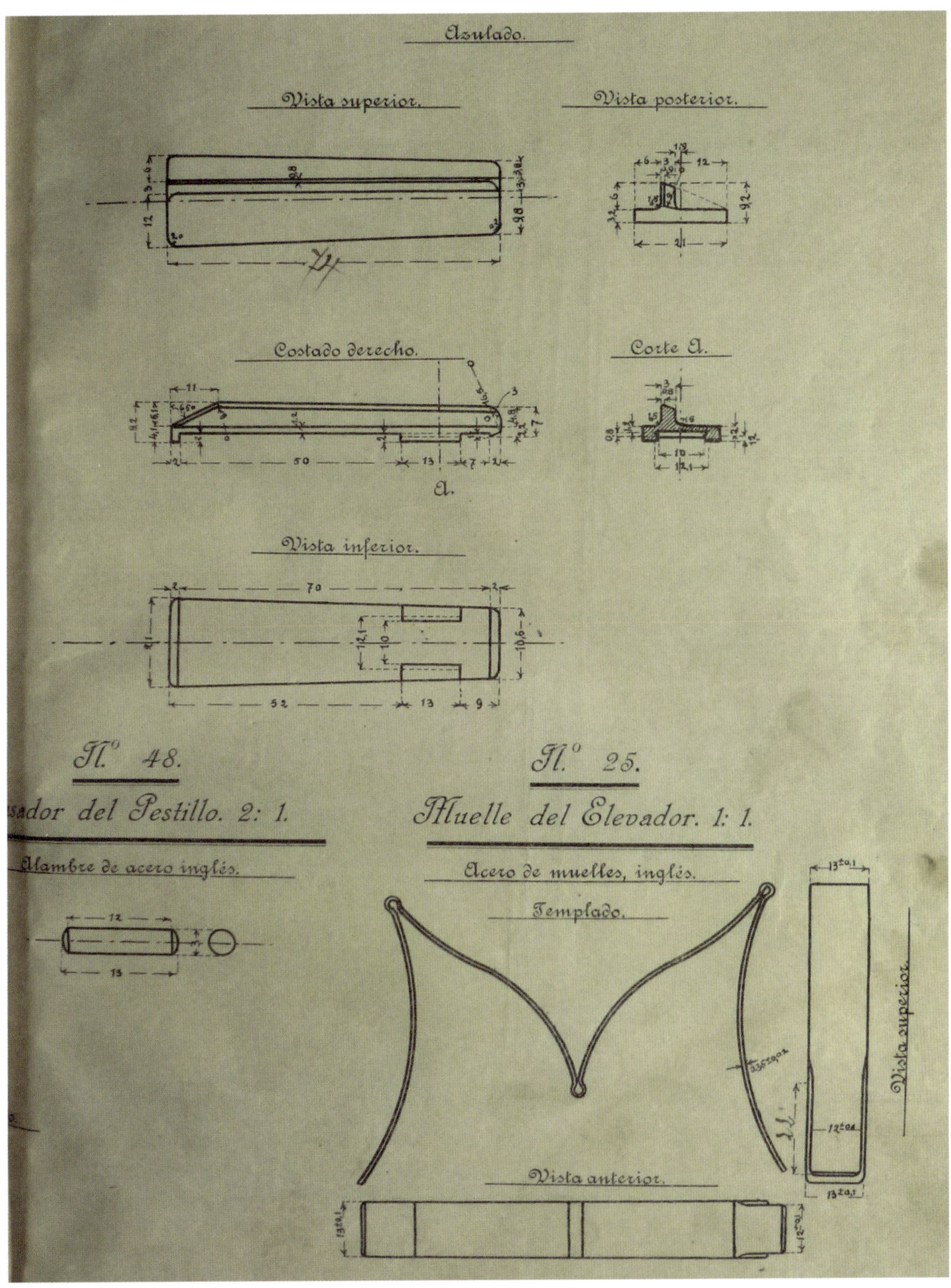

The follower and magazine leaf spring to the Chilean Model 1895.
Unknown author. 1897a. *Atlas del fusil Mauser 7mm Modelo Chileno 1895*. Berlin: Ludwig Loewe.

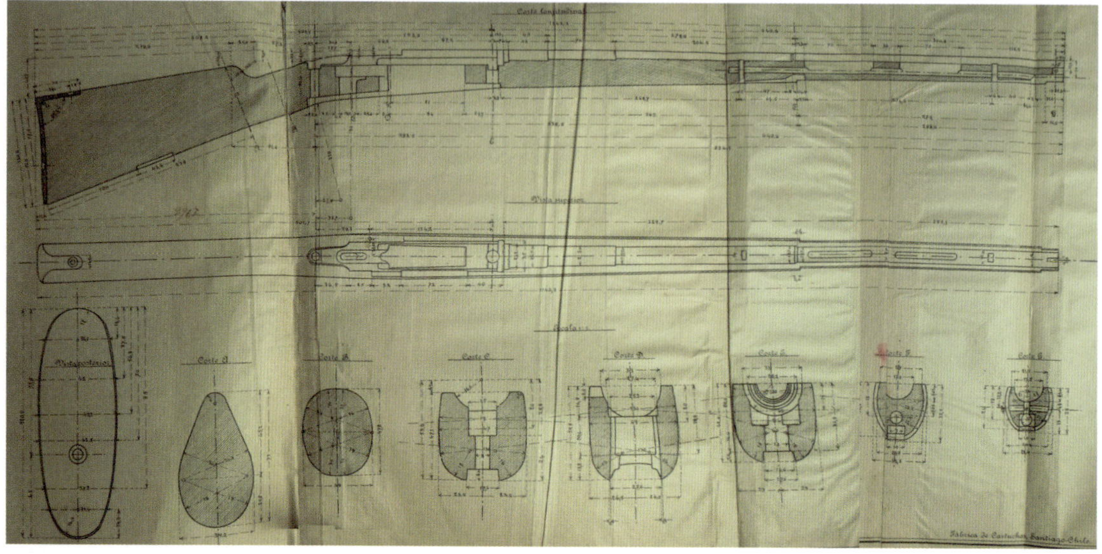

Rifle stock to the Chilean Model 1895.
Unknown author. 1897a. *Atlas del fusil Mauser 7mm Modelo Chileno 1895*. Berlin: Ludwig Loewe.

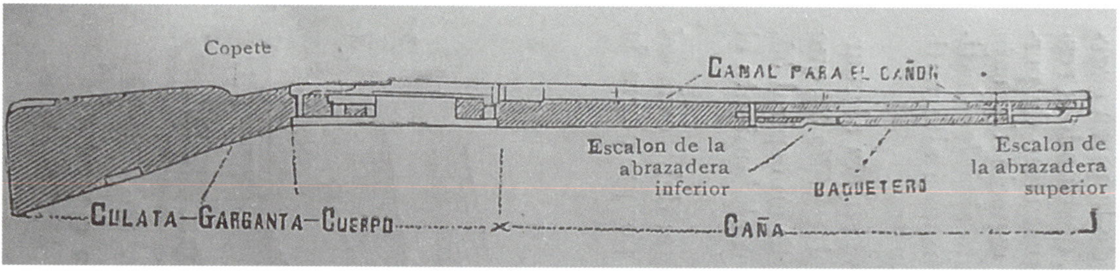

Stock to the rifle version of the Chilean Model 1895.
Boado y Castro, J. 1915. *Cartilla del fusil i la carabina Mauser Chilena Modelo 1895 por el Comandante Don José Boado i Castro i Corregida para el fusil transformado en 1912 por el Inspección de Fábricas i Maestranzas del Ejército*. Santiago, Chile: Imprenta de la Inspección de Fábricas i Maestranzas del Ejército.

When the thickness of the nose cap was included, the total length of a rifle's stock was 1,144 mm (Boado y Castro 1915, pp. 39–40).

Handguard

For the rifle, the handguard was 363 mm long (Unknown author 1897a, p. 18). All handguards—whether for rifles or both configurations of carbines—were fabricated from walnut wood. As the name implies, the primary purpose of the handguard was to protect the shooter from burning himself on a hot barrel (Boado y Castro 1896a, p. 15; 1915, p. 16).

Stock Fittings

For the rifle, the rear or lower sling swivel was pinned perpendicular to its base, allowing a limited range of rotation. The base itself was then screwed into the middle of the bottom face on the butt of the stock. For the carbines, the rear sling swivel and base—while identical to that of the rifle—were positioned differently just behind the wrist of the stock and perpendicular when compared to that of the rifle, through both primary faces of the butt of the stock. Importantly, both configurations of the carbine also had a corresponding baseplate on the right butt of the stock that allowed clamping of the two bases through the stock by means of two screws. The carbine's rear sling swivel was further distinguished by having a pronounced

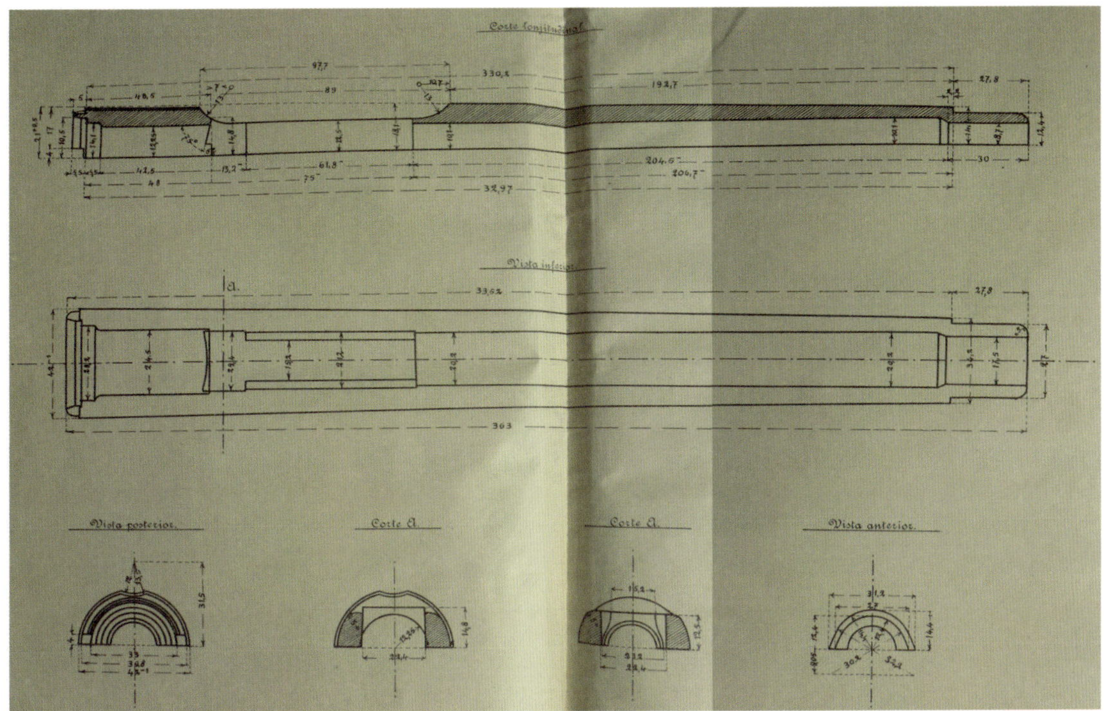

The handguard for the rifle version of the Chilean Model 1895.
Unknown author. 1897a. *Atlas del fusil Mauser 7mm Modelo Chileno 1895*. Berlin: Ludwig Loewe.

saddle ring. The lower or rear barrel band of the rifle has the sling swivel that was pinned to its underside, allowing a limited degree of rotation. For both configurations of the carbine, the front sling swivel was pinned to the left of the lower barrel band and also allowed a limited degree of rotation. The lower barrel band also served to secure the front end of the handguard to the rest of the stock, while the handguard retaining ring secured its back portion to the receiver. For the rifle and both configurations of carbine, the upper or front barrel band was identical, marked by having a pronounced stud to its underside to allow the attachment of the bayonet. The upper barrel band also enclosed the T-shaped nose cap and the pin that secured it through the stock. Upper and lower barrel bands were secured to the stock by means of L-shaped retaining springs that had projections to their forward face, allowing them to securely clip into corresponding recesses on the inside of the barrel bands. Like the nose cap, the retaining spring to the upper barrel band had a circular hole to allow the cleaning rod to pass through. The lower retaining spring had a smaller-diameter threaded hole that allowed the corresponding end of the cleaning rod to be secured. In all instances, the nose cap, butt plate, and retaining springs were identical. The butt plate was an oval design with a small projection to its upper portion and was fixed to the stock with two screws (Boado y Castro 1896a, pp. 17–18; 1915, pp. 17–18, 20). The butt plate was constructed from the same cast, low-carbon steel used in numerous components, such as the barrel bands (Unknown author 1897a, p. 16).

Cleaning Rod

The cleaning rod for the Chilean 1895 consisted of an "English spring steel" dowel 6.5 mm in diameter and, for the rifle, with a length of 438.7 mm. From observation, the cleaning rod for the extended carbine was 75 mm shorter than that of the rifle. At one end, the cleaning rod had an M4.5 mm *male* threaded portion, while on the opposite end, an identical *female* thread was tapped to allow the linking of two or more cleaning rods together

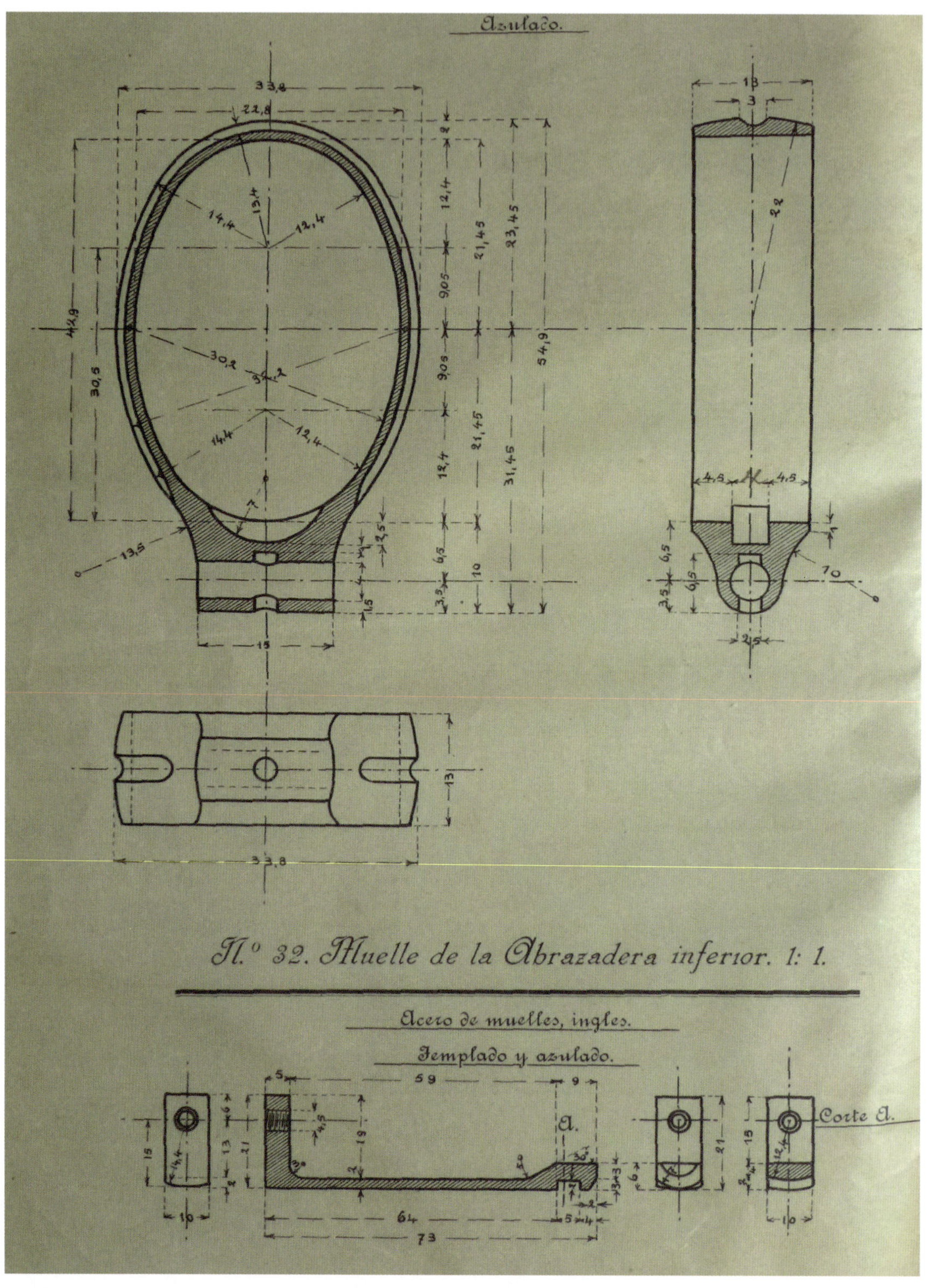

The lower barrel band and band spring of the Chilean Model 1895.
Unknown author. 1897a. *Atlas del fusil Mauser 7mm Modelo Chileno 1895*. Berlin: Ludwig Loewe.

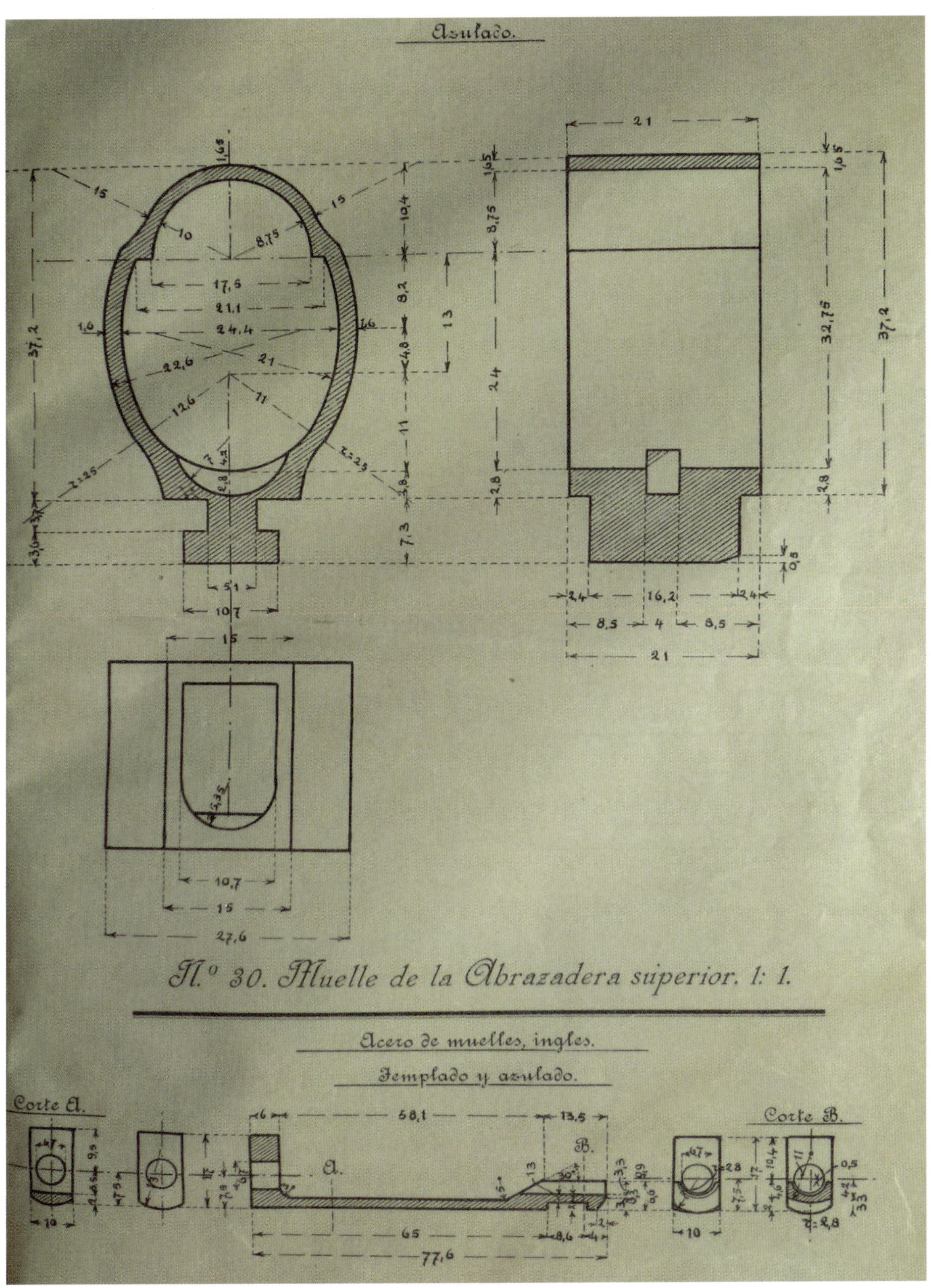

The upper barrel band and band spring to the rifle version of the Chilean Model 1895.
Unknown author. 1897a. *Atlas del fusil Mauser 7mm Modelo Chileno 1895*. Berlin: Ludwig Loewe.

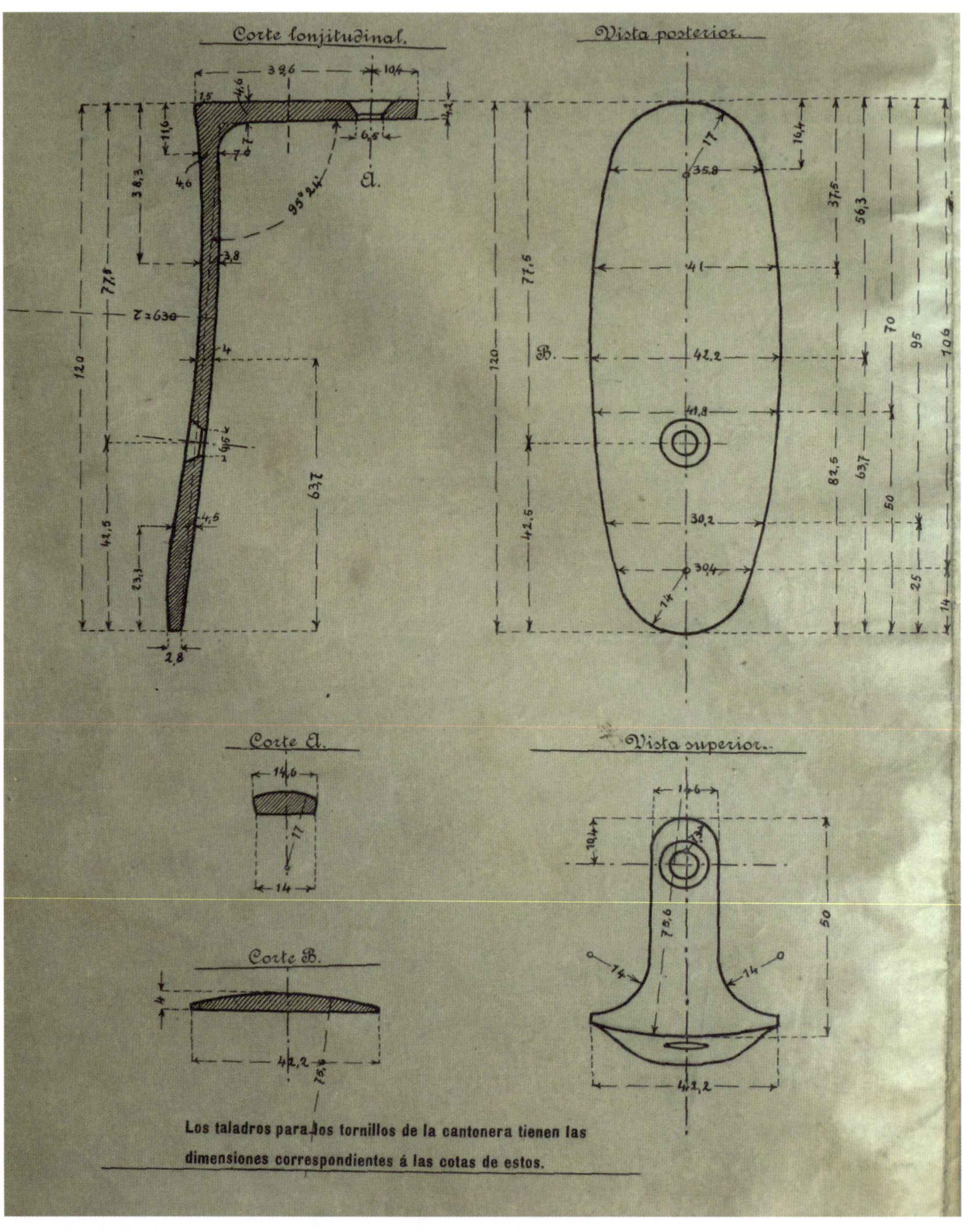

Butt plate of the Chilean Model 1895.
Unknown author. 1897a. *Atlas del fusil Mauser 7mm Modelo Chileno 1895*. Berlin: Ludwig Loewe.

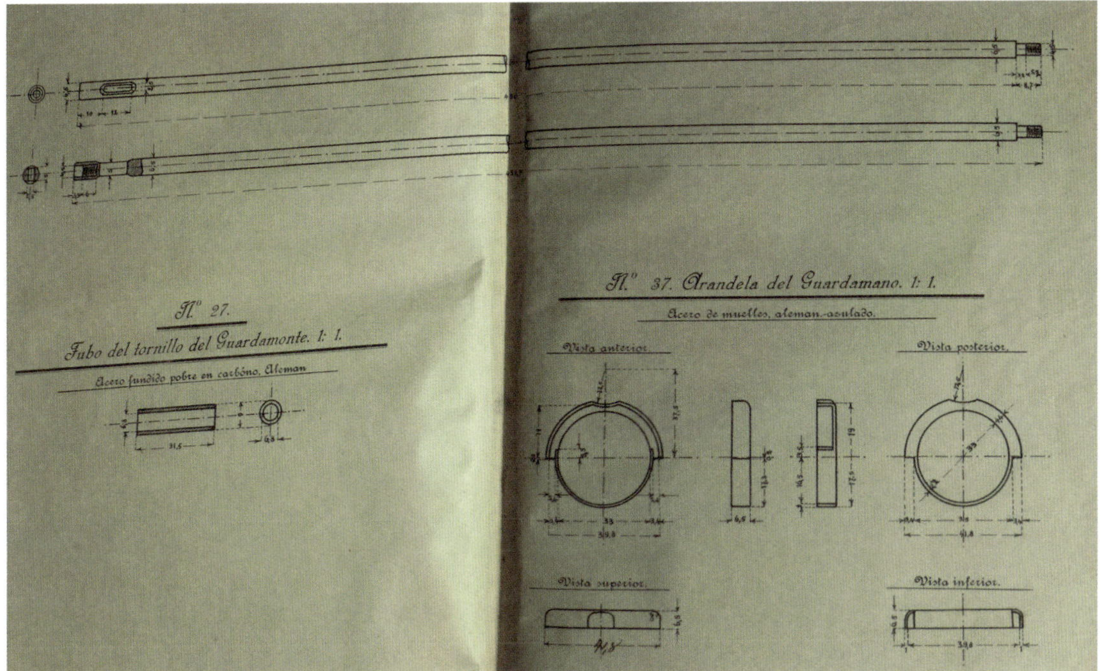

The rifle cleaning rod, handguard retaining ring, and stock pillar to the Chilean Model 1895. Unknown author. 1897a. *Atlas del fusil Mauser 7mm Modelo Chileno 1895.* Berlin: Ludwig Loewe.

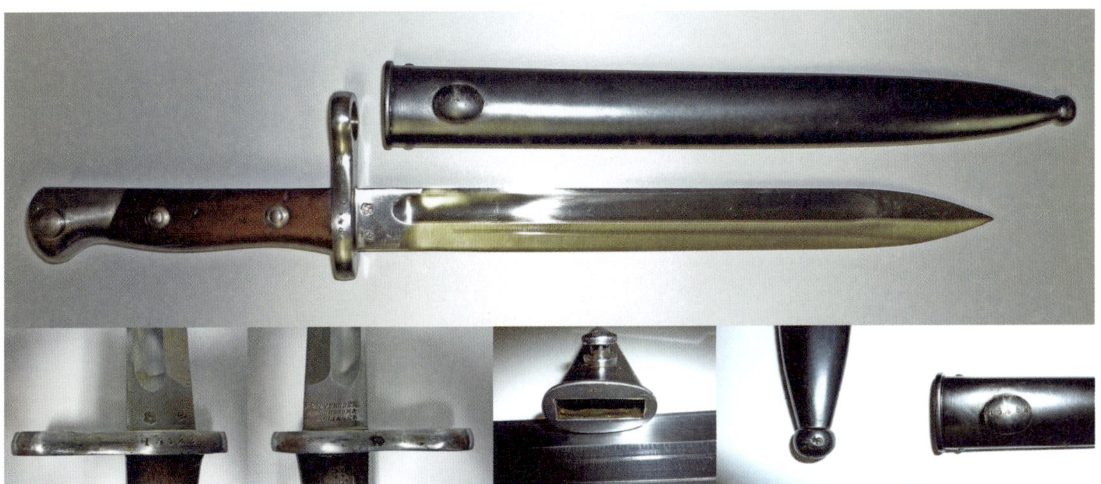

Bayonet to the Chilean Model 1895. *Author*

for cleaning. This opposite end also had a 12 × 2.5 mm oval slot that allowed a cleaning patch to be passed through the cleaning rod (Boado y Castro 1896a, pp. 15–16; 1915, p. 16; Unknown author 1897a, p. 15).

It is interesting to note that in the spare-parts contracts of 1896 and 1898 (tables 5 and 8), many thousands of special wooden cleaning rods appear to have been ordered both for rifles and carbines.

Bayonet

The bayonet had an overall length of 375.5 mm, comprising a blade with a length of 253 mm, a grip with a length of 115 mm, and a guard with a thickness of 7.5 mm (Unknown author 1897a, p. 11). It was fixed to the Chilean 1895 by sliding the hole in the top portion of the cross guard over

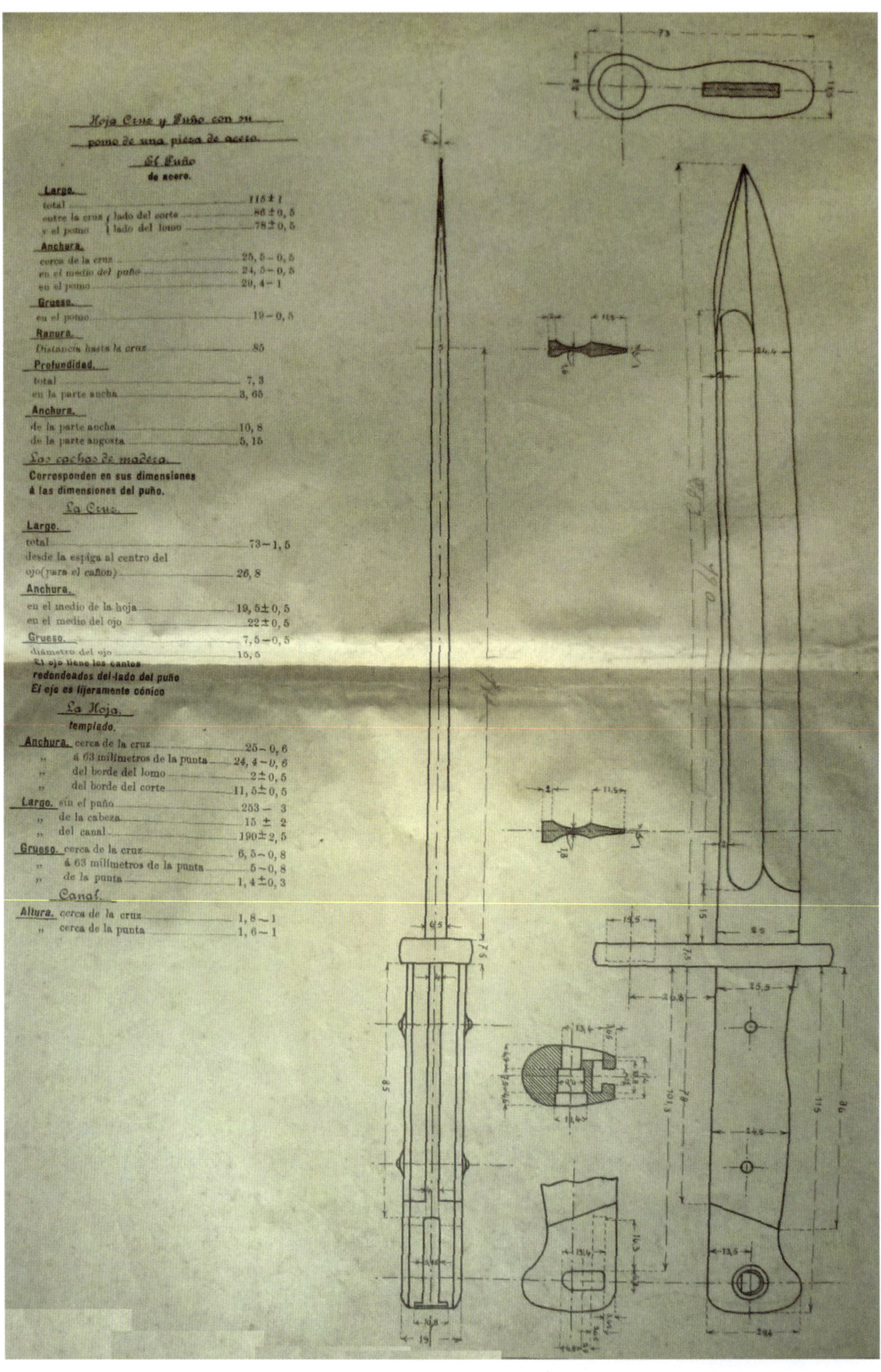

Technical drawing of the bayonet to the Chilean Model 1895.
Unknown author. 1897a. *Atlas del fusil Mauser 7mm Modelo Chileno 1895*. Berlin: Ludwig Loewe.

the front of the barrel. At its rear pommel, the bayonet slid onto the front barrel band's T-shaped projection via a matching slot. The bayonet was then locked in place by a spring-loaded button in the rear pommel. In addition to the bayonet proper, sheet-metal sheaths were also evident. These had a riveted throat insert to guide and retain the blade and a stud that was soldered to the surface of the sheath to allow its transport in a leather frog (Boado y Castro 1915, pp. 18–19).

A key point is that Model 1895s were delivered with a bayonet and sheath that were serial numbered to each individual rifle or carbine, being present on the bayonet cross guard and the frog stud to the sheath.

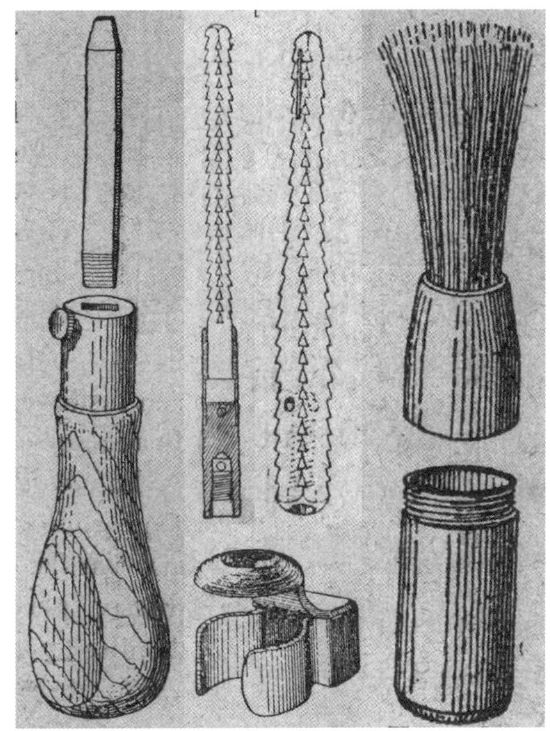

The cleaning jags, screwdrivers, muzzle covers, and brushes issued with the Chilean Model 1895.
Boado y Castro, J. 1896a. *Cartilla del fusil Mauser Chileno Modelo 1895 calibre de 7mm para uso del soldado del Ejército de Chile*. Santiago, Chile: Imprenta Mejia.

Chapter 2: The Chilean Mauser Model of 1912

Mauser Developments 1894–1898

With the development of the Model 1893, Mauser had undoubtedly revolutionized military small arms, but better was yet to come.

In the 1880s, Germany was justifiably proud of its Mauser Model 1871/84s. Just eighteen months after the Germans finished reequipping their army with 740,000 of these new Mausers in 1886, France introduced a new rifle, the Lebel Model 1886, which fired a revolutionary smokeless 8 mm cartridge that had a metal-jacketed projectile (Dorn Brose 2004, pp. 47–50; Olson 1976, pp. 35–40).

This new French threat so alarmed the Germans that a decision was made to discard the black powder 11 mm Mausers and replace them with a newer, small-bore rifle that could also fire smokeless ammunition. First, a new 57 mm cartridge case was devised that featured a rimless design credited to Col. Rubin of Switzerland. Next, a 7.9 mm cupronickel metal-jacketed projectile was designed, which was initially developed in 1874 by Lt. Col. Bode of the Prussian army, then further developed by Rubin. The result was the tremendously important 7.9 × 57 mm cartridge that would dominate German small arms until the end of World War II (Olson 1976, pp. 40–42).

Germany's answer to the Lebel was the Gewehr 1888, which was designed by a commission headed by Maj. Habrecht of the Spandau armory in Berlin. Designed around the new 7.9 × 57 mm cartridge, the Gewehr 1888 incorporated an improved Mauser 71 action with a Mannlicher magazine that was then married to a small-bore barrel with a steel jacket. In hindsight, the Gewehr 1888 can be seen as a costly mistake, since it suffered from numerous problems mostly associated with the higher pressures generated by its new smokeless ammunition, including busted barrels, double feeding, and gas escape into the shooter's face. The result was that it was not well regarded by troops and had to be replaced (Seel 1986, p. 53).

In an effort to resolve this deteriorating situation, German military authorities turned to Mauser. On 10 May 1894, Paul Mauser traveled to Spandau and presented numerous rifles that incorporated

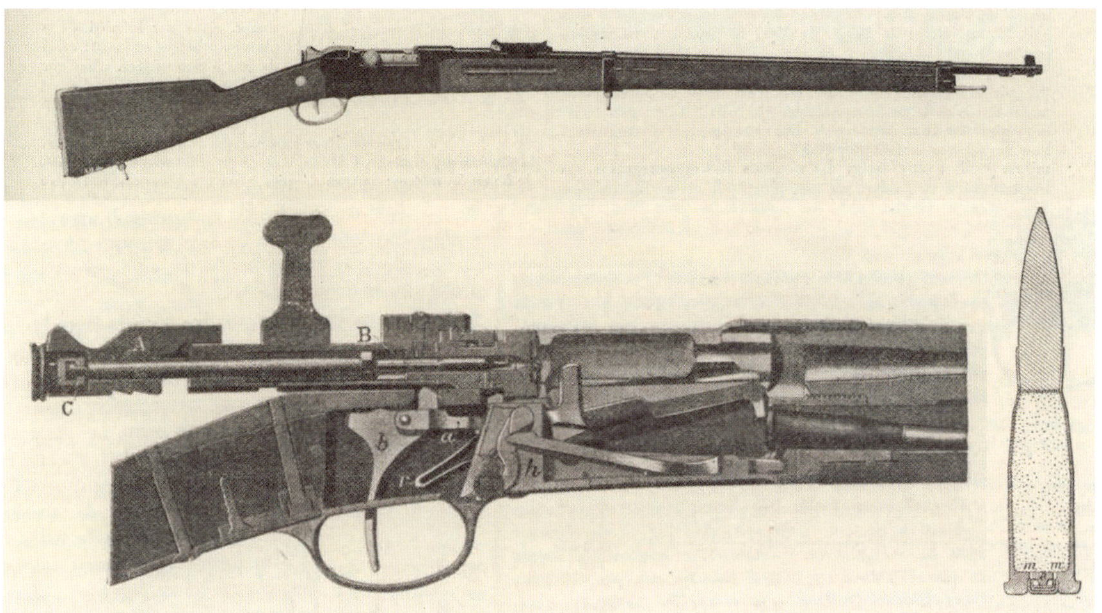

The Lebel Model 1886 rifle with the modifications of 1893.
Reynier, A. 1915. "Art militaire: Les fusils de guerre actuels." *Le Genie Civil: Revue Generale Hebdomadaire des Industries Francaises et Etrangeres* 66, no. 22: 337–344.

his latest action, magazine, and a jacketed barrel arrangement. This demonstration proved successful, and in November 1894, approximately 2,000 rifles of this type were ordered for troop trials. Issued with a production order in January 1895, these rifles, which became known as Model 95 (not to be confused with the Chilean Model 1895), were manufactured between 16 March and 27 July 1895. While all this was happening, military authorities were also reconsidering the 7.9 × 57 mm cartridge and conducted an investigation into various smaller calibers ranging from 6.5 to 4 mm. Mauser subsequently sent small-bore rifles to Spandau on 18 June 1895, followed by twenty additional rifles in February 1896. To demonstrate the viability of these smaller calibers, military authorities, via the Spandau armory, ordered approximately 2,125 rifles and 479,000 stripper clips in 6 mm caliber on 13 October 1896. The last of these rifles were delivered on 16 March 1897. In addition to these 2,125 rifles, a further sixty rifles were also manufactured and subsequently delivered to Spandau in August 1897 (Seel 1986, p. 53). Through correspondence with Jon Speed in 2017, it has been clarified that the 6 mm caliber was not adopted because its chamber pressures (over 4,000 atmospheres) were considered too high when compared to those of the 8 mm at approximately 3,200–3,600 atmospheres; it likewise became unstable at longer ranges.

Because of logistical considerations, and despite the theoretical ballistic advantages offered by the 6 mm caliber, military authorities eventually decided to stay with the 7.9 × 57 mm cartridge. On 1 September 1897, Paul Mauser again traveled to Spandau with three of his latest rifles chambered in 7.9 × 57 mm. These rifles, which included all the improvements of the previous two test models, would be the prototypes for Mauser's crowning glory: the Model 1898. In mid-January 1898, Paul Mauser again traveled to Spandau, and while there he received a rifle from Oberndorf that had a heavier receiver ring to accommodate stronger barrel threads. The Spandau armory subsequently ordered five of these rifles. Finally, on 5 April 1898, the Gewehr 98 was adopted by a cabinet decree (Seel 1986, pp. 53–54). In 1901, the first German troops—including the East Asian Expeditionary Force, the navy, and three premier Prussian army corps—were issued the Gewehr 98. The following year, the first Central American military to acquire a version of the Model 1898 was Mexico with its

Model 1902, which was essentially a 98 action in a Model 1893 stock (Ball 2011, pp. 173, 255–256). Having thus entered the Central and South American markets, the Mauser Model 1898 would afterward enjoy tremendous success.

Spare Parts, Ammunition, and the Modelo 1912

In 1895, Austria, having lost out to Germany regarding Chile's new service rifle, had to be satisfied with orders for fifty million cartridges intended for Chile's Mauser rifles and existing Mannlichers, with these orders going to Keller & Co. (Schaefer 1974, pp. 165, 267). Austria nevertheless gained a further opportunity at redemption in 1910, when Chile decided it needed more rifles, carbines, ammunition, and spare parts because the simmering Tacna and Arica question had again reached a boil.

While hard fought, the spare parts and ammunition orders were insignificant in relation to the real prize on offer in 1910–1911: more Mauser rifles and carbines. In 1910, because of escalating tensions with Peru, it was decided that Chile needed a further 30,000 rifles and 4,000 carbines. As part of the initial ammunition order for thirty million rounds of ammunition already identified in chapter 1, the decision as to which company would manufacture these weapons was transferred to the Chilean Weapons Commission in Berlin.

Despite having already signed the ammunition contract with Keller & Co. in late June 1911, the rifle and carbine supplier had yet to be decided. Between 22 and 31 August 1911, Austrian prince Windisch-Graetz went to Berlin and met several times with Gen. Pinto Concha and Col. Luis Altamirano of the Chilean Weapons Commission. During these meetings, both officers confirmed their faith in Austrian industry and also accepted

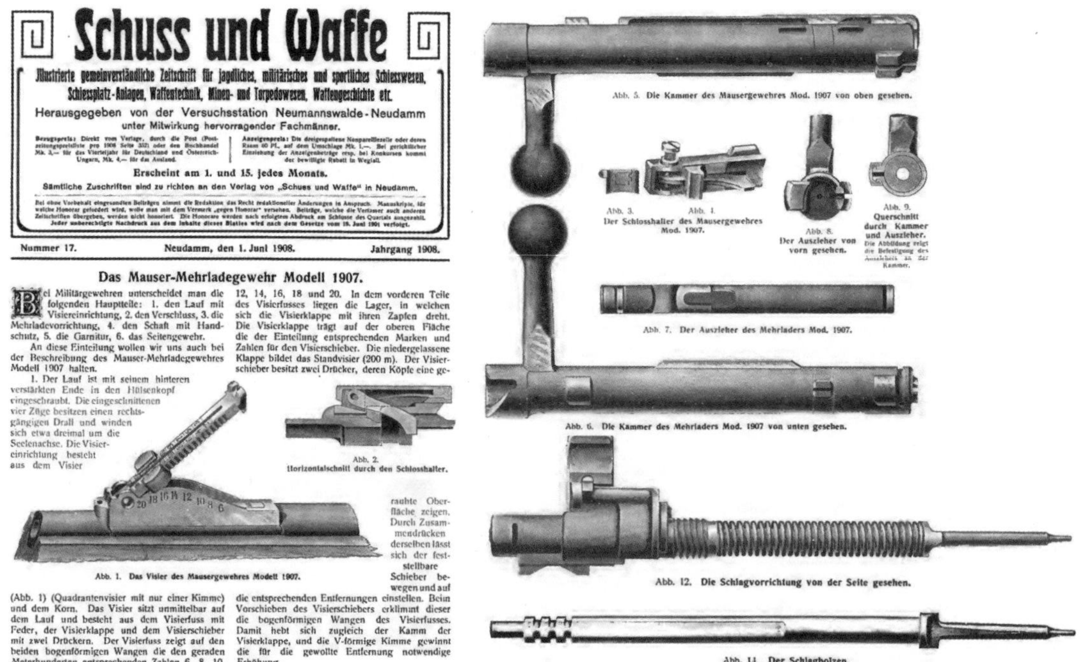

Schuss und Waffe

Illustrierte gemeinverständliche Zeitschrift für jagdliches, militärisches und sportliches Schiesswesen, Schiessplatz-Anlagen, Waffentechnik, Minen- und Torpedowesen, Waffengeschichte etc.

Herausgegeben von der Versuchsstation Neumannswalde-Neudamm unter Mitwirkung hervorragender Fachmänner.

Bezugspreis: Direkt vom Verlage, durch die Post (Postzeitungspreisliste pro 1908 Seite 352) oder den Buchhandel Mk. 3,— für das Vierteljahr für Deutschland und Österreich-Ungarn, Mk. 4,— für das Ausland.

Anzeigenpreis: Die dreigespaltene Nonpareillezeile oder deren Raum 60 Pf., auf dem Umschlage Mk. 1,—. Bei gerichtlicher Einziehung der Anzeigenbeträge resp. bei Konkursen kommt der bewilligte Rabatt in Wegfall.

Erscheint am 1. und 15. jedes Monats.

Sämtliche Zuschriften sind zu richten an den Verlag von „Schuss und Waffe“ in Neudamm.

Bei ohne Vorbehalt eingesandten Beiträgen nimmt die Redaktion das Recht redaktioneller Änderungen in Anspruch. Manuskripte, für welche Honorar gefordert wird, wolle man mit dem Vermerk „gegen Honorar“ versehen. Beiträge, welche die Verfasser auch anderen Zeitschriften übergeben, werden nicht honoriert. Die Honorare werden nach erfolgtem Abdruck am Schlusse des Quartals ausgezahlt. Jeder unberechtigte Nachdruck aus dem Inhalte dieses Blattes wird nach dem Gesetze vom 19. Juni 1901 verfolgt.

Nummer 17. Neudamm, den 1. Juni 1908. Jahrgang 1908.

Das Mauser-Mehrladegewehr Modell 1907.

Bei Militärgewehren unterscheidet man die folgenden Hauptteile: 1. den Lauf mit Visiereinrichtung, 2. den Verschluss, 3. die Mehrladevorrichtung, 4. den Schaft mit Handschutz, 5. die Garnitur, 6. das Seitengewehr.

An diese Einteilung wollen wir uns auch bei der Beschreibung des Mauser-Mehrladegewehres Modell 1907 halten.

1. Der Lauf ist mit seinem hinteren verstärkten Ende in den Hülsenkopf eingeschraubt. Die eingeschnittenen vier Züge besitzen einen rechtsgängigen Drall und winden sich etwa dreimal um die Seelenachse. Die Visiereinrichtung besteht aus dem Visier (Abb. 1) (Quadrantenvisier mit nur einer Kimme) und dem Korn. Das Visier sitzt unmittelbar auf dem Lauf und besteht aus dem Visierfuss mit Feder, der Visierklappe und dem Visierschieber mit zwei Drückern. Der Visierfuss zeigt auf den beiden bogenförmigen Wangen die den geraden Meterhunderten entsprechenden Zahlen 6, 8, 10, 12, 14, 16, 18 und 20. In dem vorderen Teile des Visierfusses liegen die Lager, in welchen sich die Visierklappe mit ihren Zapfen dreht. Die Visierklappe trägt auf der oberen Fläche die der Einteilung entsprechenden Marken und Zahlen für den Visierschieber. Die niedergelassene Klappe bildet das Standvisier (200 m). Der Visierschieber besitzt zwei Drücker, deren Köpfe eine gerauhte Oberfläche zeigen. Durch Zusammendrücken derselben lässt sich der feststellbare Schieber bewegen und auf die entsprechenden Entfernungen einstellen. Beim Vorschieben des Visierschiebers erklimmt dieser die bogenförmigen Wangen des Visierfusses. Damit hebt sich zugleich der Kamm der Visierklappe, und die V-förmige Kimme gewinnt die für die gewollte Entfernung notwendige Erhöhung.

Abb. 1. Das Visier des Mausergewehres Modell 1907.

Abb. 2. Horizontalschnitt durch den Schlosshalter.

Abb. 5. Die Kammer des Mausergewehres Mod. 1907 von oben gesehen.

Abb. 3. Abb. 4. Der Schlosshalter des Mausergewehres Mod. 1907.

Abb. 8. Der Auszieher von vorn gesehen.

Abb. 9. Querschnitt durch Kammer und Auszieher. Die Abbildung zeigt die Befestigung des Kammer.

Abb. 7. Der Auszieher des Mehrladers Mod. 1907.

Abb. 6. Die Kammer des Mehrladers Mod. 1907 von unten gesehen.

Abb. 12. Die Schlagvorrichtung von der Seite gesehen.

Abb. 14. Der Schlagbolzen.

Images from a 1908 article in *Schuss und Waffe* depicting the Mauser Model 1907.
Neumann, J. 1908. "Das Mauser-Mehrladergewehr Modell 1907." *Schuss und Waffe: Illustrierte gemeinverständliche Zeitschrift für jagdliches, militärisches und sportliches Schiesswesen, Schiessplatz-Anlagen. Waffentechnik, Minen- und Torpedowesen, Waffengeschichte, etc.* 17 (1 June 1908): 405–409.

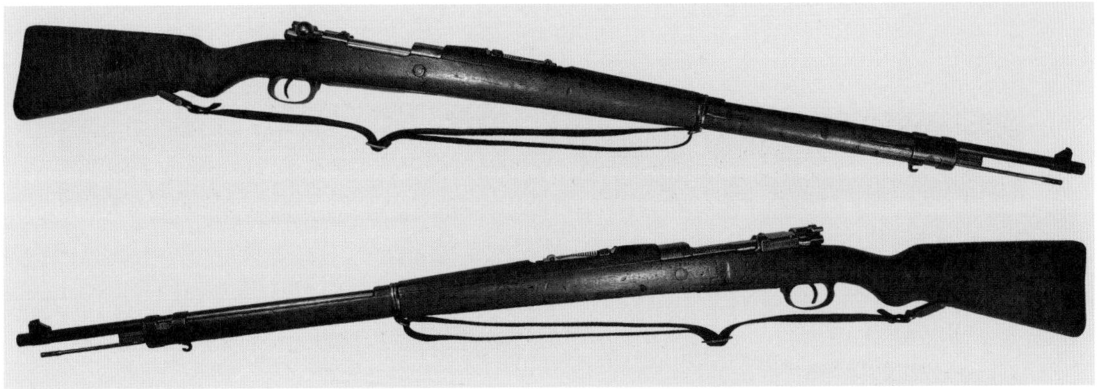

Left- and right-hand views of the rifle version of the Chilean Model 1912 that is still chambered for its original 7 x 57 mm cartridge. *Author*

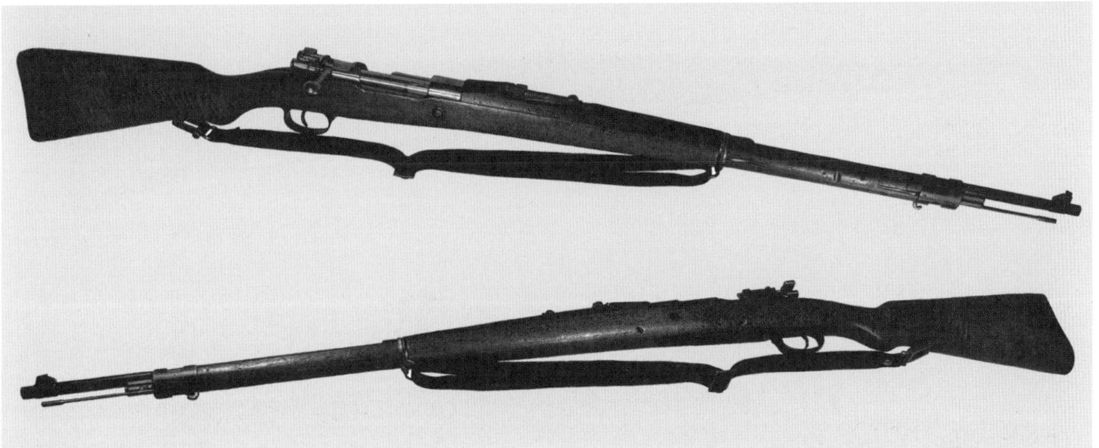

Oblique views of the Chilean Model 1912 rifle. *Author*

an offer to visit the Austrian factories of OEWG and Keller & Co. Concha consequently awarded the rifle and carbine contract to OEWG while visiting the OEWG factory. DWM was mortified when they received news of the contract and quickly mobilized its supporters in Chile to counter this decision (Sater and Herwig 1999, pp. 154–155).

In September 1911, news reached Santiago that Peru had procured numerous artillery pieces from Schneider-Canet and 15,000 to 45,000 rifles from DWM. This news coincided with the concerted attacks on OEWG in the Chilean media, particularly *El Mercurio*, which published a scathing article on 11 October 1911 that condemned the squander of approximately one million pesos on useless spare parts. It was argued that it would be simple stupidity to order rifles and carbines from a company that could not even manufacture spare parts. To avert a possible military confrontation with Peru and considering the supposed catastrophic quality of the spare parts, the Chilean cabinet, under the chairmanship of the president, met on 13 October 1911. To remedy this catastrophic situation, it was decided to immediately redirect the already agreed-on purchases of 30,000 rifles, 4,000 carbines, and thirty million rounds of ammunition from OEWG to DWM. Miraculously, the very next day after this meeting, the Chilean Weapons Commission in Berlin received a DWM quote that stipulated prices, conditions, and delivery schedules (Schaefer 1974, pp. 168–169).

It then transpired that DWM had bitten off more than it could chew. While DWM could have easily fulfilled the cartridge order, the rifles and

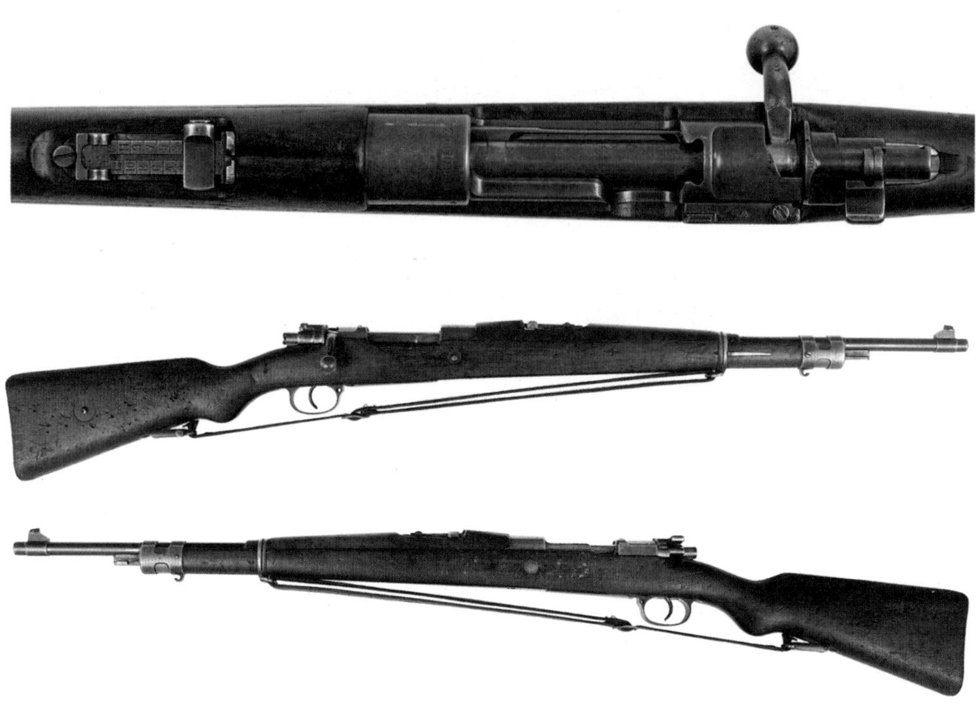

Top, left, and right views of the carbine version of the Chilean Model 1912 that is still chambered for its original 7 x 57 mm cartridge. *Pedro Bello*

Left and right views of the carbine version of the Chilean Model 1912. In all probability, the blue to the receiver is a later arsenal or civilian addition. *Jon Magnuson*

carbines were problematic because its factories were operating at full capacity; the Berlin factory was fulfilling a 100,000 Brazilian order, while the Waffenfabrik Mauser in Oberndorf was occupied with Peruvian rifles (Schaefer 1974, p. 169). Additionally, on 20 January 1909, Argentina had also contracted for the supply of 127,000 rifles and 30,000 carbines, with a further 33,000 rifles and 4,000 carbines on 4 November 1911, all of which were manufactured at the Berlin factories of DWM and were then shipped between November 1909 and April 1912 (Webster 2003, pp. 129, 179).

DWM thus became coy and proposed to cancel the order. DWM soon changed course after

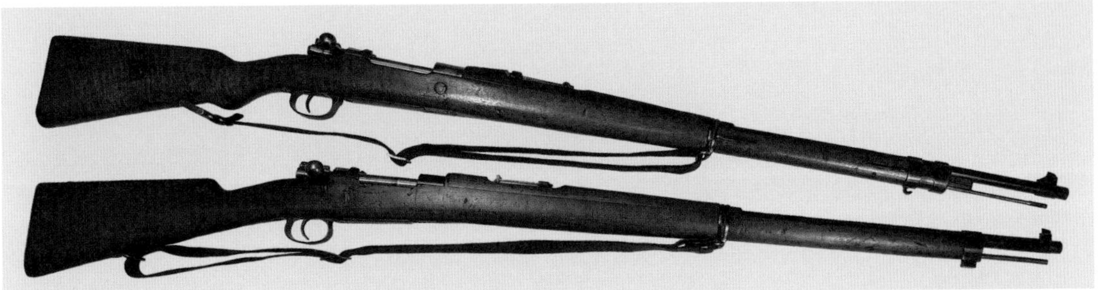

A comparison between the Chilean Model 1895 (*bottom*) and 1912 (*top*) rifles. *Author*

discovering in a conference with the Weapons Commission that if it canceled the order, it would likewise lose the ammunition order. Despite the Chileans' redirection of the rifle-and-carbine order, OEWG's lobbying efforts were still ongoing. When Austrian ambassador Styrcea contacted Chilean foreign minister Rodriguez regarding ensuring the strict and scrupulous examination of spare parts, he had also petitioned for the rifle-and-carbine contract. Quite bluntly, Styrcea proposed to Rodriguez that when the accusations against OEWG were proven groundless, he would expect an apology in the form of an order to OEWG for the new rifles and carbines. As such, on 8 November 1911, Styrcea handed Rodriguez a note that protested the redirected rifle-and-carbine order solely on the basis of malicious machinations originating from its competition (Schaefer 1974, pp. 169, 170).

Without waiting on the outcome of the spare parts inquiry, DWM informed the Weapons Commission in November 1911 that it would ensure the rapid supply of rifles, carbines, and ammunition, but only on condition that Chile promised not to procure them from OEWG. Chilean ambassador Matte was then again instructed on 14 November 1911 by the Chilean minister of war to seek updated price and delivery schedules from DWM. While all this was transpiring, Körner, who had been sent by Matte to study the production facilities of Waffenfabrik Mauser, replayed the patent dispute of 1894 and informed the Chilean ambassador that only DWM and Waffenfabrik Mauser were legally entitled to produce the Model 1898. DWM's management then assured Matte that they would make every attempt to abide by their promised delivery schedules, but in order to firmly establish them, they needed a few days' postponement. On face value this delay might have seemed reasonable, but in reality it was merely a ploy by DWM to conclude an initial agreement with OEWG. In late November 1911, it would have become increasingly clear that the spare-parts inquiry would find in favor of OEWG. As such, on 23 November, Matte organized a meeting between the directors of the two competing firms—A. Schick from OEWG and Max Kosegarten from DWM—at which it was agreed that OEWG would manufacture the rifles and carbines. But this was decided only after OEWG, furious at having been excluded from the South American market—and Chile in particular—had threatened to undercut DWM prices globally. Painfully aware that the 1905 and 1907 cartel agreements were at stake, Kosegarten therefore relented and agreed to hire OEWG as a subcontractor. DWM did have a proviso, which Kosegarten communicated to Matte on 24 November, that it would have to be paid to ensure the quality of the OEWG-manufactured rifles and carbines (Schaefer 1974, pp. 169–171).

Fully conscious that Chile had little choice, Minister of War Alejandro Huneeus subsequently invited the representatives of OEWG in Santiago to a meeting on 1 December; here he informed them that Chile would award the rifle-and-carbine contract to OEWG. As compensation, Huneeus also offered OEWG the work to convert 30,000 older Mauser rifles to the new spitzer munition (Schaefer 1974, p. 170). Interestingly, while Matte had managed to gain a very small price reduction from DWM/OEWG, the estimated cost of DWM's quality guarantee was still substantial at 200,000–300,000 francs (Sater and Herwig 1999, p. 157). In light of this and the minimum cartel price of seventy-five francs per rifle, it is estimated that Chile would have paid between 2.7 and 3.1 million

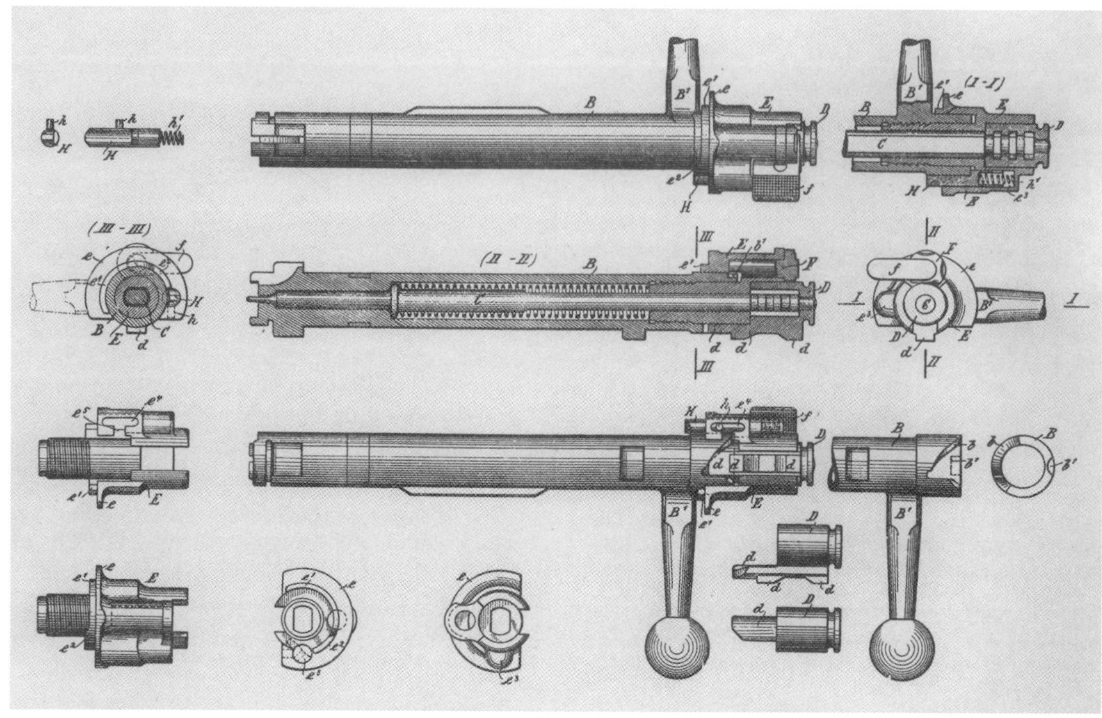

German patent 90305 as granted on 30 October 1895, showing the seminal body design to the Mauser Model 1898. Note that the firing pin is still that of the Mauser Model 1893.
Mauser, P. 1895. Germany Patent No. 90305. Kaiserliche Patentamt.

francs for its new rifles and carbines, while in all probability it was toward the higher estimate.

Following the spare-parts, ammunition, and rifle/carbine procurement shambles of 1911, both Matte and Pinto Concha lost their positions. The Chilean Weapons Commission was also disbanded by Huneeus, who then transferred the authority for future weapons purchases to the Chilean diplomatic envoy accredited to each European capital. Huneeus stated that the commission was being dismissed to ensure good public admiration and not—as some newspapers had alleged—for political reasons. Huneeus reasoned that the commission had become too independent and often acted without first consulting local diplomats. In reality, it was German ambassador to Chile Friedrich Carl von Erckert, together with DWM agent in Valparaíso, Vorwerk & Co., and a Krupp director, Otto Eccius, who had engineered the demise of the Weapons Commission, Matte, and Pinto Concha. Both Matte and Pinto Concha—Erckert hypocritically reasoned in May and June 1912—had been bought by the Austrians and had thus cost German industry about fifteen million marks in lost revenue over the last few years (Sater and Herwig 1999, pp. 154, 157).

The rifles and carbines that Chile acquired in 1911 were basically Mauser Model 1898s and are known as the Modelo 1912. These rifles existed in four sequential blocks of 10,000 serial numbers. Following standard practice, each of these blocks is distinguished by an alphabetical serial prefix that corresponds either to "A," "B," "C," or "D." If only 34,000 Modelo 1912s were produced, it would be logical to state that the highest serial number evident would be D4000. However, the author has knowledge of numerous "D" serial numbers above this, with the highest being D9718, which is still in its original 7 × 57 mm caliber. Similarly, the author is aware of a 7.62 × 51 mm converted rifle with serial number D9879. Thus, to complete the "D" serial block, at some point an additional 6,000 rifles or carbines could have been purchased and delivered. Some sources have argued that the total number of OEWG-manufactured Chilean Modelo 1912 was 43,107, claiming that this total was

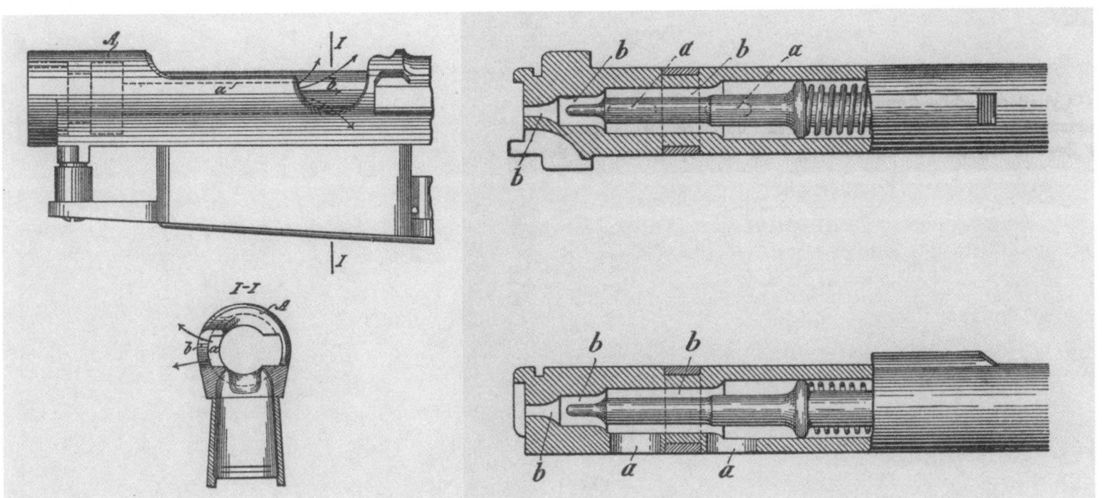

Belgian patent of 12 March 1896 for the Mauser Model 1898 gas venting. Again note the presence of the Mauser Model 1893 firing pin.
Mauser, P. 1896. Belgian Patent No. 120477. Belgian Patent Office.

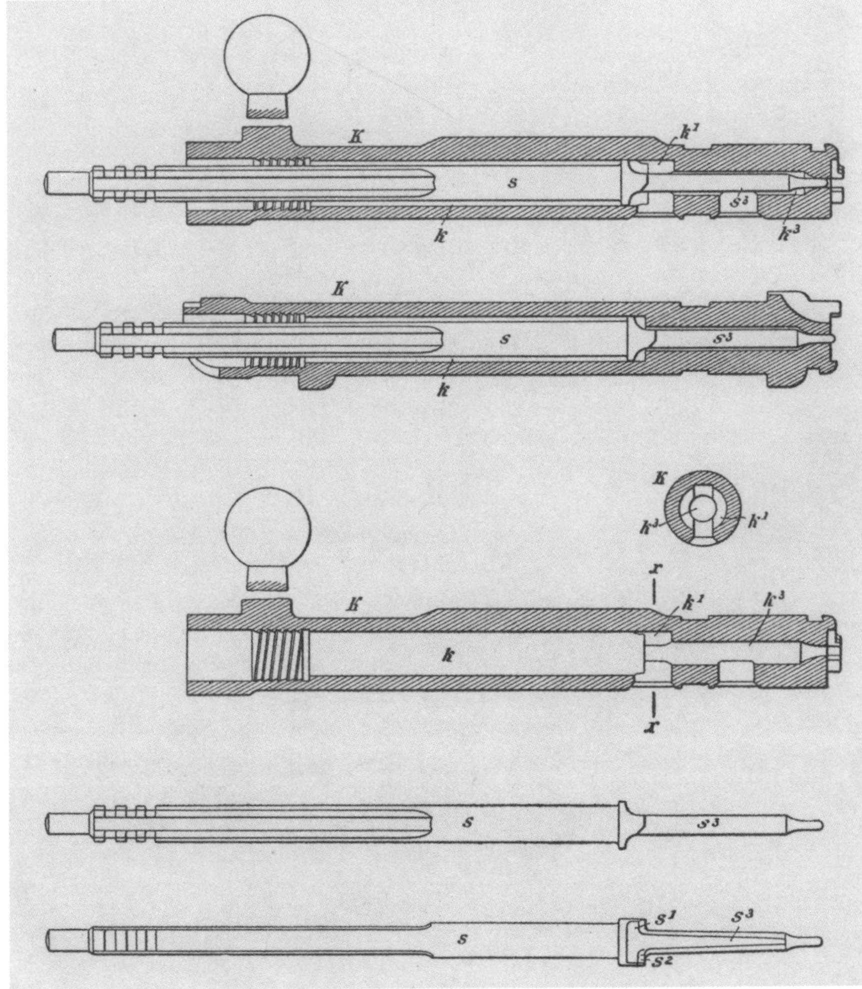

German copyright protection for Mauser Model 1898 firing-pin safety granted 22 May 1901.
Mauser, P. 1901. Germany Patent No. 154915. Deutsches Reichsgebrauchsmuster.

exclusively manufactured in 1912 (Hintermeier 2003; Neubauer 1974, p. 21). This number is largely corroborated by an internal DWM document that reported 37,500 rifles and 5,600 carbines—for a total of 43,100 units—as having been sold to Chile by OEWG in 1912 (Speed 2007, p. 432).

Remarkably, the author is also aware of two "E" serial numbers, E108 and E7031; two "F" serial numbers, F2203 and F5761; one "G" serial number, G7480; three "H" serial numbers, H1262, H4200, and H8568; one "K" serial number, K5181; and one "L" serial number, L9307. All these are described as "Mauser M.12 Cal. 7.62." Although these long arms were imported into the US in 2008 and originated in Chile, it is not known if these were OEWG-manufactured rifles.

These could in part be explained by the fact that at the outbreak of World War I, Austria was said to have commandeered 37,500 rifles and 5,600 carbines intended for Chile from OEWG warehouses (Ball 2011, p. 20). It is generally accepted that after the war, the bulk of these commandeered rifles were acquired by Yugoslavia and converted to 7.92 × 57 mm. Thus, these commandeered rifles and carbines—if they ever did exist—would never have made it to Chile. It has also been claimed that on 1 February 1912, Chile placed an order with OEWG for 97,500 rifles and 5,600 carbines following the Model 1912 specification, including bayonets, slings, muzzle protectors, and other accessories (Ortmeier 2006, p. 59). It is thus proposed by the author that the figure of 97,500 is a misprint and should in fact be 37,500.

It is therefore reasoned that the official number of Modelo 1912s produced was approximately 43,100, with 37,500 being rifles and 5,600 being carbines.

Crests, Inscriptions, Cartouches, and Proofmarks

On all Modelo 1912s—regardless of rifle or carbine designation—the left side rail of the receiver is roll-stamped with the following inscription:

An original unblued crest present on all Chilean Model 1912s. *Pedro Bello*

"WAFFENFABRIK STEYR"
"AUSTRIA"

As with almost all Mausers, the main serial number is present on the left face of the receiver's forward ring. This follows the accepted convention of an alphabetical letter followed by a four-digit number. In the case of the Modelo 1912, numerous rifles and carbines have been observed that predominantly are included in four alphabetical blocks—that is, "A," "B," "C," and "D"—with 10,000 units in each. This reasoning is confirmed by the Chilean publication *A. B. C. D. de Numeración del Fusil Mauser M.12* ("The numbering of the Model 1912: A. B. C. D.").

The full serial number is likewise present on the left side of the stock, just below the serial number on the receiver; the upper face of the stem to the bolt handle; the barrel, just ahead of the secondary torque shoulder; the forward tang of the trigger guard; the bayonet cross guard and frog stud to the scabbard of the bayonet; and the cleaning rod. The last two digits of the serial number can also be found on the rear sight ladder and its slider, the magazine floorplate, the bolt shroud, and the safety lever.

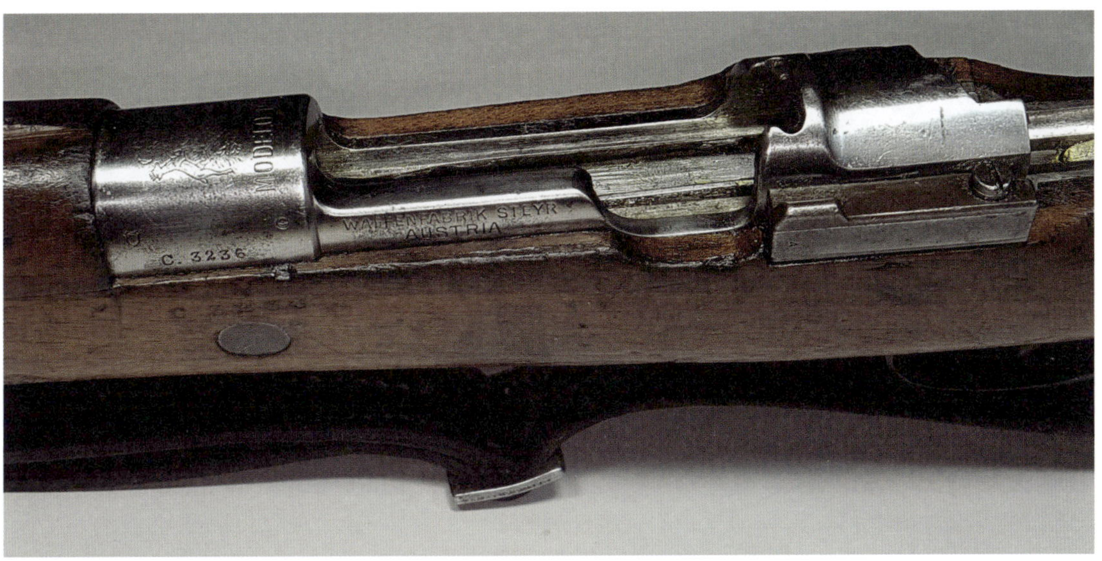

The receiver's left side rail inscription present on the Chilean Model 1912, indicating OEWG manufacture. *Author*

A large Chilean coat of arms with the words "MODELO 1912" below is roll-stamped on the upper face of the receiver's forward ring.

When compared to the Modelo 1895, the Modelo 1912 has some economy in the use of acceptance and proofing marks. The following acceptance marks are present on the Modelo 1912:

- A triangle containing a circle: front sight base, rear sight ladder and slider, ejector box and leaf spring, rear sling swivel, sear, and ball to the bayonet scabbard.
- The crossed hammer and pick: upper and lower barrel bands, bolt body, bolt shroud, safety lever, stock disk, and the rear sight base.
- A female symbol containing a dot at the center of the circular head: recoil lug and nut, trigger guard screws, extractor, the lock to the bolt shroud, and the front sight bead.
- A circle containing horizontal and vertical lines: trigger guard, magazine floorplate, barrel, and the butt plate.
- A circle containing a horizontal line with a point at its center: above and after the serial on the receiver, and the upper face of the wrist of the stock.
- A diamond containing diagonal lines that originate from the corners: cocking piece, firing pin, and the ejector.
- As with the DWM triggers of the Modelo 1895, the trigger of the Modelo 1912 has a variation of the large diamond comprising four smaller diamonds. In this instance, the symbol takes the form of a diamond with a circle at its center connected with four perpendicular lines. This variation is also found on the magazine follower.

As for the proofing marks, those present on the Modelo 1912 appear to follow a similar practice to those established on the Modelo 1895: a shield symbol stamped before and above the serial number on the left side of the receiver's forward ring; a circle with a dot at its center, with nine radiating spokes to its exterior on the ball of the bolt body; and two concentric circles connected with four spokes on the top of the barrel just ahead of the torque shoulder.

The final acceptance mark took the usual form of a stamp that was applied to the left butt of the stock, which composed the Chilean coat of arms, bounded within a circle, and had the date "1912" attached below that was itself bounded by a rectangle.

A selection of some of the acceptance marks and proofmarks present on the Chilean Model 1912. *Author and Jon Magnuson*

The cartouche present on the left butt of the stock on Chilean Model 1912s, indicating final acceptance. *Author*

The Modelo 1912 as Converted to 7.62 × 51 NATO

With the end of World War II, the Chilean communists resumed their agenda of class struggle. As part of this agenda, numerous communist ministers were subsequently appointed to the government of González Videla, who had gained power in 1946 with their help. Following a wave of increasingly violent and disruptive labor strikes organized by the communists, the Videla government soon fell out with the communists and eventually banned them in 1948.

Videla went further still; when fearing that communist countries with embassies in Santiago would ferment further unrest, his government additionally broke off diplomatic relations with these governments. He likewise removed in excess of 20,000 known communists from the voter rolls. But banning the communists did not make them simply disappear; strikes, disruptions, and inevitable military proposals for dictatorship then ensued. To add to these pressures, Videla was simultaneously faced with rising inflation, resulting in price controls and wage freezes that in turn resulted in further strikes and protests. These conditions were to worsen, and in 1952 Videla lost the presidency to former general Carlos Ibáñez (Collier and Sater 2004, pp. 246–251).

The Chilean context in the 1950s can be best described as a curious replaying of the Carlos Ibáñez and Arturo Alessandri presidencies of thirty years prior. In 1952, Ibáñez was once again elected as Chilean president on promises of economic reform, state control of the copper companies, centralization of the banks, agrarian and tax reforms, and, most importantly, an end to inflation. In 1952, some in the Chilean electorate wanted Ibáñez to assert strong leadership and were willing to trade some of their constitutional protections for an honest, reform-minded government. Chileans were destined to be disappointed, and the Ibáñez government soon deteriorated into infighting and political malaise. Seemingly frustrated by politicians, and in a supposed attempt to imitate the success of Juan Domingo Perón, who had visited Chile in 1953, Ibáñez then turned to the military. Certain parts of the Chilean military soon cozied up to Ibáñez, urging him to assume dictatorial power in a selfless endeavor to save Chile from international communism. When news of these events reached the public an outcry followed, resulting in those sympathetic members of the military being court-martialed.

Ibáñez had by then lost the faith of the majority of the electorate, who reasoned that Ibáñez was

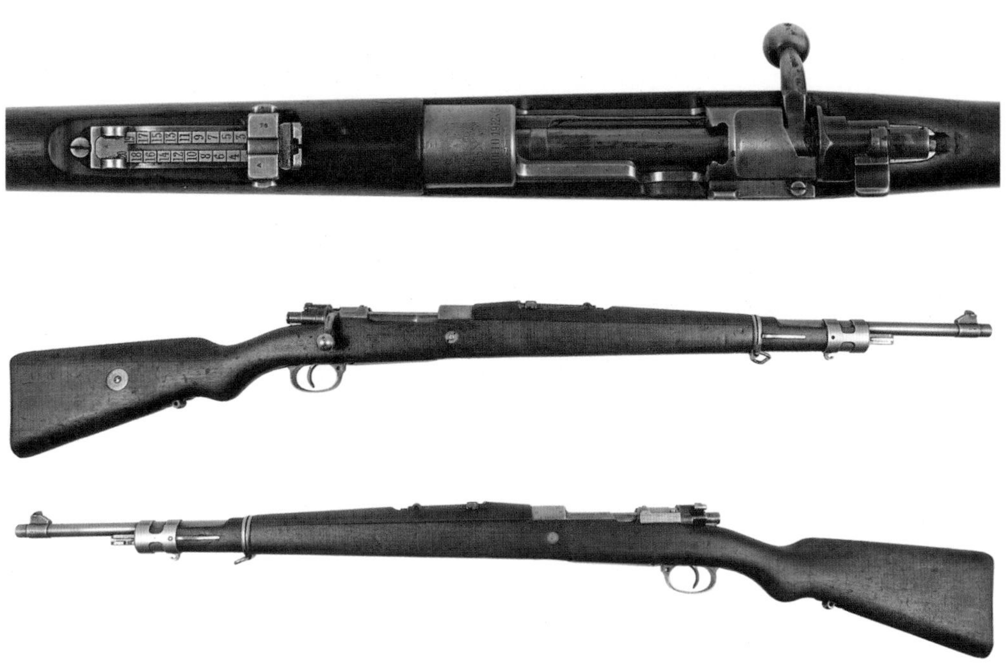

The Chilean M12-61 rechambered in 7.62 mm NATO. *Pedro Bello*

again conspiring to overthrow the democratic institutions of Chile as he had done in the late 1920s. In the context of rising inflation, strikes, protests, and mass arrests, Ibáñez was defeated in the presidential election of 1958 by Jorge Alessandri, the son of Arturo Alessandri, who had himself replaced Ibáñez almost thirty years earlier in 1932 (Collier and Sater 2004, pp. 251–258).

Before World War II, Chile—like most South American countries—heavily relied on European companies to supply their defense needs. From 1938, the United States sought to displace these alliances and convince South American nations to adopt their methods and equipment. With the outbreak of World War II and the fall of France in 1940, the United States was still competing with Germany for influence over South America. This all changed in 1941, when the United States entered the war against Germany and Japan. In 1940, the United States and all South American nations except Argentina adopted the Declaration of Reciprocal Assistance and Cooperation for the Defense of the Americas, resulting in the conclusion of bilateral defense agreements.

Likewise, the 1941 Lend Lease Act also made US arms and advisors available and granted access to military bases and strategic materials. In 1947, Videla's government signed the Inter-American Treaty of Reciprocal Assistance (TIAR), or Rio Pact, which effectively created an anticommunist Western hemisphere block backed by the United States. In concluding this mutual assistance and defense pact, the United States would support, equip, and train Latin American countries through the use of military assistance to effectively exclude the Soviet Union and communism. In 1952, Washington established military assistance donor-recipient relations—or Mutual Defense Assistance Agreements (MDAA)—with Chile, Columbia, Cuba, Ecuador, and Peru. While Brazil was the only country to receive substantial military assistance, Argentina, Chile, Peru, and Colombia received moderate arms transfers (Mott 2002, pp. 90–92).

Under the US Mutual Security Act of 1951, Latin American countries became eligible for US arms, ammunition, and training on condition that they made their natural resources available to the United States and committed to the defense of the hemisphere against the Soviet Union.

A Chilean M12-61 carbine with an experimental ten-round magazine.
Pedro Bello

Subsequently, the United States established programs such as the Excess Defense Articles (EDA) to supply "obsolete" equipment to Latin America countries, including Chile, which received twenty-four million US dollars' worth of EDA aid between 1950 and 1979. By 1979, the EDA had thus provided Chile with .45-caliber pistols, M1 and M14 rifles, M1 and M2 carbines, M1 and M3 submachine guns, and .30-caliber machine guns (Andersen and Klare 1996).

Given that they had been cut off from their traditional suppliers in Europe during World War II, the Chileans thus sought modern weapons from the United States. In 1943, they bought 1,000 Johnston Model 1941 rifles in 7 × 57 mm caliber for their mounted troops (Canfield et al. 2002). As established, after the end of the war, Chileans increasingly gravitated toward US support and were undoubtedly steered away from the 7 × 57 mm toward .30 caliber. Thus, it would be logical to conclude that after NATO adopted and standardized on the 7.62 × 51 mm in 1954, the Chileans would likewise follow suit.

In the mid-1950s, Chile adopted the FN Fusil Automatique Léger (Light Automatic rifle, or simply FAL) in 7.62 NATO (Hobart 1974, p. 198). It would therefore be rational to assume that Chile would likewise seek to progressively relegate its existing stocks of Mausers to reserve status and convert some of these to 7.62 NATO. As with the M.95-61, the Modelo 1912 was likewise converted as the M.12-61 and similarly adopted in 1961.

M.12-61s comprised the conversion both of rifles and carbines and can be distinguished by the additional lettering to the receiver's forward ring, the rear bridge, or both. On the receiver's forward ring, the numerals "-61" were added immediately after the standard "MODELO 1912." Likewise, on some observed examples the word "NATO" is also present below the standard lettering "MODELO 1912." As for the receiver's rear bridge, this has been observed with the numerals "7.62" with a large "N" below. On some examples, the receiver, stock disk, and bayonet lug have also been blued. Despite the change of caliber, all M.12-61 rifles seem to have retained their original front and rear sights; as for the carbine, the original rear sight ladder was removed and substituted with a rifle version.

A further marked difference of the carbine versions of the M.12-61 is the replacement of the original screw that secured the upper barrel band, with a second retaining spring that appears to be identical as that originally fitted to the 7 × 57 mm carbine's lower barrel band. This new retaining spring was fitted to the opposite, left-hand side of the stock. On observed versions of the M.12-61 carbines, the hole for the original upper barrel band screw is also missing. These, together with the fact that M.12-61 carbines have a 254 mm long cleaning rod, tend to indicate that the stocks used for these conversions were originally rifle stocks.

On some carbines, the barrel length is also longer than the original at approximately 600 mm and has been observed with just two lands, as opposed to the original four. To accommodate the shorter 7.62 × 51 NATO munition, magazine inserts or spacers have also been observed on some M.12-61s. As with the Modelo 1895s that were converted to 7.62 × 51 mm NATO, most M.12-61s have had their original barrels rebored and rechambered, using the method described previously. These barrels are marked by the presence of an original OEWG full serial number and proofing marks just forward of the secondary torque shoulder; in all observed cases, the serial number does not match the serial number of the receiver.

Modelo 1912s in British Service during World War I

On 6 July 1910, the Chilean congress issued a decree authorizing the award of 400,000 British pounds annually, so that Chile would always have a first-class warship under construction. To this end, the decree put forward a program to purchase six 1,500-ton destroyers, two 340-ton submarines, and two 28,000-ton battleships. Originally, the two battleships were to be named *Valparaíso* and *Santiago*, but with the death of Adm. Juan José Latorre Benavente, it was decided to rename the *Valparaíso* to the *Almirante Latorre*. As for the *Santiago*, it was renamed the *Almirante Cochrane* in honor of Thomas Alexander Cochrane, who had been the first vice-admiral of the Chilean navy during Chile's War of Independence from Spain (see "Acorazado Almirante Latorre," www.web.archive.org, 2008).

Almirante Latorre was officially ordered from the British shipyards of Armstrong Whitworth on 25 July 1911 (Livermore 1944, p. 42), laid down on 27 November and then launched two years later, on 17 November 1913. Also sourced from Armstrong Whitworth, the *Almirante Cochrane* was ordered on 29 July 1912 and then laid down on 22 January 1913 (Scheina 1987, p. 322). The six destroyers of the *Almirante Lynch* class were ordered in 1911 from the J. Samuel White shipyards (English 1984, p. 146).

At the outbreak of the World War I, work on the *Almirante Latorre* was initially halted. It was then formally purchased by the British on 9 September 1914, completed on 30 September 1915, and entered service in the Royal Navy as the HMS *Canada* (Scheina 1987, p. 322). As for the *Almirante Cochrane*, in 1914 it was only partially complete and did not have its armor installed. During the war, no further work was undertaken, and it was officially purchased only in 1918, and completed as an aircraft carrier with the name HMS *Eagle* (Gardiner and Gray 1984, pp. 38, 70). Of the six destroyers, only the *Almirante Lynch* and *Almirante Condell* were delivered before the outbreak of war. The remaining four—*Almirante Simpson*, *Almirante Goñi*, *Almirante William*, and *Almirante Riveros*—were purchased by the British and renamed the HMS *Faulknor*, *Broke*, *Botha*, and *Tipperary*, respectively. In 1920, the Chileans repurchased *Almirante Latorre* and three of the original destroyers, along with one new destroyer (Livermore 1944, p. 48).

With the purchase of these Chilean ships, and with the acquisition of a further two Brazilian warships, the British also received about 820 7 mm Mausers in September 1914. Initially, these rifles and carbines appear to have remained with

Undated photo of a British maritime crew during World War I. The depicted gentlemen are in all probability the crew members of armed merchantmen or minesweepers. While the majority are armed with Ross rifles, the crew member in the front row closest to the camera and the one second from the left in the back are armed with Chilean Model 1912s. *Solo Publications and Tony Edwards*

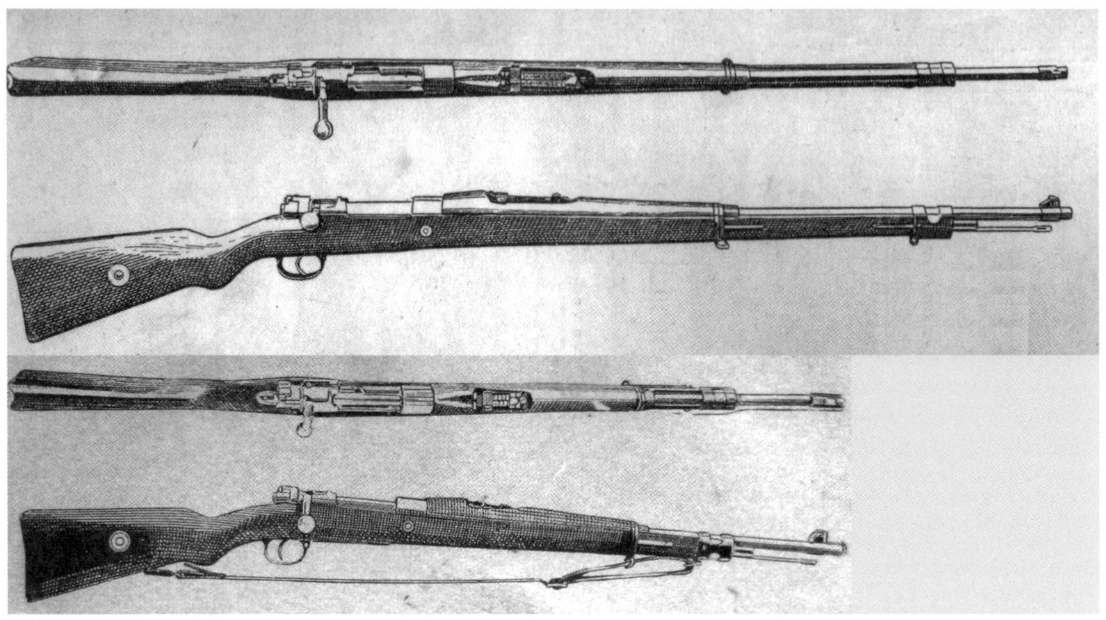

The rifle and carbine versions of the Chilean Model 1912.
Mercado, J. S. 1912b. *Cartilla de la fusil Mauser de 7 mm Modelo Chileno de 1912 para el uso de los soldados e instructores de infantería*. Santiago, Chile: José Jánez.
Mercado, J. S. 1912a. *Cartilla de la carabina Mauser de 7 mm Modelo Chileno de 1912 para el uso de los soldados e instructores de armas montadas*. Santiago, Chile: José Jánez.

their designated ships but were later withdrawn and reissued to second-line use on vessels such as minesweepers, armed merchantmen, and even dockyard guards. Five Modelo 1912s (serial numbers A3, A9, A112, A298, and A395) are today present in the collections of the British Royal Armories. Only one of these is a carbine, while the remainder are rifles. It is interesting to note that on two of these examples, the left butt of the stock has the usual final-acceptance cartouche. Further, on one of these examples, two prominent five-pointed stars are also evident, with a medium-sized one above the cartouche and a larger one just below the cartouche; the remaining example has only the medium-sized star applied below the cartouche (Edwards 2016, pp. 100–107). While not definitively known, it can be assumed that these star marks were the Chilean navy acceptance marks. It can also be supposed that approximately 400 of the 820 7 mm Mausers were Chilean Modelo 1912s.

The Chilean Mauser Modelo 1912 in Detail

In essence, the Modelo 1912 was largely identical to the German Model 98, with the most notable differences between them being the handguard and rear sight.

With a bayonet attached, the carbine had a total length of 1,316 mm and a weight of 4,100 g, while it measured 1,066 mm long and weighed 3,725 g without the bayonet (Mercado 1912a, p. 49). The rifle had a total length of 1,500 mm with the bayonet attached and weighed 4,450 g, while its length was 1,250 mm and it weighed 4,075 g without the bayonet (Mercado 1912b, p. 49).

For the Chileans, the major advantages of the Modelo 1912 over the earlier Modelo 1895 were argued as threefold: first was the tangent rear sight, which made it easier to read and adjust for distance, and likewise required only 2 cm of elevation; second was the pistol-grip stock, resulting in superior handling; and the third was the cock-on-opening bolt mechanism, which made repetition easier (Mercado 1912a, p. 48; 1912b, p. 48).

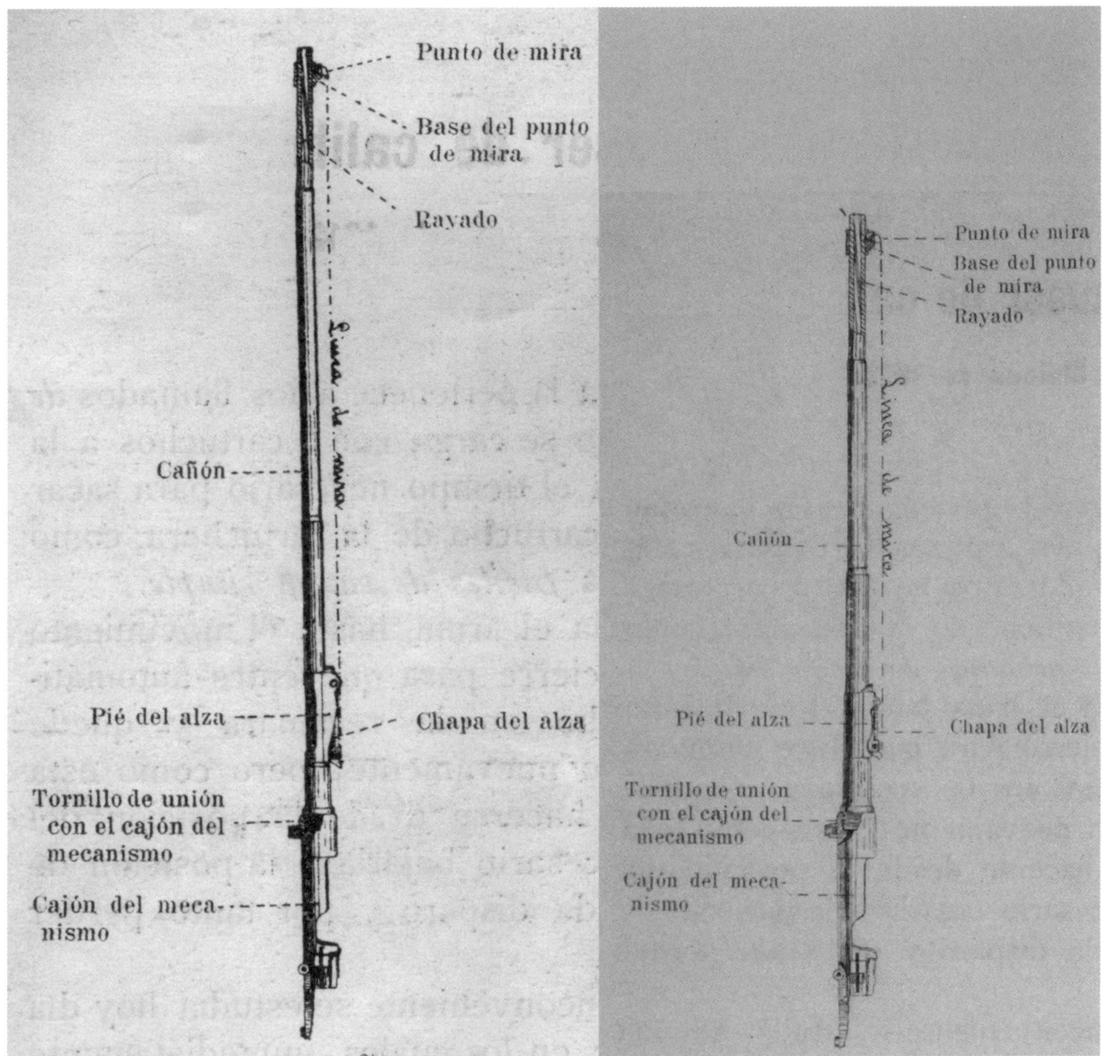

The barreled actions of rifle and carbine versions of the Chilean Model 1912.
Mercado, J. S. 1912b. *Cartilla de la fusil Mauser de 7 mm Modelo Chileno de 1912 para el uso de los soldados e instructores de infantería*. Santiago, Chile: José Jánez.
Mercado, J. S. 1912a. *Cartilla de la carabina Mauser de 7 mm Modelo Chileno de 1912 para el uso de los soldados e instructores de armas montadas*. Santiago, Chile: José Jánez.

Chilean literature details the Modelo 1912 in a manner similar to the Modelo 1895. Thus, for the sake of consistency, the discussion that follows will adhere to the conventions established earlier by the Modelo 1895.

Barrel and Sights

The barrels of the Modelo 1912 were typical of the Mauser stepped-profile design, having two torque shoulders, and were originally chambered in 7 × 57 mm. Rifle barrels were 740 mm long, while the carbine barrel had a length of 556 mm. Both for the carbine and rifle, the diameter—when measured across the lands—was 6.99 mm, while the diameter across the grooves was 7.25 mm, these having a depth of 0.13 mm. The four groove barrels had a twist rate of one turn in 220 mm and had a right-hand twist. The grooves had a width of 3.9 mm (Mercado 1912a, p. 49; 1912b, p. 49).

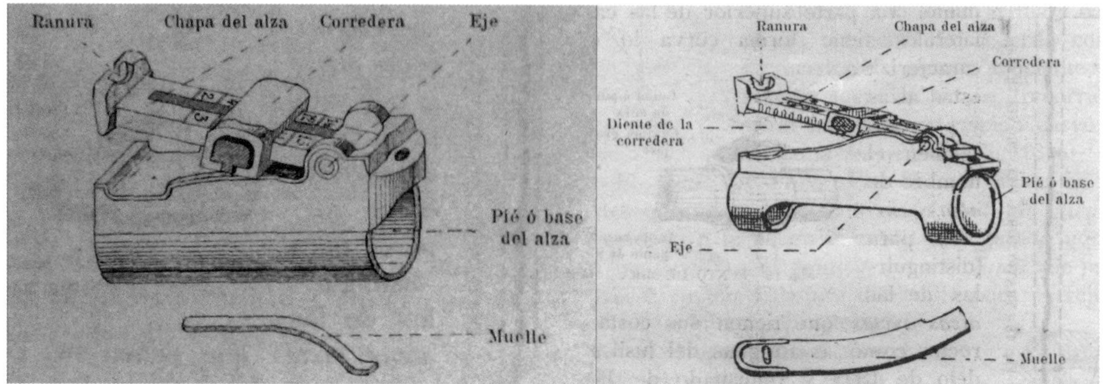

Rear sights to the carbines and rifles of the Chilean Model 1912.
Mercado, J. S. 1912b. *Cartilla de la fusil Mauser de 7 mm Modelo Chileno de 1912 para el uso de los soldados e instructores de infantería*. Santiago, Chile: José Jánez.
Mercado, J. S. 1912a. *Cartilla de la carabina Mauser de 7 mm Modelo Chileno de 1912 para el uso de los soldados e instructores de armas montadas*. Santiago, Chile: José Jánez.

Both the rifle and carbine had a tangent rear sight design that was soldered to the barrel via a sleeved base. For the rifle, the rear sight ladder was graduated from 300 m to 2,000 m in 100 m intervals. The sight ladder of the carbine was graduated from 200 m to 1,400 m in 100 m intervals. Carbine rear sight sliders had a single push button for adjustment positioned to the right; rifles had a double push-button design. Unlike the Modelo 1895, the rear sight ladder of the Modelo 1912 could not be locked in place by the slider. Front sights both for rifles and carbines were identical. The front sight base was sleeved over the muzzle of the barrel, then secured by soldering and tightening a small screw positioned below the sight bead. The front portion of the base was chamfered and checkered. The bead itself was a typical inverted "V" of Mauser design (Mercado 1912a, pp. 13–23; 1912b, pp. 13–23).

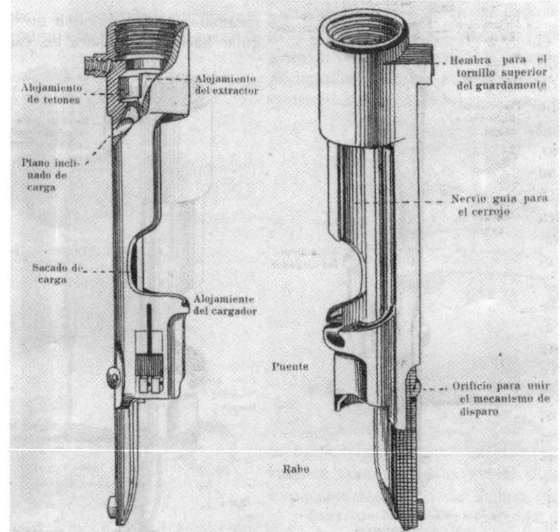

Receiver to the Chilean Model 1912.
Mercado, J. S. 1912b. *Cartilla de la fusil Mauser de 7 mm Modelo Chileno de 1912 para el uso de los soldados e instructores de infantería*. Santiago, Chile: José Jánez.
Mercado, J. S. 1912a. *Cartilla de la carabina Mauser de 7 mm Modelo Chileno de 1912 para el uso de los soldados e instructores de armas montadas*. Santiago, Chile: José Jánez.

The *Cartuchos de Guerra* used by the Modelo 1912 was the "P" spitzer version as previously discussed in the chapter on the Modelo 1895. In the literature on the Modelo 1912, certain specifics of this ammunition are listed differently: the nitrocellulose powder is mentioned either as "Troisdorf" or "Rottweil," with a powder load of 3.15 to 3.25 g (48.61–50.15 grains), which produced a maximum pressure of 3,000 atmospheres. This discrepancy reflects the fact that in 1911–12, Chile purchased thirty million cartridges from Keller & Co., and a further thirty million from DWM. In the carbine, the velocity of the projectile was an initial 840 m/s at the muzzle and 820 m/s when measured at a distance 25 m from the muzzle. For the rifle, the initial velocity when measured at the muzzle was 880 m/s, while at 25 m from the muzzle it was 860 m/s (Mercado 1912a, pp. 49–50; 1912b, pp. 49–50).

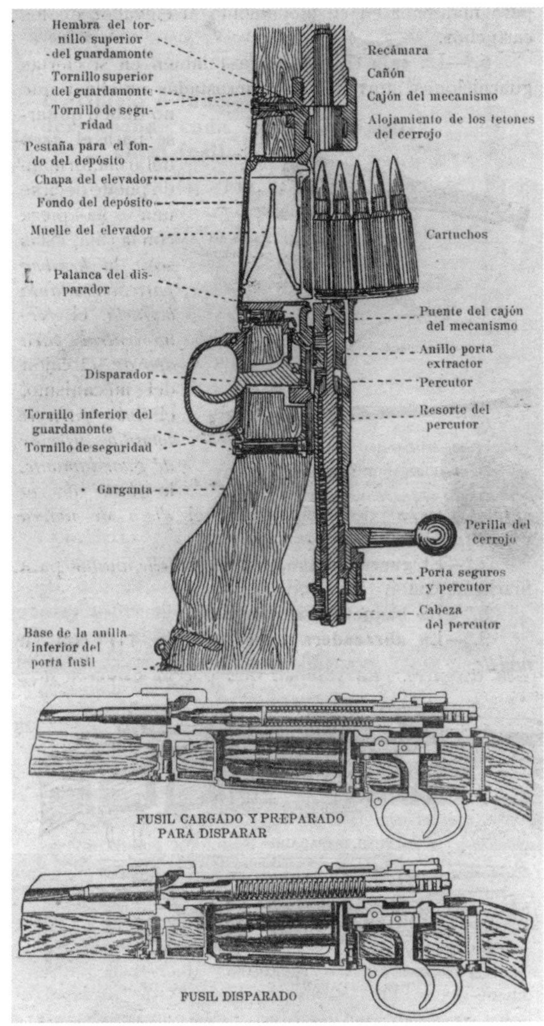

Cross sections through the action of the Chilean Model 1912. Mercado, J. S. 1912b. *Cartilla de la fusil Mauser de 7 mm Modelo Chileno de 1912 para el uso de los soldados e instructores de infantería*. Santiago, Chile: José Jánez. Mercado, J. S. 1912a. *Cartilla de la carabina Mauser de 7 mm Modelo Chileno de 1912 para el uso de los soldados e instructores de armas montadas*. Santiago, Chile: José Jánez.

Receiver

With an overall length of 222 mm and with a forward ring diameter of 36 mm that accommodated the standard 1.1 in. (28 mm) × 12 threads per inch (tpi) barrel shank, the receiver of the Modelo 1912 is not surprisingly the same as the standard-length Model 1898.

The receiver was the component that unified the major systems of the Modelo 1912: the barrel, bolt, trigger mechanism, bolt stop, and ejector and repetition mechanism. Receivers for rifles and carbines were identical (Mercado 1912a, pp. 21–23; 1912b, pp. 21–23).

Bolt

As with the Model 1898, one of the discerning features of the Chilean Modelo 1912 was the design of the bolt. As part of the development of the eventual Model 1898, Paul Mauser sought to make the Model 1893 even better. Two areas appeared to have been of particular concern: the first was the lack of adequate gas venting in the event of a cartridge failure, while the second was the desire to make the action even stronger. In an effort to resolve these issues, Mauser patented a number of innovations from 1895. Arguably the most important of these was his patent of 30 October 1895 (Deutsches Reichspatent [German Reich Patent, or simply DRP] 90,305), in which the third safety lug, improved bolt shroud and cocking piece, and the cock-on-opening arrangements first made their official appearance. Paul Mauser also copyrighted his system for the venting of gas via the thumb cut on the left rail to the receiver in Deutsches Reichsgebrauchsmuster (German Copyright Protection, or simply DRGM) number 56,068 on 9 August 1895. Likewise, the appearance of the two large, oval gas vents to the underside of the bolt body, just behind the forward-locking lugs, was patented according to Belgium Patent 120,477 on 12 March 1896. The last of these major innovations—the iconic Model 1898 firing pin—was copyrighted in DRGM 154,915 on 22 May 1901 (Korn 1971, pp. 271–290). The two cammed shoulders of this last invention prevented the firing pin from traveling forward until the bolt was completely closed.

Modelo 1912 bolts were composed of ten pieces: bolt body, extractor, extractor collar, firing pin, firing-pin spring, bolt shroud, bolt shroud lock, bolt shroud lock spring, cocking piece, and the safety lever. This complete bolt system then acts as locking, extraction, and firing and safety mechanism. The Modelo 1912 is a cock-on-opening system with two forward-locking lugs and one rear safety lug that engage in three shoulders: two to the rear of the receiver's forward ring and one to the lower face of the receiver's rear bridge. As with the Modelo 1895, the left forward-

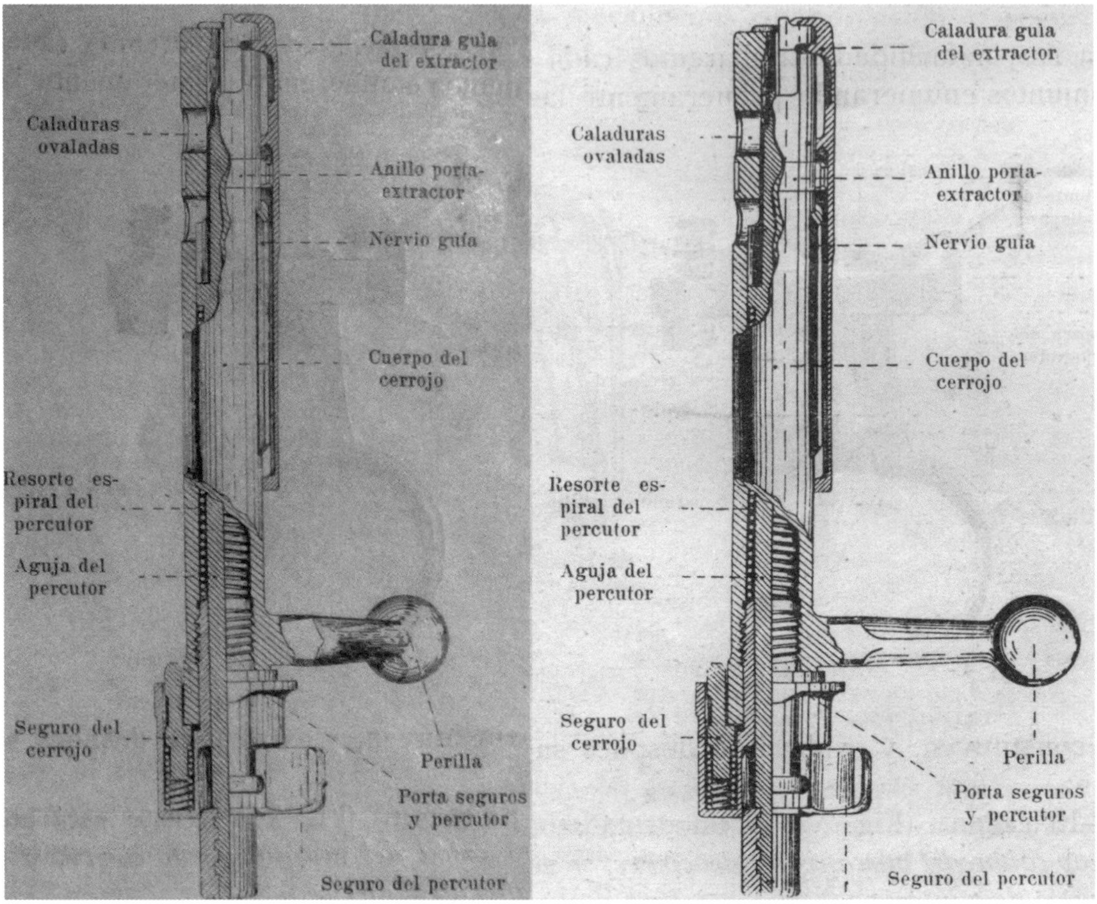

Except for the carbine's turned-down bolt handle, the bolts to the rifle and carbine versions of the Chilean Model 1912 are identical.
Mercado, J. S. 1912b. *Cartilla de la fusil Mauser de 7 mm Modelo Chileno de 1912 para el uso de los soldados e instructores de infantería*. Santiago, Chile: José Jánez.
Mercado, J. S. 1912a. *Cartilla de la carabina Mauser de 7 mm Modelo Chileno de 1912 para el uso de los soldados e instructores de armas montadas*. Santiago, Chile: José Jánez.

locking lug had a perpendicular cut to facilitate the ejector. The bolt face was round, allowing the base of the cartridge to be recessed and partly enclosed. The extractor was of a rotating claw design and was fixed to the bolt body via an extractor collar positioned behind the forward-locking lugs. The firing pin and its compression spring are contained in the hollow bolt body via the bolt shroud. Held under tension by the spring, the firing pin is actuated by the cocking piece, which is attached to the rear of the firing pin via an interrupted lug arrangement. The safety lever—which is accommodated in the bolt shroud—is a three-position design allowing for firing, bolt disassembly, and safety. Disassembly and safe positions are accomplished by the safety lever engaging a notch in the cocking piece. In addition, the safe position also locks the bolt, preventing it from

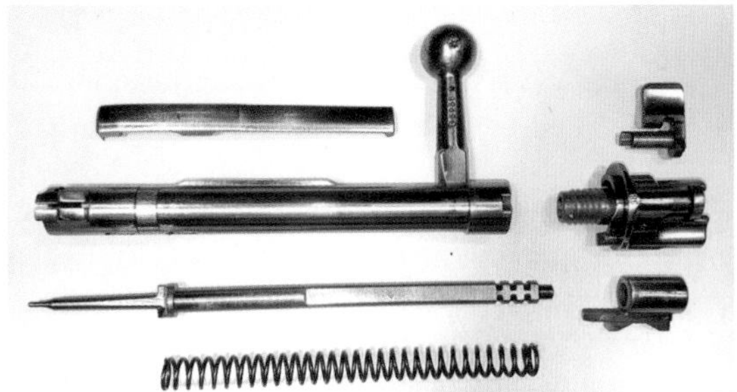
All the bolt components for the Chilean Model 1912. *Author*

rotating. Importantly, the Modelo 1912 also had a bolt shroud lock that secured the bolt shroud and enclosed cocking piece and firing pin from moving in relation to the bolt body when the bolt was opened (Mercado 1912a, pp. 23–29; 1912b, pp. 23–29).

Like the receiver, the ten pieces composing the bolt assembly were originally left unblued. In conjunction with the thumb cut to the left rail of the receiver and the large, oval gas vents to the underside of the bolt body, the wider flange to the bolt shroud also improved gas-venting abilities by presenting a greater obstacle to escaping gases from reaching the shooter's face.

On carbine versions of the Modelo 1912, the bolt handle was bent downward, while on the rifle it was straight or perpendicular to the bolt body. The union between the bolt ball and its stem was less dramatically filleted, or rounded, on the Modelo 1912 compared to the Modelo 1895.

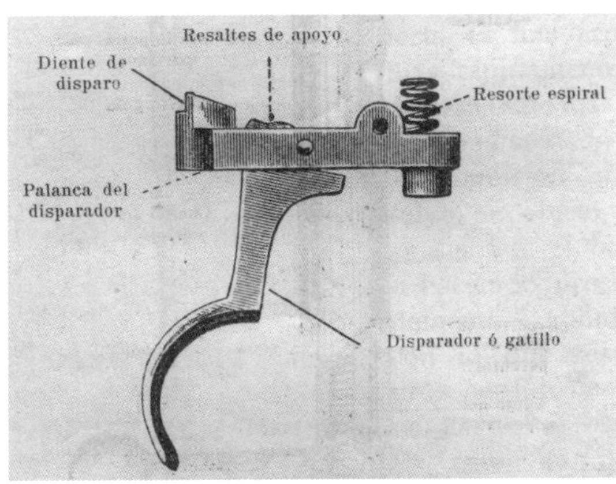

The trigger mechanism of the Chilean Model 1912.
Mercado, J. S. 1912b. *Cartilla de la fusil Mauser de 7 mm Modelo Chileno de 1912 para el uso de los soldados e instructores de infantería*. Santiago, Chile: José Jánez.
Mercado, J. S. 1912a. *Cartilla de la carabina Mauser de 7 mm Modelo Chileno de 1912 para el uso de los soldados e instructores de armas montadas*. Santiago, Chile: José Jánez.

Trigger Mechanism

In the Modelo 1912, a separate trigger and sear are pinned together to form the trigger mechanism. A further pin secured the trigger mechanism, together with an internal compression spring, to the underside of the receiver. When pulled, a raised surface, or cam, on the trigger was forced against the underside of the receiver, lowering the sear proper and disengaging the cocking piece. Unlike the Modelo 1895, the sear of the Modelo 1912 does not have the forward safety lug, since this feature was replaced by the forward cammed shoulders of the firing pin. A cut-out on the underside the cocking piece ensured that the trigger could move freely when the bolt was decocked or had been fired (Mercado 1912a, pp. 27–28; 1912b, pp. 27–28).

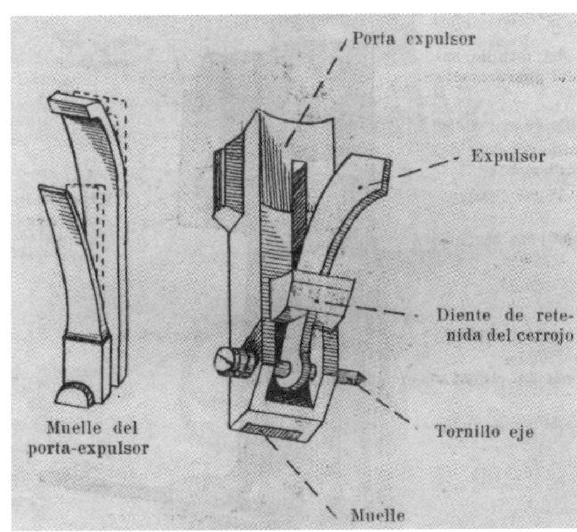

The complete bolt stop and ejection mechanism of the Chilean Model 1912.
Mercado, J. S. 1912b. *Cartilla de la fusil Mauser de 7 mm Modelo Chileno de 1912 para el uso de los soldados e instructores de infantería*. Santiago, Chile: José Jánez.
Mercado, J. S. 1912a. *Cartilla de la carabina Mauser de 7 mm Modelo Chileno de 1912 para el uso de los soldados e instructores de armas montadas*. Santiago, Chile: José Jánez.

Bolt Stop and Ejector

Attesting to their excellent initial design, the bolt stop and ejector of the Modelo 1912 are in most respects identical to those of the Modelo 1895. Attached by a small screw to the rear left portion of the receiver and kept flush via the action of an integrated leaf spring, the bolt stop serves the dual function of preventing the bolt from disengaging from the receiver and, when rotated outward to the left, allowing the removal of the bolt. The leaf spring—keyed into the body of the bolt stop—likewise served to project the ejector into the receiver and against the bolt. When the bolt was pulled rearward after firing, the ejector—also retained by the screw and having passed through the cut in the left locking lug of the bolt

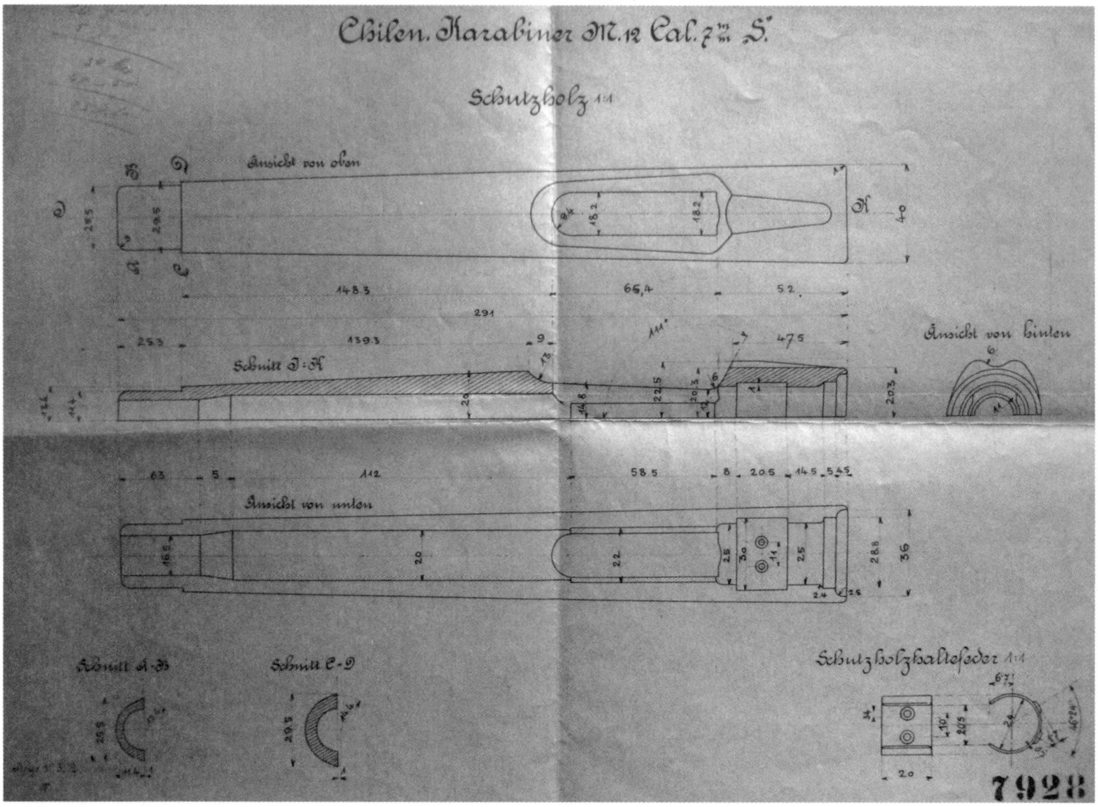

Technical drawing of the Chilean Model 1912 carbine's handguard, which is annotated in the lower left corner "Steyr 11.3.(19)12." *Jon Speed*

body—expelled the empty case by hitting its base (Mercado 1912a, p. 10; 1912b, p. 10). Ejectors to the Modelo 1912 were different from those of the Modelo 1895, in that they had a smaller radius to their inside edge.

Repetition Mechanism

As with the Modelo 1895, the repetition mechanism of the Modelo 1912 comprised the trigger guard with its integrated five-round staggered magazine. Secured to the underside of the receiver, the trigger guard was fixed via two main guard screws that were then in turn secured by two smaller lock screws. The longer of the two main guard screws was supported in the stock by a tubular stock pillar and screwed into the rear tang of the receiver. The shorter of the two was screwed directly to a threaded hole in the middle of the receiver's recoil lug. A magazine floorplate closed the bottom of the magazine by clipping into recesses cut into the

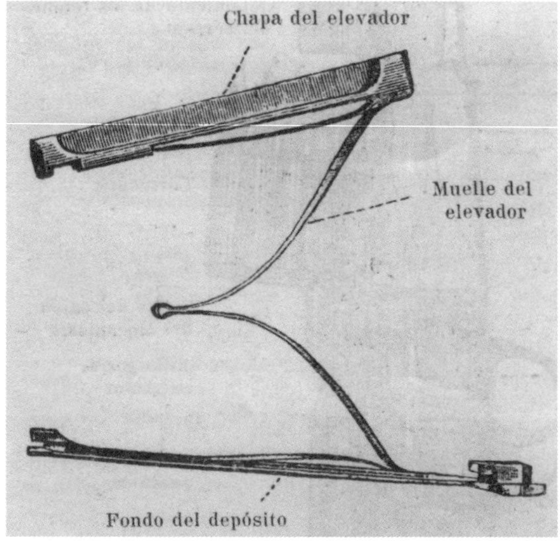

The floorplate, spring, and follower of the Chilean Model 1912. Mercado, J. S. 1912b. *Cartilla de la fusil Mauser de 7 mm Modelo Chileno de 1912 para el uso de los soldados e instructores de infantería*. Santiago, Chile: José Jánez.
Mercado, J. S. 1912a. *Cartilla de la carabina Mauser de 7 mm Modelo Chileno de 1912 para el uso de los soldados e instructores de armas montadas*. Santiago, Chile: José Jánez.

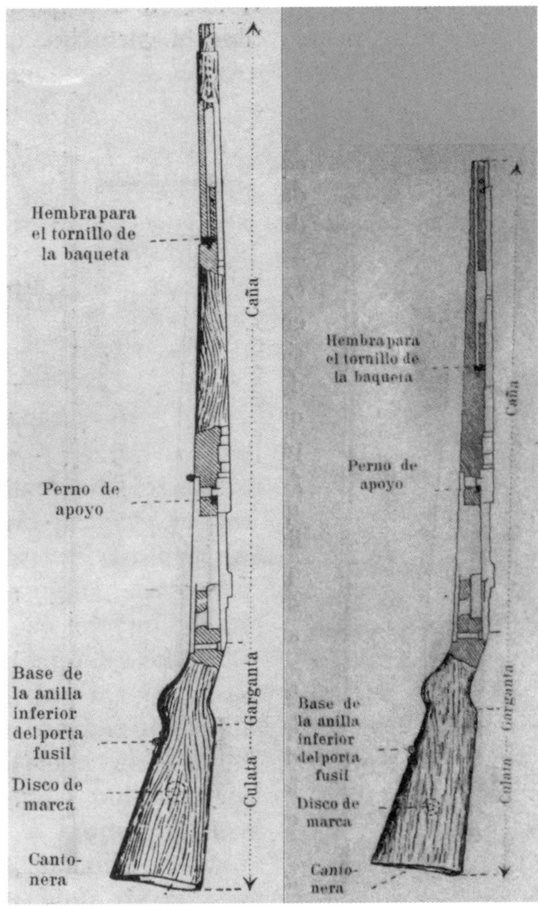

Rifle and carbine stocks of the Chilean Model 1912. Mercado, J. S. 1912b. *Cartilla de la fusil Mauser de 7 mm Modelo Chileno de 1912 para el uso de los soldados e instructores de infantería*. Santiago, Chile: José Jánez. Mercado, J. S. 1912a. *Cartilla de la carabina Mauser de 7 mm Modelo Chileno de 1912 para el uso de los soldados e instructores de armas montadas*. Santiago, Chile: José Jánez.

bottom of the trigger guard. The floorplate was secured via a small, spring-loaded button pinned into the trigger guard. A leaf spring actuated the magazine follower and was fixed into milled slots on the top side of the floorplate and the underside of the follower. Like the Modelo 1895, the rear of the follower's guide rib was chamfered to allow the bolt to close on an empty magazine. Unlike the Modelo 1895, the trigger guard to the Modelo 1912 had a small hole forward of the trigger guard proper for the fitting of the sling's quick-detach mechanism (Mercado 1912a, pp. 29–30; 1912b, pp. 29–30).

Stock and Handguard

On the Modelo 1912, the walnut stocks served to gather all the various elements of the rifle or carbine together to facilitate efficient handling and shooting. In general, stocks were divided into three main parts: the *caña* (fore end), which received the barrel, receiver, magazine, and all its associated parts; the *garganta* (wrist), with its pistol-grip design, was the part that allowed easy handling and firing of the weapon; and the *culata* (butt) served to support the weapon against the shoulder to facilitate aiming and to accommodate recoil during firing. The handguard was also constructed from walnut and served the primary purpose of protecting the soldier's hands from a hot barrel after the firing of numerous shots. Unlike the Modelo 1895, the handguard was attached at its rear to the barrel by means of a C-shaped leaf spring screwed to the underside of the handguard and then clamped over the back portion of the barrel (Mercado 1912a, pp. 30–31; 1912b, pp. 30–31).

Stock Fittings

The butt of the stock was protected by the addition of an oval butt plate that was then fixed to the stock with two recessed screws. This metal butt plate was not the same as the Modelo 1895, in that it lacked the small projection to its upper portion. Like the receiver and bolt components, the butt plate was not blued. A recessed stock disk was screwed to the right face of the butt and was intended to contain unit identification marks. In practice this appears to have never been used, since no Chilean Modelo 1912s have been observed with any unit markings and only had the acceptance mark. A quick-release sling mounting point was screwed to the underside of the butt just behind the pistol grip of the wrist. Like those of the later Modelo 1935, these were recessed into the stock and had two corresponding chamfers on either side to adequately accommodate the sling's quick-release attachment (Mercado 1912a, p. 31; 1912b, p. 31).

Unlike the Modelo 1895, the stocks of the Modelo 1912 had a cross-mounted recoil lug just ahead of the cut-out for the magazine. These consisted of a two-piece design, with the main lug having a rounded head at one end and a threaded

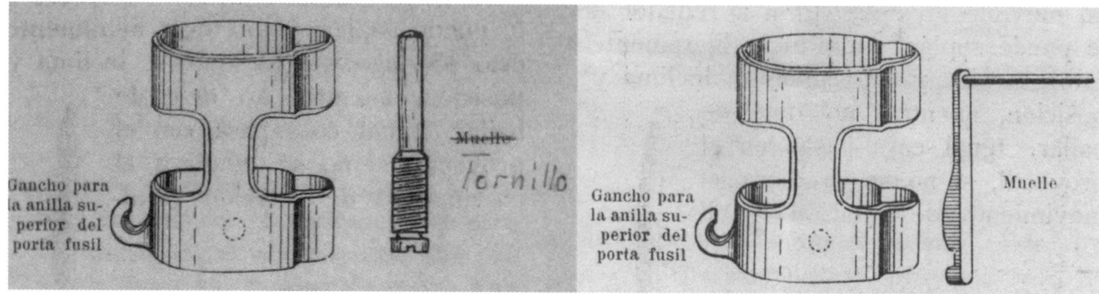

Carbine and rifle versions of the upper barrel band of the Chilean Model 1912.
Mercado, J. S. 1912b. *Cartilla de la fusil Mauser de 7 mm Modelo Chileno de 1912 para el uso de los soldados e instructores de infantería*. Santiago, Chile: José Jánez.
Mercado, J. S. 1912a. *Cartilla de la carabina Mauser de 7 mm Modelo Chileno de 1912 para el uso de los soldados e instructores de armas montadas*. Santiago, Chile: José Jánez.

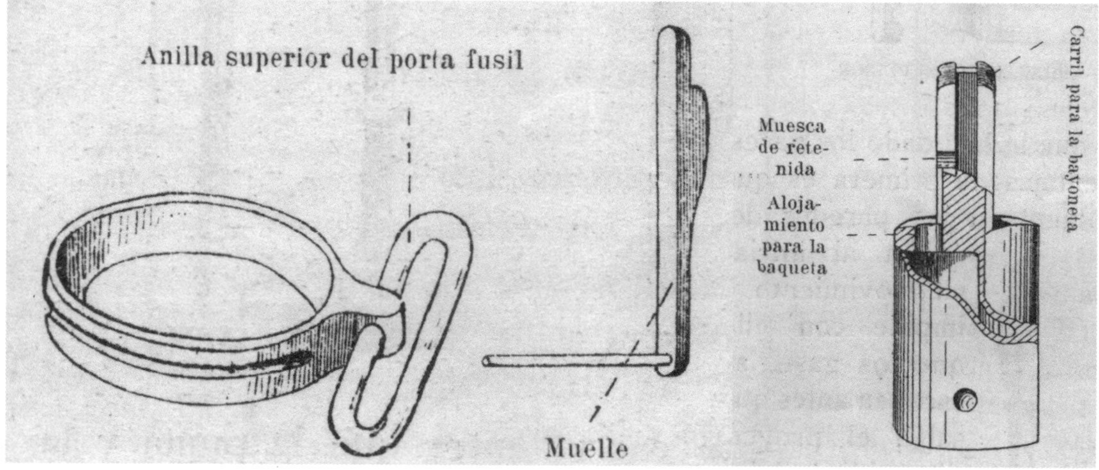

Lower barrel band and bayonet stud of the Chilean Model 1912.
Mercado, J. S. 1912b. *Cartilla de la fusil Mauser de 7 mm Modelo Chileno de 1912 para el uso de los soldados e instructores de infantería*. Santiago, Chile: José Jánez.
Mercado, J. S. 1912b. *Cartilla de la carabina Mauser de 7 mm Modelo Chileno de 1912 para el uso de los soldados e instructores de armas montadas*. Santiago, Chile: José Jánez.

shaft at the other to accommodate a round nut, with both ends being recessed into the stock.

The bayonet stud was sleeved over the forward end of the stock and then secured by a transverse pin. The bayonet was fitted by mating two longitudinal recesses running the length of the stud proper to a T-slot in the rear of the bayonet's pommel, while a round hole in the cross guard was also fitted over the muzzle of the barrel. Bayonets were locked in place via a pommel catch that engaged into a corresponding cut in the bayonet stud proper (Mercado 1912a, pp. 32–33; 1912b, pp. 32–33).

At the front of the stock, an H-shaped upper barrel band secured the barrel to the stock and enclosed the rear of the bayonet stud. On rifles, this upper barrel band was secured in place by means of a recessed spring and detent arrangement to the right of the fore end, while on carbines the spring was replaced by a transverse screw. A lower barrel band was used to secure both the barrel and the forward portion of the handguard; this also had a large swivel pinned to its base for the attachment of the sling. Both in rifles and carbines, the lower barrel band was secured by means of a recessed spring and detent

Bayonets supplied with the Chilean Model 1912 were identical in all instances. *Author*

arrangement positioned to the right of the fore end (Mercado 1912a, p. 32; 1912b, p. 32).

Cleaning Rod

Constructed from thin, round bars, cleaning rods had a threaded portion at one end and a flared portion at the other. This flared portion had a hollow center that was partially threaded and had a cut along its length. To clean rifles and carbines, a number of cleaning rods could be screwed together, and cleaning patches could be secured in the longitudinal cut (Mercado 1912a, pp. 31–32; 1912b, pp. 31–32). Rifle and carbine cleaning rods were 397 mm long. To hold the cleaning rod in the stock, threaded securing lugs were fitted directly into the underside of the stock. On rifles, this was in line with the lower barrel band; for carbines, these lugs were positioned substantially farther back in the stock.

Bayonet

From the author's observation, all Modelo 1912 bayonets were manufactured by OEWG, as evidenced by the presence of the "OE" over "WG" stamp on the ricasso of the blade. On the reverse side of the ricasso a Chilean shield and star were evident, indicating official acceptance. Likewise, on the cross guard the full serial number was evident. The length of the blade was 254 mm, and the total length of the entire bayonet was 380 mm; these figures are identical to the Modelo 1895 bayonet. To distinguish between the two, the length of the cross guard on the Modelo 1912 bayonet was significantly shorter than that of the Modelo 1895. Modelo 1912 bayonets were issued with a blued metal scabbard that had a frog stud soldered to its side near the throat, which then had the full serial number applied. To guide and secure the blade into the scabbard, the throat to the scabbard was fitted with a blued guide that was riveted in place.

Sling and Accessories

Leather slings were fitted to rifles and carbines by means of a forward looping of the sling through the swivel of the lower barrel band. While at the rear, and with the use of the quick-detach apparatus, it could be attached either to the mounting point to the underside of the butt or to the hole just forward of the trigger guard proper. In this latter arrangement, the excess length of the sling could be accommodated by the parade loop, which attached

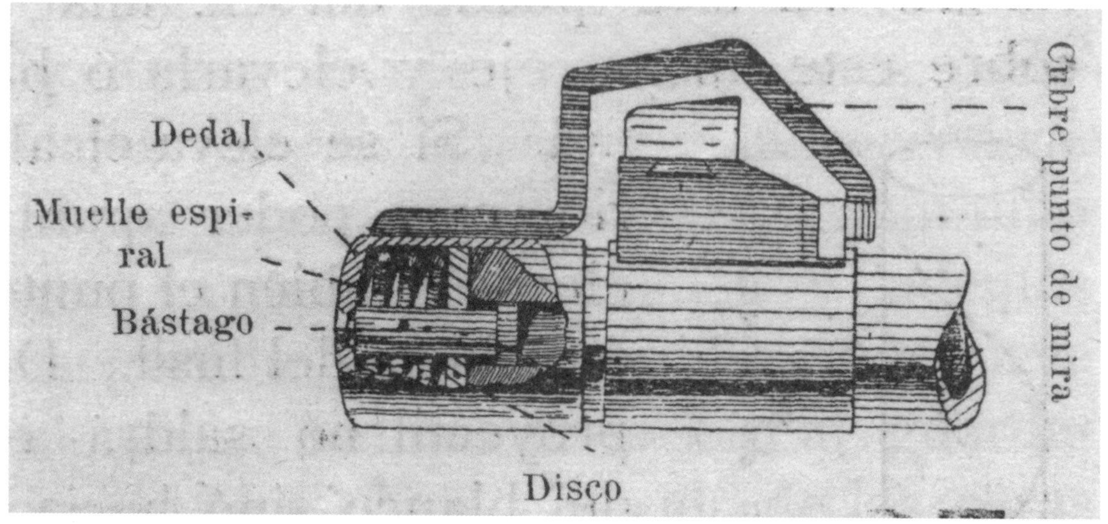

Muzzle cover for the Chilean Model 1912.
Mercado, J. S. 1912b. *Cartilla de la fusil Mauser de 7 mm Modelo Chileno de 1912 para el uso de los soldados e instructores de infantería*. Santiago, Chile: José Jánez.
Mercado, J. S. 1912a. *Cartilla de la carabina Mauser de 7 mm Modelo Chileno de 1912 para el uso de los soldados e instructores de armas montadas*. Santiago, Chile: José Jánez.

to the hook on the underside of the upper barrel band. To lengthen and shorten the sling, a blued metal buckle was provided (Mercado 1912a, pp. 33–34; 1912b, pp. 33–34).

From the author's observation, the Modelo 1912 slings were 1,050 mm long and 30 mm wide. Colors appear to have been natural, with various shades of brown and black observed. To secure the buckle to the sling, the leather was folded back on itself and then secured with three lines of parallel stitching. To secure the quick-detach mechanism to the sling, the leather was also folded back on itself and then pinned together with a removable blued steel button. Faint traces of a diagonal cross-hatch pattern have been observed on the outer faces of the sling's primary surface.

Muzzle covers were also supplied with each rifle and carbine. These were intended not only to cover the muzzle of the rifle and prevent the ingress of rain and dirt, but also to protect the front sight from accidental damage. Muzzle covers consisted of a spring-loaded bronze thimble that slid over the muzzle of the barrel. A curved sheet-steel hook was attached to this thimble; this could then be rotated over the front sight to secure the muzzle cover and ultimately protect the front sight (Mercado 1912a, p. 33; 1912b, p. 33).

Sling for the rifle version of the Chilean Model 1912. *Author*

TABLA DE TIRO

para el **Fusil** Mauser Modelo chileno de 1912 de, 7 mm., construcción de Steyr.

Velocidad inicial 880 m — Angulo de vibración—2′ 30″.

Distancias	Angulos de		Vertice de la trayectoria		Duración del trayecto	Veloci-dad restante	Enerjia del proyectil	Espacio batido para bancos de 1,70 m.	Dispersiones del 50 %	
	Proyeción	Caida	Abscisa	Ordena-da					Vertical	Horizontal
	° ′ ″	° ′ ″	m.	m.	Seg.	m.	m. kg.	m.	m.	m.
300	7 25	8 30	152	0,17	0,37	732	246	Total	0,10	0,10
400	10 25	12 25	208	0,33	0,52	678	210	"	0,14	0,14
500	13 50	17 25	265	0,56	0,68	624	178	"	0,18	0,18
600	17 45	23 25	322	0,89	0,85	570	149	"	0,23	0,23
700	22 20	32 25	382	1,35	1,06	515	122	"	0,28	0,28
800	27 45	43 00	444	1,99	1,27	462	98	171	0,34	0,34
900	34 05	56 35	508	2,86	1,52	414	80	119	0,40	0,38
1000	41 25	1 13 20	573	4,00	1,79	375	64	87	0,48	0,44
1100	49 45	1 32 30	638	5,44	2,08	343	55	67	0,56	0,49
1200	59 30	1 56 00	702	7,29	2,42	320	48	53	0,67	0,54
1300	1 10 35	2 23 15	768	9,64	2,74	302	42	43	0,78	0,59
1400	1 23 00	2 52 10	833	12,47	3,09	285	38	35	0,92	0,64
1500	1 37 00	3 25 25	897	15,70	3,43	273	35	29	1,10	0,70
1600	1 52 40	4 00 50	957	20,14	3,86	259	31	25	1,34	0,75
1700	2 09 55	4 39 00	1015	25,03	4,28	247	29	21	1,63	0,80
1800	2 28 50	5 21 05	1075	30,68	4,72	238	27	18	2,04	0,85
1900	2 49 36	6 06 55	1132	37,15	5,17	230	25	15	2,60	0,90
2000	2 12 10	6 59 00	1188	44,54	5,52	221	23	13	2,35	0,95

TABLA DE TIRO

para la **Carabina** Mauser Modelo chileno de 1912 de, 7 mm., construcción de Steyr.

Velocidad inicial 840 m — Angulo de vibración—2′.

Distancias	Angulos de		Vértice de la trayectoria		Duración del trayecto	Veloci-dad restante	Enerjia del proyectil	Espacio batido para blancos de 1,70 m.	Dispersión del 50 %	
	Proyección	Caída	Abscisas	Ordena-das					Vertical	Horizontal
	° ′ ″	° ′ ″	m.	m.	Seg.	m.	m. kg.	m.	m.	m.
200	5 15	5 49	103	0,08	0,25	722	239	Total	0,07	0,07
300	8 05	9 08	155	0,19	0,39	697	223	"	0,11	0,11
400	11 20	13 29	208	0,36	0,54	647	192	"	0,14	0,14
500	15 05	19 00	264	0,61	0,70	596	163	"	0,20	0,20
600	19 20	25 43	322	0,97	0,89	545	136	"	0,25	0,25
700	24 20	34 33	381	1,47	1,09	494	112	285	0,30	0,30
800	30 10	46 09	442	2,16	1,32	445	91	162	0,36	0,35
900	36 55	1 00 10	506	3,08	1,58	403	75	110	0,43	0,41
1000	44 40	1 17 40	570	4,28	1,85	365	61	82	0,52	0,46
1100	53 25	1 38 48	635	5,83	2,15	336	52	63	0,62	0,51
1200	1 03 35	2 01 27	700	7,76	2,46	313	45	50	0,74	0,57
1300	1 15 05	2 27 51	763	10,17	2,80	298	41	42	0,87	0,62
1400	1 28 00	2 57 38	826	13,12	3,16	282	36	34	1,00	0,67

Trajectory tables for the Chilean Model 1912 rifle and carbine.
Mercado, J. S. 1912b. *Cartilla de la fusil Mauser de 7 mm Modelo Chileno de 1912 para el uso de los soldados e instructores de infantería*. Santiago, Chile: José Jánez.
Mercado, J. S. 1912a. *Cartilla de la carabina Mauser de 7 mm Modelo Chileno de 1912 para el uso de los soldados e instructores de armas montadas*. Santiago, Chile: José Jánez.

Chapter 3: The Chilean Mauser Model of 1935

DWM, Mauser Werke, and the Treaty of Versailles

Having lost World War I, Germany signed the Treaty of Versailles on 28 June 1919. Under Article 170 of the treaty, the manufacture for, and export to, all foreign countries of arms, munitions, and war material of every kind was strictly prohibited (Allied and Associated Powers 1919, pp. 180–181). To enforce this article and other provisions, three inter-allied commissions of control were established, with authority over military, naval, and aeronautical concerns. In particular, under Article 208 of the treaty, it was mandated that military commissions of control would receive notifications from the German government as to the location of stocks and depots of munitions; the armament of fortified works, fortresses, and forts that Germany was allowed to retain; and the location of works or factories for the production of arms, munitions, and war material and their operations (Allied and Associated Powers 1919, pp. 93–96).

Waffenfabrik Mauser and DWM, like all other war-material-producing facilities, were subject to the provisions of the treaty. As for payment of war reparations, Waffenfabrik Mauser had to cede 800 machines to Yugoslavia, with a further 1,500 being surrendered to newly created Czechoslovakia. As the major recipient of these reparations, Československá Abrojovka A.S. (Czechoslovak Weapons Factory, or simply CZ), in Brno, then gradually assumed DWM's role as the preeminent supplier to Central and South America. The technical and production expertise of the Mauser and DWM factories, along with numerous Model 1898 parts, flowed east to Czechoslovakia. In the period between the two world wars, CZ exported roughly 2.5 million infantry weapons based almost exclusively on Mauser knowhow, making it the largest exporter of its kind during this period (Seel 1986, p. 75). However, from conversations held with Jon Speed and on the basis of original documentation at his disposal, it has emerged that DWM had in fact sold the Czechs three million marks' worth of older machines, spare parts, and drawings for the Mauser 1898 system before the treaty came into effect. Speed has further contended that DWM director Gontard also hid a substantial number of DWM's newer machines before the treaty inspectors arrived at its factories.

For companies such as DWM and Waffenfabrik Mauser, the end of the war meant large government contracts were immediately canceled, which in turn resulted in worker redundancies and abruptly terminated production. On 20 December 1918, production at all of DWM's plants was fully suspended, with very limited production resuming only in spring 1919. Following the end of the truce and the finalization of the treaty, the Allies demanded that DWM return to FN all machinery taken in 1914. Likewise, it was also demanded that DWM surrender its controlling stake in FN, and that it surrender or destroy all machines that could be used in the manufacture of weapons or munitions. Despite still being allowed to manufacture limited quantities of sporting arms, associated ammunition, and civilian consumer goods, DWM's market dominance and financial position steadily declined.

Compounded by the onset of hyperinflation in the early 1920s, on 30 May 1922, at a general meeting of shareholders of DWM, it was decided to rename the company Berlin-Karlsruhe Industrie-Werke A.-G. (Berlin Karlsruhe Industrial Works), with the stated aim of producing and distributing hunting and sporting goods and related ammunition articles, as well as the manufacture of all materials, products, machinery, equipment, and ball bearings that could conceivably be manufactured with the facilities of the company (Hassler and Bihl 1939, pp. 88–96). As a result of this, Waffenfabrik Mauser was officially renamed Mauser Werke A.G., Oberndorf a/N (Mauser Works Public Limited Company, Oberndorf on the Neckar River) (Speed 2007, p. 434). Initially, the Berlin-Karlsruhe Industrie-Werke proposed to relocate the entire production facility in Oberndorf to Berlin. After the Wuerttemberg government provided financial aid to Mauser Werke, paid for the construction of workers' apartments, and granted other tax concessions, this relocation was reversed in 1930, with armament production being concentrated in Oberndorf (Seel 1986, p. 86).

On 31 January 1927, the work of the inter-allied commissions of control was concluded. Despite this development, Germany was still bound by the treaty, though now ineffectively administered by the League of Nations. As such, military weapons manufacture slowly reemerged but was severely curtailed by increased competition both from FN and CZ. Bolivia was the first to order rifles, with 24,000 manufactured by Mauser Werke A.G. and delivered in 1928. The same year China also procured 22,000 rifles (Seel 1986, p. 86).

Circumventing the treaty was not a simple process if manufacture was to take place within Germany's borders. Many armaments manufacturers moved their research and production facilities to other neighboring European countries. For example, aircraft manufacturer Fokker established a proxy company in the Netherlands. From the early 1920s onward, the importation and further development of German arms technology was actively promoted and supported in Switzerland. Paradoxically, until this activity started, Switzerland had virtually no industry with the technology nor any ability to export armaments. In 1921, Schweizerische Industrie Gesellschaft (Swiss Industrial Company, or simply SIG) acquired a ten-year license from Waffenfabrik Mauser to produce its pistols for export. SIG had not exported even a single pistol when this license expired in 1931. In 1923, SIG was also involved in establishing the Patronenfabrik Solothurn A.G. (Solothurn Ammunition Factory) in Zuchwil, near Solothurn, Switzerland. Engineer Hans von Steiger, who had previously been employed by DWM, was the driving force behind this venture. Despite an initial good start, Patronenfabrik Solothurn A.G. soon encountered fierce competition from Hirtenberg Cartridge Factory, which eventually bought Solothurn in 1928–29. Solothurn Cartridge Factory was thus bought by Friedrich Mandl, who transformed it into Waffenfabrik Solothurn (Solothurn Weapons Factory) to pursue the development and manufacture of Rheinmetall products (Independent Commission of Experts Switzerland–Second World War 2002, pp. 204–209).

Arguably, with SIG's failure to sell any of its pistols, and spurred on by the evolving commercial success of competitors such as Waffenfabrik Solothurn, Mauser Werke A.G. also decided to create a dedicated Swiss manufacturing facility. The Metallwarenfabrik Kreuzlingen A.G. (Kreuzlingen

Metal Goods Factory) was thus created on 31 March 1931, with a share capital of 250,000 Swiss francs. Far from being a fully fledged production facility, Metallwarenfabrik Kreuzlingen A.G. was intended solely as a front company, with the only Swiss holding being a share of 5,000 Swiss francs owned by local Thurgau Canton Bank (Scholtyseck 2011). The establishment of Metallwarenfabrik Kreuzlingen was approved by DWM's board of directors on 12 February 1931, with an initial 90,000 Swiss francs provided directly from DWM / Mauser Werke and the remainder being financed under a loan from the local Canton Bank with 4.75 percent interest. Importantly, the Swiss subsidiary was established to allow Mauser Werke to primarily facilitate the export of military equipment, not only to Chile but also to nations such as Peru, Ecuador, Venezuela, and Turkey. While this might have been the ultimate goal, the reality was that the execution of a Chilean order would enable Mauser Werke to sustain Metallwarenfabrik Kreuzlingen until orders materialized. It equally enabled them to remain relevant as an exporter in the face of fierce competition from its rivals (Mauser Werke A.G. 1931a).

Chile's Desire for an Additional 106,000 Carbines

In Chile, the German trading houses that represented German armaments companies supported a renewed push in the 1920s for German military advisors under the leadership of Gen. Kiesling. Despite the very onerous restrictions of the Treaty of Versailles still being in place in 1924, Kiesling managed to facilitate the purchase of six Junkers aircraft for the Chilean air force. Importantly, in April 1922, Junkers—like many other German armaments manufacturers—chose to establish a production facility outside Germany. In the case of Junkers, this facility was initially in Russia, and then later in Sweden. In Germany itself, the Chilean military attaché, Col. Ludwig—who spoke perfect German—nurtured good relations with the Germany military establishment. To this end, in 1921 the German government gave the Chileans twenty machine guns destined for destruction under the provisions of the treaty. In 1927, larger orders of uniforms and other equipment were also bought in Germany for the Chilean army (Schaefer 1974, p. 211).

In 1928, the Chileans, through a Col. Sáez—who was attached to their Paris embassy—approached "Mauser Waffen Fabriken" (Mauser Weapons Factories) for the supply of Mauser carbines, as evidenced by this letter:

> Paris, November 16, 1928.
> To the Mauser Weapons Factories
>
> The Chilean Ministry of War proposes to order one hundred and six thousand Mauser rifles, 7 mm, firing a cartridge whose characteristics are as follows:
>
> - Total length of the cartridge = 78.8 mm ± 0.5 mm
> - Weight of the cartridge = 23.3 g ± 0.05 g
> - Weight of the projectile = 9.0 g ± 0.1 g
> - Weight of the propellant = 3.15 g ± 0.025 g
> - Pointed ball projectile, with a cupronickel plated steel jacket containing a core of lead (lead with antimony).
> - Velocity at 25 m from the barrel = 820 m/s.
>
> The barrels of the carbines that we currently have in service have a length of 556 mm ± 0.5 mm.
>
> If you had interest in this order, please send me an offer, taking into consideration the following conditions:
>
> 1 The armaments shall be supplied within a period of five years at the rate of 20,000 to 26,000 per annum.
> 2. The first payment will be made on signing the contract and will be 15% of the total value. The remaining payments will be 45% of the value of the lots that are then received and 40% of the value of the lots that are delivered to the shipping port. The manufacturer must present a bank guarantee to the value of the first payment.

3. The price will include shipping from a European port, in seaworthy packaging that comprises zinc-plated crates.
4. The armaments must comply with the following specifications. The barrel steel must have the following composition:

Carbon—0.60–0.75%
Silicone—0.45% max.
Manganese—0.67% max.
Sulfur and Fluorine—0.07%
Copper—0.12%
Molybdenum—1.8–2.1%

Using a round test specimen of 10 mm diameter and having a length of 100 mm, the mechanical characteristics of this must be:

R = 85–95 kg/mm^2
E = 60 kg/mm^2 minimum
A = 12–15%

The reception of the barrels will be done in batches of 1,000. Two barrels from each batch will be subject to chemical analysis and mechanical testing. If in the mechanical test, a test barrel does not give the stipulated result, the test shall be repeated with two further test specimens. If necessary, the lot can be changed, but only once. Two barrels from each lot will be subjected to overpressure proof testing by firing two cartridges that generate a pressure of 5,500 atmospheres. After this test firing, the barrel chamber will not have a deformation of greater than 0.05 mm.

Each new carbine will also be subject to the test firing of two cartridges that generate a pressure of 4,000 atmospheres. After this test, the barrel chamber will show no deformation. Each new carbine we also be subject to a precision shooting exercise that comprises five cartridges.

For the reception of the other parts of the carbine, the manufacturer can supplement these conditions with additional conditions. The Chilean Commission however reserves the right to discuss and approve these additional conditions in case of any resulting order.

The Chilean Receiving Commission shall have the right to have all manufactured parts independently verified.

(Col. Sáez representing Chilean Embassy in Paris, 1928)

According to the Treaty of Versailles, Mauser could not supply the Chilean carbines. Because 106,000 carbines was an enormous order for a company that was still trying to recover from the effects of World War I, Mauser chose to ignore the treaty and quickly established a number of proxies that would conclude the deal on their behalf. Chief among these third parties were the Hamburg trading firm H. Fölsch & Co. and Swiss SIG.

A letter dated 26 March 1929 from H. Fölsch & Co. to Mauser Werke, Oberndorf, reported on a meeting held the previous day at the Hamburg offices of Gustav Genschow & Co., attended by Director Zillinger of DWM, Dr. Seebach of Gustav Genschow & Co., and Maj. Müller of H. Fölsch & Co. The letter opened by stating that H. Fölsch & Co. had noted that according to its understanding, SIG, Neuhausen, had already submitted a binding offer for the manufacture of 106,000 carbines for Chile. All present at the meeting had then affirmed that the focus should be on progressing this endeavor as efficiently as possible, and had therefore resolved to ask SIG to pay their Chilean "friends," their middlemen, and H. Fölsch & Co. a minimum 5 percent commission. H. Fölsch & Co. requested three copies of the SIG offer so that its Santiago office could pursue the matter with due diligence (H. Fölsch & Co. 1929c). It would thus appear that before the meeting on 25 March 1929, SIG had already been approached by Mauser Werke to facilitate the execution of the Chilean order.

Subsequently, on 5 April 1929, Mauser Werke A.G., Oberndorf am Neckar, and H. Fölsch & Co. officially concluded an agreement whereby H. Fölsch & Co. was assigned the exclusive right to sell the 106,000 carbines to Chile (Mauser Werke A.G. & H. Fölsch & Co. 1929).

On 13 April 1929, Mauser Werke A.G. replied to the H. Fölsch & Co. letter of 26 March. This letter is significant because it reveals that Mauser Werke was painfully aware of the risk associated with exporting war materials and had not yet submitted an offer to the Chileans. It was then revealed that in addition to the carbines, the Chileans had also requested offers for 36,000 self-loading pistols.

Mauser Werke then informed H. Fölsch & Co. that it would soon resolve the question of exports and supply the Chileans with an offer. Considering that the real decision on the purchase of the carbines and pistols would be made in Chile, and that the Paris embassy was nothing more than a collection and mediation office for tenders, Mauser Werke then assured H. Fölsch & Co. that any offer it did make could also be available in Spanish, along with any necessary models and technical documentation. Mauser Werke then cautioned H. Fölsch & Co. that this offer was strictly conditional on H. Fölsch & Co. not representing any competitors' products and working exclusively in their interests as far as orders for rifles, carbines, and self-loading pistols were concerned. Mauser Werke concluded the letter by stating that before any offers were made, it would contact H. Fölsch & Co. to confirm any commissions due to them and their friends (Mauser Werke A.G. 1929e).

In its reply on 18 April 1929, H. Fölsch & Co. confirmed that it would exclusively represent Mauser Werke's rifles, carbines, and pistols in Chile. As such, it confirmed that Mauser Werke could submit an offer directly to the Chilean military commission in Paris and subsequently deal with any technical issues that might emerge. As such, H. Fölsch & Co. requested that any relevant correspondence be forwarded in triplicate: one copy for its records and two for its Santiago offices. The letter continued to note that H. Fölsch & Co.'s representative, Mr. Westendarp—who was intimately aware of Chile and the Chilean mentality—would travel to Paris in May and meet with Chief of the Military Commission colonel Sáez. H. Fölsch & Co. then stated that if Mauser Werke so desired, Westendarp could direct any offers, proposals, or any matters in whatever form directly to Sáez (H. Fölsch & Co. 1929a).

On the matter of the proposed 5 percent commission, H. Fölsch & Co. informed Mauser Werke on 22 July 1929 that subsequent to the meeting held on 25 March, it had received word from their Chilean "friends" and SIG. H. Fölsch & Co. emphatically stated that a minimum of 5 percent was crucial to ensure that their Chilean "friends," who were well connected to local government, remained committed. It likewise advised that Mr. Frey of SIG had disclosed that before the question of commissions was even discussed, he would first have to obtain the approval of the board of directors of SIG (H. Fölsch & Co. 1929b).

SIG's involvement was not guaranteed, as a letter written from Mauser Werke to H. Fölsch & Co. on 10 August 1929 outlines. In this correspondence, Mauser Werke confirmed that its Director Zillinger had just returned from a meeting with SIG in Neuhausen. At this meeting, it was agreed by SIG and Mauser Werke that the processing of the Chilean order would be handled by H. Fölsch & Co., and that a 5 percent commission would be paid to H. Fölsch & Co. Despite this good news, Mauser Werke then informed H. Fölsch & Co. that SIG's board of directors, led by Deputy Director Dr. Spann, had argued that its involvement was not "particularly appropriate" at that stage. This was because SIG's factories were fully occupied and the Chilean order had tremendous risk exposure.

SIG then proposed that their initial binding offer to participate in the venture would have to be withdrawn or modified. While finding the Chileans' terms of payment acceptable, SIG proposed several amendments. The first of these changes proposed that the price per carbine should not be fixed, because it was quite conceivable that during the five-year delivery period, workers' wages and salaries and the prices of raw materials might increase by more than 5 percent. The second concerned a widening of the generally accepted *force majeure* clause to include aspects such as manufacturing disturbances and difficulties in material procurement. Significantly, this second change also proposed that any negative interventions by Swiss or foreign governments would result in the Chileans having no recourse rights if the order was canceled. The third amendment concerned the materials to be used in the manufacture of the barrels. In this regard, SIG's preference was to be a subcontractor, with Mauser Werke as the contracting party. SIG then emphatically stated that if these amendments were not acceptable, Mauser Werke was free to proceed without its involvement. While accepting the first two proposals, Zillinger was fiercely opposed to the last amendment, since it would affect the issuance of the required bank guarantee. Mauser Werke could therefore not proceed until these changes had been discussed in detail by its board of directors. The 10 August letter also revealed that at that stage, the price per carbine was 143 Swiss francs (Mauser Werke A.G. 1929d). Furthermore, in a Mauser Werke pricing document written both in German and Spanish and dated 20 November 1929, it was revealed that the 106,000 carbines would have been named the Modelo 1929 (Mauser Werke A.G. 1929b).

This internal Mauser Werke pricing document is significant because it can be tied to an apparent Chilean desire not only to procure carbines, but also to partly manufacture or assemble them in its local state factories. On 21 December 1929, Mauser Werke wrote two letters to H. Fölsch & Co. The first of these informed H. Fölsch & Co. that Mauser Werke had previously supplied price lists and sample carbines of the Original-Mauser-Karabiners Kal. 7 mm. These prices were for the delivery of parts to Valparaíso in seaworthy packaging. Mauser Werke then informed H. Fölsch & Co.—as it had stressed on several occasions—that a binding offer to supply parts for domestic assembly in the state factories of Chile could be made only when it was confirmed that local assembly was indeed possible. On this last point, Mauser stated that a meeting to finally determine this matter was to be held on 3 or 4 January 1930, between Zillinger, Director Sauter of Ludwig Loewe & Co., and Westendarp from H. Fölsch & Co. (Mauser Werke A.G. 1929a). The second letter stated that in the event of Chile opting for domestic assembly, H. Fölsch & Co. would receive a 10 percent commission. However, Mauser Werke cautioned that if it was forced to lower its initial pricing due to competition, then this commission would be reduced by a corresponding amount (Mauser Werke A.G. 1929c).

A Chilean Contract for 45,727 Carbines

Original sources from December 1929 to August 1930 are unfortunately not in the author's possession. However, on 7 August 1930, Mauser Werke issued a power of attorney in Spanish to H. Fölsch & Co., authorizing the company to sign a contract on its behalf with the supreme government of Chile for the supply of 45,727 carbines under the conditions agreed upon on 16 July 1930 (Mauser Werke A.G. 1930a). This was then followed by a further letter the next day, in which Mauser Werke confirmed that this power of attorney had been issued after consultation with Westendarp, clarifying that this authorized the Santiago office of H. Fölsch & Co. to conclude the contract that had been previously submitted to Mauser Werke for the delivery of 45,727 Modelo 1912 carbines (Mauser Werke A.G. 1930b). It is fundamentally important to note that the letter is clear in its identification of the Modelo 1912 and not the earlier-mentioned Modelo 1929.

While a copy of this contract is not in the author's possession, and original documentation is again missing for the period between September 1930 and February 1931, some of the more important details are still known.

From a report written in September 1931, it became apparent that a contract was signed on 10 January 1931 between the government of Chile and Mauser Werke for 45,727 Modelo 1912 carbines. Of this total, 27,727 would be manufactured and fully assembled in Germany, and the balance of 18,000 would be assembled in Chile from parts partially supplied by Mauser Werke. The price per carbine without a bayonet and sling—which were manufactured and fully assembled in Germany—was to be 260 pesos. This price included seaworthy packaging and delivery to a railhead that connected to the Chilean arsenal in Santiago. For those carbines to be partly manufactured and assembled in Chile, the price would have been 332 pesos per carbine. For the European-manufactured carbine, a separate price of twenty-nine pesos per carbine was required for a short Model Mauser bayonet and a sling. The contract also stipulated that the price of 332 pesos for Chilean assembly did not include either a bayonet or a sling, and that these would be the subject of a special order at a later date. The total contract price was indicated as having been 13,989,103 pesos. According to Article 16 of the contract, four sample Chilean Modelo 1912 carbines and existing technical documentation were to be sent to Europe: three of the carbines were for Mauser Werke and one for the Chilean "European Study Commission." Article 3 of the contract stated that Mauser Werke was to have started Chilean domestic manufacture by 10 July 1931. This article also stipulated that one year after signing the contract (i.e., by 10 January 1932), it would also have delivered 5,000 carbines manufactured in Europe. The report also stated that Mauser Werke had not mandated an initial payment on signing the contract because it had absolute faith in the Chilean government's ability to honor its financial obligations (Colonel Berrios representing Dirección de los Servicios de la Ministerio de Guerra 1931).

Similarly, in internal Mauser Werke costing estimates that were attached to its annual report of 1930–31, it was assumed that all parts of the carbine would be manufactured in Oberndorf, with the exception of a few final machining operations and assembly to be carried out in Kreuzlingen that would be invoiced at 10 percent of the Oberndorf costs. Final revenue was to have been proportioned on the basis of respective production cost incurred either at Oberndorf or Kreuzlingen. It was therefore proposed that the total production cost per complete European-manufactured carbine would be 76.03 Reichsmark (RM), with 78 percent (59.57 RM) being proportioned to Oberndorf and the remaining 22 percent (16.46 RM) to Kreuzlingen. For those parts to be manufactured in Oberndorf and then delivered to Chile, the production costs would be 26.06 RM. In an effort to contextualize these production costs, a comparison was then made between the proposed Chilean carbine and the Mauser Pistol Model of 1896 (C96), with caliber 7.63 × 25 mm. This indicated that on the basis of the production cost of 76.03 RM and adding a profit of 40 percent (30.41 RM), the final price would have been 106.41 RM (Mauser Werke A.G. 1931a).

While the signing of the contract would have been a tremendous relief to Mauser Werke, it was plagued by numerous significant difficulties. In a confidential letter dated 23 May 1931, H. Fölsch & Co. informed Mauser Werke—without stating any reasons—that both its Hamburg and Santiago branches were going into liquidation. H. Fölsch & Co. then relayed that it intended to establish a new company in Chile, for which capital had already been made available by a third party. The staff of this new entity was listed as relevant gentlemen of the previous company who were intimately involved in the handling of the contract. H. Fölsch & Co. cheerfully announced that the new company would not bear any burden whatsoever in relation to the liquidated concern. H. Fölsch & Co. concluded the letter by stating that it hoped that it could count on the continued support, trust, and cooperation of Mauser Werke as per their previously concluded representation agreement (H. Fölsch & Co. 1931).

Mauser Werke's reply to this letter, written on 30 May 1931, opened by stating that the news of the liquidation was an "embarrassing surprise" that presented the company with a very serious and difficult situation. It abruptly ended by Mauser Werke emphatically stating that until it knew the full reasons as to H. Fölsch & Co.'s liquidation, it could not make a judgment and therefore reserved all its rights (Mauser Werke A.G. 1931d).

But more was yet to come; on 6 August 1931, Col. Pedro A. Barros, writing on behalf of the Chilean embassy in Paris, informed Mauser Werke that because of a dire financial crisis in Chile, all progress on the contract was to be immediately suspended. Barros instructed that it was thus imperative to suspend the proposed departure of Mauser personnel to Chile and the manufacture of the carbines (Barros 1931).

With this latest news, Mauser Werke was placed in an exceedingly difficult position, and in an attempt to salvage the rapidly deteriorating situation, it chose to reengage with the Santiago branch of H. Fölsch & Co., known as H. Fölsch y Cia. (with "Cia." an abbreviation of "Compañia"). In a long letter of 13 August 1931, Mauser Werke stated that the Chilean government's suspension of the contract had caused the company to substantially increase its financial risk because of loans taken out to finance the endeavor and a large amount of work that had already been undertaken. Mauser Werke then outlined eight areas in which it had incurred significant expenses. The first was the construction and equipping of production facilities, both locally in Oberndorf and internationally in Kreuzlingen. This first point is important, since it seems to confirm that the Swiss and SIG were still active in the Chilean contract. While no clear evidence is available, it can be hypothesized that this was an endeavor to circumvent the restrictions of the Treaty of Versailles.

The second point outlined that costs had been incurred to repair and supplement the technical material and gauges to be used during the manufacture, revision, and acceptance stages. The third was the remanufacturing of machines and tools, while the fourth involved repair, revision, and correction of technical material, gauges, and instructional material received from Chile. The ordering of the entire stock of raw materials, including the barrel and stock blanks, was then listed as the fifth item. Sixth was the hiring of a number of qualified technical personnel for deployment to Santiago, while the seventh was the extensive technical work undertaken by Mauser Werke's work preparation office to ensure that the contract was processed on time and on schedule. Eighth was the repair and reconstruction of machines and equipment for the Santiago armory and its seaworthy packaging.

Mauser Werke then acknowledged that its commitment to the Chilean contract had resulted in having to decline certain other business opportunities with other governments. After further stressing the point as to its faith in Chile, being entirely cognizant of the difficult situation that Chile then found itself in, and not requiring an initial payment on signing of the contract, Mauser Werke then offered to suspend the implementation of the contract for a three-month period, until mid-November 1931 (Mauser Werke A.G. 1931b).

The decision to suspend the implementation of the contract—including the sending of Mauser Werke personnel to Chile—was likewise communicated to Col. Barros on 15 August 1931. This communique similarly included the view that Mauser Werke was prepared to consider some requests from the Chilean government, on the proviso that they were contractually possible and caused no financial hardship (Mauser Werke A.G. 1931e).

H. Fölsch y Cia. appears to have assumed its new position of trust with vigor. On 22 September 1931, it reported to Mauser Werke on a meeting that it had facilitated between Mr. von Olshausen—the German ambassador to Chile—and a Mr. Leute from Banco Germánico. At this meeting, von Olshausen confirmed that he was well informed as to the contract and stated that despite the current difficulties, the Chilean government had always been aware of the commitments that they assumed and had thus always honored their obligations. Leute was then asked if he shared this opinion, to which he affirmed that he did. He added that no special risk was to be expected, since, on the one hand, the currency exchange rate had been fixed in the contract, while on the other hand, express interest payments were allowed in the event of a default. It was then revealed that Leute would continue to work on this matter, since he had substantial contacts in the Chilean government and had previously helped other German concerns in similar difficulties. Before any further action was to be taken, the consensus in the meeting was to wait until the Chilean presidential elections—due on 4 October—were concluded. The letter finished with a strong emphasis that whatever the outcome of these elections, Mauser Werke could be assured that it would enjoy appropriate "first-class relations at all levels" with the Chilean government (H. Fölsch y Cia. 1931b).

To demonstrate these first-class relations, H. Fölsch y Cia. then forwarded to Mauser Werke translations of two confidential Chilean reports on 30 September 1931. The first of these reports was written by Maj. Julio E. Béjares of the Departamento de Artillería y Material de Guerra (Department of Artillery and War Material) to the Chilean ministry of war. The body of this report was virtually a word-for-word copy of the Mauser Werke letter to H. Fölsch y Cia. on 13 August 1931. The last two points were the only aspects that differed. The first of these stated that to simply cancel the contract would result in a significant monetary outlay with absolutely no benefit. However, this monetary outlay could be fully utilized if the long-term goals of the contract were considered (i.e., the establishment of a domestic manufacturing capability). If the contract was argued from this fundamental perspective, the Chilean government could, for example, request that the initial three-year payment schedule be extended to five with corresponding interest. The second and final of these points stated that the Chilean government should not miss the significance of the execution of the contract in terms of its value to the army and the country: not only would they receive a significant quantity of modern and desperately needed carbines, but also the transfer of technical knowledge to manufacture Mauser's weapons well into the future (Major Béjares representing Departamento de Artillería y Material de Guerra 1931).

Some of the contents of the second report have already been outlined. What is also of significance in this report are additional facts that detail Chile's financial commitments to the contract and the country's desire to establish a local manufacturing capability. As per Ministerial Decree C-2 No. 258 of 27 February 1931, the amount of 116,754.66 pesos was made available to prepare the Santiago arsenal for the domestic manufacture of carbines. The vast majority of this money was allocated via Ministerial Decree M-2 No. 685 (issued on 15 May 1931) to a contract with Siemens-Schuckert for the sum of 82,036 pesos to supply equipment to enlarge the Santiago Arsenal's electrical Substation No. 3. It was also decreed on 13 June 1931 that the sum of 9,937 pesos be made available to the local firm of Louis Roman to conduct the building work for the extension to Substation No. 3. It was similarly proposed that 7,214.85 pesos was to have been used to construct a forge and associated coal bunker. The report then went on to list Mauser Werke's damages as outlined in the letter to H. Fölsch y Cia. on 13 August 1931. The report then advised that it would be impossible to cancel the contract, since the compensation that Mauser Werke had demanded would amount to several million pesos (Colonel Berrios representing Dirección de los Servicios de la Ministerio de Guerra 1931).

Having considered the findings of the two reports, Gen. Agustin Moreno, representing the Chilean ministry of war, then wrote to H. Fölsch y Cia. on 8 October 1931 and proposed a number of amendments to the contract, the most important of which was that the total number of 45,727 carbines would be fully assembled in Chile, and the major components supplied from Europe. Mauser Werke was thus expected to convert its quantity of 27,727 finished carbines to an equivalent volume of individual parts or kits. The delivery schedule was also extended, since it had become dependent on the performance of the Santiago factory. It was also proposed that payment schedules should be extended by one or two years. To save the cost of an acceptance commission, the Chileans proposed that Mauser Werke accept the raw materials and their finished parts. And to add insult to injury, the Chileans finally proposed that Mauser Werke grant them a price reduction. Gen. Moreno then concluded by bluntly stating that if no mutual agreement could result from these proposals, then Chile would have little choice but to cancel the contract (General Moreno representing Dirección de los Servicios de la Ministerio de Guerra 1931).

The contents of Gen. Moreno's letter were dutifully forwarded by H. Fölsch y Cia. to Mauser Werke the very same day. H. Fölsch y Cia. asked Mauser Werke what price reduction or degree of restructuring it would like to implement: a price reduction from 332 pesos to 300 for the originally contracted 18,000 carbines that were to have been assembled in Chile, or a flat price of 310–315 pesos for all 45,727 carbines (H. Fölsch y Cia. 1931a).

Mauser Werke replied to H. Fölsch y Cia. on 9 October 1931, but this letter did not respond to the proposed alterations to the contract; instead, the letter reaffirmed Mauser Werke's commitment to the suspension of the contract until mid-November. It also stated that because of the unexpected devaluation of the British pound, the originally contracted prices needed to be confirmed; namely, 289 pesos for 27,727 *carabiners* with bayonet and sling and 332 pesos for the remaining 18,000, according to the gold–British pound parity ratio of one pound to 20.40 RM, with 1 RM = 1/2790 kg gold (Mauser Werke A.G. 1931f).

Mauser Werke's silence on Moreno's proposals did not mean it was not actively considering them. What appears to be an internal Mauser Werke document from 19 November 1931 makes clear that the production capacity of its factories was, at that point, dramatically underutilized. Because of this shortage of work, and subject to the approval of its board of directors, Mauser was preparing a counterproposal. The first point of this counterproposal stated that it was ready to accept the assembly of all 45,727 carbines at the Santiago factory. Mauser Werke was also prepared to accept an extension of the originally mandated delivery schedule of three years to four years but was not prepared to make the delivery schedule dependent on the performance of the Chileans'

Santiago factory. Instead, it was proposed that any shortfall in Chilean-produced parts would be made up with Oberndorf-manufactured parts, with an estimate that at least 10,000 complete sets of parts would be needed.

Regarding price, Mauser Werke was prepared to lower the originally quoted price of 332 pesos for the 18,000 carbines to approximately 315–320 pesos. At this price, an estimated profit of 750,000 marks was still achievable, but it was made clear that this would have to be subject to further accurate and careful calculation. To secure the price in relation to the value of gold, it also proposed that payment should be made in US dollars at a rate of 315 pesos, equaling 37.65 US dollars. Chile's request for an extension to the payment schedule was rejected, since the original contract already contained an option that allowed for the final payment to be made within one year of final delivery. The initial contract had also stipulated that any interest paid by the Chilean government was to be calculated at a rate fixed by the Central Bank of Chile for private customers. Mauser Werke proposed that this be changed to the interest rate payable on the loan to the German Golddiskontbank, which was financing Mauser Werke's side of the Chilean contract. To guarantee the payment of salaries and wages of its staff in Santiago, Mauser Werke also proposed that the Chilean government deposit 200,000 pesos into its Santiago bank account every three months. Likewise, Mauser Werke was also seeking the payment of 300,000 marks before any work commenced. Finally, the document also indicated Mauser Werke's willingness to carry out the acceptance processes on behalf of Chile, but proposed that this would be done according to "Bannor," or Standard Model Contract (Mauser Werke A.G. 1931c).

The issue of Mauser Werke's representation in Chile was partly resolved in a letter sent to a Mr. Herbert Müller c/o H. Fölsch y Cia. dated 30 December 1931. In this communication, Mauser Werke informed Müller that while a final agreement was still to be reached, the company's representation with H. Fölsch & Co. in Hamburg had been revoked. The letter then informed Müller that Mauser Werke representatives had met with a Mr. Otto Haer, who had stated that on his return to Chile, he and Müller would establish a Chilean company independent of Fölsch concerns after its final liquidation. Mauser Werke then offered—subject to later final liquidation—the right to represent its interests in Chile and requested that Haer take their proposals to the relevant Chilean government authorities with all due diligence. It also requested that Haer and Müller report on the progress of any negotiations, as well as any news on political and financial matters that could have an impact on Mauser Werke's risk exposure (Mauser Werke A.G. 1931g).

The new firm—Otto Haer Oficina Técnica (Technical Office of Otto Haer)—dutifully fulfilled its mandate by sending regular reports to Mauser Werke on the political and financial situation in Chile. As to the execution of the contract, it had no success, since 1932 was a period of tremendous upheaval in Chile. Starting in 1927, Chile gradually became a dictatorship under former army officer Carlos Ibáñez, who was initially very popular because of his economic policies, particularly a large-scale public-works program. Importantly for this publication, it was Ibáñez who created the 19,000-strong National Police Force (*Carabineros*) in 1927 and concluded the Treaty of Lima in 1929, which finally resolved the Tacna-Arica question. After the Wall Street crash of 1929, the large foreign loans that had underpinned his policies collapsed; Ibáñez then became increasingly unpopular.

In 1930, Chile owed a total of sixty-two million British pounds to American, British, and Swiss banks, with this total being twice Chile's foreign debt in 1920. Chile's finances were largely derived from duties imposed on exports of nitrates and copper. When these two commodities suffered dramatic production losses and price deflation, the repayment of these foreign loans became increasingly impossible. Under the growing pressure of public discontent and economic austerity, Ibáñez was forced into exile on 27 July 1931. Under these circumstances, the Chilean congress declared the presidency vacant and appointed Juan Esteban Montero to act as the Chilean head of state until elections could be held in October. To compound an already complicated situation, a naval mutiny then occurred. Having crushed this rebellion, Montero then won the presidential election on 4 October 1931. However, one crisis led to the next, and in June 1932 Montero faced another, more serious mutiny that resulted in his downfall. Montero was then replaced by one of the ring leaders of the coup, Carlos Dávila, who proclaimed himself provisional president of the Socialist Republic of Chile on 8 July 1932. Typical of that period, Dávila's tenure did not last long; he too was replaced, on 13 September by Gen. Bartolomé Blanche, who in turn declared a presidential election for 30 October 1932. This election resulted in a win for Arturo Alessandri, who then very slowly but methodically restored stability and subsequently created the conditions for four decades of democratic expansion in Chile (Collier and Sater 2004, pp. 214–234).

In the context of these unfolding events, Mr. Otto Haer wrote to Mauser Werke on 18 May 1932. This letter opened with Haer stating that despite having written to Mauser Werke on numerous occasions in the preceding four months, he had still received no reply. Haer then outlined that the contract—like almost everything in Chile—depended solely on the question of financing. He then stated that despite the personal interventions and representations of the Chilean minister of war to the minister of finance, there was absolutely no way of progressing the issue; Chile simply did not have the money to buy the carbines. Haer then added, as he had in his letter of 2 March, that there might be another way to secure the required funding: Chile still had a significant amount of Mauser Model 1895s and 1912s, along with many millions rounds of non-spitzer ammunition. Given the deteriorating international situation in Manchuria that might provoke a war potentially involving Russia, Japan, and China, Haer suggested that these Mausers might be sold through Mauser Werke's export connections to either party to generate funds to pay for the contract (Haer 1932).

On 17 June 1932, Mauser Werke finally replied to Otto Haer and stated that with eighteen months having passed, it regretfully concluded that the Chilean government was in legal default. Having consulted Mauser Werke's attorney—Dr. Sekler of Stuttgart—the deduction was that out of a total contract price of 7,134,442.50 marks, Mauser Werke could be entitled to damages of approximately 1.9 million marks. Again, it was reiterated that the contract had resulted in significant hardship to the company, but that it remained cognizant of Chile's difficulties. Mauser Werke then proposed to further suspend the contract until 30 June 1933, but on the express condition that the Chilean government pay a deposit of 476,680 marks on the fixed exchange rate of 4.2 marks to 1.0 US dollar. The deposit amount corresponded to the value of Mauser Werke's cash expenses to that date in fulfillment of the contract. This deposit would then be credited to the Chilean government and deducted from any future payments in relation to the contract (Mauser Werke A.G. 1932).

Cancellation, Compensation, and a Final Contract for Carbines and Ammunition

Following Mauser Werke's letter of 17 June 1932, the availability of original documentation is once again lacking until 1935. On 14 August 1935, Otto Haer again wrote to Mauser Werke. This letter confirms that in May 1935, Mauser Werke and the Chilean government had come to a confidential agreement to finally settle the issue of payment of compensation and to cancel the initial carbine contract. Remarkably, with the cancellation of this contract, another was then agreed to purchase a further quantity of carbines and ammunition for the Chilean Carabineros. The letter makes equally clear that the matter of the ammunition and new carbine contracts was detailed in official government decrees: one from the ministry of the interior that authorized the purchase of carbines and ammunition, and another from the ministry of finance that authorized payment for these. One of the decrees was dated 21 June 1935.

Haer then wrote that the Chilean government was insistent that the new carbine and ammunition contracts were to be treated as totally separate items from the settlement of compensation. Thus, on face value, the public decrees presented only carbine and ammunition purchases. The Chilean government was very concerned that the issue of compensation was to have been kept in the utmost confidentiality, since the payment of this was the subject of a further secret decree. In a very complicated ruse, the payment decree outlined the delivery of 12,000 barrel blanks, a certain number of stocks blanks, and technical materials as concealment for the payment of the compensation. Haer then stressed that the presentation of invoices—which were to be supplied at the various stages of delivery—should mirror and respect these local arrangements in all regards. Haer then concluded by stating that the payment of the amounts would be forwarded to the Chilean Central Bank for immediate transfer (Haer 1935a).

The carbine contract that Haer mentioned was formally concluded on 21 August 1935 and reads as follows:

> On 21 August 1935, in Santiago, Chile, the following contract was agreed between the Government of Chile, on the one hand, representing the General Directorate of the Chilean Carabineros, by General Humberto Arriagada Valdivieso, empowered by Decree No 2665 of 21 June 1935, which was issued by the Ministry of the Interior, and on the other hand, the Mauser Werke AG, Oberndorf (Hereafter referred to as Mauser Werke), represented in this contract by Mr. Otto Haer, who is empowered to fully represent the Mauser Werke:
>
> The Government of Chile orders from Mauser Werke the following equipment of the Carabineros of Chile; namely, 10,000 Mauser carbines, Chilean Model 1935, caliber 7mm Mauser, for Spitzer bullet, Model P with Mauser tangent sights graduated up to 1,400 m. The rest of the technical characteristics of this carbine will be as per the attached construction and specification documents, which are intended to detail the manufacture and acceptance of the carbines. These two attached documents must be signed by both parties as they form part of this contract.
>
> The price per complete carbine, with muzzle cap and sling, including seaworthy packaging in wooden crates lined with zinc inserts, is 65 Reichsmark. Shipping will be from Hamburg, where the Government of Chile will receive the carbines, to Valparaíso. All the shipping costs and marine insurance of the carbines will be paid by Mauser Werke and are to be paid in full before the departure of the consignment from Hamburg. Marine insurance will cover all usual risks, such as total or partial loss, regardless if this occurs at sea or in harbor. The Government of Chile will pay all costs, such as customs duties, associated with the carbines that relate to their importation into Chile. The shipping documents shall be issued to the General Directorate of the Chilean Carabineros.
>
> The 10,000 carbines shall be delivered in two installments: 5,000 at the end of 1935 and the remaining 5,000 at the end of the first half of 1936. The second delivery installment is subject to no further agreements being concluded between the Government of Chile and the Mauser Werke.
>
> Payment of the carbines shall be made in Reichsmark by means of a Berlin bank, against the delivery of the shipping documents for each dispatched consignment. For the purpose of payment, Mauser Werke will communicate the amount and value of each consignment, by means of its representative, so that the Chilean Government can deposit the corresponding amount at the agreed-on Berlin bank.
>
> The acceptance of the carbines will be carried out at the premises of the Mauser Werke by the recognized German authority, who is responsible for the control of the manufacture and the acceptance of small arms destined for the German Government and foreign Governments. To this end, the General-Directorate of the Chilean Carabineros has requested the Chilean Ministry of Foreign Affairs to submit a request directly to the Ministry of Interior of Wurttemberg, headquartered in Stuttgart, that this acceptance task is to be carried out by the personnel of the Wurttemberg State Proof-House for Handheld Firearms. The acceptance protocol must be signed and certified by this State Proof-House in the presence of a notary and a competent Chilean consular official and then delivered to the General Directorate of the

Chilean Carabineros, through the representative of Mauser Werke in Santiago, Chile.

Signed: Otto Haer
Representative of the Mauser Werke in Santiago, Chile

Signed: Humberto Arriagada Valdivieso
General Directorate of the Chilean Carabineros
(Haer and Arriagada Valdivieso 1935)

Haer wrote a further letter to Director Zillinger of Mauser Werke on 28 August 1935, detailing difficulties that concerned the demands for commission payments by Gustav Genschow & Co. Haer wrote that as far as he was concerned, Gustav Genschow & Co.'s involvement with the initial contract of 1931 had been terminated along with H. Fölsch & Co. To complicate this matter, Gustav Genschow & Co.—now referred to as GECO in his letter—had also become involved in the new carbine and ammunition contracts. This was apparently a result of Haer having informed GECO of his initial negotiations, and as the reader will see, it was responsible for the production of a certain portion of the ammunition contract. Haer then detailed that when the Carabineros issued the initial invitation to supply the carbines and ammunition, they had done so publicly.

Considering that other manufacturers had supplied quotes that were substantially cheaper than Haer could manage, Haer then colluded with GECO to keep them from submitting a further competitive and cheaper quote for Mauser products. Haer then argued that this agreement with the local representative of GECO had thus enabled him to win the carbine contract on prices that were much higher than they would have been without such an agreement. Therefore, Haer proposed that GECO should be entitled to at least a 2.5 percent commission on the total value of the new carbine contract. Furthermore, Haer revealed that he and GECO had also colluded on the contract for the ammunition. Again, he outlined that international completion—particularly Hirtenberg and the representatives of Solothurn pistols, along with London Chemical—had offered prices that were much cheaper than his. It was then proposed that in the interests of German companies, Berlin-Karlsruher Industrie Werke (Berlin Karlsruhe Industrial Works, or simply BERKA)—being the successor to DWM munitions activities—would quote for the carbine ammunition, while GECO would quote for the pistol ammunition. Haer then stated that without this collusion, the contract on individually submitted prices would never have been won. Haer then commented that the award of the carbine ammunition contract to an international supplier was "surprising," considering that the Chilean arsenal had the capacity to produce it locally. Importantly, the final inclusion of additional millions of rounds of carbine ammunition had been included only in April 1935 (Haer 1935b).

Mauser Werke's compensation payment would be further delayed. In this regard, Haer wrote on 30 August 1935 and informed that because of complicated banking arrangements between the Chilean and German central banks, on the one hand, and the Deutsche Überseeische Bank and the Banco Alemán Transatlántico, on the other, the payment had been delayed. In the compensation agreement, it was promised that all monies would be paid in RM and free of exchange. The first complication revolved around the question of which company would pay the 0.25 percent transfer fee, while the second concerned the fact that on paper the payment of the compensation was disguised as the delivery of certain materials and technical documents. This, the banks contended, was a violation of Chilean foreign-exchange laws, since payments of this type could be done only via a letter of credit, which were strictly limited at that time. To resolve the first of these issues, Haer then informed that he had sought and obtained necessary government approvals, with Chile paying the transfer fee. The second issue was likewise resolved, with Deutsche Überseeische Bank issuing the required irrevocable letter of credit to Mauser Werke, which had to be redeemed by 31 December 1935. This was subject to the delivery to Chile of the required ammunition, materials, and technical documents by no later than November 1935. According to this letter of credit, the following partial payments were to be made against the delivery of the following shipping documents: 64,650 RM for one million BERKA-produced 7 × 57 mm cartridges; 129,300 RM for a further two

Side views of the Chilean Model 1935. *Jon Magnuson*

million BERKA-produced 7 × 57 mm cartridges; 60,525 RM for 1.5 million GECO-produced 9 mm Steyr cartridges; and, importantly, 286,645 RM for the materials and technical documents, which also included the compensation. The total of these items was listed as having been 541,120 RM. Haer then concluded by warning that all these dealings should be subject to strict confidentiality (Haer 1935c).

While agreed on earlier, the official cancellation of the contract was signed by Zillinger on behalf of Mauser Werke only on 9 December 1935. In this document, the secret decree was identified as A.4 No. 91 of 9 August 1935. It was confirmed that according to Article 2 of the secret decree, payment of 541,120 RM would be made subject to the delivery of certain utensils, materials, and technical information specified according to Article 3 (Zillinger 1935a).

Zillinger wrote to Otto Haer on 12 September 1935 to congratulate him on the effort and time that he had devoted to resolving the issue of the 1931 contract and the payment of the compensation, and for bringing the new contracts of 1935 to agreement. Zillinger then detailed exactly what Chile would get for its 286,645 RM payment. First was detailed mass and tolerance documentation that covered parts that were to have been parallel manufactured in Germany and Chile for the Modelo 1912. This documentation, which was originally supplied by OEWG, had then been updated by Mauser Werke and assessed against its master gauges. The second inclusion was a report that detailed the testing carried out to accommodate some changes proposed by the Chileans regarding certain parts and their specification. The third was the inclusion of production plans, machining and tool specifics, acceptance and inspection protocols, and other technical documents that covered the forty-six components that were to have been manufactured in the Santiago factory, and the organization of that facility. As for actual materials, the Chileans were to receive 12,000 barrel blanks originally supplied by Böhler, packaged, which were ready for shipment to Santiago, as well as tools and equipment for the Santiago factory that were indispensable in the manufacture and inletting of stocks and handguards. This machinery, together with a complete bluing facility, was valued at 20,300 RM. (It is unclear whether this amount was required as an additional payment or if its value was merely being recorded.) Zillinger then stated that with these documents, Chile had the capacity to engage in full serial manufacture of forty-six of the most-rudimentary parts for the Modelo 1912. He then stated that the Santiago factory was currently not capable of producing the remaining twenty-two more complex and important parts. To remedy this situation, he proposed that if Chile later decided to manufacture any of these, then Mauser Werke would directly supply them with the technical knowhow and facilitate the procurement of any required machines. Zillinger then assured Haer that Mauser Werke would do everything possible to assure delivery of all the items before the letter of credit expired on 31 December 1935 (Zillinger 1935b).

Argentina's Model 1933 and Its Chilean Connection

On 30 December 1932, the chief of police of the province of Buenos Aires, the firm of Simon Hermanos, and Mauser Werke concluded a contract for 1,000 Original-Mauser-Repetier-Gewehre (Original Mauser Repeating Rifles), Standard Model, in 7.65 mm caliber spitzer munition. These rifles were specified to include a bayonet and have a walnut stock, a Mauser tangent rear sight graduated to 2,000 m, a 600 mm long barrel, and a total length of 1,100 mm. The Argentines also ordered a further 500 Modelo C.H. (Model Chilean) carbines in 7.65 mm caliber with walnut stock. Unlike the previous 1,000 rifles, these carbines were to have had a Mauser tangent sight graduated to 1,400 m and a barrel length of 556 mm. This contract also included 1,500 spare magazine springs and 1,500 spare bolt shroud lock springs (Provincia de Buenos-Aires et al. 1932, p. 2).

On 3 January 1933, the firm of Simon Hermanos officially ordered the 1,000 rifles and 500 Karabiner Kal. 7.65 mm Mod. C.H. from Mauser Werke. The subsequently produced work authorization form, dated 5 January 1933 and bearing the number 101161, specified that all 1,500 units were to have been supplied with slings and muzzle covers (Mauser Werke A.G. 1933a).

In an internal Mauser Werke document that detailed the *Lieferplan* (delivery schedule) of the 1,500 Argentine units, it is identified that parts could have been taken either from Standard Model, Karabiner 1898 (K98), or Chile production, with parts such as the ejector, extractor, bolt body, and upper barrel band and its cross screw conceivably coming from Chilean production. Interestingly, the barrel, handguard, receiver, and complete front sight were specified as having been subject to special or custom production (Mauser Werke A.G. 1933b).

It has been identified that Model 1933 rifles and carbines were indeed manufactured, with numerous but minor differences between the two. The rifle has an overall length of 1,107 mm, an overall weight of 3.901 kg, a rear sight starting at 200 m and graduated in 100 m intervals to 2,000 m, and a total barrel length of 600 mm; the carbine has slightly different specifications of 1,062 mm, 3.825 kg, and 200 m graduated in 100 m intervals to 1,400 m (Webster 2003, p. 223).

From the above arguments, it has been shown that Chile's contract in 1930 was for Modelo 1912 carbines. Likewise, chapter 2 of this book detailed that the carbine version had a barrel that was 556 mm long and a tangent rear sight starting at 200 m and then graduated in 100 m intervals to 1,400 m. In chapter 1, it was argued that the 556 mm long barrel had its initial Chilean debut in the extended carbine, or M.95-12.

From this argument, it can be proposed that the 500 "C.H." carbines delivered to the Buenos Aires Provincial Police were largely an alternatively chambered Chilean Modelo 1912 with various changes, such as the lack of a stock disk, a longer bayonet stud, and an additional recess in the stock for the bolt handle.

Crests, Inscriptions, Cartouches, and Proofmarks

The following wording is inscribed on the left-hand side of the receiver of all Modelo 1935s:

"MAUSER-WERKE A.G. OBERNDORF A/N."

All Modelo 1935s had the Carabineros' coat of arms crested onto the top portion of the receiver's forward ring. The words "CHILE" and "ORDEN Y PATRIA," with "MODELO 1935" below, were applied to the top and bottom of the coat of arms. "ORDEN Y PATRIA" was the motto of the Carabineros, meaning "Order and Fatherland." The distinctive Mauser Werke logo is applied to the receiver's rear bridge.

Uebersetzung.

30.12.32

Endgültiger

Kontrakt

für die Beschaffung von Mauser-Gewehren und

Karabinern Kal.7,65 mm .

Zwischen dem Chef der Polizei der Provinz Buenos-Aires, Republik Argentinien, Vertreter der Regierung der genannten Provinz, und der Firma Simon Hermanos Ltda., handelnd im Namen und auf Rechnung der Firma Mauser-Werke A.-G., Oberndorf a.N.,Württemberg, welch letztere ausschliesslich verantwortlich bleibt für die Ausführung des gegenwärtigen Kontraktes, ist folgendes vereinbart worden:

Artikel 1.

Die Regierung der Provinz Buenos Aires, die kurz "die Regierung" genannt wird, kauft bei der Waffenfabrik Mauser das nachfolgend bezeichnete Material, welches diese sich verpflichtet, zu den Preisen und Bedingungen des gegenwärtigen Kontraktes zu liefern:

1000 Original-Mauser-Repetier-Gewehre, Standard-Modell,Kal.7,65 mm, komplett, für Verfeuern der S-Munition, Zugsystem und Patronenlager analog dem argentinischen Modell 1909, mit Nussbaumschaft, Mauser-Kurvenvisier bis 2000 m, 600 mm langem Lauf, ganze Länge 1100 mm,

1000 Seitengewehre für diese Gewehre,

500 Karabiner Kal.7,65 mm, Modell C.H., mit Nussbaumschaft, Mauser-Kurvenvisier bis 1400 m, Lauflänge 556 mm

1500 Satz Spezial-Zubehörteile, d.h. 1500 Zubringerfedern und 1500 Schlagbolzenfedern

15 Satz Werkzeuge zum Zusammensetzen und Auseinandernehmen und Putzzeug,

2 Satz Kontrollwerkzeuge.

Diese Waffen müssen genau der Qualität der Waffen gleicher Herstellung entsprechen, welche früher der argentinischen Regierung

-2-

The first page of the Argentine contract for Mauser carbines signed on 30 December 1932.
Provincia de Buenos-Aires, Firma Simon Hermanos, and Mauser Werke A.G. 1932. “Kontrakt für die Beschaffung von Mauser-Gewehren und Karabinern Kal. 7,65mm.” Contract in Archive Jon Speed, Heilbronn, Germany.

Lieferplan für 1500 argentinische Karabiner.

	Fg	Fl	Fr	Wb	Wm	Wz	Kann entnommen werden aus :
Abzug	sofort	5.2.	12.2.	-	-	-	K 98-k-Fertigung
Abzugfeder	-	-	12.2.	-	-	8.2.	" "
Abzuggabel	-	5.2.	12.2.	-	-	-	" "
Abzugstift	-	-	-	-	-	-	K 98-k-Lager
Abzuggabelstift	-	-	-	-	-	-	" "
Auswerfer	-	5.2.	12.2.	-	-	-	Chile-Fertigung
Auszieher	sofort	-	12.2.	5.2.	-	-	Chile-Fertigung
Auszieherring	sofort	5.2.	12.2.	-	-	-	K 98-k-Fertigung
Druckbolzen	-	-	12.2.	5.2.	-	-	" "
Druckbolzenfeder	-	-	12.2.	-	-	8.2.	" "
Haltebolzen	-	-	12.2.	5.2.	-	-	" "
Haltebolzenfeder	-	-	12.2.	-	-	8.2.	" "
Haltebolzenstift	-	-	-	-	-	-	" -Lager
Halteschr.z.Kreuz	-	-	12.2.	5.2.	-	-	" -Fertigung
" " Verb.	-	-	12.2.	5.2.	-	-	" "
Handschutz	-	4.3.	-	-	-	-	Sonder-Fertigung
Hülse	sofort	-	14.2. hart	14.2. hart	-	-	" "
Kammer	sofort	-	14.2. hart	7.2.	-	-	Chile-Fertigung
Kasten	sofort		14.2.	10.2.	-	-	K 98-k-Fertigung
Kastenboden	-	-	12.2.	5.2.	-	-	" "
Klammerfuss	-	-	18.2.	-	-	14.2.	Stand.-Fertigung
Klammerfussschr.	-	-	-	-	-	-	Lager
Kolbenkappe	-	14.2.	18.2.	-	-	-	K 98-k-Fertigung
Kolbenkappenschr.	-	-	-	-	-	-	Lager
Korn	-	-	14.2.	-	-	8.2.	Sonder-Fertigung
Kornhalter	-	-	14.2.	-	-	8.2.	" "
Kornhalterschraube	-	-	-	-	-	-	K 98k-Lager
Kreuzschraube	-	-	10.2.	-	-	-	-
Lauf	-	14.2.	14.2.	-	-	-	Sonder-Fertigung
Oberring	sofort	-	29.2.	-	24.2.	-	Chile-Fertigung
Oberringschraube	-	-	29.2.	24.2.	-	-	" "
Putzstock	-	-	18.2.	14.2.	-	-	Standard-Fertigung
Putzstockhalter	-	-	18.2.	14.2.	-	-	So.

Delivery plan for the 1,500 Argentine carbines.
Mauser Werke A.G. 1933b. "Lieferplan für 1500 argentinische Karabiner." Delivery schedule in Archive Jon Speed, Heilbronn, Germany.

Direktion Kom.-Nr. 101161.

Nr. **1** **Auftrag**

Bestelldat. 3.1.33 Eingang d. Best.: Ausgest. am: 5.1.33

Auftraggeber: Simon Hermanos,
Paris.

Pos.	Stückzahl und Gegenstand	Bemerkungen
	Für Administracion de la Policia de la Provincia de Buenos-Aires.	
	1000 Standard-Sportgewehre Kal. 7.65 mm, mit Seitengewehr m/Stahlscheide, Tragriemen, Mündungsschoner	
	500 Karabiner Kal. 7.65 mm, Mod. CH mit Lauf 556 mm lang, mit Tragriemen, Mündungsschoner.	
	Der stat. Schein ist beizufpgen!	Wert: Rmk. 120488.--

Versandvorschriften: f o l g e n

Verpackung und Zeichen:

Ablieferungstermin: ab Werk Ende Februar 1933!

Werkstatt-Termin: Erledigt:

Nachtrag	1	2	3	4	5	6	7	8	9	10
Eing.										

Kv. 3 — 5 — RG. XII. 32.

The internal Mauser official order for the 1,500 Argentine carbines as per the contract of 30 December 1932. Mauser Werke A.G. 1933a. "Direktion Auftrag." Work instruction in Archive Jon Speed, Heilbronn, Germany.

The crest as applied to the receiver's forward ring on the Chilean Model 1935. *Jon Magnuson*

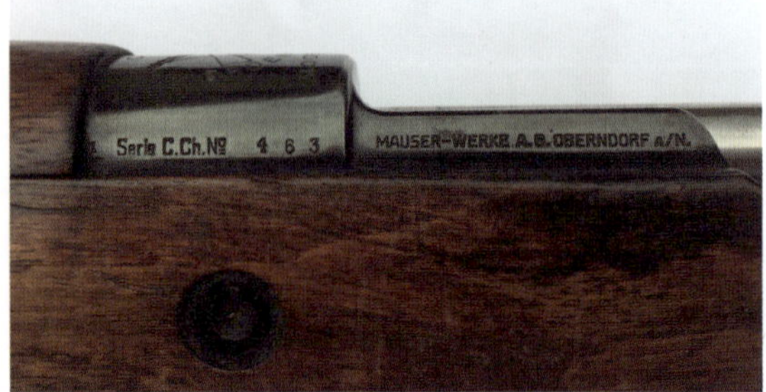

The receiver's side rail inscription as found on the Chilean Model 1935. *Jon Magnuson*

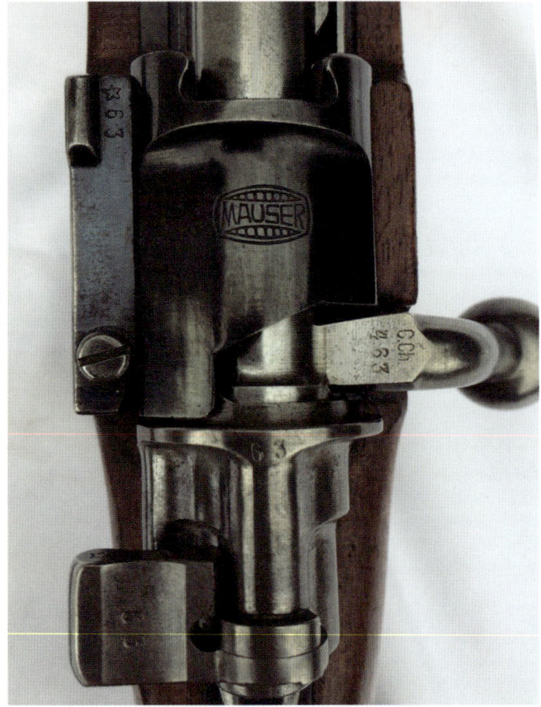

Mauser Werke logo as evident on the receiver's rear bridge of the Chilean Model 1935. *Jon Magnuson*

As for the serial numbering of the Modelo 1935, these were composed of numerals from 1 to 10,000. The usual practice of applying an alphabetical serial number prefix was abandoned in the Modelo 1935 and replaced with the words "Serie C.Ch Nº," which translates to "Series for the Carabineros of Chile, Number," on the left side of the receiver's forward ring. Likewise, the full numeric serial number was applied to the barrel, bolt body, trigger guard, and cleaning rod, preceded by the letters "C.Ch.," supposedly standing for "Carabineros of Chile." The left face of the butt of the stock had two cartouches applied. The first consisted of the Chilean national coat of arms contained within a circle, with the date below bounded by a rectangle; the date was indicated as 1935 and can be argued as referring to the model designation as opposed to the year of the contract. If the earlier precedents of the Modelo 1895 and Modelo 1912 are applied to the Modelo 1935, then it is clear that the Chilean coat of arms with the date below was the final-acceptance mark.

The second cartouche consisted of two large letters "C" and "E," with a smaller "A" and possibly an apostrophe between, all contained within a circle. Because the exact connotation of these letters is unknown, their meaning has to be hypothesized.

In 1903, Chilean authorities created the Regimiento Gendarmes, with its manpower coming from the Cazadores, Lanceros, Dragones, and Guías cavalry regiments of the army. Acting under the orders of mayors and provincial governors, these four squadrons were then deployed to combat banditry in Chile's remote provinces. The Regimiento Gendarmes was then reorganized on 13 January 1906 and changed its name to Cuerpo de Carabineros, with the mission of ensuring public

The stock cartouches of the left butt of the stock of the Chilean Model 1935. *Jon Magnuson*

safety and maintaining law and order, particularly in rural areas and on roads and railways. As for Chile's cities, these were policed by separate municipal police forces: *prefectura de policía* or *policía fiscales*. On 8 September 1924, the separate *fiscales* were amalgamated into a single force that comprised the six zones of Iquique, Valparaíso, Santiago, Talca, Concepción, and Valdivia. A *dirección general de policías* (general directorate of the police) was tasked with the organization and distribution of personnel and services. On 27 April 1927—a short while before becoming Chile's president—Carlos Ibáñez, who was then minister of the interior, merged the newly combined *policías fiscales* with the Cuerpo de Carabineros to form the Carabineros de Chile. On 27 September 1927, the *dirección general de carabineros* (general directorate of the Carabineros) was formed under the auspices of the Chilean interior ministry. Under this general directorate, four subdirectorates of security and order, personnel, administration, and health were created. Interestingly, the administration subdirectorate had responsibility for armaments and ammunition (Museo Histórico Carabineros de Chile 2012).

It has also been shown in chapter 1 that a number of the Model 1895 navy examples—with what appear to be their original stocks—had the cartouche of the Chilean navy both on the receiver's forward ring and the left butt of the stock, with the cartouche on the butt indicating final acceptance. If this and the above description of the Carabineros are considered, then it is highly probable that the Modelo 1935 second cartouche was indicating acceptance by the Carabineros under the auspices of the ministry of the interior.

There is surprising economy when the proof and acceptance marks present on the Modelo 1935 are compared to the Modelo 1895 and Modelo 1912. On the Modelo 1935, the acceptance mark takes the form of a five-pointed star that was then stamped onto the barrel, cleaning rod, front sight base sleeve, bayonet stud, front and rear barrel bands, rear sight ladder and its slider, rear sight base, receiver, cocking piece, bolt body, firing pin, bolt shroud, extractor, safety lever, ejector box, recoil lug, trigger guard and its screws, floorplate, rear base to the sling swivel, butt plate, and stock (on the lower wrist). The full serial number was present on the receiver, barrel, bolt body, trigger guard, floorplate, handguard, stock (inside the barrel cut), cleaning rod, and rear sight ladder. The last two digits of the serial number could be found on the front and rear barrel bands, extractor, bolt shroud, safety, cocking piece, firing pin, and ejector box.

Four proofing marks—that is, those marks applied after the firing of overpressure rounds, subsequent inspection, and certification—were present on the underside of the barrel, just ahead of the secondary torque shoulder, and on the left side of the receiver. These marks comprise a series of "Crowned-B," "Crowned-G," "Crowned-N," and "Crowned-U" stamps and are clearly those of the German proofing laws of 19 May 1891, since their rules, marks, and tables were propagated on 22 June 1892, came into effect on 1 April 1893, and were amended on 8 May 1895.

The "Crowned-B," "Crowned-G," "Crowned-N," and "Crowned-U" proofmarks as evident on the forward receiver ring of the Chilean Model 1935. *Jon Magnuson*

In this context, it is clear that the "Crowned-B"—with the "B" representing *Beschuss* (fired)—was a proofmark indicating that the proof loads had been fired; the "Crowned-G," with the "G" standing for *Geschoss* (projectile), was a proofmark applied to rifled barrels that fired a solid projectile; the "Crowned-N," with the "N" standing for nitrocellulose, was a mark that the weapon had been proofed for smokeless powders; and the "Crowned-U," with the "U" standing for *Untersuchung* (examination), was a final definitive proofmark for handheld firearms in their finished state. The latter was always used together with the "Crowned-B," which certified that the carbines had been inspected for defects after the proof firing.

This last point is relevant because the Modelo 1935 bolt body had both a "Crowned-B" and "Crowned-U." It is also interesting to note that barrels in the immediate area surrounding the proofmarks also have certain other marks: an "S," supposedly for a spitzer ammunition; the numbers "222.5" for the bore plug gauge measurement, which equates to 7 mm; and "7.0" representing

Further proofmarks visible on the underside of the handle of the bolt of the Chilean Model 1935. *Jon Magnuson*

the 7 mm metric bore diameter (Meyer 2016; "Germany 1890–1945," www.shotguns.se, 2015). A further "Ch46" is also evident on the barrels, and it would be tempting to ascribe this as a further inspection of the barrels by the Chileans in 1946. However, this is not the case, since this same marking has been observed on a Brazilian Model 1935, while a "Ch.29" has been observed on Model 1933 carbines sold to the Buenos Aires Provincial Police in Brazil. On 21 February 1933, the head of Mauser Werke's test-firing department, Mr. Premaour, sent a report to Mr. Wirthle as the technical director. Here it was stated that a 200-round shooting test was conducted on a group of Argentine Model 1933s and that two types of steel were used in the manufacture of the barrels: B.J. grade from Bismarkhütte Steelworks (today the Huta Batory Steelworks) and Ch.40 from Böhler Uddeholm (Mr. Premaour for the Mauser Werke 1933). Following this line of argument, it is therefore likely that the "Ch46" indicated the grade or lot of the steel used in the manufacture of the barrel.

The Mauser Chileno Modelo 1935 in Detail

There can be little doubt that the Modelo 1935 bore many similarities to Mauser's Standard Model or "Banner Rifle." World War I had shown that the ballistic performance of a 600 mm long

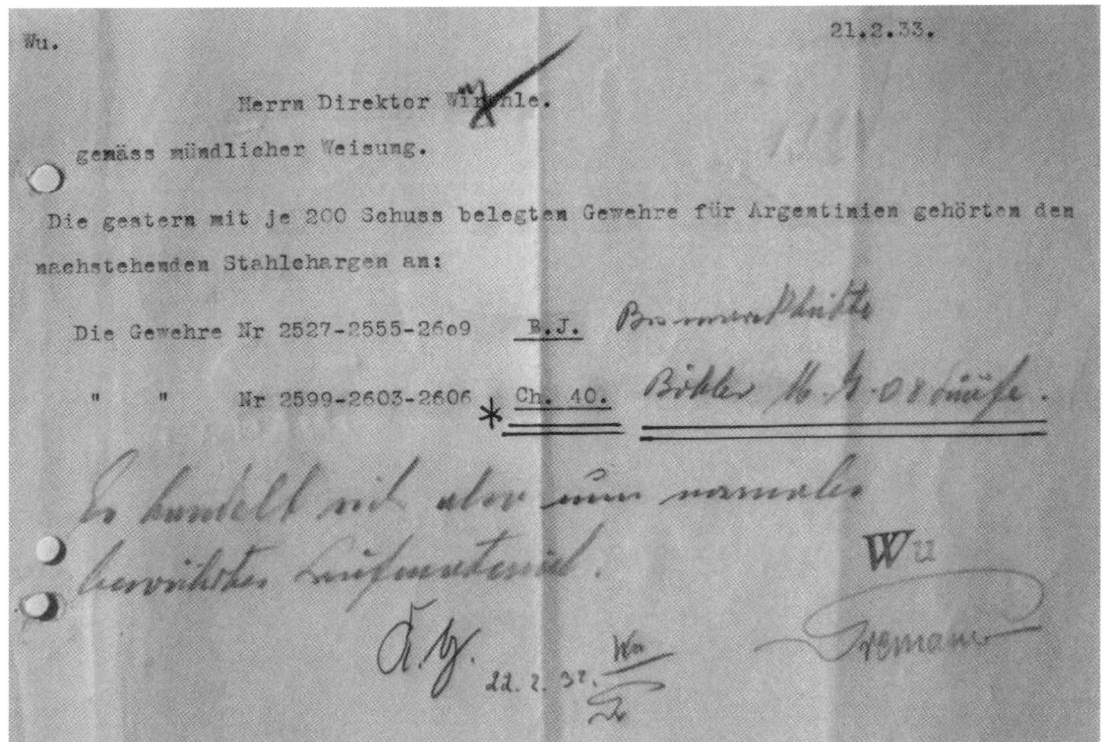

Wu. 21.2.33.

Herrn Direktor Wirthle.

gemäss mündlicher Weisung.

Die gestern mit je 200 Schuss belegten Gewehre für Argentinien gehörten den nachstehenden Stahlchargen an:

Die Gewehre Nr 2527-2555-2609 B.J.

" " Nr 2599-2603-2606 Ch. 40.

Wu

Test report concerning Argentine Model 1933 barrels manufactured both from B.J. and Ch.40 steels.
Mr. Premaour for the Mauser Werke. 1933. *Herrn Direktor Wirthle*. Report in Archive Jon Speed, Heilbronn, Germany.

barrel, when combined with spitzer ammunition, produced satisfactory performance at almost all combat distances. Consequently, in 1924, Mauser Werke developed—possibly as a collaboration with FN and CZ—a standard weapon both for infantry and cavalry. This rifle had similar construction details as the German infantry rifle Model 1898, differing primarily by its shorter barrel and modified rear sight. Against fierce competition from FN and CZ from 1931 onward, Mauser Werke brought its Standard Model into the market, chambered in various calibers (Seel 1986, p. 95). It has been reliably proposed that total Standard Model production was approximately 190,000 units—most of which were exported, with many being delivered to China between 1930 and 1938 (Speed 2007, p. 474).

Despite its overall similarities, the Modelo 1935 had numerous differences that made it unique when compared to the Standard Model. The first of these distinctive features was the front sight, which is similar to the contemporaneous Mausers manufactured by CZ for countries such as Persia; it is conversely remarkably similar to that of the Swiss carbine model of 1931. The rear, quick-release sling attachment is a further feature that is distinctive, in that it is essentially a combination of the earlier sling quick release and a saddle ring. This arrangement supposedly allowed for the sling to be mounted either on the left wrist or on the lower face of the stock. In practice, the quick release could not be removed, since it was permanently fixed to the left of the stock's wrist. The rear sight (which was graduated to 1,400 m as opposed to the usual 2,000 m), the bent bolt handle, and the handguard (which extended all the way to the receiver) were three further distinctive features.

It would be pointless to simply restate the functional details of the Modelo 1935, since these are, in most cases, the same as for the Modelo 1912. Therefore, the detailed explanation of the components of the Modelo 1935 that follows will focus primarily on those components that are different or unique. It will also importantly

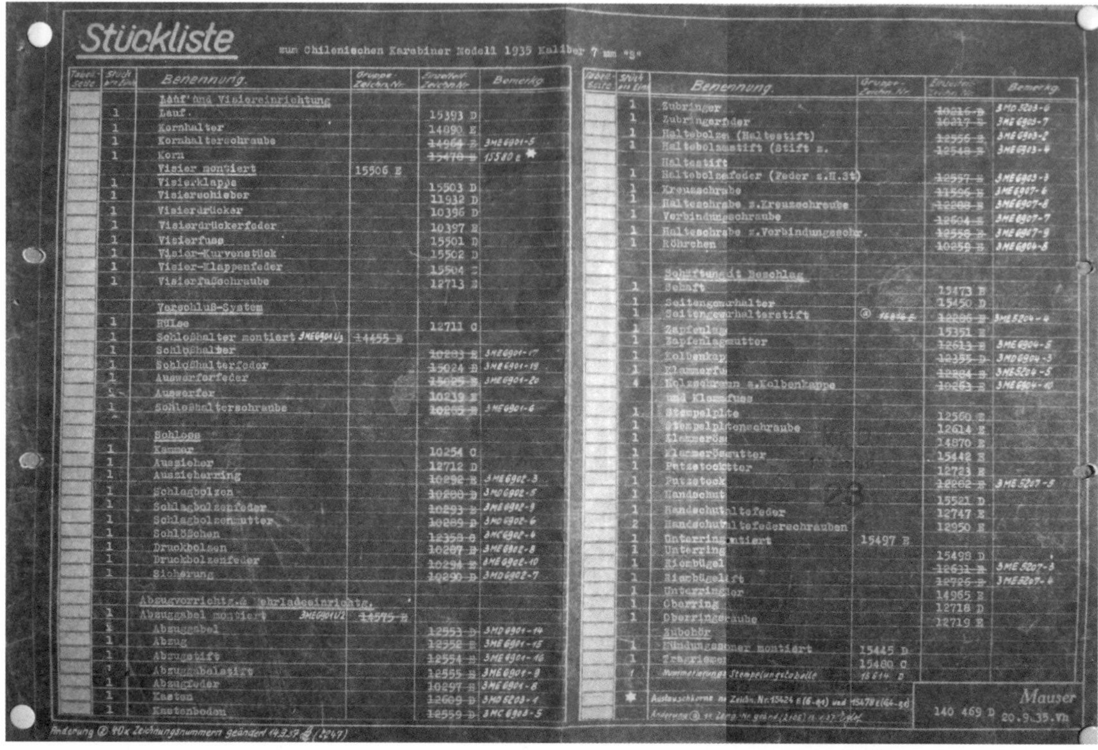

Stückliste zum Chilenischen Karabiner Modell 1935 Kaliber 7 mm "S"

Tabell.-Seite	Stück je Einh.	Benennung	Gruppe-Zeichn.-Nr.	Einzelteil-Zeichn.-Nr.	Bemerkg.
		Lauf und Visiereinrichtung			
	1	Lauf		15393 D	
	1	Kornhalter		14890 E	
	1	Kornhalterschraube		~~14964 B~~	3ME6901-5
	1	Korn		~~15470 B~~	15580 E *
		Visier montiert	15506 E		
	1	Visierklappe		15503 D	
	1	Visierschieber		11932 D	
	1	Visierdrücker		10396 D	
	1	Visierdrückerfeder		10397 E	
	1	Visierfuss		15501 D	
	1	Visier-Kurvenstück		15502 D	
	1	Visier-Klappenfeder		15504 E	
	1	Visierfußschraube		12713 E	
		Verschluß-System			
	1	Hülse		12711 C	
	1	Schloßhalter montiert 3ME6901U3	~~14455 B~~		
	1	Schloßhalter		~~10283 E~~	3ME6901-17
	1	Schloßhalterfeder		~~15024 B~~	3ME6901-19
	1	Auswerferfeder		~~15025 B~~	3ME6901-20
	1	Auswerfer		10239 E	
	1	Schloßhalterschraube		~~10285 B~~	3ME6901-6
		Schloss			
	1	Kammer		10254 C	
	1	Auszieher		12712 D	
	1	Ausziehering		~~10292 E~~	3ME6902-3
	1	Schlagbolzen		~~10288 D~~	3MD6902-5
	1	Schlagbolzenfeder		~~10293 B~~	3ME6902-9
	1	Schlagbolzenmutter		~~10289 D~~	3MD6902-6
	1	Schlößchen		~~12358 C~~	3MC6902-4
	1	Druckbolzen		~~10287 B~~	3ME6902-8
	1	Druckbolzenfeder		~~10294 E~~	3ME6902-10
	1	Sicherung		~~10290 D~~	3MD6902-7
		Abzugvorricht. & Mehrladeeinrichtg.			
	1	Abzuggabel montiert 3ME6901U2	~~14575 B~~		
	1	Abzuggabel		~~12553 D~~	3MD6901-14
	1	Abzug		~~12352 E~~	3ME6901-15
	1	Abzugstift		~~12554 B~~	3ME6901-16
	1	Abzuggabelstift		~~12555 B~~	3ME6901-9
	1	Abzugfeder		~~10297 E~~	3ME6901-8
	1	Kasten		~~12609 D~~	3MD6203-1
	1	Kastenboden		~~12559 D~~	3MC6903-5

Änderung ② 40x Zeichnungsnummern geändert 14.3.37 [illegible] (2247)

Tabell.-Seite	Stück je Einh.	Benennung	Gruppe-Zeichn.-Nr.	Einzelteil-Zeichn.-Nr.	Bemerkg.
	1	Zubringer		~~10216 B~~	3MD5203-6
	1	Zubringerfeder		~~10217 E~~	3ME6903-7
	1	Haltebolzen (Haltestift)		~~12556 B~~	3ME6903-2
	1	Haltebolzenstift (Stift z. Haltestift		~~12548 B~~	3ME6903-4
	1	Haltebolzenfeder (Feder z.H.St)		~~12557 B~~	3ME6903-3
	1	Kreuzschraube		~~11596 B~~	3ME6907-6
	1	Halteschraube z.Kreuzschraube		~~12288 B~~	3ME6907-8
	1	Verbindungschraube		~~12604 B~~	3ME6907-7
	1	Halteschraube z.Verbindungsschr.		~~12558 B~~	3ME6907-9
	1	Röhrchen		~~10259 B~~	3ME6904-8
		Schäftung mit Beschlag			
	1	Schaft		15473 B	
	1	Seitengewehrhalter		15450 D	
	1	Seitengewehrhalterstift	④ ~~[illegible]~~	~~12286 B~~	3ME5204-4
	1	Zapfenlage		15351 E	
	1	Zapfenlagemutter		~~12613 B~~	3ME6904-5
	1	Kolbenkappe		~~12355 D~~	3MD6904-3
	1	Klammerfuss		~~12284 B~~	3ME5204-5
	4	Holzschrauben z.Kolbenkappe und Klammerfuss		~~10263 B~~	3ME6904-10
	1	Stempelplatte		12560 E	
	1	Stempelplattenschraube		12614 E	
	1	Klammeröse		14870 E	
	1	Klammerösenmutter		15442 E	
	1	Putzstockmutter		12723 E	
	1	Putzstock		~~12262 B~~	3ME5207-5
	1	Handschutz		15521 D	
	1	Handschutzhaltefeder		12747 E	
	2	Handschutzhaltefederschrauben		12950 E	
	1	Unterring montiert	15497 B		
	1	Unterring		15498 D	
	1	Riembügel		~~12631 B~~	3ME5207-3
	1	Riembügelstift		~~12726 B~~	3ME5207-4
	1	Unterringfeder		14965 E	
	1	Oberring		12718 D	
	1	Oberringschraube		12719 E	
		Zubehör			
	1	Mündungsschoner montiert	15445 D		
	1	Tragriemen	15480 C		
	1	Nummerierungs-Stempelungstabelle	15614 D		
	*	Austauschkorne m. Zeichn. Nr. 15424 E (6.-41) und 15478 E (64-68)			

Änderung ④ [illegible]

Mauser 140 469 D 20.9.35.Vn

Parts list for the Chilean Model 1935 dated 30 September 1935. *Jon Speed*

emphasize certain often-overlooked aspects, such as material specification and heat treatment.

Barrel and Sights

The barrel of the Modelo 1935 is typical of the generic Model 1898 design, with a stepped-contour profile having two torque shoulders with an overall length of 556 mm, chambered in 7 × 57 mm, with the standard Chilean twist rate of one turn in 220 mm and having four lands and grooves. As partially explained, the rear sights exhibited a tangent arrangement, with the rear sight ladder's graduations starting at 100 m and being calibrated in 100 m intervals to 1,400 m. The single push button of the sight ladder slider is on the right, and actions locking grooves are to the left of the sight ladder. Typical of the Model 1898 design, the handguard is partly retained via a large, flat-headed screw on the front of the rear sight base. The front sight base, which is sleeved, soldered, and screwed to the barrel, has pronounced protection lobes.

The rear sight of the Chilean Model 1935. *Jon Magnuson*

Härtetabelle nach Rockwell
zum Chile Karabiner Mod 1935.

Lfd. Nº	Bestandteil	Rockwell Prüfung in wieviel %	Härtegrad n. Rockwell m. Prüfdiamant Belastung 30 Kg	150 Kg	Härtegrad zu prüfen mit Schlichtfeile	an wieviel %	Härtetiefe in mm	Welche Art von Härtung	Bemerkungen
1	Abzug	100	70÷80				0,3÷0,4	Druckpunktfläche und Bohrung glashart sonst federhart	
2	Abzuggabel	100		50÷65				am Stollen hart im übrigen federhart	
3	Abzugstift und Abzuggabelstift				ja	10		federhart	
4	Putzstock	100		40÷48				federhart	
5	Auswerfer	100		40÷55				federhart	
6	Auszieher	100		40÷45				federhart	
7	Ausziehering				ja	10		Krapfen glashart	
8	Druckbolzen	100		40÷55				federhart	
9	Halteschrauben zu Kreuz u. Verbindungsschr.				ja	10	0,1	Oberfläche glashart	
10	Haltebolzen (Haltestift)	10	70÷78				0,2÷0,3	Oberfläche glashart	
11	Holzschrauben				ja	10		Oberfläche glashart	
12	Hülse	100	I 75÷85	II 5÷25 Kernprüfung	ja	100	0,1÷0,2	Verschluß- Zapfenlager- Druckpunktfläche- [illegible] sonst federhart	
13	Kammer	100	69÷80				0,2	Oberfläche bis auf Stengel glashart	
14	Korn				ja	10		Korndach federhart	
15	Kornhalterschraube				ja	10		Oberfläche glashart	
16	Kastenboden				ja	10		Krapfen u. hintere Stirnfläche glashart	
17	Kurvenstück	100	67÷80				0,3	Kurvenbahn glashart	
18	Kreuz u. Verbindungsschraube	10	62÷78				0,1	Oberfläche glashart	
19	Oberringschraube				ja	10	0,1	Oberfläche glashart	
20	Schlagbolzen	100		35÷50				Kupplungsende u. Schlagspitze federhart	
21	Schlagbolzenmutter	100	69÷80				0,5÷0,6	Oberfläche glashart	
22	Schloßhalter	100		40÷55				federhart	
23	Schloßhalterschraube				ja	10	0,1	Oberfläche glashart	
24	Schlößchen	100	62÷76				0,2	Oberfläche glashart	
25	Sicherung	100	69÷80				0,3	Oberfläche glashart	
26	Seitengewehrhalterstift				ja	10		federhart	
27	Seitengewehrhalter				ja	100		Aufpflanzzapfen glashart	
28	Stift zum Haltestift				ja	10		Federhart	
29	Visierfuß				ja	10		am Charnier glashart	
30	Visierdrücker	100		40÷55				federhart	
31	Visierklappe	100		30÷55				federhart	
32	Visierschieber	100		40÷55				federhart	
33	Visierfußschraube				ja	10	0,1	Oberfläche glashart	
34	Unterringfeder				ja	10		federhart	
35	Zapfenlager	100	62÷78				0,2	Oberfläche glashart	
36	Zapfenlagermutter				ja	10		Oberfläche glashart	
37	Zubringer	100	70÷78				0,2÷0,3	Oberfläche glashart	
38	Klammeraosenmutter				ja	10		Oberfläche glashart	

Mauser-Werke A.G. Oberndorf a.N. 140479 D

Hardness chart for the individual parts of the Chilean Model 1935.
Jon Speed

Oberndorf a/N., 10. Dez. 1935.
Wk/Eb./L.

Zusammenstellung
der Schleif- und Polier-Operationen sämtlicher Gewehrteile
für Chile.

Bei der Zusammenstellung der Gewehrteile, wie sie in der Schleiferei geschliffen und poliert werden, sind genaue Angaben über Körnung, des verwendeten Kunstkorundes, sowie über Grösse und Material der Schleifwerkzeuge (Schleifscheiben & -Zapfen) angegeben. Hierbei ist zu erwähnen, dass die Materialbezeichnungen dieser Werkzeuge wie folgt zu verstehen sind:

Kernlederscheibe.ist eine Holzscheibe angegebener Breite, auf die ein glatter Kernlederriemen mittels Leim radial befestigt wird.

Chromlederscheibe ist eine fertigbezogene Schleifscheibe (Patentscheibe "Fortschritt"), bei welcher kleine Chromleder-Stückchen axial auf dem Umfang einer Holzscheibe festgepresst und verleimt sind.

Die Filzscheibe besteht vollständig aus Filz,ohne Holzkern.

Unter Profilscheibe ist eine Schleifscheibe aus oben bezeichneten Material zu verstehen, bei der die Scheibe am Umfang nicht eben, sondern in der dem zu schleifenden Werkstück entsprechenden Form angedreht ist.

Die entsprechende Unterscheidung ist bei der Verwendung von Schleifzapfen nach Chromleder-, Kernleder-, Filz- und Profilzapfen gemacht.

Auf sämtliche oben erwähnte Schleifwerkzeuge wird das zum Schleifen verwendete Schleifmaterial (Kunstkorund) auf dem Scheibenumfang aufgeleimt.- Als Schleifböcke sind ein- und zweiseitige Spindelstöcke in Verwendung, mit ca. 1800 Umläufen pro Min. bei Scheiben- und ca. 5000 Umdr. pro/min. bei Zapfen-Maschinen.

Gegenstand & Bearbeitung	Werkzeug		
	Material	Grösse	Körnun

1\. Lauf.

Der in der Lauffertigung an der Rundschleifmaschine auf Mass vorgeschliffene Lauf gelangt erst nach Weissmontage, Beschu und Auflöten des Visierfusses und Kornhalters zum Fertigschleife und Polieren.

Gegenstand & Bearbeitung	Material	Grösse	Körnung
Lötnhat zwischen Visierfuß und Lauf vorschleifen	Chromleder	Ø 350/55	90
Lauf am Visierfuss vorschleifen	Chromleder	Ø 28/50	1
	Filz	Ø 40/35	1
Feinschleifen	Filz	Ø 28/50	0
Kornring vorschleifen	Chroml.-Profil	Ø 60/18	1
	Chromleder	Ø 40/8	1
Kornring feinschleifen	Filz-Profil	Ø 60/18	0
	Filz	Ø 40/8	0
Handschutz am Visierfuß schleifen	Chromleder	Ø 350/30	0
Lauf zwischen Visierfuss & Laufbund schleifen	Chromleder	Ø 350/40	0
Den ganzen Lauf feinschleifen	Chromleder	Ø 350/70	0
Lauf bürsten	Fibrebürste	Ø 400/12	

2\. Hülse.

Gegenstand & Bearbeitung	Material	Grösse	Körnung
Übergang am Hülsenkopf schleifen	Chromleder	Ø 350/100	90

Das Vorschleifen der Hülse erfolgt vor dem Stempeln des Hülsenkopfes. Die Hülse gelangt erst wieder nach der Weissmontage, Beschuss, und Auflöten des Visierfusses und Kornhalters zum Fertigschleifen und Polieren.

Gegenstand & Bearbeitung	Material	Grösse	Körnung
Hülse schleifen an der Zapfenmaschine	Chromleder	Ø 22/50	1-90
	"	Ø 55/45	1-90
	"	Ø 50/22	1-90
	"	Ø 20/28	1-90
	"	Ø 18/10	1-90

Gegenstand & Bearbeitung	Werkzeug		
	Material	Grösse	Körnung
Hülse feinschleifen an der Zapfenmaschine	Filz	Ø 22/50	0
	"	Ø 55/45	0
	"	Ø 50/22	0
	"	Ø 20/28	0
	"	Ø 10/18	0
Hülse vorschleifen an der Scheibe	Chromleder	Ø 350/55	90
	"	Ø 350/40	1
	"	Ø 350/35	1
	Chroml.Profil	Ø 350/30	1
Hülse fertigschleifen an der Scheibe	Chromleder	Ø 350/55	0
	"	Ø 350/40	0
	"	Ø 350/35	0
Hülse bürsten	Fibre	Ø 400/8	
3. Kammer.			
Übergänge an der Kammer am Zapfen schleifen	Chromleder	Ø 50/15	1
	"	Ø 30/25	1
	"	Ø 35/8	1
	"	Ø 45/10	1
	"	Ø 25/15	1
	"	Ø 25/13	1
	"	Ø 25/5	1
	"	Ø 15/8	1
Kammer schleifen und polieren an der Scheibe	Filz	Ø 400/25	90
	"	Ø 350/100	90
	Chromleder	Ø 350/25	0-1
	"	Ø 350/20	0-1
	Chroml.Profil	Ø 350/33	0-1
	" "	Ø 200/10	0-1

Gegenstand & Bearbeitung	Werkzeug		
	Material	Grösse	Körnung
Kammer schleifen und polieren an der Scheibe	Chroml.Profil	Ø 215/15	0-1
	Kernleder	Ø 350/20	0-1
	"	Ø 250/10	0-1
	"	Ø 250/15	0-1
	"	Ø 300/45	0-1
	Filz-Profil	Ø 150/12	0-1
	"	Ø 400/25	000
Kammer bürsten	Fibre	Ø 300/8	

Nach der Weissmontage und Nummerieren der Kammer wird dieselbe mit der Fibre-Bürste nochmals behandelt, um beim Stempeln entstehende Aufwerfungen zu beseitigen.

4\. Schlösschen.

Gegenstand & Bearbeitung	Material	Grösse	Körnung
Übergänge & Radius schleifen am Zapfen	Kernleder-Prof.	Ø 55/10	90
	" "	Ø 22/10	90
	" "	Ø 15/8	90
	Filz- "	Ø 35/15	90
	" "	Ø 25/25	90
	" "	Ø 25/10	90
	" "	Ø 15/15	90
Feinschleifen am Zapfen	Kernleder- "	Ø 55/10	000
	" "	Ø 22/10	000
	" "	Ø 15/8	000
	Filz- "	Ø 35/15	000
	" "	Ø 25/25	000
	" "	Ø 25/10	000
	" "	Ø 15/15	000
Vorschleifen mit der Scheibe	Kernleder	Ø 350/50	1
Feinschleifen mit der Scheibe	Chromleder	Ø 350/35	0-1

The first four pages of the grinding and polishing specification for all applicable parts of the Chilean Model 1935. Mauser Werke A.G. 1935b. "Zusammenstellung der Schleif- und Polier- Operationen sämtlicher Gewhrteile für Chile." Grinding and polishing operations of all parts for the parts for the Chilean carbine, in Archive Jon Speed, Heilbronn, Germany.

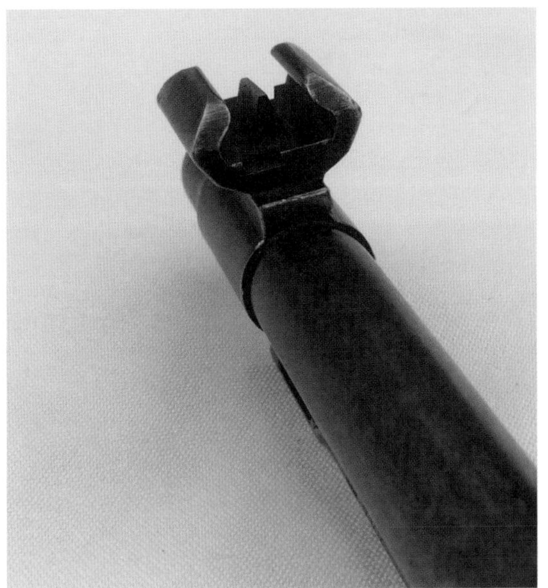

The front sight of the Chilean Model 1935. *Jon Magnuson*

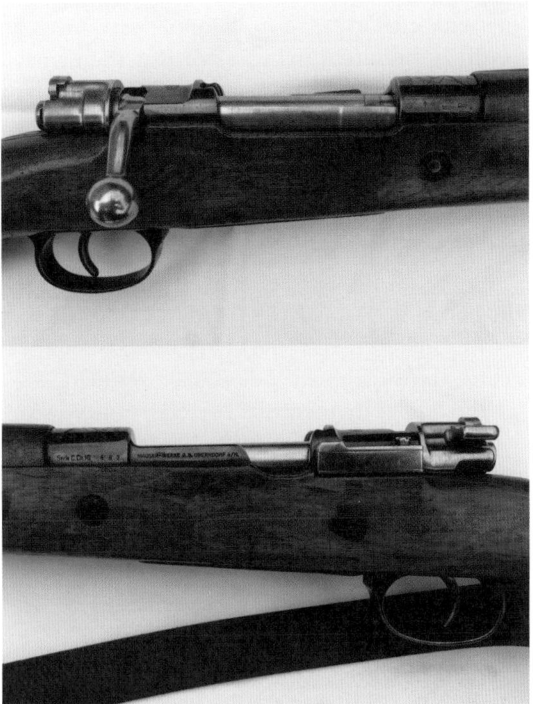

Right- and left-hand views of the receiver of the Chilean Model 1935. *Jon Magnuson*

Atypically for a Mauser, the front sight bead does not have the conventional left-right placement; rather, it follows a diagonal adjustment design. All parts of the barrel and sights except for the upper numbered surfaces of the rear sight ladder were blued.

From the material specification, the rear sight ladder was constructed from St.35.61 steel with an average carbon content of 0.35 percent and then hardened to 25–40 degrees Rockwell (°R); the handguard retaining screw was constructed from St.38.13, and the rear sight leaf spring was constructed using an alloyed spring steel that was then hardened to 48–52°R. Interestingly, while the spring and screw were *Blauen in Blaubad* (hot-water blued), the ladder was subject to final bluing finish, or *Brünieren*. The spring also went through further internal verification processes to test both its maximum deflection of 3 mm and final shape after continuous loading (Mauser Werke A.G. 1935a, pp. 5, 11–12).

Receiver

As with the Modelo 1895 and Modelo 1912, the receiver was considered the crucial component that unified the barrel, bolt, trigger mechanism, bolt stop and ejector, and repetition mechanism. True to its Standard Model heritage, the technical specifics of the receiver of the Modelo 1935 were in all respects the same as those of the Mauser Model 1898; that is, it had a bolt body that was 161.5 mm long, an internal magazine dimension of 84 mm, and a forward receiver ring that was 36 mm in diameter and accommodated a barrel, with the threaded portion measuring 28 mm in diameter.

Modelo 1935 receivers were machined from St.50.11 steel with a carbon content of 0.35 percent. The hardening process involved a pre-treatment process in which plugs were inserted into all threaded portions to prevent hardening and damage, the trigger sear hole and its projecting lug were packed with clay, and then the whole trigger area and rear tang portion were dipped in a protective coating. The receiver was then immersed in molten salt for twenty minutes at 850–860°C (1,562–1,580°F), removed, and left to air cool. Individually, the receiver's forward ring and the area cover with the protective coating were reheated to 780–800°C (1,436–1,472°F) and then oil quenched. The thread plugs, protective coating, and clay were then removed and the receiver was then subjected to 3.5–4 volts copper galvanization for thirty minutes. The receiver was then rinsed with cold water and tempered in a bluing bath for four minutes at 300°C (572°F). The final hardness of the receiver was 10–30°R, and its finish was *Brünieren* (Mauser Werke A.G. 1935a, p. 13).

Bolt

The bolt of the Modelo 1935, apart from proofing and acceptance marks, can be regarded as identical to that of the carbine version of the Modelo 1912.

The bolt body was constructed from the same material as the rear sight ladder (i.e., St.35.61 steel). To harden the bolt body to an eventual 35–45°R, it was first soaked in molten salt at 860–870°C (1,580–1,598°F) for thirty minutes and then left to air cool. It was then reheated to 820°C (1,508°F), petroleum quenched, and tempered in an oil bath for thirty minutes at 180–200°C (356–392°F). The bolt handle and the forward shoulder that surrounded the bolt face were then reheated until red hot and left to anneal. After this extensive heat treatment was complete, the bolt body was then polished and left unblued (Mauser Werke A.G. 1935a, p. 19).

Extractors were constructed from St.60.61 steel that had an average carbon content of 0.60 percent. Heat treatment involved heating the covered extractor in a muffle furnace to 780°C (1,436°F), quenching in oil, and then tempering for seven to eight minutes in molten salt at 430°C (806°F) to attain a final hardness of 40–55°R. Extractors—like the bolt bodies—were then polished and left unblued (Mauser Werke A.G. 1935a, p. 20).

Firing pins were machined from St.60.61 steel. The heat treatment involved only the rear interrupted thread portion and the front firing-pin tip. These areas were successively heated in a molten lead bath to 780°C (1,436°F)and then quenched in oil. After brushing both areas, the firing-pin tip was then reheated to a yellow color with a gas torch, while the interrupted threaded portion was later tempered by immersing it in the bluing bath at 340–360°C (644–680°F). The resulting hardness of the firing-pin tip was tested by using a file, while the interrupted thread portion had a hardness of 35–50°R (Mauser Werke A.G. 1935a, p. 21). Firing-pin springs were made from bright-drawn spring wire that had a carbon content of 0.8–0.9 percent. Post-manufacture, each spring was then subject to two verification tests: the first was continuous loading that lasted six hours, and the second verified the loaded length of 67 mm, within a tolerance of 4 mm, when the spring was subject to a load of 9.5 kg (Mauser Werke A.G. 1935a, p. 22).

The bolt shroud, safety lever, and cocking piece all were constructed from St.16.61 steel with an average carbon content of 0.16 percent, and all were finished by polishing. Bolt shrouds were heat treated by immersing them in a molten salt bath at 850°C (1,562°F) for forty-five minutes, quenching them in a petroleum bath, and then tempering them in an oil bath at 180–200°C (356–392°F) for thirty minutes, resulting in a final hardness of 15–40°R (Mauser Werke A.G. 1935a, p. 25). Cocking pieces were essentially case hardened. The interior interrupted threaded portion of the cocking pieces were first packed with clay and then, together with charcoal and leather scraps, placed in a sealed container and heated to 860–870°C (1,580–1,598°F) in a muffle furnace to a depth of 0.4–0.5 mm. They were then removed from the container and quenched in oil, after which they were tempered in a further oil bath at 180–200°C (356–392°F) for thirty minutes. The resulting surface hardness was 50–63°R (Mauser Werke A.G. 1935a, p. 24). To harden the safety levers, they were first heated by being soaked in molten salt for one and a half to two hours at 900–920°C (1,652–1,688°F), quenched in oil, and then tempered in another oil bath for thirty minutes at 180–200°C (356–392°F) to achieve a final hardness of 40–65°R (Mauser Werke A.G. 1935a, p. 26).

Trigger Mechanism

There is nothing unique in the construction of the trigger mechanism of the Modelo 1935. Constructed from St.60.61 steel, the sear of the Modelo 1935 was heated to 780–800°C (1,436–1,472°F), quenched in petroleum, and tempered for thirty minutes in an oil bath at 180°C (392°F) to achieve a required hardness of 57–63°R. To finish the sear, only the sear projection proper was then sanded. The trigger was machined from St.16.61 steel, which was then heated to

900–920°C (1,652–1,688°F) in molten salt for one and a half to two hours. After this initial heating, the trigger was then quenched in petroleum and tempered in an oil bath for thirty minutes at 180–200°C (356–392°F) to achieve a final hardness of 40–55°R. The lower half of the trigger was then hot-water blued at 370°C (698°F) (Mauser Werke A.G. 1935a, pp. 30–31).

Bolt Stop and Ejector

As with the trigger mechanism, there is nothing distinctive about the bolt stop and ejector, which were constructed from St.60.61 steel. Heat treatment of the bolt stop involved heating to 780°C (1,436°F), quenching in petroleum, and tempering in an oil bath for twenty to thirty minutes at 180°C (356°F) to attain a final hardness of 40–55°R. Ejectors were heat treated by heating in a muffle furnace to 780°C (1,436°F), quenching in oil, and then tempering in molten salts at 380–400°C (716–752°F) for three to four minutes to produce a final hardness of 40–55°R. The leaf spring to the bolt stop was fabricated from spring steel that had a carbon content of 0.6–0.7 percent. Heat treatment involved heating in a muffle furnace to 780°C (1,436°F), quenching in oil, and tempering in molten salt at 380°C (716°F) for four minutes to produce a final hardness of 40–50°R. Bolt stops, with their leaf spring and ejectors, were all finished by hot-water bluing (Mauser Werke A.G. 1935a, pp. 14–15, 17).

Repetition Mechanism

Trigger guards of the Modelo 1935 are the same as that of the Modelo 1912. Trigger guards are distinguished from most other parts of the Modelo 1935 by having had no heat treatment, simply being fabricated from St.34.11 steel with a carbon content of 0.12 percent and finished with *Brünieren*. Magazine floorplates were fabricated from St.50.11 steel, which were then heat treated by first being dipped into potash, then heated to 820°C (1,508°F), quenched in petroleum, and tempered in an oil bath at 180–200°C (356–392°F) for thirty minutes. The final hardness was tested by filing, after which a *Brünieren* finish was applied. The follower to the Modelo 1935 had a chamfered rear shoulder to the middle rib, allowing the closing of the bolt with an empty magazine. Machined from St.16.61, the follower was heat treated by warming to 860–870°C (1,580–1,598°F) in molten salt, quenching in petroleum, and then tempering for thirty minutes in an oil bath at 180–200°C (356–392°F). Like the floorplate, the follower's hardness was tested with a file and was finished by polishing, and thus left unblued. The magazine spring was constructed from ribbon spring steel that had a carbon content of 0.85–1.1 percent. Heat treatment involved heating to 780°C (1,436°F) in a muffle furnace, quenching in oil, and tempering in molten salt at 400–430°C (752–806°F) for five minutes. Springs were then verified by subjecting them to a continuous load for six hours, after which the shape and dimensions should have conformed to "gauge number 2" (Mauser Werke A.G. 1935a, pp. 34–36).

Trigger guard screws were machined from St.38.13 with a carbon content of 0.11–0.18 percent. They were heat treated by heating for forty-five minutes in molten salt to 860–870°C (1,580–1,598°F), quenching in water, and then tempering in an oil bath at 180–200°C (356–392°F) for thirty minutes to attain a hardness of 20–40°R (Mauser Werke A.G. 1935a, p. 41).

Stock and Handguard

The walnut stock and handguard of the Modelo 1935 can be argued as being identical to the carbine version of the Modelo 1912. However, one observable difference on the stock is the placement of the retaining spring to the lower barrel band, which is positioned a few millimeters forward to accommodate the wider barrel band of the Modelo 1935.

The material specification dictated that the wood used be air dried, with no insect or rot damage, and be free from harmful knots and cracks. Likewise, in the wrist and receiver portions of the stock, wood fibers were not allowed to run transversely. An *Oelen* (oil) finish was applied to stocks (Mauser Werke A.G. 1935a, p. 46).

Stock Fittings

From observation, the butt plate and stock disk—to the right face of the butt—are identical to that of

The sling swivel, saddle ring, and permanently attached "quick-detach" fixture to the left wrist of the Model 1935's stock. *Jon Magnuson*

the Modelo 1912. The Modelo 1935 has numerous fittings that are different from the Modelo 1912: the recoil lug has a central concave depression, supposedly for bolt disassembly on the non-threaded side; the rear sling swivel to the lower face of the butt is positioned deeper into the stock and thus has two corresponding chamfers on either side to accommodate the sling quick-detach attachment; and the upper barrel band lacks the sling retaining hook to its underside. As explained, a unique feature of the Modelo 1935 was the addition of distinctive quick-release and a saddle-ring fitting to the left face of the stock's wrist. This feature was attached to the stock via a threaded shaft that projects through the wrist and is then fastened in a manner similar to the recoil lug. Likewise, the lower barrel band is completely different to that of the Modelo 1912, in that it is the broader Standard Model design, with a fixed sling mount to the left, and has the further addition of a hole at the bottom.

It is interesting to note that while no examples of Modelo 1935 have been observed with the hook to the upper barrel band, the material specification clearly illustrates it as being present (Mauser Werke A.G. 1935a, p. 67).

The bayonet lug was constructed from stainless steel that was then heat treated by heating for fifteen minutes in molten salt to 840°C (1,544°F), quenching in oil, and then tempering in a further oil bath at 180–200°C (356–392°F) for thirty minutes. Final hardness was determined by filing, and the finish was sanded and thus unblued (Mauser Werke A.G. 1935a, p. 46).

While the upper barrel band was constructed from St.8.23, the lower barrel band was constructed from St.42.11 with a carbon content of 0.25 percent; both received no heat treatment and had a *Brünieren* finish (Mauser Werke A.G. 1935a, pp. 63, 67).

The recoil lug was fabricated from St.16.61 steel that was then heat treated by spending thirty minutes in molten salt to reach a temperature of 860–870°C (1,580–1,598°F), quenched in petroleum, tempered for thirty minutes in an oil bath, and then transferred to the bluing bath at 450°C (842°F). The final hardness was determined by filing, and the finish was an initial polishing of the area that contacted the recoil lug with eventual *Brünieren* (Mauser Werke A.G. 1935a, p. 49).

Like the trigger guard, the butt plate received no heat treatment. Being fabricated from St.42.22, the butt plate received no bluing, having had only a polished finish (Mauser Werke A.G. 1935a, p. 51).

Like all screws on the Modelo 1935, the screws to the butt plate and the rear sling swivel were fabricated from St-38.13, then heated treated by heating for fifteen minutes in molten salt at 840–850°C (1,544–1,562°F), quenching in petroleum, and then tempering in an oil bath for thirty minutes

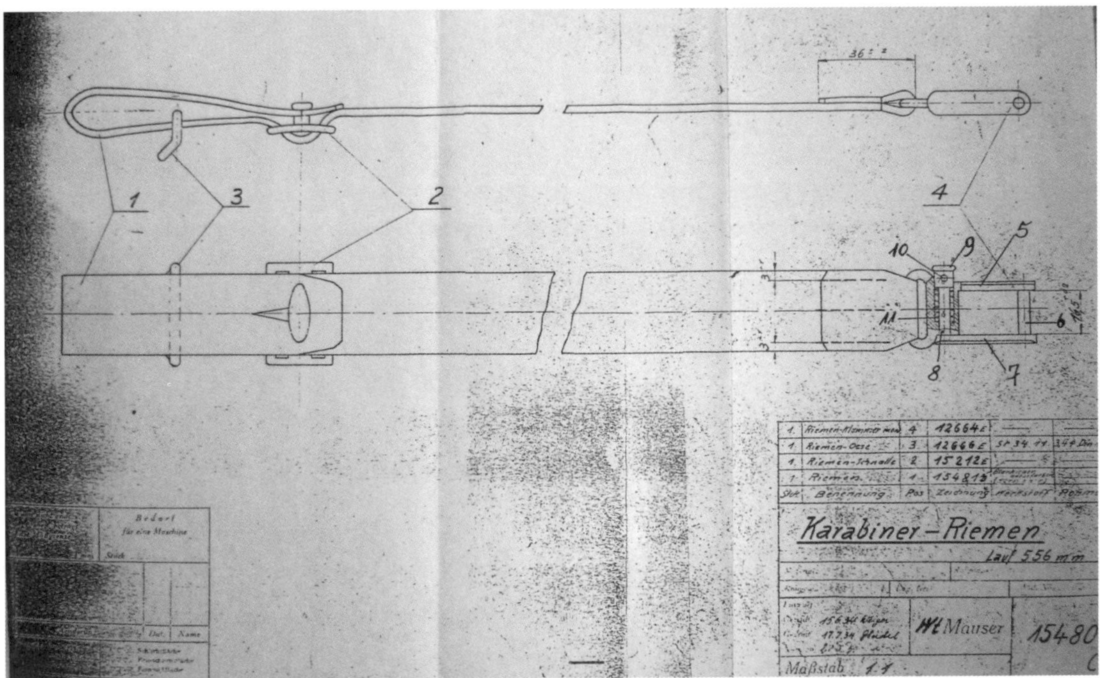

Technical drawing of the sling of the Chilean Model 1935.
Mauser Werke A.G. 1935a. "Chilen. Karabiner Kal. 7mm "S" Modell 1935—Werkstoffliste und Wärmebehandlung bzw. Letze Oberflächenbehandlung." Material and hardening specification in Archive Jon Speed, Heilbronn, Germany.

at 180–200°C (356–392°F). Final hardness was determined by filing, and the finish was hot-water bluing at 330–350°C (626–662°F) (Mauser Werke A.G. 1935a, p. 55).

An interesting feature often found on Modelo 1935s is the presence of numerous small, round depressions on the right face of the butt of the stock. Assumedly, these were caused by Carabineros troops depressing the point of the firing pin during disassembly into the wood of the butt, rather than into the recess in the recoil lug.

Cleaning Rod

The cleaning rod was constructed from St.60.61, then heat treated by heating it to 780°C (1,436°F) in molten salt, quenching it in oil, and then tempering it by immersion for five minutes in a hot-water bluing bath at 380–400°C (716–752°F). Despite this initial bluing, any traces were removed by subsequent polishing. Finished cleaning rods were then twice evaluated for bending by suspending them at their two ends and having a unspecified load applied to the midpoint (Mauser Werke A.G. 1935a, p. 59).

Bayonet

It is not known whether Chile bought bayonets for the Modelo 1935. From observation in 2016 of the Carabineros troops who guard the Chilean La Moneda (Presidential Palace) in Santiago, the bayonets are visually those of the Modelo 1912. Also of interest is that these troops have the ammunition pouches originally intended for mounted troops as originally specified in 1895.

Sling and Muzzle Cover

Slings were fabricated from the highest-quality, natural-colored, top-grain leather that had a diagonal cross-stitch pattern applied. Skins were specified to be as free as possible from damage, cuts, and the like, while the resulting leather had to be tanned, durable, and acid free. To test the strength of the leather, it was mandated that with its grain to the outside, it should be bent over a

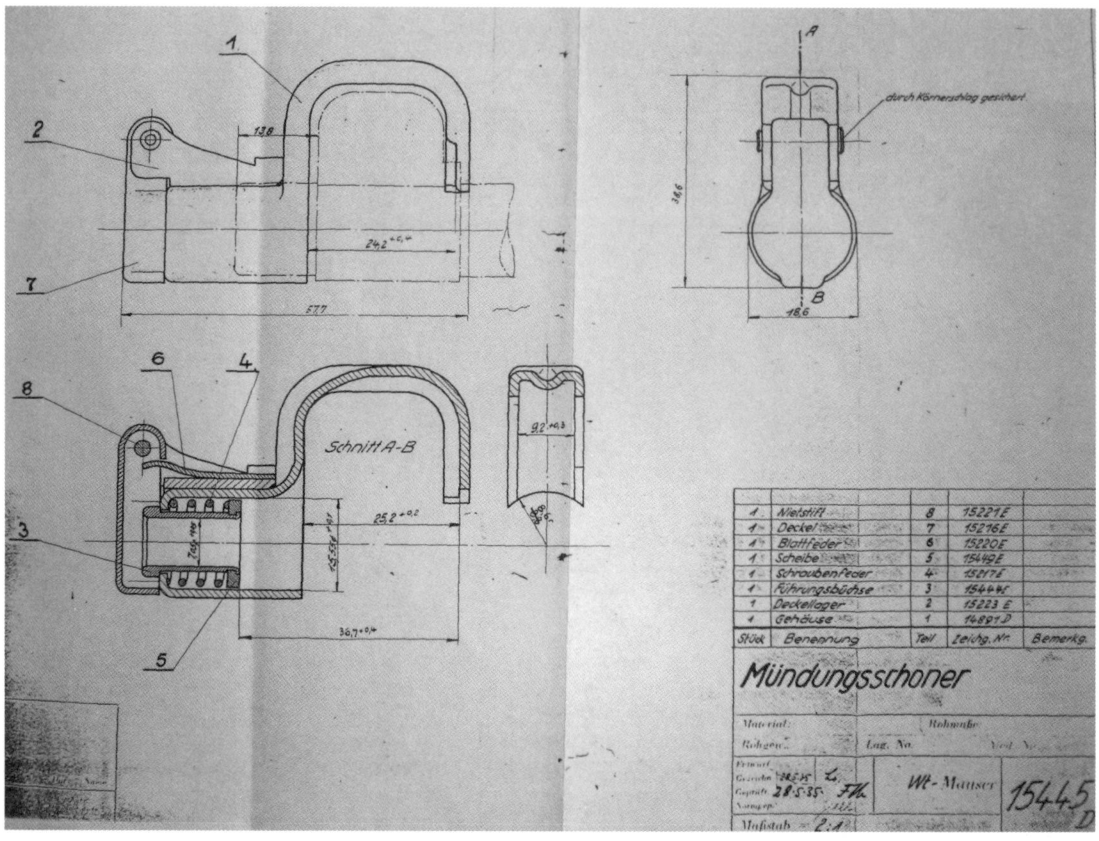

Technical drawing of the muzzle cover of the Chilean Model 1935.
Mauser Werke A.G. 1935a. "Chilen. Karabiner Kal. 7mm "S" Modell 1935—Werkstoffliste und Wärmebehandlung bzw. Letze Oberflächenbehandlung." Material and hardening specification in Archive Jon Speed, Heilbronn, Germany.

mandrel that was twice the thickness of the leather and not break (Mauser Werke A.G. 1935a, p. 77). It is curious to note that slings were still specified as having the parade loop, despite the lack of the hook to the upper barrel band.

Modelo 1935 muzzle covers were a variation of the blued, pressed-steel flip-up design commonly encountered on later Mausers.

Bibliography

"Acorazado Almirante Latorre." 2008. https://web.archive.org/web/20080608084301/http://www.armada.cl/site/unidades_navales/336.htm.

Allied and Associated Powers. 1919. *The Treaty of Peace between the Allied and Associated Powers and Germany*. London: His Majesty's Stationary Office.

Andersen, D., and M. Klare. 1996. *A Scourge of Guns: The Diffusion of Small Arms and Light Weapons in Latin America*. Washington, DC: Arms Sales Monitoring Project, Federation of American Scientists.

Arellano, S. H., and A. T. Goycoolea. 2009. "Historia y situación actual de los fuertes de la Infantería de Marina en la Bahía de Concepción." *Revista de Marina* 4: 377–385.

August Schriever & Compagnie. 1895. *The Repeating Rifles on the Mannlicher System of the Oesterreichische Waffenfabriks Gesellschaft, Steyr, Austria*. Liège, Belgium: August Bénard.

Ball, R. W. D. 2011. *Mauser Military Rifles of the World*. 5th ed. Iola, WI: Krause.

Barreyre, N. 2011. "The Politics of Economic Crises: The Panic of 1873, the End of Reconstruction, and the Realignment of American Politics." *Journal of the Gilded Age and Progressive Era* 10, no. 4: 403–423. doi:10.1017/S1537781411000260

Barros, P. A. 1931. "Ich überschreibe Ihnen das soeben erhaltene criptograma (Kabel in Geheimcode) aus Chile, welches lautet." Letter in Archive Jon Speed, Heilbronn, Germany.

Bester, R. 2003. *Small Arms of the Anglo Boer War, 1899–1902*. Brandfort, South Africa: Kraal.

Boado y Castro, J. 1895. *El fusil Mauser espanõl, modelo de 1893: Descripción, municiones, accesorios, funcionamiento, nomenclatura, desarme, cuidados que exige, noticias de su fabricación, reconocimientos, tiro de precisión, marcas y empaques, propiedades balísticas y datos nunéricos*. Madrid: Estudio Tipográfico "Sucesores de Rivadeneyra."

Boado y Castro, J. 1896a. *Cartilla del fusil Mauser Chileno Modelo 1895 calibre de 7mm para uso del soldado del Ejército de Chile*. Santiago, Chile: Imprenta Mejia.

Boado y Castro, J. 1896b. *Le fusil Mauser espagnol de 7 mill., Modelé 1893*. París: Imp. de Berger-Levrault.

Boado y Castro, J. 1896c. *El fusil Mauser espanõl, modelo de 1893: Descripción, municiones, accesorios, funcionamiento, nomenclatura, desarme, cuidados que exige, noticias de su fabricación, reconocimientos, tiro de precisión, marcas y empaques, propiedades balísticas y datos numéricos*. 2nd ed. Gijón, Spain: Carretera de Villaviciosa.

Boado y Castro, J. 1897. *Cartilla del fusil Mauser Chileno Modelo 1895 para uso del soldado del Ejército del Chile*. 3rd ed. Coruña, Spain: Imprenta y Estereotipia de Vicente Abad.

Boado y Castro, J. 1915. *Cartilla del fusil i la carabina Mauser Chilena Modelo 1895 por el Comandante Don José Boado i Castro i Corregida para el fusil transformado en 1912 por el Inspección de Fábricas i Maestranzas del Ejército*. Santiago, Chile: Imprenta de la Inspección de Fábricas i Maestranzas del Ejército.

Boonen Rivera, J. 1888. *Estudio sobre la reorganización i planta del ejército*. Santiago, Chile: Imprenta de La Época.

Budge, E. 1901. *Chile at the Pan-American Exposition: Brief Notes on Chile and General Catalogue of Chile Exhibits*. Buffalo, NY: Commission of Chile to the Pan-American Exposition.

Bulnes, G. 1893. "Señor Ministro: Con cumplimiento de las instrucciones que recibí de V.S., hoy firme con la Casa de Ludwig Loewe y Cía." Ministerio de Guerra, vol. 2238. Letter in Archivo Nacional de Chile, Santiago.

Bulnes, G. 1894. "Ministro du Guerra, del 27 de Octubre a VS., el telegrama siguiente." Ministerio de Guerra, vol. 2241. Letter in Archivo Nacional de Chile, Santiago.

Buxbaum, B. 1919. "Der deutsche Werkzeugmaschinen- und Werkzeugbau im 19. Jahrhundert." *Beiträge zur Geschichte der Technik und Industrie: Jahrbuch des Vereins Deutscher Ingenieure* 9:97–129.

Canfield, B. N., R. L. Lamoreaux, and E. R. Johnson. 2002. *Johnson Rifles and Machine Guns: The Story of Melvin M. Johnson, Jr. and His Guns*. Lincoln, RI: Andrew Mowbray.

Canto, E. del. 1894a. "A la Fabrique National d'armes de Guerra à Herstal." Legación de Chile en París, 1892–1894, vol. 2089. Letter in Archivo Nacional de Chile, Santiago.

Canto, E. del. 1894b. "Monsieur Chartraine, Directeur Gérant de la Fabrique Nationale d'Armes de Guerra de Herstal." Legación de Chile en París, 1892–1894, vol. 2089. Letter in Archivo Nacional de Chile, Santiago.

Canto, E. del, J. Boonen Rivera, and J. D. Vial. 1893. "Reunida la Comisión de estudio de armamento." Legación de Chile en París, 1892–1894, vol. 2089. Letter in Archivo Nacional de Chile, Santiago.

Canto, E. del, J. D. Vial, E. Körner, and A. Matte Pérez. 1894. "Remitas el Señor Ministro de Chile en Francia." Ministerio de Guerra, vol. 2089. Letter in Archivo Nacional de Chile, Santiago.

Chantraine, J. 1894a. *La Fábrica Nacional de Armas de Guerra, Herstal*. Ministerio de Guerra, vols. 2238 and 2089. Archivo Nacional de Chile, Santiago.

Chantraine, J. 1894b. "Monsieur le Président." Legación de Chile en Paris, 1892–1894, vol. 2089. Letter in Archivo Nacional de Chile, Santiago.

Chantraine, J. 1895. "Nous avons appris que votre gouvernement se propose de décider prochainement une nouvelle commande de fusils et de cartouches pour votre infanterie." Legación de Chile en Francia e Inglaterra, vol. 400. Letter in Archivo Nacional de Chile, Santiago.

"Chilean Navy Mausers M1895." 2015. http://forums.gunboards.com/showthread.php?393698-Chilean-Navy-Mausers-M1895&highlight=chilean+1895.

"Chilean Navy, Torpedo Ships, Almirante Simpson." 2015. www.navypedia.org/ships/chile/chi_dd_almirante_simpson.htm.

Collier, S., and W. F. Sater. 2004. *A History of Chile, 1808–2002*. 2nd ed. Cambridge, UK: Cambridge University Press.

Colonel Berrios representing Dirección de los Servicios de la Ministerio de Guerra. 1931. *Bericht über den Vertrag mit Mauser, Santiago, September 1931*. Report in Archive Jon Speed, Heilbronn, Germany.

Colonel Sáez representing Chilean Embassy in Paris. 1928. "A la firma Mauser Waffen Fabriken." Letter in Archive Jon Speed, Heilbronn, Germany.

Comisión Militar de Chile Sección de Recepción de Municiones. 1896. *Culot*. Legación de Chile en Francia, 1893–1898, vol. 373. Technical drawing. Archivo Nacional de Chile, Santiago.

"Deutsche Dampfschifffahrts-Gesellschaft Kosmos—DDG Kosmos." 2004. www.theshipslist.com/ships/lines/kosmos.shtml.

Dirección del Material de Guerra. 1924. *Calcificación y nomenclatura del armamento, vehículos de tren, atalajes, munición y otros pertrechos de guerra*. Santiago, Chile: Dirección del Material de Guerra, Inspección de Depósitos de Armamentos y Material de Guerra.

Donoso, A. 1947. *Recuerdos de cincuenta años: Prólogo y notas de Ricardo Donoso*. Santiago, Chile: Nacimiento.

Donoso, E. M., J. H. Gonzalez, and V. E. Palma. 1982. *Historia del Ejército de Chile: Reorganización del ejército y la influencia alemana (1885–1914)*. Vol. 7. Santiago, Chile: Ejército de Chile.

Dorn Brose, E. 2004. *The Kaiser's Army: The Politics of Military Technology in Germany during the Machine Age, 1870–1918*. Oxford: Oxford University Press.

Edwards, A. O. 2016. *British Secondary Small Arms, 1914–1919*. Vol. 1. Canterbury, UK: Solo.

English, A. J. 1984. *Armed Forces of Latin America*. London: Jane's.

Fabrique Nationale d'Armes de Guerra. 1895. "Comme suite à la lettre que nous avons eu l'honneur de vous adresser en date du 2 courant et au télégramme ci-inclus que nous venons de recevoir de Berlin de Mr. Legrand." Legación de Chile en Francia e Inglaterra, vol. 400. Letter in Archivo Nacional de Chile, Santiago.

Fonson, A. 1894a. "J'ai l'avantage de vous acenser la réception de votre estimée rappelée." Ministerio de Guerra, vol. 2241. Letter in Archivo Nacional de Chile, Santiago.

Fonson, A. 1894b. "A sa rentrée de Berlin Monsieur Van Makkelenberg." Ministerio de Guerra, vol. 2241. Letter in Archivo Nacional de Chile, Santiago.

Francotte, A., and C. Gaier. 1989. *FN 100 Years: The Story of a Great Liege Company, 1889–1989*. Translated by A. McDonald. Brussels: Didier Hatier.

Fuente, J. 1894. "El fusil Mauser español." *Memorial de Ingenieros del Ejército* 49, no. 12: 361–369.

Garcia-Huidobro Correa, F. 1999. "Centenario del primer viaje de instrucción de la Corbeta General Baquedano." *Revista de Marina* 5:1–2.

Gardiner, R., and R. Gray, eds. 1984. *Conway's All the World's Fighting Ships: 1906–1921*. Annapolis, MD: Naval Institute Press.

General Moreno representing Dirección de los Servicios de la Ministerio de Guerra. 1931. "In Beantwortung Ihres Schreibens vom 12 September des Jahres ist es mit angenehm Ihnen mitzuteilen." Letter in Archive Jon Speed, Heilbronn, Germany.

"Germany 1890–1945." 2015. www.shotguns.se/html/germany_1890-1945.html.

Groncki, E. 1894. *An die Fabrique National d'Armes de Guerra, Herstal les Liège*. Ministerio de Guerra, vol. 2089. Archivo Nacional de Chile, Santiago.

H. Fölsch & Co. 1929a. "Wir bestätigen danken Ihr Schreiben vom 13.ds. Mts." Letter in Archive Jon Speed, Heilbronn, Germany.

H. Fölsch & Co. 1929b. "Wir bestätigen unser heutiges Telegramm." Letter in Archive Jon Speed, Heilbronn, Germany.

H. Fölsch & Co. 1929c. "Wir beziehen uns auf die gestrige Besprechung am Kontor der Firma Gustav Genschow & Co." Letter in Archive Jon Speed, Heilbronn, Germany.

H. Fölsch & Co. 1931. "Vertraulich! Zu unserem Bedauern sehen wir uns heute genötigt, Ihnen davon Mitteilung zu machen." Letter in Archive Jon Speed, Heilbronn, Germany.

H. Fölsch y Cia. 1931a. "Auszug aus privat-vertraulichen Mitteilungen in Ergänzung der offiziellen Korrespondenz." Letter in Archive Jon Speed, Heilbronn, Germany.

H. Fölsch y Cia. 1931b. "Betr.: Chile-Auftrag: Mit Gegenwärtigen teilen wir Ihnen zunächst höfl. mit, dass wir gestern vormittag zusammen mit dem Gerenten des Banco Germanico." Letter in Archive Jon Speed, Heilbronn, Germany.

Haer, O. 1932. "Ich nehme höflichst Bezug meine Schrieben vom 15 Februar, 2 und 23 März, 12 April und 3 ds.Mts." Letter in Archive Jon Speed, Heilbronn, Germany.

Haer, O. 1935a. "Betr. Liquidation des Chile Vertrages." Letter in Archive Jon Speed, Heilbronn, Germany.

Haer, O. 1935b. "Ich bitte Sie gütigste zu entschuldigen, wenn ich heute erst auf Ihr Geehrtes vom 28 Juni der Angelegenheit der Firma Genschow & Co." Letter in Archive Jon Speed, Heilbronn, Germany.

Haer, O. 1935c. "Meinem letzten Schreiben vom 23 d.s, mussten Sie entnehmen, dass mit dem Depot der Staatkasse bei der Banco Central die R.M. 541,120." Letter in Archive Jon Speed, Heilbronn, Germany.

Haer, O., and H. Arriagada Valdivieso. 1935. "In Santiago de Chile wurde am 21 August 1935 der folgende Vertrag abgeschlossen zwischen der Hohen Regierung von Chile." Contract in Archive Jon Speed, Heilbronn, Germany.

Hassler, F., and A. Bihl, eds. 1939. *50 Jahre Deutsche Waffen- und Munitionsfabriken Aktiengesellschaft*. Berlin: VDI-Verlag.

Hintermeier, H. 2003. *In der Stunde der Not: Fremdländische Gewehrmodelle in Österreich-Ungarn 1914–1918* Vienna: Stöhr.

Hobart, F. W. A., ed. 1974. *Jane's Infantry Weapons 1975*. London: Jane's Information Group.

Independent Commission of Experts Switzerland–Second World War. 2002. *Switzerland, National Socialism and the Second World War*. Zurich, Switzerland: Pendo.

Jones, D. 2003. *Crown Jewels: The Mauser in Sweden, a Century of Accuracy and Precision*. Cobourg, ON: Collector Grade.

Keller & Co. 1895a. "La Commission Militaire du Chili à Berlin: Pour les articles suivant livres conformément au 3 contrat." Legación de Chile en Francia e Inglaterra, vol. 400. Delivery confirmation in Archivo Nacional de Chile, Santiago.

Keller & Co. 1895b. "A la légation du Chili à Paris: Monsieur Mandle a eut l'honneur d'avoir été reçu par votre excellence et il a été confié à notre établissement un nouveau contract en vue de nouvelles fournitures ultérieures." Legación de Chile en Francia e Inglaterra, vol. 400. Letter in Archivo Nacional de Chile, Santiago.

Keller & Co. 1895c. "A la légation du Chili à Paris: Nous avons été honorés par votre très estimée lettre du 6 courant." Legación de Chile en Francia e Inglaterra, vol. 400. Letter in Archivo Nacional de Chile, Santiago.

Keller & Co. 1895d. "A son Excellence Monsieur le Ministre Matte: Nous référant à l'entretien que nous avons eu l'honneur d'avoir avec votre Excellence ce matin." Legación de Chile en Francia e Inglaterra, vol. 400. Letter in Archivo Nacional de Chile, Santiago.

Keller & Co. 1898. "A la Legacion du Chili, Paris: Votre estimée du 30 de l'eole." Legación de Chile en Francia, 1893–1898, vol. 373. Letter in Archivo Nacional de Chile, Santiago.

Keller & Co. and Comisión Militar de Chile. 1898. "Cahier des charges pour la reception des cartpuches cal 7mm Mauser Modele Chilien 1896." Legación de Chile en Francia, 1893–1898, vol. 373. Specification in Archivo Nacional de Chile, Santiago.

Korn, R. H. 1971. *Mauser—Gewehre & Mauser—Patente*. Graz, Austria: Akademische Druck Verlagsanstalt.

Körner, E. 1894a. "Distinguido Señor y amigo." Archivo Sergio Larrin, vol. 138. Letter in Archivo Nacional de Chile, Santiago.

Körner, E. 1894b. "No: 15 no puede ponerse en duda que los propósitos del Supremo Gobierno." Ministerio de Guerra, vol. 2238. Letter. Santiago.

Körner, E. 1894c. "Señor Ministro de Guerra." Ministerio de Guerra, vol. 2238. Letter in Archivo Nacional de Chile, Santiago.

Krnka, K. 1892. US Patent No. 475061. US Patent Office.

Kruck, A. A. 2000. *Patronentaschen, Patronengürtel und Banduliere 1850–1950*. Münster, Germany: Druckhaus Aschendorff.

Lara, A. E. 1929. *Los oficiales alemanes en Chile: Influencia que ejercieron con sus lecciones en la instrucción y alto prestigio que el Ejército de Chile ha alcanzado*. Santiago, Chile: Imprenta Condor.

Laylin, J. K. 1993. *Nobel Laureates in Chemistry, 1901–1992*. 3rd ed. Washington, DC: American Chemical Society.

Leconte, L. 1910. *Les armes portatives des troupes belges de 1830 à 1910*. Paris: Henri Charles Lavauzelle.

Legación de Chile en Francia. 1893. "Contrat entre Monsieur Augusto Matte, Envoyé Extraordinaire et Ministère Plénipotentiaire du Chile en France." Legación de Chile en Francia, 1893–1898, vol. 373. Contract in Archivo Nacional de Chile, Santiago.

Legación de Chile en Paris. 1892. Legación de Chile en París, 1892–1898, vol. 2088. Archivo Nacional de Chile, Santiago.

Legrand. 1895. "Envoyez d'urgence Paris prix séparés avec certificats Brésiliens constatant fabrication." Legación de Chile en Francia e Inglaterra, vol. 400. Letter in Archivo Nacional de Chile, Santiago.

Léopold, L. P. M. V., and C Pontus. 1889. *Adoption d'un fusil a répétition de petit calibre pour les troupes de l'infanterie et du génie*. Brussels: Moniteur Belge Journal Officiel.

Livermore, S. W. 1944. "Battleship Diplomacy in South America: 1905–1925." *Journal of Modern History* 16, no. 1: 31–48.

Ludwig Loewe & Cie. 1893. "Excellence: Afin de rendre inutile une modification éventuelle des outils commandes sous le contrat." Ministerio de Guerra, vol. 2238. Letter in Archivo Nacional de Chile, Santiago.

Ludwig Loewe & Cie. 1894. "Monsieur—Par la preesente nous avons." Ministerio de Guerra, vol. 2241. Letter in Archivo Nacional de Chile, Santiago.

Ludwig Loewe & Cie. 1895a. "Ayant expédié le 27 Août à l'adresse de votre Haut Gouvernement 13 caisses contenant des pièces de rechange pour le fusil Mauser." Legación de Chile en Francia e Inglaterra, vol. 400. Letter in Archivo Nacional de Chile, Santiago.

Ludwig Loewe & Cie. 1895b. "D'après le certificat ci-inclus la Comission Militaire du Chili de cette ville à reçu pendait le mois écoulé 6450 fusils ainsi que 600 carabines." Legación de Chile en Francia e Inglaterra, vol. 400. Letter in Archivo Nacional de Chile, Santiago.

Ludwig Loewe & Cie. 1895c. "D'après le certificat ci-joint, nous avons délivré pendant le mois d'Août à la Commission Militaire du Chili de cette ville en Août 14700 fusils et 500 carabines." Legación de Chile en Francia e Inglaterra, vol. 400. Letter in Archivo Nacional de Chile, Santiago.

Ludwig Loewe & Cie. 1895d. "En réponse à votre très honorée lettre du 15 courant." Legación de Chile en Francia e Inglaterra, vol. 400. Letter in Archivo Nacional de Chile, Santiago.

Ludwig Loewe & Cie. 1895e. "En réponse à votre très honorée lettre du 15 courant." Legación de Chile en Francia e Inglaterra, vol. 400. Letter in Archivo Nacional de Chile, Santiago.

Ludwig Loewe & Cie. 1895f. "Honorés de la lettre du 23 courant, nous en avons retiré un chèque de Frs 33,657.50." Legación de Chile en Francia e Inglaterra, vol. 400. Letter in Archivo Nacional de Chile, Santiago.

Ludwig Loewe & Cie. 1895g. "La commission militaire du Chili de cette ville ayant reçu pendant le mois de septembre 11,100 fusils et 2700 carabines." Legación de Chile en Francia e Inglaterra, vol. 400. Letter in Archivo Nacional de Chile, Santiago.

Ludwig Loewe & Cie. 1895h. "Nous avons l'honneur de vous accuser la réception de votre très estimée du 10 courant." Legación de Chile en Francia e Inglaterra, vol. 400. Letter in Archivo Nacional de Chile, Santiago.

Ludwig Loewe & Cie. 1895i. "Nous avons l'honneur de vous informer que d'après ce certificat ci-joint, la Comission Militaire du Chili de cette ville a reçu." Legación de Chile en Francia e Inglaterra, vol. 400. Letter in Archivo Nacional de Chile, Santiago.

Ludwig Loewe & Cie. 1895j. "Nous avons l'honneur de vous remettre ci-inclus le contrat fait entre Votre Excellence et Monsieur le Directeur Riese." Legación de Chile en Francia e Inglaterra, vol. 400. Letter in Archivo Nacional de Chile, Santiago.

Ludwig Loewe & Cie. 1895k. "Nous vous accusons réception de votre très estimée lettre du 10 de ce mois et en réponse nous avons l'honneur." Legación de Chile en Francia e Inglaterra, vol. 400. Letter in Archivo Nacional de Chile, Santiago.

Ludwig Loewe & Cie. 1895l. "A son Excellence Monsieur Augusto Matte Ministre Plenipotentiaire du Chili en France." Legación de Chile en Francia e Inglaterra, vol. 400. Letter in Archivo Nacional de Chile, Santiago.

Ludwig Loewe & Cie. 1895m. "A son Excellence Monsieur Augusto Matte Ministre Plenipotentiaire du Chili en France, Excellence." Legación de Chile en Francia e Inglaterra, vol. 400. Letter in Archivo Nacional de Chile, Santiago.

Luger, G. 1892. *Herrn Kommerzienrat Mauser, Oberndorf am Neckar*. Archive Jon Speed, Heilbronn, Germany.

Major Béjares representing Departamento de Artillería y Material de Guerra. 1931. *Bericht über den Mauser-Vertrag, Santiago, September 1931*. Archive Jon Speed, Heilbronn, Germany.

Makkelenberg, A. van. 1894. "Par sa lettre du 24 du cousant Monsieur August Fonson." Ministerio de Guerra, vol. 2241. Letter in Archivo Nacional de Chile, Santiago.

Mardones, V. M. 1995. "El Apostadero Naval del Talcahuano, los Arsenales de Marina y Asmar." *Revista de Marina* 6:1–13.

Matscoss, C., and G. Schlesinger. 1930. *Ludw. Loewe & Co. Aktiengesellschaft, Berlin, 1869–1929*. Berlin: VDI-Verlag.

Matte Pérez, A. 1893a. "Por carta privada habíamos participado al Señor Don Francisco Pinto." Legación de Chile en París, 1892–1894, vol. 2089. Letter in Archivo Nacional de Chile, Santiago.

Matte Pérez, A. 1893b. "Señor Ministro de la Guerra." Legación de Chile en París, 1892–1894, vol. 2089 Letter in Archivo Nacional de Chile, Santiago.

Matte Pérez, A. 1893c. "Señor Presidente de la Comisión Militar." Legación de Chile en París, 1892–1894, vol. 2089. Letter in Archivo Nacional de Chile, Santiago.

Matte Pérez, A. 1894a. "Señor Ministro de la Guerra." Ministerio de Guerra, vol. 2089. Letter in Archivo Nacional de Chile, Santiago.

Matte Pérez, A. 1894b. "Señor Ministro: Recibí de V.S., los cablegramas siguientes, que test realimente dicen." Ministerio de Guerra, vol. 2089. Letter in Archivo Nacional de Chile, Santiago.

Mauser, P. 1889. US Patent No. 402605. US Patent Office.

Mauser, P. 1890. US Patent No. 440955. US Patent Office.

Mauser, P. 1891. US Patent No. 449352. US Patent Office.

Mauser, P. 1892a. Germany Patent No. 67343. Kaiserliche Patentamt.

Mauser, P. 1892b. *Herren Theodore Dohse*. Archive Jon Speed, Heilbronn, Germany.

Mauser, P. 1892c. Germany Patent No. 65225. Kaiserliche Patentamt.

Mauser, P. 1893a. Germany Patent No. 70114. Kaiserliche Patentamt.

Mauser, P. 1893b. Germany Patent No. 74162. Kaiserliche Patentamt.

Mauser, P. 1895. Germany Patent No. 90305. Kaiserliche Patentamt.

Mauser, P. 1896. Belgium Patent No. 120477. Belgium Patent Office.

Mauser, P. 1901. Germany Patent No. 154915. Deutsches Reichsgebrauchsmuster.

Mauser, P., II. 1893a. "Herren Ludwig Loewe & Co, Berlin 1." Letter in Archive Jon Speed, Heilbronn, Germany.

Mauser, P., II. 1893b. "Herren Ludwig Loewe & Co, Berlin 2." Letter in Archive Jon Speed, Heilbronn, Germany.

Mauser, P., II. 1893c. "Herren Ludwig Loewe & Co, Berlin 3." Letter in Archive Jon Speed, Heilbronn, Germany.

Mauser, P., II. 1893d. "Herren Ludwig Loewe & Co, Berlin 4." Letter in Archive Jon Speed, Heilbronn, Germany.

Mauser, P., II. 1893e. "Herren Ludwig Loewe & Co, Berlin 5." Letter in Archive Jon Speed, Heilbronn, Germany.

Mauser Werke A.G. 1929a. "Betr: Chilenische Karabiner-Fabrikation." Letter in Archive Jon Speed, Heilbronn, Germany.

Mauser Werke A.G. 1929b. "Lista de precios de Piezas componentes del la Carabina Mauser Modelo 1929." Pricing document in Archive Jon Speed, Heilbronn, Germany.

Mauser Werke A.G. 1929c. "Wir bestätigen Ihnen hiermit, dass wir Ihnen auf die Preise der Ihnen heute übersandten Liste." Letter in Archive Jon Speed, Heilbronn, Germany.

Mauser Werke A.G. 1929d. "Wir empfingen Ihre gefälligen Schreiben von 2 und 5 ds.Mts." Letter in Archive Jon Speed, Heilbronn, Germany.

Mauser Werke A.G. 1929e. "Wir nahem Bezug auf die Unterredung, welche unser Herr Direktor Zillinger am 25.v.Nts im Büro der Firma Gust." *Genschow & Co A.G.* Letter in Archive Jon Speed, Heilbronn, Germany.

Mauser Werke A.G. 1930a. "Autorizamos por este documento a la firma Fölsch y Cía., Santiago de Chile." Power of Attorney in Archive Jon Speed, Heilbronn, Germany.

Mauser Werke A.G. 1930b. "Nach Rücksprache mit Herrn Westendarp von der Firma Fölsch & Co in Hamburg." Letter in Archive Jon Speed, Heilbronn, Germany.

Mauser Werke A.G. 1931a. *Annual Report 1930–31*. Archive Jon Speed, Heilbronn, Germany.

Mauser Werke A.G. 1931b. "Auf den Inhalt Ihrer rechtzeitig in unseren Besitz gelangten Briefe No. 21, 22, 23, 24, 25, 26 & 27 werden wir gesondert zurückkommen." Letter in Archive Jon Speed, Heilbronn, Germany.

Mauser Werke A.G. 1931c. *Bert. Chile: Vorausgesetzt, dass der Aufsichtsrat beschließt, auf eine Abänderung des mit der chilenischen Regierung abgeschlossenen Vertrages einzugehen*. Memorandum in Archive Jon Speed, Heilbronn, Germany.

Mauser Werke A.G. 1931d. "Direktion: Ihre gefl. Zuschrift vom 23.ds. Mts. haben wir erhalten, was wir dankend bestätigen." Letter in Archive Jon Speed, Heilbronn, Germany.

Mauser Werke A.G. 1931e. "Wir bestätigen den Empfang Ihrer Nota No. 725 und erlauben uns, Ihnen zu Ihrer Information mitzuteilen." Letter in Archive Jon Speed, Heilbronn, Germany.

Mauser Werke A.G. 1931f. "Wir bestätigen der Ordnung halber den rechtzeitigen Eingang Ihrer Briefe No 30-33 vom 9, 3, 16 und 22 September und danken Ihnen für Ihre eingehende Berichte." Letter in Archive Jon Speed, Heilbronn, Germany.

Mauser Werke A.G. 1931g. "Wir teilen Ihnen hierdurch mit, dass wir der Firma H. Fölsch & Co., in Hamburg unsere Vertretung, die wir ihr Unterm 13 April 1929 übertragen haben." Letter in Archive Jon Speed, Heilbronn, Germany.

Mauser Werke A.G. 1932. "Wir bestätigen den Empfang Ihrer verschiedenen Berichts, von denen wir mit Interesse Kenntnis genommen haben." Letter in Archive Jon Speed, Heilbronn, Germany.

Mauser Werke A.G. 1933a. "Direktion Auftrag." Work instruction in Archive Jon Speed, Heilbronn, Germany.

Mauser Werke A.G. 1933b. "Lieferplan für 1500 argentinische Karabiner." Delivery schedule in Archive Jon Speed, Heilbronn, Germany

Mauser Werke A.G. 1935a. "Chilen. Karabiner Kal. 7mm 'S' Modell 1935—Werkstoffliste und Wärmebehandlung bzw. Letze Oberflächenbehandlung." Material and hardening specification in Archive Jon Speed, Heilbronn, Germany.

Mauser Werke A.G. 1935b. "Zusammenstellung der Schleif- und Polier- Operationen sämtlicher Gewhrteile für Chile." Grinding and polishing operations of all parts for the parts for the Chilean carbine, in Archive Jon Speed, Heilbronn, Germany.

Mauser Werke A.G. and H. Fölsch & Co. 1929. "Entwurf: Zwischen der Firma Mauserwerke A.G., Oberndorf am Neckar." Agreement in Archive Jon Speed, Heilbronn, Germany.

Mercado, J. S. 1912a. *Cartilla de la carabina Mauser de 7 mm Modelo Chileno de 1912 para el uso de los soldados e instructores de armas montadas*. Santiago, Chile: José Jánez.

Mercado, J. S. 1912b. *Cartilla de la fusil Mauser de 7 mm Modelo Chileno de 1912 para el uso de los soldados e instructores de infantería*. Santiago, Chile: José Jánez.

Meyer, S. 2016. "Gun Marks: A Proof Mark Primer, 1891–1939." German Gun Collectors Association. www.germanguns.com/tech-corner.html.

Miller, J. M., and L. G. Stahl. 1909. *The Twentieth Century Atlas of the Commercial, Geographical and Historical World with a Description of Every Known Land, Both Near and Remote, Ancient and Modern, Embracing Complete, Original and Authentic Maps of the Present Development of All Countries, Empires and States of the World Comprising Graphic Description of the People: Their Civilization, Their Religion, Their Government, Their Cities, Their Imports and Exports, Their Wealth, Their Railways, Their Canals, Their Cables, Their Telegraphs, etc., etc., Including Useful and Timely Statistics, Educational, Industrial Military, Naval*. 3rd ed. Chicago: L. W. Walter.

Ministerio de Guerra. 1893. "Contract." Ministerio de Guerra, vol. 2238. Contract in Archivo Nacional de Chile, Santiago.

Ministerio de Guerra. 1894. "Contrat supplémentaire." Ministerio de Guerra, vol. 2238. Contract in Archivo Nacional de Chile, Santiago.

Mott, W. H. 2002. *United States Military Assistance: An Empirical Perspective*. Westport, CT: Greenwood.

Mr. Premaour for the Mauser Werke. 1933. *Herrn Direktor Wirthle*. Report in Archive Jon Speed, Heilbronn, Germany.

Museo Histórico Carabineros de Chile. 2012. *200 años de historia policial*. Edited by D. Miranda Becerra. www.museocarabineros.cl/sitio/200-anos-de-historia-policial/.

Navarro, R. O., J. H. Gonzalez, and V. E. Palma. 1982. *Historia del Ejército de Chile: La Primera Guerra Mundial y su influencia en el ejército (1914–1940)*. Vol. 8. Santiago: Ejército de Chile.

Neubauer, H. 1974. "Österreichische Waffenfabriks gesellschaft bzw. Steyr-Werke A.G.: 1914–1934." PhD diss., Universität Wien, Vienna.

Neumann, J. 1908. "Das Mauser-Mehrladergewehr Modell 1907." *Schuss und Waffe: Illustrierte gemeinverständliche Zeitschrift für jagdliches, militärisches und sportliches Schiesswesen, Schiessplatz-Anlagen; Waffentechnik, Minen- und Torpedowesen, Waffengeschichte, etc.* 17 (1 June): 405–409.

Nova Vidal, J., J. A. de Lavalle, and M. C. Zaldivar. 1883. Tratado de paz de Ancon. www4.congreso.gob.pe/comisiones/1999/exteriores/chile/ANCON.htm.

Nunn, F. M. 1970. "Emil Körner and the Prussianization of the Chilean Army: Origins, Process, and Consequences, 1885–1920." *Hispanic American Historical Review* 50, no. 2: 300–322.

Olson, L. 1976. *Mauser Bolt Rifles*. 3rd ed. Montezuma, IA: F. Brownell & Son.

Ortmeier, M. A. G. 2006. "Chile und Mauser." *Deutsche Waffen Journal* 6:57–61.

Pinto Concha, A., L. Altamirano, E. Medina, and J. Bennet. 1911. *Informe: Sobre los supuestos defectos de los repuestos para fusiles y carabinas entregados por la Oesterreichische Waffenfabriksgesellschaft, Steyr*. Berlin: Commission Militar de Chile.

Provincia de Buenos-Aires, Firma Simon Hermanos, and Mauser Werke A.G. 1932. "Kontrakt für die Beschaffung von Mauser-Gewehren und Karabinern Kal. 7,65mm." Contract in Archive Jon Speed, Heilbronn, Germany.

Rector, J. L. 2005. *The History of Chile*. New York: Palgrave Macmillan.

Resende Santos, J. 2007. *Neorealism, States, and the Modern Mass Army*. Cambridge, UK: Cambridge University Press.

Résimont, A. 1890a. "Cher Monsieur Mauser 2." Letter in Archive Jon Speed, Heilbronn, Germany.

Résimont, A. 1890b. "Cher Monsieur Máuser 1." Letter in Archive Jon Speed, Heilbronn, Germany.

Reynier, A. 1915. "Art militaire: Les fusils de guerre actuels." *Le Genie Civil: Revue Generale Hebdomadaire des Industries Francaises et Etrangeres* 66, no. 22: 337–344.

Riese, A. 1895a. "Nous venons de recevoir la lettre de Mr. le secrétaire Domingo Vega." Legación de Chile en Francia e Inglaterra, vol. 400. Letter in Archivo Nacional de Chile, Santiago.

Riese, A. 1895b. "Votre Excellence, par la très honorée du 13 courant a bien voulu diriger notre attention à ce que deux fusils." Legación de Chile en Francia e Inglaterra, vol. 400. Letter in Archivo Nacional de Chile, Santiago.

Sater, W. F., and H. H. Herwig. 1999. *The Grand Illusion: The Prussianization of the Chilean Army*. Lincoln: University of Nebraska Press.

Schaefer, J. 1974. *Deutsche Militärhilfe an Sudamerika: Militär- und Rüstungsinteressen in Argentinien, Bolivien und Chile vor 1914*. Düsseldorf: Bertelsmann Universitastverlag.

Scheina, R. L. 1987. *Latin America: A Naval History, 1810–1987*. Annapolis, MD: Naval Institute Press.

Scheina, R. L. 2003. *Latin America's Wars: The Age of Caudillo, 1791–1899*. Sterling, VA: Brassey's.

Scholtyseck, J. 2011. *Der Aufstieg der Quandts: Eine deutsche Unternehmerdynastie*. Munich: C. H. Beck.

Sears, J. H., and B. W Wells. 1893. *The Chilean Revolution of 1891*. Washington, DC: Government Printing Office.

Seel, W. 1986. *Mauser von der Waffenschmiede zum Weltunternehmen*. Zurich, Switzerland: Verlag Stocker-Schmid AG.

Serrano, J. 1894. *Cronica extranjera: Los fusiles Daudetau, Mannlicher y Mauser estudiados por una comision chilena en Europa Revista tecnica de infantería y caballería*, V(X), 477–480.

Société Française des Munitions de Chasse, de Tir et de Guerre. 1894. "Monsieur le Chef de l'Etat-Major General du Chile a Santiago." Legación de Chile en Francia e Inglaterra, 1819–1903, vol. 400. Letter in Archivo Nacional de Chile, Santiago.

Speed, J. 2007. *The Mauser Archive*. Cobourg, ON: Collector Grade.

Tower, W. S. 1913. "The Nitrate Fields of Chile." *Popular Science Monthly* 83 (September): 209–230.

Unknown author. 1891a. "Lieutenant Colonel Korner Says the Mannlicher Rifle Is the Best Made, but Suggest a Reduction of the Caliber." *New York Herald*, 19 September.

Unknown author. 1891b. "Official Report of the Battle." *New York Herald*, 3 September.

Unknown author. 1892a. *Annual Report of the Chief of Ordnance to the Secretary of War for the Fiscal Year Ended June 30 1892*. Washington, DC: Government Printing Office.

Unknown author. 1892b. *Memorandum de la Revolución de 1891: Datos para la historia recopilados por un ayudante del Estado Mayor Jeneral del Ejército de Chile*. Santiago, Chile: Imprenta Cervantes.

Unknown author. 1893. *The International Columbian Naval Rendezvous and Review of 1893 and Naval Manoeuvres of 1892*. Washington, DC: Government Printing Office.

Unknown author. 1894. *Notes on the Year's Naval Progress*. Washington, DC: Government Printing Office.

Unknown author. 1895. "Overseas News." *Financial News*, 17 June, quoting the *Journal do Commercio*.

Unknown author. 1897a. *Atlas del fusil Mauser 7mm Modelo Chileno 1895*. Berlin: Ludwig Loewe.

Unknown author. 1897b. "The Mauser Magazine Rifle Caliber 7mm Model 1893–95 and Its Ammunition." In *The Mauser Magazine Rifle*. Edited by W. Mauser. Berlin: H. S. Herman.

Unknown author. 1905. *Escuela de caballería, revista final, 19 diciembre 1905*. Santiago, Chile: Biblioteca Escuela Militar.

Unknown author. 1911. "Con el Ministro de Guerra Señor Alejandro Huneeus." *El Mercurio*, 9 November: 23.

Unknown author. 1912a. "El asunto armamentos: Le segunda nota de Ministro en Berlín al Ministerio de Guerra." *El Mercurio*, 24 April: 15.

Unknown author. 1912b. "La adquisición de armamentos a la casa Steyr: Antecedentes completos de este asunto que tan viva preocupación ha causado en el público." *El Mercurio*, 9 April: 14.

Unknown author. 1912c. "La adquisición de repuestos en la casa Steyr: Nuevos antecedentes y documentos oficiales; La historia de esta negociación." *El Mercurio*, 10 April: 16.

Unknown author. 1912d. "La adquisición de repuestos en la casa Steyr: Nuevos antecedentes y documentos oficiales." *El Mercurio*, 10 April: 16.

Unknown author. 1912e. "Los repuestos de armamentos: Señor don Ismael Valdés Vergara." *El Mercurio*, 10 April: 5.

Unknown author. 1938. *Geschichte der Mauser-Werke*. Berlin: VDI Verlag.

Vega, D. 1894. "Señor Ministro de Guerra." Ministerio de Guerra, vol. 2089. Letter in Archivo Nacional de Chile, Santiago.

Webster, C. 2003. *Argentine Mauser Rifles, 1871–1959*. Atglen, PA: Schiffer.

Wengenroth, U. 2002. "Industry and Warfare in Prussia." In *On the Road to Total War: The American Civil War and the German Wars of Unification, 1861–1871*. Edited by S. Forster and J. Nagler, 249–262. Cambridge, UK: Cambridge University Press.

Yorulmaz, N. 2014. *Arming the Sultan: German Arms Trade and Personal Diplomacy in the Ottoman Empire before World War I*. London and New York: I. B. Tauris.

Zillinger, H. 1935a. "Annuliering des Vertrages Zwischen der Hohen Regierung von Chile und der Firma Mauser-Werke A.G. in Oberndorf a.N." Contract cancellation in Archive Jon Speed. Heilbronn, Germany.

Zillinger, H. 1935b. "Liquidation des Chilevertrages und Erläuterungen der Positionen a bis j des chilenischen Zahlungsdekrets." Letter in Archive Jon Speed, Heilbronn, Germany.